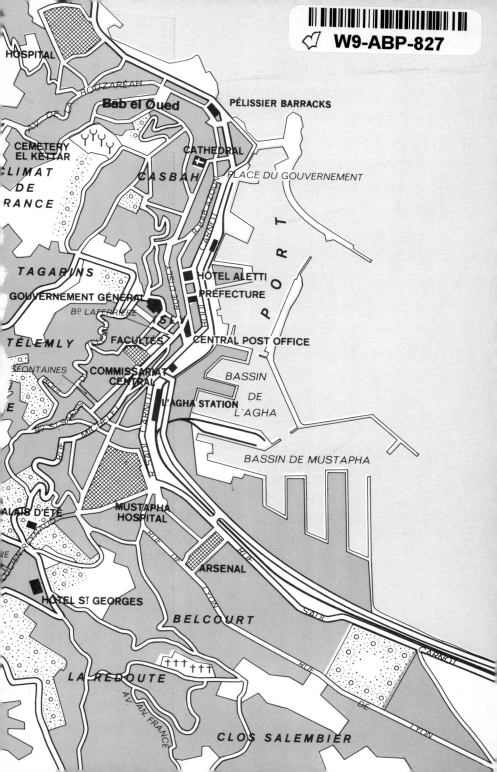

W9-ABP-827

WOLVES
in the CITY

THE DEATH OF
FRENCH ALGERIA

Paul Henissart

Simon and Schuster
New York

FIRST PRINTING

SBN 671-20513-7
Library of Congress Catalog Card Number: 76-101877
Designed by Irving Perkins
Manufactured in the United States of America
Printed by Mahony & Roese Inc., New York, N.Y.
Bound by H. Wolff, New York, N.Y.

For SYLVIE

A Note

The time span of this work covers the period when opposition to General de Gaulle's self-determination policy for Algeria went underground, in contrast with earlier open resistance.

A book of this sort does not get written without the help of numerous people. I was aided along the way by many in all camps—those who initiated and carried out French Government policy; those who bitterly opposed the abandonment of French Algeria, and often sacrificed much in defense of an ideal; those who played an active part in the struggle for Algeria's independence and accepted sacrifices at least as great. Many gave freely of their time and hospitality during the course of my research. My thanks are herewith expressed to them all.

Special thanks go to Lucien Bitterlin, who allowed me to read his unpublished manuscript, *"Des Hauts de la Casbah,"* upon which I drew for some material concerning the *barbouzes*.

CONTENTS

8   *Contents*

List of Principal Characters

French Government

GENERAL CHARLES DE GAULLE
MICHEL DEBRÉ, Premier
PIERRE MESSMER, Minister of the Armed Forces
ROGER FREY, Minister of the Interior
LOUIS JOXE, Algerian Affairs Minister
ALEXANDRE SANGUINETTI, *chargé de mission* attached to Frey's staff for anti-OAS operations in France
BERNARD TRICOT, Algerian policy adviser to de Gaulle
GENERAL CHARLES AILLERET, commander in chief of French forces in Algeria, June 1961 to April 1962
JEAN MORIN, Delegate General for Algeria, November 1960 to March 1962
VITALIS CROS, Prefect of Police, Algiers, November 1961 to June 1962
GENERAL JOSEPH KATZ, Army commander in Oran
PIERRE LE THIAIS, Prefect of Police, Oran, July 1961 to February 1962
LOUIS GRASSIEN, chief of Algiers' first anti-OAS police brigade

Activists (Code names appear in parentheses)

GENERAL RAOUL SALAN (Soleil), leader of the OAS, formerly commander in chief of French forces in Indochina and in Algeria
JEAN-JACQUES SUSINI (Jeannine), in charge of OAS propaganda and political action under Gardy, then virtual head of the Algiers OAS

9

after Salan's arrest; formerly president of the Algerian Student Association

COLONEL YVES GODARD (Claude), chief of all OAS intelligence activities; former director of Algiers Sûreté

COLONEL JEAN GARDES (Fleur), head of OAS enrollment, fund-raising, etc.; former head of the Cinquième Bureau (Psychological Action), Algiers

DR. JEAN-CLAUDE PEREZ (Paulette), head of OAS offensive operations and intelligence-gathering

LIEUTENANT ROGER DEGUELDRE (Delta), Perez's deputy in charge of "Delta" terrorist teams; deserter from the French Foreign Legion

COLONEL ANTOINE ARGOUD (Albatros), coleader of the OAS "Madrid Group"

COLONEL HENRY DUFOUR, second in command of the Oran OAS in spring 1962

COLONEL JOSEPH BROIZAT (Bravo), participated in April 1961 putsch, then edited OAS magazine for Army officers

CAPTAIN JEAN FERRANDI (Fernande), Salan's aide-de-camp

CAPTAIN PIERRE SERGENT (Sierra), OAS leader in France

GENERAL EDMOND JOUHAUD (Compagnon), OAS chief for Oran and western Algeria; former Chief of Staff, French Air Force

GENERAL MAURICE CHALLE, leader of the April 1961 putsch; former commander in chief of French forces in Algeria; former commander in chief, Allied Forces, Europe Center, Fontainebleau

GENERAL ANDRÉ ZELLER, conspirator in the April 1961 putsch; former Chief of Staff, French Ground Forces

GENERAL PAUL GARDY (Guy), replaced Jouhaud as Oran OAS chief in spring 1962; former Inspector General, French Foreign Legion

PIERRE LAGAILLARDE, coleader of the OAS "Madrid Group"

JEAN SARRADET, Algerian student leader

DR. BERNARD LEFÈVRE, member of the OAS "Madrid Group"

MAURICE GINGEMBRE (Tacite), "treasurer of the OAS"; Algiers industrialist

CHARLES MICHELETTI, civilian leader of the Oran OAS

ANDRÉ CANAL, leader of OAS Mission III to France

Algerian Nationalists

BELKACEM KRIM, vice-president, then Minister of the Interior in the Algerian Provisional Government; signatory to the Évian cease-fire agreement

BEN YOUSEFF BEN KHEDDA, president of the Algerian Provisional Government, August 1961 to July 1962

SI AZZEDINE, chief of the *zone autonome d'Alger*, April to June 1962

DR. CHAWKI MOSTEFAI, chief FLN member of the Provisional Executive, at Rocher Noir, March to June 1962

ABDERRAHMANE FARÈS, president of the Provisional Executive

Others

JACQUES CHEVALLIER, former mayor of Algiers

JEAN-MARIE TINÉ, French industrialist of Algiers

JACQUES DAUER, president of the pro-Gaullist Mouvement pour la Coopération

LUCIEN BITTERLIN, secretary general of the Mouvement pour la Coopération in Algeria

O my poor kingdom, sick with civil blows!
When that my care could not withhold thy riots,
What wilt thou do when riot is thy care?
O, thou wilt be a wilderness again,
Peopled with wolves, thy old inhabitants!

       —SHAKESPEARE,
        King Henry IV, Part II

PROLOGUE

Algeria, SUMMER 1961

THEY HAD been waiting for more than an hour to murder him. It was now close to midnight, and they were ready.

When Police Inspector Roger Gavoury stepped into the darkened apartment and saw the pale astral glow of the city beyond, he had a sudden presentiment of danger. He was tired, he had received threats, but he had refused to have a bodyguard.

Something stirred behind him; three shadows pressed forward in the room, hemming him in as he tried to turn. He shouted for help just before the board smashed down on his head and fingers wrapped themselves expertly around his throat.

The blade leaped out like a sliver of light and drove at his heart, once and once again.

❀ ❀ ❀

Algiers awoke on the morning of July 14, 1961, to one of those perfect Mediterranean dawns, shot through with pale washes of opaline and salmon, that prefigure a fair, fragrant summer day; it awoke to the equally agreeable prospect of a three-day weekend, for the Fourteenth fell on a Friday. The mood of the population, nonetheless, was apathetic. Although Algiers is an early-rising city, few pedestrians were abroad and fewer cars. As the sun rose higher and grew more oppressive, windows remained shuttered; this was unusual and was not intended merely to keep the heat out. Tricolor flags flew from the masts of official buildings but were visible nowhere else; they were conspicuously missing from the wrought-iron balconies in residential quarters, where they had proliferated in an unbroken front in earlier years. A curious lethargy muted the entire city—from the port to Bab el Oued, from the Casbah to the ocher sun-struck villas on the heights overlooking the checkerboard of architecture, modern and colonial, that sprawls around the half-moon bay. Europeans and Moslems alike were boycotting Bastille Day.

A crossroads of races, ambitions and manners, Algiers (El Djezair as Moslems called it), the old stronghold of Barbary pirates, normally celebrated July 14 with an uninhibited patriotism no longer in vogue in France itself—a patriotism that reflected the city's exuberance and self-confidence, not to speak of a native fondness for fiestas. At daybreak, European men, women and children—Frenchmen and Italians, Malts, Jews, Majorcans, some of whom spoke French quite haltingly—flowed out into the narrow streets, shoving and crying, bellowing their allegiance to France and their enthusiasm for the French Army (which protected them against all manner of vague but everpresent evils.) The Fourteenth of July was the occasion for a paroxysm of flag waving and fireworks and identification with the mother country. In this way the *pieds noirs* persuaded themselves annually that they were loyal Frenchmen, perhaps more faithful to France than the tight-lipped, cold-blooded *pathos* to the north.* The chauvinistic frenzy was so contagious that it swept up many Moslems, who had still less reason to consider themselves French. But all this was in the past. The popularity of the national holiday was running down; the drawn-out war had affected everybody's temper; last year government representatives had been roundly booed, and cursed during the sounding of Taps.

This year, Pierre Messmer, the French Minister of the Armed Forces, thought twice about the wisdom of going ahead with any of the customary ceremonies. He knew that weekends often bred trouble in Algiers; both the Barricades and the Generals' Putsch, after all, had begun on a Saturday. He also realized that numerous Army units would be in town for the parade, and it was symptomatic that the Army was no longer regarded as a force to preserve order but one that potentially threatened it. At length Messmer hit upon a compromise—which, like all compromises, suited practically no one.

---

* *Pieds noirs:* Europeans of Algeria. *Pathos:* a derogatory term in Algeria for Frenchmen of France.

This year, he decided, there would be no patriotic appeals and no wreath-laying; and as a further precaution he ordered the ceremonies transferred away from the Plateau des Glières, scene of past riots, to a neutral site.

A reviewing stand had accordingly been erected facing the sea along Boulevard Carnot between the Prefecture and the Hôtel de Ville, and the area immediately around it had been cleared of bystanders. In the early morning, officials and their guests began taking their places. Those present included Vice-Admiral Jean-Marie Querville, commander of French naval forces in Algeria; the police prefect; and the archbishop of Algiers, Monseigneur Léon-Étienne Duval, whose episcopal residence in St.-Eugène had been bombed, for the second time, just the evening before as a warning not to meddle in politics. Otherwise, attendance was scant. The first row of seats reserved for war veterans remained insultingly empty. The public grandstands near by were vacant. Security troops braced themselves behind rows of interlocked iron palings to contain troublemakers (a superfluous precaution). It was all this which led one newsman to refer to the "tragic isolation of the authorities."

At about 8:15 A.M., Jean Morin and General Charles Ailleret, Delegate General and commander in chief of French forces in Algeria respectively, drove down Rue Michelet in a command car. Derisive hoots greeted them. The two men took no notice. Morin, dour and brusque, and Ailleret, a scrappy balding ex-artillery officer, did not get on well, but they shared a stanch loyalty to General de Gaulle's government eight hundred miles away in Paris. This was why they had been picked for their assignments.

Those who attended the ceremonies recall the atmosphere that day as extraordinarily lugubrious. First, Morin and Ailleret passed in review some two thousand men drawn up at attention along the waterfront, then they bestowed medals on a deserving few—all this, and what followed, in dead silence. No *pieds noirs* were allowed to come close, but their presence could be felt, hostile and mute, as they watched from behind shut windows. The parade itself was opened, inexplicably, by a squadron of *gardes mobiles,* the most detested unit in Algiers, followed by zouaves, *tirailleurs,* an Air Force platoon, and *fusiliers-marins* (the French equivalent of the United States Marines), all marching perhaps a bit more hurriedly than usual. Sky-blue caps, maroon berets, white kepis—superficially, at least, it resembled the smart-stepping turnouts which the French had staged with so much awareness of the rainbow of Empire before World War II, when much of the map of Africa, a huge swath from the Mediterranean to the Congo, was inked in green to denote French possession. The gaudy march-pasts in those years had stirred a great deal of uncritical pride. This year, clearly, nobody's heart was in it, neither participants' nor spectators'; it seemed a tactless reminder of better days and glories vanished. The green berets of the Foreign Legion paratroop regiments were conspicuously absent; in euphemistic official language, the Legion was "in the process of reorganization." In fact, the government had disbanded one crack regiment, placed most of its officers under arrest, and shipped them back in disgrace to France.

The handful of onlookers broke into scattered applause when a company of former colonial paratroopers—the 3ème Régiment Parachutiste d'Infanterie de Marine—advanced, automatic pistols at the ready, executing their familiar cadenced step. A few cries of *"Algérie française"* and *"Vive Salan!"* rose tentatively, but then subsided without response. The Moslems' reaction was uncompromising; at one point, they turned their backs to the passing troops.

By 9:15 A.M. the sorry affair was over. Morin and Ailleret, relieved that no serious trouble had occurred, sped off in their car, avoiding the center of the city. Workmen began to disassemble the grandstands. It was the last time French troops would parade in the white vibrant seaport, and it had been the most lackluster Bastille Day in Algiers' history.

The contrast offered at this same moment in Paris could not have been greater.

In spite of buffeting winds, thousands of onlookers mingled with vendors of peanuts and cardboard periscopes and pickpockets on the Champs Élysées, transformed temporarily into a mile-long fairground. Bands blared, troops strutted, tanks rumbled, Mirages swooped low, designing tricolor contrails in the clouds. Amid this show of pomp, if not real power, the magnet of greatest attraction, near the Rond-Point, was President Charles de Gaulle himself—seventy, ponderous, autocratic, solitary. He was flanked by generals and admirals and by service attachés in their splendid dress uniforms. Profoundly conservative in his ordering of ritual and profoundly liberal in his vision of the world, what de Gaulle thought of this trite

pageant, no one could tell. Ironically, two of the units he was now sa-
luting—the 501st Armored Regiment of Rambouillet and the 2nd Hussars of Orléans—had shown signs of open revolt against him only
three months before. The general, unmoved, waited until the last
drumbeat, then invited the official party to a reception in the salons
and gardens of the Élysée Palace. July 14 had proceeded according
to schedule.

The Parisian daily *Le Figaro* found reasons to be optimistic. "There
was not a discordant cry, not even a rumor of factiousness to mar
the holiday," it reported, adding in high-flown prose: "The dangers of
tragic division now removed, it was to the Army—united, disciplined,
at the orders of the Nation—that the crowd's homage was addressed."
The phrase "tragic division" referred to the short-lived Generals'
Putsch in April. To what extent the newspaper's sanguine outlook for
the future was justified remained to be seen.

It was an uncertain summer. The sirocco blew from the wastes
in the south, and in the citrus groves of the Tell and the grazing
lands of the Hauts Plateaux the temperature soared to 105 degrees.
Drought spread. The wheat harvest was threatened; deaths among
livestock spurted alarmingly; the Délégation Générale announced
emergency measures: flocks of Algerian sheep barred from France
would be authorized, exceptionally, to feed in Alpine pastures.

Algeria was in its sixth year of war. Within the French Army the
objective of military victory in the field was being reluctantly sup-
planted by the less inspiring prospect of a political settlement—or,
as a vociferous minority claimed, a sellout. It was a war that had
been carried on by junior officers in outposts scattered across immense and lonely stretches of rugged terrain; but since May 20,
offensive operations were at a standstill. Infantry regiments continued to man the electrified frontier defenses, claiming a few prisoners here and there; but paratroop commandos no longer scoured
the arid *djebels* (hills) on seek-and-destroy missions.

The peace negotiations were dragging on interminably. Broken
off at Évian in June, they were expected to resume shortly at Lugrin;
but although the situation had never been more strained, neither
delegation seemed ready to make peace. The FLN denounced the
unilateral truce as "blackmail," a trick to lower morale among guerrilla forces of the interior; it hotly refused to follow suit. For their

part, the French continued to claim full sovereignty over the Sahara; in Paris it was observed that pipelines carrying oil from the wells of Hassi Messaoud and Edjele to Tunisia could be guarded indefinitely "like Roman roads"—an expensive proposition but one that had a reassuring ring, even when uttered by politicians. De Gaulle threatened partition as a last resort in the event of a breakdown of negotiations; Europeans and Moslems viewed the remedy as worse than the disease, and the French government still summed up its policy in the negative slogan: "Algeria without Moslems is unthinkable, Algeria without Europeans would be unlivable." Unofficially, the same idea was expressed by *pieds noirs* bluntly: "We are condemned to live together."

The coastal cities of Algeria sweltered in the exceptional heat, and the European minority of a million waited—for what exactly they would have been unable to say. The country's economy was paralyzed. The unilateral truce had led to a resurgence of terrorism. Near Algiers, a ten-year-old European girl was discovered stoned to death, her skull fractured, in the forest of Sidi-Ferruch. Swift retaliation came when a group of European youngsters returning from the funeral stopped a streetcar toiling up the grade toward the basilica of Notre Dame d'Afrique, ordered all Europeans out, then stoned the Moslems trapped inside.

In the Casbah and the mushrooming shantytowns on the heights of Algiers, the Moslems, at least the older ones, showed more political sophistication as they awaited further talks. But occasionally they did foolish things too, as on the day Moslem cleaning women turned up with chits to be signed by their European employers, that would give the maids possession of the apartments "once the French left." The FLN tightened its hold on the population, Arab and Berber; in early July it ordered a general strike to show the threat of partition was unenforceable. Work stopped at plants and docks, bakery ovens shut down, fruits and vegetables rotted at the Halles Centrales. The next day, heavy rioting broke out, leaving 80 dead and 266 wounded.

Far off, on a five-day tour of Lorraine, speaking before compact audiences in mining towns and farming communities, General de Gaulle everywhere underscored the idea which his audience wanted to hear: the war in Algeria was practically over; the Army had done its duty; association between the two countries was the commonsense solution of the future. In private, before a group of deputies, he growled that those who still believed in *Algérie française* were frauds. Publicly, for the first time in referring to Algeria, he pronounced the binding words: "an independent and sovereign state."

He repeated them for greater effect in a nationwide television address on July 12. In Algiers, saboteurs blew up the coaxial cable carrying the general's image; but no one was naïve enough to think that the explosion could settle the problem. The *pieds noirs* concluded grimly that France was preparing to clear out and leave them in the lurch.

Among Europeans, a new underground movement was recruiting and raising funds—another of the self-reproducing cells that appeared, agitated briefly, then disappeared in the city's political ferment. No one, the police least of all, knew much about the OAS (Organisation Armée Secrète)—who ran it, what it could do. In June it issued a tract, with queer echoes of the Third Reich, summing up its program: "One aim: Bring down the Fifth Republic. One slogan: *Algérie française*. One leader: Salan." The press guessed, wrongly, that it consisted principally of students. Nightly now, the streets reverberated to the thud of plastique bombings, for which the OAS next day claimed credit. The organization was also beginning to kill. In May, an ambitious police inspector named Roger Gavoury began, on his own, to investigate the movement and called in the wives of several suspects for questioning; when he was found stabbed to death in his apartment soon afterward, no one was surprised.

Relations between the major power groups in Algeria were at flashpoint. The Army felt cheated of victory, but was chary of the European extremists. The *pieds noirs* felt abandoned—by France, by their old ally the Army, by the world at large. The Moslems distrusted de Gaulle's motives; the old, interdependent relationship between European and Arab was frayed. Change was in the air; French rule was drawing to a close after 130 years, but on what conditions no one knew. Some dreaded the change, others eagerly awaited it; but concern overshadowed anticipation.

For the moment, however, life continued, outwardly serene and uncomplicated as in the past, under the peerless blue skies of North Africa. A boy would buy two dollars' worth of gas and drive a girl on his motorbike to one of the beaches at Zeralda. Most seaside eating places provided plank tables where one unwrapped one's lunch and bought only a glass of beer. Bourgeois families spent weekends in their villas at Alger-Plage and Surcouf. The Moslems went by tradition to the cluttered and not very attractive bathing establishments at Pointe Pescade. With a slight effort of imagination it seemed as if, politics and plastique explosions notwithstanding, life would continue in this timeless way. So the summer wore on, inconclusive, unpredictable, hazardous.

The prospects of the summer of 1961 proved deceptive. The war did not end during these torrid months; a full year still lay ahead before ultimate independence. The final year was the strangest, grimmest, most sterile, in character quite unlike the preceding years of conflict; the roving drawn-out sporadic struggle between the French Army and the FLN in mountains, ravines and impoverished settlements was replaced by a shapeless, nameless vicious war in the cities. It was a war of underground networks, gunmen, deserters, police informers, liaison agents and double agents. Sometimes security forces clashed in the open with European extremists in the streets of Algiers and Oran, but for the most part it remained a twilit war.

Eventually the new war spread to France and affected neighboring countries—Spain, Switzerland, Belgium. It was centered, however, in Algeria's coastal cities, where tempers, stretched to the breaking point, finally broke. An American observer of this period wrote: "As the inevitability of Algerian independence became clear, the opposition of the European minority there turned to a blind rage of senseless violence and, in one of the most extraordinary finales to any event in recent history, a *Götterdämmerung* of self-immolation. . . ."*

By the time the final throes died down, Algeria was independent, but hope of coexistence and cooperation between the two communities, European and Moslem, was wrecked. France passed through a moral crisis that shook the Republic.

The final year of French Algeria saw the culmination of increasingly unbearable pressures, frustrations and miscalculations. As the summer of 1961 progressed, three groups found themselves upon a collision course—Moslems who wanted Algeria independent, Euro-

---

* Charles Gallagher, *The United States and North Africa.*

peans determined to prevent it at all cost, and the French Army, which, haplessly, was caught in the middle.

This is the story of that final year.

PART ONE

The police defend the State as though it were a city;
the military attack the State as though it were a fortress.

—Curzio Malaparte,
Technique du coup d'état

1

Le Chinois

THE HOTEL PRINCESA no longer stands in Madrid. Several years ago it was torn down to make way for one of the capital's rising steel-and-stone skyscrapers. In its day, though, the Princesa passed for a dignified and restful—indeed, exceptionally attractive—establishment appreciated by guests who knew exactly what they required from the staff and seldom disputed a bill. Set in a well-watered semitropical park, boasting a high standard of unobtrusive service, the two-story structure, in the words of one former resident, represented an "oasis of verdure" among the otherwise shabby, arid surroundings of the Calle Princesa near the hustling Plaza de España.

In January 1961, General Raoul Albin Louis Salan was staying in ground-floor Suite Number 4 of the hotel. Its old-fashioned air of leisurely respectability appealed to him.

He could often be met, turned out in neat, heavy tweeds, crossing the lobby or in the lounge taking a whisky. Journalists kept an attentive eye on him. So did the Spanish and French secret police.

Salan was not a guest who went unnoticed. For a general he was smallish, measuring not more than 5 feet 6 inches, but he cut a memorable figure, with a disciplined stocky build, milk-white skin astonishing on the part of a soldier who had spent most of his life in Asia and Africa, and unmistakable, thick, flowing, silvery hair streaked violet from the rinse he used habitually to keep his scalp clean. In spite of deliberate impassivity, his face was far from expressionless; he had shrewd blue eyes, a tough jaw, and a mobile mouth folded by turns into certitude and skepticism. Often his features were overlaid by profound, weary mournfulness.

Salan had reached sixty-one. A few months before, he had slipped across the French frontier—unhindered but almost furtively; at any rate, in a way unbecoming his rank—and taken up residence in Spain. The French Army still carried him on its rolls as a five-star *général d'armée*, retired; his position nonetheless was peculiar and uncomfortable.

He had had a distinguished military career: starting out in the Colonial Service, which is not a traditional steppingstone to the top echelons of the French Army, he had risen to command all French fighting forces in Indochina and Algeria. He had done this by dint of application, intelligence, courage, and a strong dose of common sense. In the process he became the country's most decorated soldier; row upon row of ribbons, including the esteemed Médaille Militaire, flamed at his chest.

By coming to Spain, he entered into direct conflict with the French government. There are not many precedents for a retired general abruptly packing up and departing for a foreign country to carry on political opposition. A retired general is usually a safe general.[*] It is rarer still to see a general go off on such a mission alone, without other generals. What drove Salan was galling humiliation, cold anger, and alarm over the way the Algerian problem was being handled. To which must be added that he had been listening to some of the most virulent right-wingers in France.

There were paradoxes in his behavior. A political writer summed it up thus: "The mystery of Salan is not that he was mysterious but that he should have gone from skepticism to fanaticism . . . from the mysteriousness that was his usual way of life and even a mania with him, to the most rigid sort of commitment." To which a Foreign Legion officer retorted: "The time he joined the OAS was the only time he was honest with himself in his whole life."

Salan cultivated caginess and unfathomability. He veiled his opinions and feelings, perhaps most of all from close friends. "He is as cold as a prison door—unfathomable when you don't know him,

---

[*] The April 1961 putsch would demonstrate the contrary and its consequences.

and also when you do," observed one high-ranking colleague. It was not surprising that in the Army he was attacked as a politician in general's clothes. A fellow general called him—and it was not meant as a compliment—"a born subversive leader." But, above all, he was *"Le Chinois,"* the Chinaman.

An uncle in the family had sailed in the South China Sea. One can appreciate the spell cast on a boy in a staid provincial French town at the turn of the century by tales—no doubt embellished—of an Orient teeming with desperate and romantic figures and bursting with high adventure, an Orient such as the hero of Conrad's *Youth* discovered with gratified eyes.

Salan himself discovered the Orient in the Twenties. He arrived in Indochina as a young captain after St.-Cyr, a baptism of fire in World War I and service in the Levant. Reality, for once, matched and surpassed boyhood tales. He lived upcountry and learned Laotian. He fought river pirates and local war lords. At one point he entered the Deuxième Bureau.

The Colonial Army and the Deuxième Bureau were two major influences that shaped his character with lasting effect. Salan sprang from a tradition of officers with simple tastes, from relatively modest milieux, who entered the Colonial Army and served in outposts of Empire, some balmy, some fetid. Colonial officers were a hard-drinking, profane, convivial group; they had little in common with the aristocratic officer corps stationed in France itself. Years later, Salan spoke movingly of the Empire he had known in its heyday, the Empire "of Gallieni and Lyautey." Significantly, he felt deepest attachment not to France but to the French Empire; he knew the latter better than the former. As for the Deuxième Bureau, it suited him eminently—he was astute and capable, courageous but wary.

Few officers start out to make a career in Intelligence; most are tapped for it, some then take a fancy to it. A psychologist might theorize that it corresponds to a subterranean streak of the outlaw and the actor in their makeup. This may have been Salan's case; at any rate he found himself not unhappy engaged in the sordid but stimulating cat-and-mouse game of intelligence-gathering and spying. He smoked opium; and according to writer Claude Paillat, he covered up officially for the opium trade which provided the

French counterespionage services in the Far East with extra funds.* By this time, he was gaining a reputation as an opportunist adept at tacking with prevailing political winds. Within the Army he was far from popular—he was judged too cold and prudent—but he won the lasting allegiance of some subordinates and impressed his superiors.

In 1939, Interior Minister Georges Mandel dispatched him to Ethiopia on an undercover mission to scout out the possibility of an uprising by native tribes against the Italians—and no doubt to stir one up, if feasible. Salan went ostensibly as a correspondent of *Le Temps;* the cover name he used was Hugues.† The outbreak of war in Europe ended his mission before it ever properly got underway. He was thirty-nine. He married a Vichy hotel owner's blond daughter, who was quite struck by the pragmatic, ambitious, reserved officer. She soon developed considerable ambition of her own —on his behalf.

Salan's record during World War II may leave the reader bemused. He claimed to be "neither Pétainist not Gaullist but interested in winning the war"—a statement that later dumbfounded Jean-Jacques Susini, his political mentor in the OAS, who coldly wondered how one can fight a war without being committed. On this point there was no meeting of minds between the two men. In 1944 Salan liberated Toulon from the Wehrmacht, and the grateful citizens of nearby Solliès-Ville named a street in his honor. He emerged from the war a general.

Inevitably he returned to Indochina—as second in command under the most flamboyant general produced by the post-Liberation French Army, Marshal Jean de Lattre de Tassigny. The river pirates of Salan's early days were a vanishing breed; in their place, Communist guerrillas swarmed through the Tonkin hills. During the winter of 1951, when the French Expeditionary Corps made fitful forays against the Viet Minh, Salan won favorable notice from de Lattre for his detailed preparations before joining battle. *"Il ne s'embarque jamais sans biscuit,"* de Lattre wrote of his subordinate in a report that was to become famous. After de Lattre's death in 1952, Salan replaced him.

---

* Later, the opium trade was a major stake in the Indochina war. The Viet Minh tried to corner this lucrative business, so it was natural, according to the French, to try to block them and channel the trade into French hands.

† The name he subsequently gave to a son, who died at age three and is buried in Algiers.

The change at headquarters was immediate and striking. The new commander in chief, unlike his predecessor, gave few interviews and shunned publicity; the receptions of the past were discontinued. An atmosphere of secrecy and ambiguity enveloped staff work. Salan exercised little of de Lattre's personal sway over the troops. He was at home in the Colonial Army, but for the bulk of the Expeditionary Corps he remained a stranger. He preferred to stay out of Saigon, with its perpetual civilian meddling in military affairs, and set up personal headquarters in Hanoi. He professed some admiration for the elusive enemy in the jungle.

The war was prosecuted. Salan launched an occasional blow against the Viet Minh "so daring that de Lattre himself might have thought twice about undertaking it"; but then he relapsed into periods of indolence. Bizarre stories circulated about his belief in omens—one bit of gossip pretended that he had watched white mice run up a ladder and interpreted this as a sign of victory, then snapped out of his lethargy and ordered a battalion into action. Given Salan's chill sense of realism, it is unlikely that he paid much attention to these stories, although they may have amused him. Fellow officers found it impossible to make him out.

They called him Le Mandarin and Le Chinois. The names stuck for good. They were not undeserved. Salan showed a strong disposition for meditation. Jade beads, Oriental astrology, opium—one can overstress the role of these accessories in Salan's life, but they were indisputably present. Moreover, he admired Asians' composure and reserve, and his ingrained penchant for multifaceted intrigue—a legacy of the Deuxième Bureau—was by this time notorious.

He also developed a marked streak of unsociability; at times he went for days without uttering a word, and asked his aide, Captain Jean Ferrandi, a sharp-tongued Corsican who followed him devotedly for the next eleven years, to assume the burden of conversation with unwanted dinner guests. Ferrandi noted with obvious disappointment in his memoirs: "It is the commander in chief who seems to know where he wants to go who inspires a certain amount of sympathy *a priori* from his staff officers."

Nine months before Dien Bien Phu, Salan turned over his command to General Henri Navarre and left with his reputation intact as a good defensive general. He had witnessed the approaching breakup of Empire, and it angered and disturbed him.

Socialist Premier Guy Mollet assigned Salan in 1956 to Algeria, where he arrived with the awkward label of being a Freemason, a "liberal" general, a commander responsible for losses in Tonkin— in short, in the eyes of hypermistrustful Rightists, a devil who might be ready to liquidate French Algeria. Almost all this was inaccurate—for example, he was not a Protestant but a lapsed Catholic, and it would have been truer to describe him as a disbeliever —but his own reticence and mysteriousness were partly to blame for the exagerrated reports.

It speaks worlds about the neurotic atmosphere in Algiers that hearsay sufficed to trigger a murderous conspiracy against him. Less than two months later, a former paratroop officer, Philippe Castille, poked a bazooka out of a nearby window, aimed it at Salan's office and fired; the shot went off just seconds after Salan had stepped outside, and it killed one of his aides.

The government did little to discover the instigators of the affair, and Salan himself—for reasons that are not entirely clear—ultimately forgave Castille, if not all of his would-be assassins. (The reader has been advised that in many episodes in Salan's life, murkiness is the rule and clarity an exception.)*

His arrival in Algiers coincided with the outbreak of urban terrorism. Criticism of Salan's lack of combativity now proved premature. He brought in General Jacques Massu's 10th Parachute Division to neutralize FLN terrorists of the Casbah. The result was the third-degree, torture and the unresolved deaths of a number of European and Moslem suspects—but the daily terror attacks ceased. Salan became convinced that the vast majority of Moslems wanted no part of the FLN. In 1961 and 1962 he continued to cling to this idea, although meanwhile the situation had changed radically.

The story of de Gaulle's return to power in 1958 has been told elsewhere. Salan's role in the chain of events was brief but revealing. Aware that pressures within the Army of Algeria were building up beyond the danger point, he dispatched a warning report in early May to the President of the Republic, René Coty. The report stressed the need to maintain French presence in Algeria. A timorous

---

* The terrorist group that sought to kill Salan was identified, but rumors linger to this day that one originator of the plot was a former premier of the Republic. The charge has never been proved.

government interpreted it as an ultimatum—which it was certainly not meant to be—and panicked.

On May 15, Salan stood on the balcony of the huge, T-shaped Government General building in the center of Algiers, and confronted a tumultuous mob that had just brought down the Fourth Republic. At first he was booed and promptly withdrew; mistrust of his motives persisted among the *pied noirs*. To please this insurgent crowd, and because he could think of nothing else to say, he reluctantly shouted: *"Vive de Gaulle!"* A great roar rose in response. The crowd mistakenly believed that *"Vive de Gaulle"* corresponded to *"Vive l'Algérie française,"* and it included Salan in the ovation. The consequence was disastrous: Salan became convinced that de Gaulle's return to power was due to him. The popular acclaim went to his head—as several years earlier it had gone to the head of another innately cautious man, Jacques Soustelle.

The ironies of Salan's career began to thicken. His basic affinities were with the Socialists of the Fourth Republic, who after all had appointed him commander in chief; but in May he became the top military representative and "loyal vassal" of de Gaulle, for whom he had no particular liking or admiration. Furthermore, he was now identified with a cause whose champions had tried only recently to eliminate him. In this paradoxical situation, Salan preserved an enigmatic silence.

In the late spring of 1958, de Gaulle toured Algeria, and on June 6, for the first and only time, he made the far-reaching mistake of crying out at Mostaganem: *"Vive l'Algérie française!"* On the strength of this single appeal, and in spite of the fact that de Gaulle regularly admonished officers about the need for change in Algeria, the Right in France would later base its entire accusation of monstrous and Machiavellian double-dealing. It has been suggested that Salan, through his privileged position, early became aware of de Gaulle's intention to break the promise contained in the slogan. It has also been suggested that Salan remained silent because he believed events would oblige de Gaulle to change his policy of self-determination or retire from office. All this is supposition. Salan, since his release from prison, has furnished no explanation. The facts are that Salan carried out de Gaulle's directives that summer, with misgiving but unprotestingly. It is true that it would have required extraordinary courage to challenge de Gaulle at a time when he was borne by a wave of immense popularity and hope.

At the end of the year, Salan, the "loyal vassal," was recalled to France. He made no secret of his conviction that, after the loss of Indochina, France must retain Algeria for strategic and moral reasons. His ideas were certainly influenced and buttressed by his wife, a hard-driving woman wholly committed to the concept of *Algérie française*. In Salan's judgment, he turned over a "more than favorable military situation" to his successor, General Maurice Challe. Logically, therefore, this was the time to proceed with the Army's pet scheme of integration of Europeans and Moslems. When integration showed signs of slowing down, instead of moving forward, Salan's alarm grew over the trend of the government's Algerian policy.

Personal humiliation added to his resentment. He expected to be given the newly created post of Inspector General of National Defense, in recognition of his services in Indochina and Algeria. Temporarily, however, he was named Military Governor of Paris, a purely social assignment. Time passed. The anticipated appointment was not announced. With exquisite disparagement the government made quarters available to his family—in a country house notorious as a former place of assignation. Mme. Salan reacted violently. When Salan finally learned that the new post was being abolished without ever having been filled, he decided grimly that de Gaulle had tricked him to get him out of Algeria because of his political views.

He began to meet with extreme-Right backers of *Algérie française*, including Yves Gignac, secretary general of the powerful Veterans Association of the French Union, and lawyer Jean-Louis Tixier-Vignancour. They reminded Salan that he had been instrumental in "giving" power to the man now bent, in their view, on treasonably abandoning a part of French soil. Undoubtedly they also urged him to redress the error by speaking out.

On June 9, 1960—the day preceding his scheduled retirement from the Army at the age limit of sixty—Salan attended a luncheon in his honor at the Élysée Palace. De Gaulle, who knew a good deal about his new political connections, cautioned him: "Don't get mixed up in a dirty business." Salan listened in noncommittal silence. The two men parted on that note.

A retired general in France automatically belongs to the General Staff Reserve and so needs prior authorization of the Armed Forces Minister to make a public statement. Salan chose to ignore the regulation. On September 14 he addressed a war veterans' congress, and stated flatly: "It is not within the power of any authority to decide upon the relinquishment of a part of the territory where France exercises her sovereignty." This, in itself, amounted to a declaration of hostilities.

That month, Salan further defied the government by sailing with his family for Algiers to take up residence in the villa he had acquired on the heights of Hydra—knowing beforehand that it would be construed as a controversial gesture.

When the *Kairouan* arrived with the Salans aboard, there was no official turnout; but shortly afterward, Delegate General Paul Delouvrier drove up the hillside to inform Salan that his presence in Algeria was undesirable. Delouvrier pointed out that it was unheard-of for a former commander in chief to return in retirement to a theater of operations where he had served in the midst of a war and what he euphemistically called "an unsettled political situation." The Delegate General got nowhere.

As he had feared, Salan's presence encouraged the European activists, who now looked upon him as a leader providentially sent to revive the faltering *Algérie française* movement. Anti-Gaullist Army officers fell into the habit of paying a courtesy call on their former commander to voice their dissatisfaction.

All this naturally struck the government as close to insubordination, and within a month Minister of the Armed Forces Pierre Messmer summoned Salan to Paris to do some explaining. This time, Delouvrier recalls, "I did not drive back up the hill. I called Salan to my office, handed him the message and when he expressed astonishment, told him it had been sent at my request."

Salan reluctantly heeded the order, leaving his wife in Algiers, it was claimed, to act as "his eyes and ears" during his absence. He affected to believe that he was well within his rights, that the government was persecuting him needlessly, and that the unpleasantness would be quickly settled. But in Paris he was told that he could not reenter Algeria.

His testy relations with the government had reached a stage

where he must either give way or expect further sanctions. He knew that he was under surveillance by the Sûreté, and it added to his irritation. Tixier-Vignancour proposed putting him in touch with the Spanish ambassador to France.

The ambassador, not surprisingly for one of Franco's envoys, dreaded the result for Spain if the "Communist FLN" gained control of the southern shore of the Mediterranean. At a meeting in his residence on Avenue Foch, he urged Salan to move to Spain, where he would be treated properly, if he feared being put in prison by the Gaullist regime.

Captain Ferrandi, who accompanied Salan to the meeting, believes in retrospect that these fears were unfounded and resulted from listening to self-seeking and distorted advice. There is something to be said for this view; certainly, some extreme Rightists in France, while ready to exploit Salan's name and prestige, found it expedient to encourage his departure, which left them a clear field for their own ambitions. Delouvrier thinks that in the long run Salan would have been less exposed in Algiers than in Paris to reckless political influences.

For several days after the meeting, Salan stayed at the Hotel Astor with Ferrandi. Le Chinois was not even sure that he would be allowed to leave France; one reason for the next step, accordingly, was to determine whether or not he enjoyed freedom of movement. On October 30 the two men boarded a train to Bordeaux—or rather, this is what they said they were going to do. In fact, they briefly visited Georges Bidault at his country house near Rambouillet, and informed the former premier—now also embroiled in right-wing circles—of their plans; then they traveled by train to Nîmes, gave the remaining police still on their trail the slip at Perpignan, rented a car and drove quickly to Port-Bou at the Spanish frontier.

They showed their passports and were waved on; it was as simple as that. The frontier post had received no order to detain them.

2

The Tower of Madrid

SALAN ARRIVED in Spain smarting with resentment, convinced of de Gaulle's "treason," national and personal, but with no precise plan for doing anything about it. Free of day-to-day police surveillance, he hoped to organize political action to preserve French Algeria. He had no intention of going underground or remaining in Spain indefinitely; Algiers was the goal.

He stayed for a few days in Barcelona, then Madrid, and at the Hotel Londres in San Sebastián. Ferrandi made himself indispensable in a number of roles, as aide-de-camp, private secretary, press secretary, counselor and confidant, and traveling companion. He thought the flight from France impetuous and not well thought out, but he followed loyally and forbore from raising the matter too often. A small, elderly French general, Paul Gardy, former Inspector General of the Foreign Legion, called on the two men, and informed Salan of a putsch being prepared in Algeria. With very little prompting, Gardy soon gave up the ennui of retirement in Bayonne to join Le Chinois.

In December, Salan moved again—back to Madrid, into the Hotel Princesa. At the Princesa no one ever mistook the new guest for anything but what he was, a retired general who bore himself in conservative, aloof style. His well-ordered life proceeded on two

levels, one blameless, the other less so. He spent mornings reading newspapers and periodicals in French and Spanish. He appeared
at about eleven and went on an hour's walk, his only form of exercise, at his brisk but stiff gait. He lunched at a table reserved at
the far end of the hotel dining room, with Ferrandi and occasional
guests including Franco's brother-in-law, Serrano Suñer, the former
Spanish Defense Minister, and officers and activists from Algiers;
and the frugal meals sometimes featured one of the general's favorite
dishes, chick peas cooked in oil imported from North Africa. In the
afternoon he rested during the siesta, and phoned to his wife in
Hydra; he appeared at the bar at six or seven, remained until about
nine, dined, then capped the night with a game of poker.

It was, not wholly by choice, a circumspect and retiring existence.
For in spite of what the Spanish ambassador had promised, Franco's
government was not overjoyed at Salan's presence. Franco depended on the Fifth Republic to buy Spanish oranges, and he
wanted de Gaulle's support to enter NATO. Although the Spanish
government sympathized with Salan on political grounds, for economic reasons it set careful limits on its welcome. It asked him to
engage in no political activity; and it can be assumed that privately
it stipulated that, if he disregarded the request, he do so discreetly.
Salan was still on the Army rolls, and the French Embassy eventually sent round a counselor to sound him out on his plans. The
diplomat learned little, primarily because Le Chinois had no intention of telling him anything, but also because his plans were vague.
Ferrandi, who was still on active duty, meanwhile received orders
to report to Fréjus, but he ignored them.

At another level, the important part of Salan's day came when he
met with the fugitives from the Barricades Trial in Paris, who had
also arrived by prearrangement in the Spanish capital.

The Barricades Trial opened on November 4, 1960. Nineteen defendants appeared before a military court, seventeen of them
charged with an attempt on the internal security of the state; all
had participated, directly or indirectly, in the week-long January
insurrection that took twenty-four lives. Less than halfway through
the trial, the judge inexplicably set at liberty the most outspoken
defendant and one of the ringleaders of the uprising, Pierre Lagail-

larde.* He promptly fled the country to Spain—soon followed by three fellow defendants including Jean-Jacques Susini.

Both Lagaillarde and Susini were protégés of the French Army's Cinquième Bureau, set up in 1957 to apply psychological-warfare methods during the Algerian War to the Moslem population. Both, while enrolled at Algiers University, had devoted as much time to agitation as to studies. Both were stalwarts of the *Algérie française* movement. There, the similarity between the two ended.

The high point of Lagaillarde's flamboyant career occurred on May 13, 1958, when, in uniform, armed and with a handful of followers—"not more than twenty men," he later affirmed—he broke into the Government General building and occupied it, setting in motion the events that led to the downfall of the Fourth Republic. This exploit won him fame in Algeria and led to his easy election as a deputy. Trim russet beard, chin resolutely set into an adverse wind, flashing eyes—this is stuff out of which tabloids manufacture heroes, and Lagaillarde, a sort of Algerian Errol Flynn, made the most of it. But once elected to the National Assembly, he hovered between swashbuckling ardor and parliamentary prudence, losing many of his followers. Among his compatriots in Algiers, his reputation revived during the Barricades, when he set up an armed camp on the university grounds and, a week later, marched out of his beleaguered command post at the head of a column of insurgents, amid military honors normally reserved for a serious enemy. Typically, he challenged the court to indict him for his earlier action in May 1958 and railed at de Gaulle as "an old man obsessed with death."

Susini cut a less colorful but surely more interesting figure. Physically he was unprepossessing—blond, skinny, with a huge forehead and pallid complexion; one writer described him as a "tubercular beanpole, sickly and sarcastic," while he reminded a *New York Times* correspondent of "a silent man in an old Western movie," which was unfair and inaccurate. Intellectually, he stood head and shoulders above most activists, if only through an ability

---

* Lagaillarde was set at temporary liberty under circumstances that appeared scandalous and have remained unelucidated. A veteran French court reporter notes that only twenty-four hours before, the National Assembly had voted, by 219–201, to keep Lagaillarde in confinement. He says the judge's ruling came as a complete surprise: ". . . it was the first time in memory that a court had done this in mid-trial." J. M. Theolleyre, *Ces Procès qui ébranlèrent la France.*

to juggle complex political ideas with considerable deftness. Brainy and ambitious, he was obsessed with popular insurrection, raising an army of citizen-soldiers on the Israeli model, and the organizational methods of totalitarian groups. The tactics of the enemy—in this instance, the FLN—fascinated him. (A relentless anti-Communist, he chose a citation from Lenin as the epigraph for his book on the OAS.) A close friend defended Susini's ambition as that of any "highly intelligent man." But there was something abstract and frigid about his political preoccupation, and the same friend compared him to a computer into which all the relevant data about a political problem could be fed, and an answer would automatically come out.

A *pied noir* of Corsican descent, he had studied medicine in Strasbourg and Lyons, dabbled briefly in student right-wing politics, then joined café owner Joseph Ortiz's ultra movement, the Front National Français. Susini became its most effective orator. Because he was a facile and inexhaustible talker, who spoke with authority, people listened; he talked to them about the "unnatural alliance" between the French government and the FLN, and about Algeria and its future, in which he believed passionately.

Susini participated in Barricades Week as one of Ortiz's lieutenants. Before a crowd of two thousand at an FNF rally he shouted: "The hour to overturn the regime has struck. The revolution will start in Algiers and go to Paris." But within activist circles he was still relatively obscure; when he launched upon a harangue condemning the Army's unreliability as an ally, Ortiz coldly told him to shut up—and Susini complied, then enjoyed the melancholy consolation of being proved right.

Subsequently put on trial, he startled the court by a proclamation that reflected Fascist doctrine. "I wanted," he said, "to reconcile the movement of social emancipation, which is shaking the entire world, and the fact of nationalism. I have attempted . . . to take up in an over-all synthesis these two currents that have shaken the twentieth century." Anybody who has met Susini will recognize the tone and the pretentiousness of this statement; at the time he made it, he was twenty-seven, the youngest of the defendants, but no false modesty inhibited him then or later. Undoubtedly concerned by the effect this statement made on the bench, his lawyer interposed: "It is a crying abuse of language to tax him as a National Socialist because, like others, he dreamed of a synthesis of nationalism and socialism." The distinction remains obscure.

When the court recessed in December, Susini, Marcel Ronda, a captain of the Unités Territoriales (the Algiers Home Guard) and Jean-Maurice Demarquet, a former Poujadist deputy, fled to Beziers, contacted Marcel Bouyer, also a former Poujadist deputy, and with his help bolted across the Pyrenees.* Like Salan, they arrived in Spain expecting to stay only a short time.

Susini's opinion of his fellow activists, never very high, had plummeted during Barricades Week. He reached Madrid with a wealth of ideas, but no power base and no one to lend his ideas an aura of authority and prestige. Then he met Salan. The meeting was to have a momentous effect on the subsequent last-ditch attempt to preserve French Algeria.

He experienced some admiration for this battle-scarred general in his sixties who was running risks to his career, reputation and security to defend a cause, and who, once his mind was made up, disliked half measures. Le Chinois's imperturbable calm impressed him. But he also decided that Salan was a man "who did not create circumstances but was superb at exploiting them," a tactician rather than a strategist. This seemed a welcome state of affairs to Susini, whose limitless ambition was to create, himself, an entirely new set of circumstances, as part of what he believed was a revolution. He did not make the mistake of considering Salan a mere figurehead, but set out to convert him to his ideas. These, briefly put, consisted of mass revolutionary action and social reform.

The notion of a twenty-seven-year-old agitator undertaking to sway a sixty-one-year-old general may seem either shallow or preposterous. It was neither. Salan was restless and vindictive; he wanted to checkmate de Gaulle for various reasons already described, but he lacked a plan of action and a program, and he was adrift—brusquely, if voluntarily, cut off from career-long friendships and environment. It must not be assumed that he was acting altogether in a void; right-wingers in France backed him, but practically his contacts at this stage were limited to a few dissident senior officers. So he listened increasingly to Susini.

Among the activists in Madrid, Susini's only potential rival for

* The verdicts handed down by the court in March 1961 were even more surprising. Susini, in spite of his flight from justice, received a *suspended* sentence of two years; Lagaillarde, ten years (the prosecution asked for twenty). Ortiz was condemned to death *in absentia*. Thirteen defendants were acquitted.

influence was Lagaillarde; but Lagaillarde was extravagant, unruly, bombastic. He exclaimed that he was ready to die for Algeria but wanted a general to die beside him—which earned the retort, "Who said anything about dying?" His free-spending habits in bars, restaurants and, in particular, the nightclub L'Elefante Blanco quickly became legendary. At first, he stayed in the American-style Plaza Hotel, near but grander than the Princesa, then he moved across the square into a top-story suite of the Torre de Madrid, a luxury apartment building, which boasted Sophia Loren among its tenants and some of the highest rents in the capital. None of this did much to ingratiate him with a man of Salan's careful nature. Then, too, *le barbu* suffered from being a mere reserve paratroop lieutenant, while Susini enjoyed the enormous advantage of being a civilian— Salan could talk on relatively equal terms with the latter, not with the former. But above all, Susini was no ordinary twenty-seven-year-old agitator. Other men, experienced and discerning men twenty years his senior, would later consent to take orders from him, struck by his emphasis on efficiency, his total commitment and an icy fanaticism—characteristics which would lead one observer, who was not an unmitigated admirer, to describe him as the "most intelligent, most capable and most ambitious of the civilian leaders of the OAS."

During December, in spite of various stresses, Salan, Lagaillarde and Susini maintained daily contact. Like most political malcontents without troops, they took refuge in writing tracts. One, addressed to Europeans of Algeria and also signed by Ronda, said: "Four Frenchmen have met in a Madrid hotel. We do not pretend to represent you, but we shall do all we can soon to share your efforts and suffering." Fifty-eight thousand copies were prepared for distribution.

A few days later, Lagaillarde, on his own, dispatched another tract in a more belligerent vein. It said bluntly: "Unite among yourselves, for we are going to fight."

On December 9, General de Gaulle landed in his presidential Caravelle at Tlemcen on the first stage of a scheduled three-day visit to Algeria. A singular reception awaited him at the hands of military and civilian extremists. Since they disagreed with his policy, they planned to kill him.

The plot was the work of the Front de l'Algérie Française, the latest among countless home-grown movements to maintain French rule in Algeria and thwart the establishment of an independent republic. Formed in June 1960, its stated purpose was to represent the entire European minority and all anti-FLN Moslems. It set about doing this with considerable fanfare. Operating legally, it opened a recruiting office across the street from the Prefecture, with local officials' blessings, and it solicited contributions. The *bachaga* Said Boualem, a wealthy Moslem landowner in western Algeria with pro-French leanings, was named honorary president. The immediate results were impressive. *Pieds noirs* formed lines to join (they pressured Moslems into doing likewise), and soon FAF, as it was called, claimed membership exceeding 500,000, though official estimates scaled this down to 200,000, which was still considerable.

In fact, the emphasis on legality was so much nonsense, for simultaneously a secret branch was organized, like the *apparat* which operates alongside a Communist party cell. FAF's above-board activity served two purposes: it created a not entirely true impression of unity and resolve among the *pieds noirs*, and it masked a far-reaching subsurface conspiracy. The secret branch, known as *le FAF clandestin*, stored arms (many left over from Barricades Week), maintained contact with sympathetic Army officers and Paris-based extremists, and drew up a detailed plan for a putsch against the government.

The chief architect of the plan was a retired Air Force general and *pied noir*, Edmond Jouhaud. A heavy-set, vigorous and choleric man, with strong emotional ties to his native country, he had risen to the rank of chief of staff of the Air Force, then Inspector General, after which he asked to be retired prematurely because of whole-hearted opposition to de Gaulle's policy of self-determination for Algeria's ten million inhabitants. He then returned to Algiers, where he plunged into local activism, using as cover a position in a card-board-manufacturing firm. One of the few high-ranking *pied noir* generals residing in Algeria, he became the link between the Army and FAF.

Jouhaud's plan hinged on exploiting a city-wide general strike and street demonstrations to provoke clashes between European youths and security forces. In the midst of these disorders, certain picked units of paratroopers would side with the demonstrators and fire on *gendarmes mobiles* and CRS.* Some conspirators wanted de Gaulle himself to be taken prisoner or, better still, "accidentally" killed while touring eastern Algeria, either at an officers' mess or in

* Compagnie Républicaine de Sécurité, riot-control troops.

the isolated countryside. The resultant confusion would bring to power in France an Army-backed government pledged to defend *l'Algérie française*. In short, this represented a more elaborate and ambitious version of Barricades Week. As was the case in the earlier uprising, the plan presupposed the Army's active intervention on the side of the Europeans—a tacit admission that without the Army the *pieds noirs* could do little or nothing.

Considerable but uninspired work went into the plan. Jouhaud, for example, drew up a list of 150 persons to be arrested in Algeria; reflecting a dearth of political realism, the list included Monseigneur Duval and "progressive" schoolteachers, whom Jouhaud disliked, but not *gendarmerie* commanders, whose arrest could—as any revolutionist could have told him—make a significant difference. The FAF clandestine committee, which ran the secret branch, consisted of six men, all civilians; in the event, they knew more about carrying out a *coup de force* than did the general, and they haggled endlessly with him over details. Shortly before the target date, Jouhaud informed Salan of the plan, and Le Chinois, who was in San Sebastián, approved it and agreed to come to Algiers.*

On the eve of de Gaulle's trip, the French government unwittingly played into the plotters' hands by announcing its own plans to hold a referendum the following month on administrative reforms in Algeria. FAF promptly denounced the referendum, issued a strike call, and appealed to all Europeans to assemble next morning "without arms, calm and resolute. The time has come to affirm our fierce will to remain French. . . ." On the surface, this sounded reasonable enough, but it camouflaged a signal to launch operations.

Early December 9, gangs of European youths moved out into the streets of Algiers and began to bombard *gendarmes mobiles* with lead pellets and cast-iron bolts. The youngsters had the advantage of being fast on their feet: at the first sign of a counterattack they raced uphill and waited until the pursuers, mostly older men, stopped out of breath and started back down the hill; then the youths re-formed, attacked, and the chase recommenced.

The FAF clandestine committee directed operations from a garage on Boulevard Saint-Saëns, in liaison with Jouhaud, who was in a villa on the heights surmounting the city. His plan called for riots

---

* Salan never succeeded in reaching Algiers on this occasion. He disappeared from his hotel and dodged both the Spanish police and French counterespionage service, but the plot collapsed and he reappeared at the hotel.

the first day, to be followed by the paratroopers' intervention the second day, when de Gaulle was to be assassinated.

On December 10, harassment continued as foreseen. *Pieds noirs* poured oil on hillside trolley tracks, and parked their cars athwart intersections. The strike spread, and strikers swelled the number of demonstrators. *Gendarmes mobiles* and CRS troops riposted with tear gas and grenades, but at times were submerged and even disarmed. FAF commandos briefly surrounded the Palais d'Été, the summer residence of French governors general. There were four paratroop regiments stationed around Algiers, and FAF called for prompt support by its allies. Nothing happened—for the simple reason that the regimental commanders wavered.

At the end of the day, Dominique Zattara, a local schoolmaster and member of the clandestine committee, called on Jouhaud and expressed his concern. The general asked him to keep up the rioting a third day, and promised that one regiment, at least, would intervene. Zattara reluctantly agreed. At ten o'clock that evening, he saw trucks of the 18ème Régiment de Chasseurs Parachutistes driving in from the suburb of Birmandreis—"I thought we were going to win," he recalls.

The weather is no ally of politics. A drenching rain fell that night on Algiers, dampening the already weakening spirit of the demonstrators. On the third day, the barrage of projectiles resumed, though halfheartedly, against security forces, but by this time it was too late.

It was at about 10 A.M. that the unforeseen occurred. From the housing developments of Diar-el Mahcoul and Diar-el Saada, from Clos Salembier and Belcourt, a horde of club-wielding Moslems flowed down the hillside on a broad front, flourishing the outlawed green-and-white banner of the FLN. At first they chanted, *"Vive de Gaulle,"* but this swiftly gave way to *"Vive le FLN!"* and *"Ferhat Abbas au pouvoir!"**Moslem women and girls appeared in the forefront of the procession—some wearing green blouses and ribbons, the nationalist color—screaming and urging the men on. Nothing like it had ever been seen before in Algiers. The counterdemonstrators broke through roadblocks and overflowed into the European

---

* Supporters of Algérie Française accused Political Affairs Counselor François Coulet of covertly organizing the Moslem counterdemonstration to show support for de Gaulle; if so, it was easily taken over by FLN agents, who transformed it to their own ends.

quarters, where hysterical *pieds noirs,* who had hitherto done all the demonstrating with impunity, opened fire on them from rooftops and balconies. Eventually the Moslems were turned back by CRS and paratroopers of the 18ème RCP, who had rolled into town for a different purpose; but the challenge was launched, and photographers were there to record the event.

It is impossible to overestimate the importance of December 11. French historians are nearly unanimous in pinpointing it as the turning point of the entire Algerian War. The psychological jolt was enormous. The counterdemonstration graphically drove home the lesson that the Moslems could, if they chose, play at the Europeans' game and win it, for they far outnumbered the Europeans; and suddenly they realized their own force. The *pied noir* ultras more than ever distrusted the Army, which had let them down once again, as during Barricades Week. Within the Army, many officers experienced second thoughts about the great hope of May 1958. Integration, it seemed, had never existed, or it had been outstripped by events. The ensuing despair of some soldiers and civilians led, stage by stage, to the formation of the OAS. "All the basic characteristics of the OAS," wrote Paul-Marie de la Gorce, "are comprised in the history of those twenty-four hours. . . . December 11, 1960, explains the existence of the OAS, its psychology, its methods and even its mythology."

De Gaulle's potential assassins, meanwhile, had lost their nerve. During the riots, the President of the Republic stayed out of Algeria's coastal cities and traveled through the hinterland. Jeered by Europeans and hailed by Moslems, he advised the population imperturbably to forget "outworn slogans." Then, a day before schedule, he flew back to Paris, unscathed. The government never openly acknowledged the assassination plot, but Information Minister Louis Terrenoire, in a speech at the Mutualité hall on December 15, hinted at it, referring to "a diabolical plot . . . in which everything was foreseen, prepared, organized." Fed up with the European extremists, de Gaulle ordered FAF dissolved and its leaders arrested.

The clandestine committee disbanded in confusion; Zattara and several other committee members identified with the "legal" FAF were imprisoned. The secret branch had received a body blow. As for the exiles in Spain, who had been awaiting the announcement of de Gaulle's death to rush back to Algiers, they were left stranded. And more bad news was in store for them.

On January 8, 1961, voters in France and Algeria replied to two propositions. The first was the French government's plan to establish executive bodies in the twelve Algerian departments. The second would authorize the government to hold an Algeria-wide referendum "when security permits."

Shorn of administrative jargon, the intent was clearly to provide Algeria with more autonomy in the short term; while preparing it, in connection with a cease-fire, for some measure of independence in the long run. It implied giving de Gaulle carte blanche to apply his solution to the Algerian impasse. In France, both the extreme Left and the extreme Right opposed the two propositions, and Algérie Française supporters predicted an overwhelming "No" vote.

But referendums and plebiscites have a way of reflecting the wishes of governments in power; this is why governments organize them, and January 8 proved no exception. Seventy-five percent of the ballots cast in France gave de Gaulle the "frank and solid Yes" he had called for in three major speeches on December 20 and 31 and January 6. However, some six million registered voters abstained—a notably high percentage, which revealed dissatisfaction with the way the problem had been put to the electorate.

In Algeria, the FLN ordered all Moslems to boycott the referendum, and 40 percent of the Moslem voters did. Of the rest, 69 percent voted "Yes," but a breakdown by localities showed that a heavy Yes vote came from the countryside, where it was not inconceivable that Moslems had cast their ballots under pressure from local authorities, both European and Moslem. In the major cities, where Europeans abounded, "No" votes sometimes amounted to 75 percent of the total.

De Gaulle, satisfied, drew several significant conclusions from the over-all results. He saw January 8 as putting an end to the pressure exercised by the Right on behalf of *Algérie française;* and he told Terrenoire that, no matter how the abstentions were interpreted, a majority *in France itself* had given him a free hand to negotiate. Finally, the success of the FLN boycott impressed him.

Convinced that nothing had been done from 1830 to 1958, the date of his return to power, to settle the Algerian problem,* the

* He said as much, in a speech on July 12, 1961.

General was not one to waste time on further minute analysis of the referendum. On February 27, following several diplomatic approaches, he conferred for six hours in the fourteenth-century château of Rambouillet with Tunisia's President Habib Bourguiba. The communiqué issued after this meeting spoke of "positive and rapid progress" toward direct negotiations between France and the GPRA, the Algerian Provisional Government.

The effect of these developments on the exiles in Madrid can be imagined. "We are going to fight . . ."; the truculent tone of Lagaillarde's tract belied a certain despair. The December putsch had backfired, the January referendum, contrary to expectations, had given de Gaulle a stable majority. It seemed as if they had fled from France for nothing—further opposition to the General appeared hopeless and foredoomed. Worse still, there was no unanimity among them about ways to reverse the current. Relations between Salan and Lagaillarde had inevitably chilled, and by late January couriers arriving from right-wing groups in France found two distinct activist headquarters in Madrid, one at the Princesa, the other at the Torre de Madrid. Susini conducted liaison between the two headquarters.

In spite of the unfavorable outlook, Susini and Lagaillarde agreed on two central points: the need to resist de Gaulle's self-determination policy by force, and the need for this resistance to take a different form than in the past. Both favored the formation of a single civilian and military combat organization. In early February, at a series of meetings in Lagaillarde's suite at the Torre de Madrid, they worked out some guidelines. The entire European population of Algeria was to be enrolled and mobilized in the new movement; all existing activist groups would be fused into it; it would function in close liaison with backers in France. Over-all leadership was to be carried on by a central committee of six, which would entrust the direction of all operations to Salan.

At one meeting, Susini proposed calling the new movement O.S., for "Organisation Secrète," but the FLN had already appropriated the initials for its own paramilitary organization founded in 1947. Lagaillarde suggested O.A.S. for *"Organisation armée secrète"*),*

* Translated into English, this becomes "Secret Armed Organization." Later, the two terms, *Organisation armée secrète* and *Organisation de l'Armée*

and the set of letters was adopted. So began, under an essentially uninspired name and in the unlikely setting of a modernistic luxury skyscraper, the OAS, on which Susini pinned his hopes for a revolutionary new party that, as he said, "would be closer to the Yugoslav partisans than the Spanish *Opus Dei*." The emphasis, realistically, was on armed organization; it did not pretend to be an army, but counted on the French Army's support (the lesson of December 11 had not been fully assimilated); for the moment—with the exception of two retired generals, Salan and Gardy—it was in the hands of civilians.

It came into being gradually, one may say, almost imperceptibly; the OAS in the late winter of 1961 was more a wish among a small group than a reality. In Paris, Jacques Soustelle thought that French Algeria could still be saved, but he acknowledged that the prospects were slim.

Ferrandi first heard of the proposed new movement that week from Susini. Susini was optimistic and predicted that the OAS would absorb all existing activist groups in Algeria and put an end to internal bickering. When Ferrandi repeated what he had heard, Salan's reaction was less hopeful. He dismissed the idea as "acceptable until something better comes along." As for the new set of letters, coming as it did after FAF, FNF, FR and MP-13,* he exclaimed: "Poor Algerians!" (When he learned later from his wife that someone had scrawled "OAS" on the walls of his villa, he asked distractedly what it meant).

At the end of February, a liaison agent named André Saada left for Algiers with a directive from Lagaillarde instructing his followers to regroup under the new designation. The directive stressed the need to form "an essentially civilian apparatus for revolutionary combat."

The mood in Algiers was receptive. The activists, though stunned by the December debacle, were beginning to regroup cautiously,

---

secrète ("Secret Army Organization") were used interchangeably and loosely. Susini said in an interview: "Those who created the term OAS wanted to recall the existence of a Secret Army in France during the last war"; but he said this five months after the fact. Ferrandi said that Susini wanted a term "that suggested force, cohesion, mystery," but this is also a *post hoc* explanation. For many, the key word throughout remained "organization" rather than "army."

* FR, France-Résurrection; MP-13, Mouvement Populaire du 13 Mai. Both were right-wing movements.

and they were still deadly. On January 25, at noon, two men called on Maître Pierre Popie, a liberal barrister, who, in spite of death threats following his defense of an FLN militant in court, continued to work at his lonely office on Rue de l'Abreuvoir, near the Palais de Justice. The two men belonged to a clandestine terrorist group working with, though not directly under, FAF. They found Popie alone, stabbed him to death after a terrible fight, and fled.

Zattara, released from prison, resumed contact with other members of the clandestine committee, and meetings took place in his villa at Rue des Pins, in Hydra, and at the home of Claude Capeau, an employee of the Électricité et Gaz d'Algérie. The secret branch took note of Lagaillarde's directive, but reacted negatively to his insistence on being recognized as sole leader of the new movement. A leader, they reasoned, must be physically present in Algiers; when Lagaillarde showed no hurry to return, they dismissed his claim to leadership.

But his instructions to regroup were followed, and contact was made with France-Résurrection and Jeune Nation, the other activist groups in the city. It would take months to build a unified organization—and the work was never wholly terminated—but out of these initial meetings a first, wary and tentative effort at coordination emerged. Zattara estimated the new movement now totaled about one thousand active supporters throughout Algeria.

So, on March 6, for the first time, inhabitants of Algiers going out into the streets found walls, doorways and tree trunks daubed with a set of still unfamiliar initials: OAS.

3

Captains, Colonels and Civilians

IN THE same spring of 1961 the Sûreté Nationale furnished Premier Michel Debré with a list of officers it considered unreliable in the event of a putsch. The list contained hundreds of names, including those of forty generals.*

The Armed Forces Ministry knew about the problem, of course, and took steps to remedy it—steps that were, however, tentative, timid and largely inadequate. It shuffled a few officers here, and disciplined a few there; units suspected of activism were transferred to the Algerian frontiers, far from the hotbed of city dissidence, or to regions where they had no link with the *pieds noirs*.

What was worrisome about the situation in 1961 was that restiveness in the military establishment was not limited to a definable group; it was tenuous, intangible but widespread—which accounted for the length of the list.

Ever since the Barricades of January 1960, and in a sense long before then, the position of the French Army had been ambiguous; and the government had good reason to be concerned.

* In France it is the function of the Sûreté, which is an arm of the Interior Ministry—together with other investigative agencies including Military Security—to keep tabs on the political leanings and aspirations, the contacts and friendships, of an Army that is supposed to stay out of politics. The Republic has learned through painful experience that to be informed is, sometimes, to be forearmed. Besides which, it is the view of the French police that its duty is to know about everything and everybody in the nation.

The word at the time to describe the unhealthy atmosphere within the Army was *malaise;* it connotes lingering, indefinable disaffection, and it was all the harder to cope with for being so vague.

The immediate cause of disaffection was Algeria and the obsessive certitude in some military circles that de Gaulle was about to betray their interests and those of the nation; but there were deeper and more tangled roots. The story of the inner travail of the French Army after the collapse of 1940 has been told innumerable times; at the core was the fundamental conflict between those who, like de Gaulle, rebelled and resisted, and those who followed orders from a legally constituted government, a course of action they had been systematically taught to regard as their supreme duty. Many, like Salan, adopted an intermediate and neutral position. When the war ended, the conflict was unresolved.

The Army that slowly re-formed after the Liberation was, in consequence, a patchwork of sharply differing concepts and ideals. The officer corps was haunted by ghosts named Giraud, Darlan and Pétain. In 1946 the professionals boarded ship for Indochina, where they suffered a new, hard defeat at the hands of a numerically inferior but more mobile enemy. The lesson they drew from this defeat had less to do with military operations than with political manipulation. They had come upon Mao Tse-tung's precepts on guerrilla warfare and subversion. It is curious that to the rigidly logical French mind, the proposition of employing Communist techniques to battle Communism did not seem paradoxical. On the contrary, it appeared practicable, even irresistible—an expeditious and painless way of indoctrinating local populations and winning a new type of war, provided that one overlooked or ignored those passages in Mao that explicitly relate military success to revolutionary goals. Such goals were out of the question for the French Army, which was fighting on behalf of a most unrevolutionary society.

When the same career officers arrived in Algeria in 1954 to put down the dawning rebellion in the Aurès mountains, the lessons of Indochina remained alive and were quickly put into practice. In some areas, officers made an honest, thoroughgoing and indeed admirable effort to promote social reform—always, however, under the French flag, and often in the teeth of resistance by European settlers. Professor Raoul Girardet, a right-wing observer of military mores, has noted that already, at this date, *Algérie fraternelle* possessed greater appeal for junior officers in the field, many of whom had little sympathy for the *pieds noirs,* than the suspect slogan "*Algérie française,*" with its connotations of vested interests and rigid racial segregation. Officers and enlisted men alike grew attached to Algeria. Many persuaded themselves that the success of integration here—the development of a Franco-Algerian state—would redeem past failures elsewhere.*

The Army's illusions about integration ended brutally on September 16, 1959, the day de Gaulle proposed three solutions to the Algerian problem: "*francisation*" (which was a Gaullist way of saying integration); association; and secession (which was another way of saying independence). Until then, many officers had argued that de Gaulle's intention was to honor the commitment he had so imprudently made at Mostaganem, where he was persuaded to shout "*Vive l'Algérie française!*" Abruptly, the same officers realized that integration was viewed in Paris as only one of three remedies, and not necessarily the best.

So opened what was called the "great schism" between the French Army and de Gaulle.

The Army had never wholly liked, trusted or accepted him. At St.-Cyr, he was considered overweening and aloof. Later he was viewed, with some jealousy, as Pétain's protégé, recalled providentially, through the intercession of the Marshal, from dull assignments in dreary provincial garrisons to staff duties. The views on modern tank warfare expressed in the slim book, *Vers une Armée de métier,* won only a limited audience. Moreover, Charles de Gaulle was an officer who, unlike the great colonial soldier-administrators, Lyautey, Weygand, Juin, had never served a day in North Africa. All in all, he was resented both by the hidebound element of the Army, which could not forgive his call to disobedience in June 1940, and by the new crop of politically minded young officers, who could not fathom and did not trust his aims in Algeria.

De Gaulle, in turn, made no secret of his disdain for the Army. His impatience was notorious with the slowness and the unimaginativeness and other shortcomings of the military mind. To impress de Gaulle, a general must be a statesman, a visionary, a reformer and a poet—Rameses II, Mohammed, Saint Louis and Peter the Great no doubt commanded his admiration—but men "of all seasons" are in short supply, in the French and other armies. Whether or not

---

* Suez added to the Army's frustrations. Blaming U.S. intervention, some segments of the Army became as anti-American as the Navy was anti-British.

the antimilitaristic aspect of de Gaulle's makeup has been exaggerated, he was aware of the Army's limitations, especially in the field of greatest interest to him, foreign policy. Here the breach was complete. "For de Gaulle," wrote one observer, "France's position in the world depended on a calculation of dozens of factors; for much of the Army, all of France's honor, esteem and success centered on a single issue—Algeria."*

During the decade of exile at Colombey-les-Deux-Églises, he had lost contact with the new French Army that came into being in the Fifties. It was not the old, traditionalist anonymous Army of homogeneous social background and interests that flourished until World War II. The new Army was a mirror of various social classes; it was interested in politics, and not averse to public relations, and in Algeria it had discovered a cause and a crusade. In Jean-Louis Guillaud's phrase, the "heady perfume of disobedience" permeated it. Officers fell into the habit of going outside channels to get their way; orders were no longer issued to be carried out automatically, but became, in one memorable phrase of the time, "a basis for discussion." The intermittent warfare dictated by the terrain and the enemy allowed senior officers ample time for soul-searching and brooding over the faults of civilians, while junior officers carried on whatever localized military action was deemed necessary. De Gaulle misjudged the Army's temper; he ascribed its restlessness and lack of internal discipline to the weakness of the Fourth Republic, and was persuaded that his own prestige would suffice to bring it to heel. Barricades Week proved him wrong; but after the threat was reduced he concluded, mistakenly, that the troublemakers within the Army had shot their bolt. And never one to conceal his opinion, he indulged in sarcasm at the Army's expense: "It cannot see further than the nearest hill," he stated mercilessly (*"L'armée qui ne voit plus loin que le bout de son djebel"*).

Meanwhile, the Army's worries about where de Gaulle was leading it subsided momentarily in 1959, when the new commander in chief, Maurice Challe, created an operational reserve, composed of paratroopers and Legionnaires, as the spearhead of an offensive strategy aimed at actively seeking out and destroying FLN guerrillas in the *djebels,* sealing off each *wilaya* (province) and securing the frontiers. The new strategy paid off—perhaps not as spectacularly as claimed by the communiqués, but the number of *mou-*

* George Kelly, *Lost Soldiers*

*hadjinnes** killed in the field undeniably rose, morale within the *wilayas* slumped, and among French Army officers it soared.

The burst of euphoria was short-lived. For while militarily the tide was turning, it led nowhere politically, certainly not to a reassertion of French sovereignty in Algeria, which was the Army's objective. Politically, indeed, the situation remained at dead center in 1960. Bernard Tricot, one of de Gaulle's closest counselors, called it "a lost year."† Then as the new year began—in the wake of the December 1960 riots—de Gaulle moved toward direct negotiations with the detested GPRA. In February he met with Bourguiba. In March, the French cabinet publicly expressed its hope of opening talks "with an official delegation" on the self-determination of the Algerian peoples. Several days later, Évian was chosen as a meeting place. And on March 30, the French government and the GPRA announced in a joint communiqué that cease-fire negotiations would start on April 7.

The officers of the Army of Algeria followed this seemingly ineluctable progression of events with mounting anger and anxiety. They saw de Gaulle's new policy as the epitome of duplicity, a flagrant and cynical repudiation of all the earlier statements— *"Je vous ai compris,"* in Algiers; *"Vive l'Algérie française!"* at Mostaganem; and "Who can doubt that anything would bring greater joy . . . to de Gaulle than to see the Moslems choose . . . the solution that would be the most French?"‡ They saw military victory virtually within the Army's grasp being scrapped and abandoned by Paris; and they saw the government going back on solemn commitments to the Moslem population, including tens of thousands of Moslem auxiliaries—*harkis, moghaznis* and self-defense groups— fighting alongside French forces. The *malaise* deepened. Army opposition to de Gaulle underwent a significant change. *"De Gaulle se trompe* [De Gaulle is making a mistake]" was heard less and less; it was replaced by uglier criticism: *"De Gaulle nous a trompé*

---

* Combatants, or soldiers.

† Tricot noted, in conversation with the author, that the government concentrated on an economic effort in Algeria (the Constantine Plan) during 1959–60, rather than on political solutions. The mysterious Si Salah affair, nonetheless, occurred in mid-June 1960. De Gaulle secretly met with Si Salah and Si Mohamed, two *wilaya* chiefs, by night at the Élysée Palace; they showed some readiness to conclude a separate peace, but de Gaulle dropped the contact, preferring, according to his critics, to deal with the GPRA, thereby letting the war drag on another year and a half.

‡ Television address on January 29, 1960.

[De Gaulle has betrayed us]." Officers' messes buzzed with scandalous anecdotes about his alleged gamy behavior in his earlier days, the limitlessness of his aspirations which had already isolated him at St.-Cyr, and his dangerous opportunism. Activist officers wondered whether they were not guilty of the accusation leveled by right-wing journalist Lucien Rebatet, who charged the Army with "committing the worst error in postwar French history by bringing the wrong man to power in May 1958." But what could they do about it?

The reactions of three young officers forecast some of what was to come.

Lieutenant Michel de la Bigne, one of six brothers serving in the French Army, heard of the Moslem demonstrations of 1960 with what he later recalled as "indignation and shock." He was on active duty with the 1st Foreign Legion Paratroop Regiment in the Constantinois area, and he refused to lead his platoon on further missions against the enemy. He saw no point henceforth in risking his men's lives, he announced, when the FLN was allowed to mass in the streets of Algiers and unfurl its flag.

De la Bigne was transferred out of Algeria to Annecy in the foothills of the French Alps. This was intended as punishment—but punishment, it turned out, of an extremely gentle sort. His new commanding officer chided him, but other senior officers went out of their way to express "understanding" of his motives. His opinion on the situation in Algeria was sought and appreciated. He was under no special surveillance, and he was granted generous leave. He used it to contact fellow malcontents.

Captain Pierre Sergent found himself, by choice, in the thick of the European demonstrations of 1960. A tense young Foreign Legion officer who took himself with utmost seriousness, he volunteered to carry on liaison with the FAF clandestine committee. At the height of the riots, eyewitnesses described him as emotionally distraught and totally involved in the *pieds noirs'* cause; already convinced that the renunciation of Algeria was tantamount to cowardice.

Sergent was likewise transferred out of Algeria to an undemanding assignment at Chartres. When he declared that he disagreed with government policy and threatened to resign his commission, his superiors were aghast, and made a concerted effort to dissuade him. By Sergent's own account, a general in mufti invited him to lunch, praised his attitude, and urged him to persevere in his opposition *from within the Army*. It was the sort of irresponsible adulation likely to go to a young officer's head—and it did.

The third officer, Lieutenant Roger Degueldre, likewise carried on liaison with FAF in the initial planning stage of the December 1960 demonstrations, then turned over the task to Sergent. A strapping, somber figure who had risen from the ranks—and of the Foreign Legion, at that—Degueldre by instinct shunned publicity and played a less conspicuous though equally illegal role in the riots themselves; he was chosen to act as the detonator within his regiment, raising it against security forces in the city. He planned simultaneously to seize Radio Algiers.

Suspecting his involvement, the Army reassigned him in January to one of the Legion's *compagnies portées,* or motorized units, in the Sahara, far from political turmoil. Degueldre's reaction was characteristically sharp; he ignored the transfer order. He remained with his regiment, the 1er Régiment Étranger Parachutiste, at its rear base at Zeralda, ate at the officers' mess as in the past, and drove about Algiers in an Army jeep, renewing contact with civilian activists. No one found this strange. He was AWOL, but the Army went to no special trouble to locate or arrest him. He deserted, but it was a comfortable desertion, during which he continued to be fed, clothed and housed by his regiment.

The colonels—the refractory colonels known for their unyielding stand on French Algeria, and their readiness to overthrow the government, if necessary, to gain their way—were now in a state of semi-disgrace. Without exception they had been relieved of their commands in Algeria after Barricades Week and December 1960, and packed off, like the junior officers, to provincial garrisons in France and West Germany to dampen their rebelliousness. Antoine Argoud (Massu's former chief of staff at Algiers Army Corps headquarters, a little man with an extraordinarily agile mind; ascetic, cold and supercilious) was chief of staff of the 6th Military Region at Metz. Joseph Broizat (former commander of the 1er RPIMA—colonial paratroopers—and Massu's divisional chief of staff; a stern-faced, shaven-skulled erudite seminarian turned career soldier) was deputy to the commanding general at Châlons-sur-Marne. Yves Godard (former chief of the Algiers Sûreté, credited with infiltrating and cracking the FLN terrorist networks of the Casbah in 1956–57, a subtle and ruthless paratrooper whose taste for secrecy-ridden operations outdid Salan's) was languishing in command of a subdivision at Nevers. Henry Dufour (voluble and breezy, the former commander of the crack 1er REP) was at divisional headquarters in Offenburg, in the Black Forest.

To this list belong two other names. Charles Lacheroy (Salan's former information officer in Algiers; the bluff popularizer of *action psychologique*) was giving lectures at the École Militaire in Paris to reserve officers. Jean Gardes (Lacheroy's successor as head of the Cinquième Bureau in Algiers; a zealous but notoriously naïve specialist in Moslem affairs) had just been acquitted at the Barricades Trial and was likewise assigned to Metz.

Each would play a significant role later; each, by this time, was an overpublicized figure, often commanding more prestige and wielding more influence than the generals under whom they served. The Right saw the colonels as symbols of military honor and selfless commitment to a cause; in the eyes of the government, they were first-rate officers regrettably embroiled in Algerian power politics; the Left saw them as inveterate neofascist schemers itching to establish a dictatorship, like some Latin American camarilla. The truth was more prosaic. To a greater or lesser degree they had all fallen victim to the simplistic notions of psychological warfare in which they put so much stock.

The colonels were under intermittent surveillance by Military Security; which did not prevent them from coming and going as they chose, maintaining contact wth one another and Rightist politicians. The government's belief that reassignment would dilute their latent insubordination proved ill-founded. They were men in their late forties and early fifties, set in their opinions; for the most part, they had fought in World War II and almost continuously thereafter. "Few armies in the world possess a generation of officers who have fought so much," wrote the military correspondent of *Le Monde*. In their own estimate, the French Army shaped up as a first-class professional force second to none in Europe, with continuous battle experience since 1942 and firsthand acquaintance with Communist military and political tactics. At their new postings, the colonels continued to be obsessed by Algeria; they were unprepared to accept another capitulation, and their sense of urgency grew; they met, and more than ever, they conspired.

The common denominator between the colonels and the captains in the spring of 1961 was the determination to act before the French government signed a cease-fire with the GPRA. In this they were supported by some civilians.

They met often in an apartment on Rue Vavin in Montparnasse. Among those who attended were a prominent publisher, a doctor, a Protestant clergyman, and a professor of military science.

The door sometimes was opened by two dark-eyed Eurasian children incongruously got up in paratroop uniforms. The apartment belonged to Colonel Roland Vaudrey, a veteran of Indochina, who had married a Vietnamese girl and had less control over youngsters than over troops.

These meetings were not taut and stealthy affairs, lasting well past midnight in a smoke-obscured room behind drawn drapes. The civilians met in the afternoon, around an occasional glass of anisette, and they separated sedately at dinnertime. Whenever they found a pretext to travel to Paris, seven officers joined them. De la Bigne, who was present at several gatherings, recalls the atmosphere as "sincere and calm . . . we were seeking a way to overcome technical problems and attain an objective."

The objective was to carry out a putsch in Algeria, bring down the government, and pave the way for a Rightist-dominated Sixth Republic. The mood was dedicated, for they were convinced that their action would save France from far-reaching dangers: in their view, the drift toward decadence, the reduction to small-power status and the Communization of the southern shore of the Mediterranean. The most illuminated saw French Algeria as the stake in a forthcoming European civil war between the Christian West and the totalitarian East.

Vaudrey, their host, had served as deputy director of the Sûreté in Algiers; subsequently relieved of his command in Collo, in eastern Algeria, for his outspoken political views, he had returned to France and was using accrued leave to cultivate trade-union contacts and to plot.*

---

* A fellow conspirator has recalled that Vaudrey, as a matter of principle, would not take leave for rest and relaxation. Using it for sedition was another matter.

Letters from officers in Algeria described the regiments' readiness to rise. The entire professional Army of Algeria, seething with discontent (the conscripts were not taken into account), was willing and eager to throw its weight into a coup—or so it seemed at the time. And similar meetings were taking place elsewhere through the city.

The plot was, so to speak, permanent; it was in essence the same as Jouhaud's in 1960, but this time it was being orchestrated in Paris and scored not for several regiments but for the entire Army, in Algeria, France and West Germany. The problem was to find a general to whom the putsch could be entrusted.

Salan's name cropped up and was immediately eliminated because of the bizarre stories dating back to Indochina about his cryptic manner, his unsavory contacts with various secret services, and his political opportunism. If he led a revolt, it was thought extremely unlikely that many officers would follow.

Massu's name also came up. In March, two colonels, Argoud and Broizat, called on the former commander of the 10th Paratroop Division at his country house in Montargis, in central France. They found him tending his garden after more than a year of enforced inactivity following an all-too-publicized interview with a West German newspaper.* Noting that in spite of his misadventure he remained a loyal Gaullist, Massu turned down the colonels. What of the *pieds noirs* if de Gaulle handed over Algeria to the FLN? "They'll have to learn to wear a fez," replied Massu, whose gift for gruff explicitness was more sophisticated than most imagined. The colonels came away disconsolate.

Time passed. The captains, tiring of inaction, weighed the idea of launching their own putsch; the plan came to nothing, but pressure on the colonels to find a leader mounted. They were in the awkward position, for organizers of a *coup de force,* of having too many potential troops and not a single general (or so it seemed; in the end, the troops would be lacking too).

It was some time in March that Gardes first mentioned Challe's

* On January 18, 1960, Munich's *Süddeutscher Zeitung* published an interview by its correspondent, Hans Kempski, in which Massu intimated the French Army was ready to compel de Gaulle to change his self-determination policy in Algeria. The ensuing uproar led to Massu's recall and the start of Barricades Week. Massu claimed his remarks were not made for publication.

name. The reaction was mixed. Vaudrey thought he would be of little use. Broizat recalled Challe as being "incapable of taking a decision" during Barricades Week. Gardes disagreed and argued that Challe had far more chance than Salan of rallying the Army. The other colonels hesitated. It was only after Massu's refusal that Argoud and Broizat approved Gardes's suggestion.

However, Challe's own position remained unclear—when sounded out he said that he sympathized with their views, but he asked for time to consider. Throughout the latter half of March, the various plotters in Paris thought seriously of carrying out the putsch under the leadership of the *comité des colonels,* Argoud, Broizat, Dufour and Gardes—a solution urged by some junior officers, including Sergent. Sergent took the position that, no matter which general was given nominal command, real control of the insurrection must remain in the hands of the colonels.

In point of fact, there was dangerously little agreement between the captains and the colonels, between the military and the civilians, between Paris and Algiers, over ways and means to attain the main objective. Paris bred theory, not action. Drawing rooms of the seventh and sixteenth *arrondissements* served as rostrums for an ill-assorted collection of monarchists and nationalists, antirepublican agitators, ultraconservative bourgeois, and traditionalist officers. Their aims differed radically; their only common link was de Gaulle. For these plotters, the French President—like Roosevelt in the Thirties among Republicans—was a favored, insatiable hate topic about whom they fulminated for hours. It was all quite antiseptically removed from the stench and poverty and growing pains of Algeria. Junior officers experienced a pang of sharp disillusion when they came to Paris for concrete assistance and were welcomed with a tirade. They encountered some difficulty making the transition from *djebels* to salons, from particular military problems to considerations of breathtaking generality, as, for instance, the defense of the West. And since this was France, wives and mistresses conspired too, vehement in their rage against de Gaulle, talented as liaison agents, but helpless when it came to the organizational brass tacks of plotting. From this muddle one central fact emerged: Paris concluded that Algiers must be the first to rise, then it would follow, while Algiers, before rising, looked in vain to Paris for practical leadership. The military wanted to concentrate on military problems, and leave politics to the civilians, which was naïve; the civilians complacently set trust in the Army's competence to make tactical plans. So a hazardous standoff existed. Under the circumstances, it is easy to understand the disenchantment of one industrialist, who said: "When I saw how we prepared for the putsch, I thought it was perhaps better that we did not win."

One frequent visitor to these clandestine meetings was a short, cocksure, goateed paratroop officer, Colonel Pierre Château-Jobert. Château-Jobert, the creator of the French Army's present-day paratroop regiments, had led the drop on Port Said during the 1956 Suez War, served in Algeria, and now was up for reassignment to Niamey, in central Africa. He had stalled for time as long as he dared; on the eve of his departure he asked a fellow officer, Colonel Yves Godard, to take his place among the conspirators.

Godard, later to be one of the main actors in the story of the OAS, agreed and so became involved in *Arnat*.

A transparent contraction of *armée* and *nation,* the code word *Arnat* was assigned to an undercover operation to win over three armored units stationed in the Paris area—at Orléans, Rambouillet and Chantilly—to the putschists' side. By no means all of the officers and men in these units were favorable to the idea of a putsch. The scheme therefore consisted of replacing hostile (that is, pro-Gaullist) officers by reserve officers; recalcitrant troops by civilians drawn from right-wing paramilitary groups. Coinciding with the outbreak of insurrection in Algeria, the three regiments would march on the capital, encircle it with a ring of armor, and capture the Élysée Palace. The Chantilly regiment was also expected to halt the miners of northern France if they marched on Paris to the aid of the government. The activists saw the nightmarish spectacle of a "red army of 80,000" massing in the coal fields of the Pas de Calais; but, as later events demonstrated, this figure existed nowhere except in their imagination. At a final meeting, the organizers of *Arnat* calculated with reckless optimism that they could count on five thousand volunteers.

In early April, Godard—a veteran of antisubversive warfare during the Battle of Algiers, now a bona fide subversive in his own right—was assigned, with unconscious complicity by the Army, to a course in subversive warfare at Versailles, the result of which was to bring him from Nevers to Paris and make contact with his fellow conspirators easier. He was unenthusiastic about *Arnat;* he thought, then as later, that Algiers, not Paris, was the key to the solution of the Algerian problem. A week later he received a telephone call. A fellow officer broke the news that put an end to the drawn-out theoretical discussions in Colonel Vaudrey's apartment, and gave rise to a sense of quickened anticipation among all the conspirators, civilian and military. Challe had said yes.

Challe in the spring of 1961 was a retired general, like Salan, in his mid-fifties, a calm, pipe-smoking southern Frenchman, of medium height, thick in the waist, still muscular but going a bit flabby, unhurried. The Fourth Republic considered him to be a Gaullist—so dangerously so that just prior to May 13, 1958, the Defense Ministry transferred him from Algiers to Brest, where police escorted him to the maritime prefecture and placed him under temporary arrest. De Gaulle restored his freedom and several months later promoted him.

A product of the French Air Force—which is less stuffy in its views than either the Army or the Navy—Challe had forged a highly regarded career as a strategist, planned the successful amphibious landings at Port Said, then in December 1958 succeeded Salan as commander in chief in Algeria.

Hopes ran high as a result of the appointment. Two authoritative French writers, Jacques Fauvet and Jean Planchais, subsequently summed up the period: "Nineteen fifty-nine was the year when Algeria was headed by the most brilliant team it had ever seen— Maurice Challe and Paul Delouvrier." The two men, both technocrats, proceeded to fulfill these hopes, the Delegate General by carrying out the five-year Constantine Plan for economic development, the commander in chief by launching offensive operations— "Jumelles," "Pierres Précieuses," "Ariège"—that brought the *wilayas* close to defeat.

Campaigning in the field, after years of headquarters duties, profoundly marked Challe. He entered into daily contact with the new generation of junior officers, whose dedication impressed him, and his belief grew in a definitive military victory.

The motivations of the men who participated in the end of French Algeria are to be found without exception in events that preceded the final phase; in Challe's case, it was Barricades Week. When European hostility erupted on January 24, 1960, it struck him as a wasteful interruption, all the more so since he disliked the *pieds noirs*. His primary ambition was to get on with operations against the FLN in the countryside and win the war. During that entire tense week, Challe and Delouvrier lived together at Quartier Rignot, the combined staff headquarters in Algiers. Delouvrier has recalled that he dared not let Challe out of his sight: on the commander in chief hinged the reaction of the Army, and Challe came under increasing pressure by the colonels, in particular Argoud and Broizat, who urged him to side openly with the Europeans and force Paris to abandon its self-determination policy. When Delouvrier decided to move out of the frenzied atmosphere of Algiers itself, Challe balked at following him. Then Delouvrier made an odd and prophetic remark.

"Don't become a Salan," he said.

"I don't plan to," Challe replied.

He emphatically did not want to become involved; unlike Salan, he had scant basic interest in politics, least of all the stew of Algerian politics. He had counted on Massu to keep the *pieds noirs* under control, but Massu was gone, recalled in disgrace. Challe felt some kinship with the headstrong colonels, and an obligation to remain with his troops; so he wavered, listening neither to Argoud and Broizat nor to the Delegate General. Eventually he followed Delouvrier to La Reghaia, the Army's headquarters outside Algiers, but by this time the activists blamed him for squandering a unique opportunity, and the government thought he might have reacted more vigorously against the barricaded insurgents.

A few months later he was recalled and made commander in chief of Allied Forces, Europe Center, at Fontainebleau. He accepted the assignment without enthusiasm. Although it entailed strategic responsibilities, he considered himself sidetracked. Like so many other Frenchmen—like Robert Lacoste, Jacques Soustelle and Salan—he had come under the imprecise spell of Algeria; he remained emotionally committed to the Army left behind with regret in Kabylia and the Nemencha Mountains. Aggravating this state of affairs was the evident fact that, following his departure, the war was not being won or even very actively pursued. Challe's mood strikingly resembled Salan's a year earlier—a mischief-making compound of frustration, exasperation and slow-burning anger. General Étienne Valluy said Challe "was like a craftsman who does the best work he can, it is almost done . . . then it is taken from him and

given to another." One of the most perspicacious French newsmen
of the period, Jean Daniel, summed up Challe's attitude: "He was
given an assignment. He fulfilled it. Then it was sabotaged." But,
noted Daniel, Challe never attempted to fathom the political consequences of a partial military victory. At Fontainebleau, Challe grew
as alarmed about de Gaulle's hostility toward the Atlantic Alliance
as about his Algerian policy. He confided his worry to American
fellow officers at Allied headquarters. In January 1961 he requested
premature retirement.

The indefatigable colonels Argoud and Broizat called on him
again in the spring and found the moment favorable, or nearly so,
for their purposes. There is an unresolved mystery here about the
evolution of Challe's views. What prompted him to lead the putsch?

One major consideration was the imminence of the Évian meeting.
The colonels argued that if action was not taken now, it would be
too late afterward; former Premier Mendès-France had just
launched a plan for an international conference to settle Algeria's
future in the event that negotiations faltered—and internationaliza-
tion was a prospect that the colonels found almost as distasteful as
direct dealings with the FLN. For the moment, they argued, France
was still in a strong bargaining position. Argoud pressed the point
that the cadres in Algeria, ready to rise, wanted Challe as their
leader. One consideration, certainly, was his knowledge that, with
or without him, the putsch would be launched—his feeling that he
was morally obligated to the Army in the field (after wavering during
Barricades Week), and that with him the rising enjoyed a greater
chance of succeeding. He wanted to use his influence to shunt aside
the *pied noir* activists, "the people in Jouhaud's wake," as he put it
—FAF and the OAS—whom he despised.

Still, he hung fire. He stayed away from all the conspiratorial
meetings in Paris. He waited for de Gaulle's press conference on
April 11, scheduled following the postponement of the Évian talks.*

What de Gaulle said proved conclusive. He was in a loquacious
and penetrating mood, and he spoke his mind in a statement of unusual length on Algeria, which showed the importance he attached to
the subject. "An Algerian state will be created within and without,"

---

* The GPRA announced on March 31 that it would not go to Évian after
French Minister for Algerian Affairs Louis Joxe declared that he was ready to
meet with the FLN's rival faction, the MNA (the Messalists), as well as with
the FLN. But neither side construed this as anything other than a temporary
maneuver by the GPRA.

the General declared, adding matter-of-factly: "Our interest, and consequently our policy, lies in decolonialization." His ultimate aim could not have been clearer, and the effect on various groups was electric.

In Tunis and Rabat, a strong feeling permeated Algerian nationalists that independence was virtually within sight. Ahmed Francis, the Algerian Provisional Government's finance minister, had just returned from Moscow with a pledge of Soviet diplomatic and material aid. *Afrique-Action* wrote: "The FLN will go to Évian to make peace in concrete terms as one goes to a notary to establish a deed of ownership." There is no evidence that Challe read this story, but those in his entourage came across similar accounts, and the sentiment grew that something must be done soon.

Challe reached a sudden decision and, having done so, decided that there was no time to lose. Within forty-eight hours of the press conference, word reached the conspirators in Paris that the putsch would take place in just one week, on April 20.

4

A Clear Night

POLITICAL EXILE cannot be devoted entirely to elaborating schemes
for grabbing power; there recur unavoidable stretches of idleness.
To while away the glacial early spring in Madrid, Salan and Ferrandi visited the Prado and the Escorial, toured a bull-breeding
ranch in the north, and made an excursion to Seville. The Princesa
group gossiped in cafés, read and waited, and gambled at cards on
rainy days—under the vigilant eye of the Seguridad. At the Torre de
Madrid, conviviality abounded, and the drinking was heavy; then
Lagaillarde made a five-day retreat with Spanish Jesuits. *Pieds
noirs* arrived mysteriously, lectured all within earshot on what
should be done, then departed just as abruptly. Tassou Georgopoulos,
an Oran restaurant manager, and Pancho Gonzales, manager of an
Oran driving school, were frequent visitors to Lagaillarde's suite—
they would later turn up as chieftains of the OAS in that city. Susini
discussed revolutionary tactics with Falangist youths in a Madrid
suburb. "We did not take him very seriously," recalls one exile, Fernand Feral, now principal of the Lycée Français in Alicante; but it
became progressively more difficult to catch Salan's ear without Susini's help. Susini's own contacts with the general were facilitated
through Ferrandi, a fellow Corsican.

The signal they were awaiting was brought in early April by a silver-haired French general on inactive duty, Jacques Faure.* He came with news of Challe's decision and details about the putsch. There was no excessive joy in Salan's reaction. This was understandable. He had fled to Spain, at some sacrifice, to organize action to defend French Algeria, and the OAS was gradually forming under his sponsorship; the colonels' choice of another general to lead the putsch was almost insulting. Although Salan shared with Challe a reputation as a Leftist-leaning general, nothing else united the two men, neither military background nor personal tastes, nor even much mutual esteem. Challe considered Salan, with distaste, as a "political general." Salan viewed Challe as exclusively "military," unsuited to mount a conspiracy in depth. The relationship was aggravated by Salan's clear resentment of his successor's popularity in the Army of Algeria. Then, Faure had traveled to Madrid not to seek Salan's approval but merely to inform him of the colonels' choice, a distinction to which Le Chinois responded without warmth.

Faure stayed several days in the capital. During meetings at the Princesa, he assured the activists that Challe planned to mobilize Algeria's *pieds noirs* and launch a paratroop drop on Paris, two steps Susini thought vital if the insurrection was to succeed. An inveterate antirepublican plotter but not overly bright, Faure had no justification, apart from wishful thinking, for making these promises; he was translating vague remarks into firm commitments.

Taking Faure's reassurances on faith, Salan agreed that a radio code message, *"La chambre de la bonne a été cambriolée* [The maid's room has been burglarized]," would be the signal to fly to Algiers and join Challe. There is no reason to believe that Challe gave Faure the mission of inviting Salan to participate in the putsch. Here again, Faure acted on his own. But Le Chinois had little choice: he was perfectly aware that, whether or not he accepted, Challe could proceed with the coup.

It was also obvious to Salan that the longer he remained isolated in Madrid, the less influence he would exercise once he landed in Algeria. Susini and Ferrandi concurred, and urged him to get to Algiers before the putsch. This proved more difficult than they thought. The Spanish police showed no inclination to cooperate and

---

* Faure had already participated in an abortive plot in January 1957 while commanding a division in Algiers. The plot was uncovered through Faure's own loose tongue, and he drew thirty days' fortress arrest. After the Barricades, he was placed on the inactive list.

indeed made it clear that if they tried to leave Spain overtly, they would be stopped. Susini was prepared to do business, as he put it, "with anybody," to charter a boat and slip out of a Mediterranean port; yet, surprisingly, he found no serious bidders. One gang of Rumanians, former Iron Guard members, proposed embarking Salan and fellow passengers on a fishing boat bound for Melilla, on the coast of Spanish Morocco; but from there they would be forced to make their way overland into Algeria through an area swarming with troops of the ALN.* The impractical scheme was dropped, and the Princesa group again settled down to a nerve-racking wait. Salan meanwhile sent Jacques Achard, a former colonial administrator, to check at first hand the situation in Algiers and maintain direct liaison with Mme. Salan. Achard, a resident of Algiers, had no trouble entering and leaving Spain.

Madrid was—and still is—a haven for right-wing exiles, Pétainists, Rexists, Peronistas. One man whose advice the exiles valued, and on whom they paid respects upon arriving in the capital, pulled a long face when he heard about their plans for a military revolt. His own experience had left him skeptical. After the July 1944 attempt on Hitler's life, he had arrested a roomful of suspect Wehrmacht generals, to whom it did not occur to flee although only two SS guards barred the way. Many, as a result, went straight to their death at the Gestapo's hands. This man felt that generals do not make good conspirators. He was former SS Standartenführer Otto Skorzeny.

Louis Grassien, deputy director of the Sûreté Nationale in Algiers, at the outset noted two things about the new movement. It claimed, with some justification, to be a sort of federation of all activist groups in the city; and, in contrast to previous movements, it operated wholly in the dark. Unlike FAF, it carried on no overt activities, and unlike Ortiz's FNF, its militants wore no membership pins on their shirts.

A story made the rounds of an illiterate fishmongeress in Bab el Oued who explained that the three white letters OAS stood for "O Armes Sitoyens." Tracts circulated surreptitiously—stuffed before

---

* Armée de Libération Nationale, FLN troops stationed in reserve on the Tunisian and Moroccan frontiers, who did little actual fighting but were of nuisance value against the French Army.

dawn into letterboxes, scattered in stairways and gutters—continued to be signed, at first, by the Front de l'Algérie Française. Then in early April, a tract appeared for the first time openly bearing the new name, Organisation Armée Secrète. The context was much the same as before, but the tone was, if anything, more aggressive. Taking credit for a series of explosions in the Algiers region, the Organization added austerely: "These actions—mere reprimands—are only a prelude to harsher measures." The tract carried a terse warning, adopted from FAF and soon to become notorious in a slightly different form: "*L'OAS frappe ou elle veut, quand elle veut* [OAS strikes where it wants, when it wants]."

From a local priest, Grassien learned something of the new movement's composition. It shunned middle-class Algérie Française agitators of pre-1958 days—the "ultras," as they were known then—and it recruited, for the first time, among petty bureaucrats, factory, rail and dock workers, fishermen and students from low-income groups. Most had no previous police record and thus were hard to identify. Grassien, however, had several other leads. It had taken the Algiers police only two weeks, beginning with a set of fingerprints found in a bathroom where the murderers had washed their hands, to arrest Maître Popie's assassins: a twenty-five-year-old former paratroop corporal, Claude Peintre, and a thirty-five-year-old deserter from the Foreign Legion, Léon Dauvergne. The two, in the course of interrogation, disclosed that extremists had promised them $400 apiece to execute the lawyer. The new movement's link with the Army, in short, appeared to be—also for the first time—through enlisted men, noncoms and junior officers, rather than at higher echelons. Finally, a flurry of clandestine traffic by cutter, trawler and small pleasure boat between Spain and Algeria indicated a coordinated effort with activists abroad. One tract also boasted of increasing aid and determination by "patriots" in Metropolitan France.

Identifying the OAS and its sources of recruitment and ramifications was one matter; evaluating the threat it posed, quite another. The Organization had not spelled out precisely what it wanted or what it planned to do, beyond threatening alleged FLN agents, turncoats, and in general, all "traitors to the cause of French Algeria." It appeared logical that since the activists no longer had the run of the streets to demonstrate, following the December 1960 debacle, they would turn increasingly to terrorist attacks to make their point. Grassien, an unemotional man, judged that the OAS should be taken seriously "but not dramatically."

The same conclusion was reached by other officials at the Délégation Générale. Algiers was awash in extremist groups, some potentially dangerous, others so wild-eyed and ineffectual that they were ridiculous. The city was a breeding ground for fantastic rumors. Daily, members of the Délégation Générale received death threats and reports of impending putsches. They had, inevitably, grown a bit blasé. So, when curious newsmen raised the question of the new set of letters at morning briefings, Information Officer Jacques Coup de Fréjac, publicly at least, dismissed the OAS as a "myth."

Privately it was taken with somewhat—but not much—more alarm. Two other tracts appeared on April 19 and were examined routinely by the police. They were not forwarded at once to the Délégation Générale; had they been, there is no reason to think they would have aroused special interest. But they contained the strongest hints yet of forthcoming action. One was issued by Robert Martel, the weird and fanatical leader of the Mouvement Populaire du 13 Mai, an activist group in the Mitidja farm area pledged not only to preservation of French Algeria but to religious purification of the community. After enjoying some prestige in the tumultuous period before May 1958, Martel was now an object of distrust among the new wave of European conspirators, who considered him invidious and mad; Susini tartly defined him, once and for all, as the "Rasputin of the Mitidja." He had not been invited to join the OAS, but he had heard of its formation. Bulletin No. 21 of his seditious publication, *La Voix du maquis,* announced that his group as well as others were merging within the OAS. It praised Salan as the only soldier "whose voice is raised against the liquidators of Empire. . . . The opposition is organizing, unifying, growing stronger and stronger. May the French Army understand that in supporting Salan, it is helping us to save the West."

The second tract, signed by the OAS, was addressed to security forces in Algeria. "The moment of choice is near," it warned. "Remember the fate of the Miliciens—ten thousand were shot for thinking the Fatherland can be bargained away. Be ready to join the national army at the hour of insurrection!"

This almost gave the game away.

Challe planned to draw exclusively on units of the Operational Reserve (which he had created) to take Algiers, since they could move without orders from the commander in chief and had their own autonomous transport. Once the first stage of the putsch was carried out, regular troops would rally to Challe's orders. As an Air Force general (and this applied likewise to Jouhaud), he could expect probable cooperation, or quiescent support at the least, at most air bases. He foresaw no trouble with the Navy, which contained elements favorable to French Algeria and was occupied patrolling offshore waters for clandestine cargoes of FLN arms. One of the few difficulties Challe anticipated was with the Army Corps commander at Oran, General Henri de Pouilly, whose support remained doubtful, but he would be rapidly neutralized by the presence of the Foreign Legion at Sidi bel Abbès only fifty miles away to the south. To win over the Legion, Challe counted on Gardy.

The 1st Foreign Legion Paratroop Regiment, the crack 1er REP, a hotbed of activism, to which Degueldre, Sergent and de la Bigne all belonged, would serve as the spearhead of the insurrection. It was resting up, after months in the field, at its rear base at Zeralda, only a half hour's drive from Algiers. All together, Challe made plans for the commitment of twelve elite regiments, which would furnish him with a well-honed force of some 21,000 men; from this nucleus the insurrectional movement would swiftly spread and engulf the entire 500,000-man Army of Algeria. The situation would become untenable in Paris for de Gaulle.

Challe's strategy proceeded on the basic assumption that his arrival in Algiers and an appeal to the troops would set off a chain reaction. Everything hinged on this. No one questioned it. Challe's prestige in the Army was a byword among the colonels; he believed in it himself. Speed was imperative; Challe hoped to consolidate his power within forty-eight hours. He made no plans, according to available evidence, for carrying the putsch to France, but the conspirators in Paris did; they reasoned that the threat of a strike by two paratroop regiments against the capital would suffice to drive de Gaulle into retirement, but in the event that he showed signs of resisting, the threat could be carried out, abetted by armor from the Paris area and West Germany.

Between April 13 and 20, Challe informed Jacques Soustelle and at least one Socialist party leader of his plans, in general terms. No revolutionary, Challe intended to carry out the putsch without bloodshed, and—so to speak—respectably, almost as though it were not a putsch at all; although he rejected *pied noir* support, he wanted responsible political backing in France. The results of his soundings were unencouraging. Soustelle thought Challe "out of his depth" and would have preferred to see Salan in charge. The Socialist expressed vague sympathy, said nothing to dissuade Challe and apparently did not notify the government; but, on the other hand, he made no commitments.

Challe also met with right-wing parliamentarians of the Vincennes Committee, an informal study group created in 1960, which included, apart from Soustelle and Bidault, diehard partisans of French Algeria in the National Assembly.

Two fellow generals came to Challe's Left Bank apartment on Boulevard de la-Tour-Maubourg. Jouhaud was one—the heavy-handed organizer of the December 1960 riots, escaping scot free after that fiasco, had campaigned equally unsuccessfully against the January referendum. In the following months, French administrative logic—and laxity—permitted him to conspire relatively unimpeded: the police watched his movements in Algiers, since he was a *pied noir*, but not in Paris. The second visitor was André Zeller, a sixty-three-year-old logistics specialist, former chief of staff of the Ground Forces. Stubborn and quick-tempered, Zeller, who perpetually bore the ruffled look of an angry hen, had twice quit the Army in the space of four years, the first time in a row over the recall date of conscript units from Algeria, the second time in angry dissent from de Gaulle's self-determination policy. Oddly, after his first resignation, it was the Gaullist government that recalled him to active service, an opportunity he promptly exploited to build up a clique of activist officers in key posts throughout Army headquarters at Boulevard Saint-Germain. Of the three generals, Zeller alone sprang from a pure military background; he was the son of a general, the brother of another, and the father-in-law, brother-in-law, uncle, first cousin and nephew of other officers. "Zeller," one military critic said, "is a fellow who even conspires through channels." This, however, in many ways held true of the entire trio. None was made of revolutionary fiber; there was no deep-seated tradition of revolt in the French Army, the *malaise* was recent, and they were newcomers to sedition. They were sturdy conventional men in advanced middle age, of limited intellectual insight, who wanted to reverse government policy (and possibly the regime), and to even a profound grudge against de Gaulle. Reshaping existing social structures and creating a new society in Algeria lay well outside their scope. For all their lofty ruminations about peace, bread, justice and fraternity, what they planned was a classic military pronunciamento. And to make it stick, they were counting on a phalanx of present-day centurions—paratroopers and Legionnaires—who would re-establish order and clarity, a *Pax Gallica,* in the mountainous marches of North Africa, in damning contrast with the decadence of imperial Paris.

Paris in the spring, unaware of forthcoming salvation, speculated worriedly about the Bay of Pigs disaster, a lesson in Hamlet-like irresolution. The three generals met in the dim, self-contained world of conspiracy—Challe, trying to make amends for his own indecision during Barricades Week, and now more than ever under the colonels' influence; Zeller, presumably praying to family gods of war and retribution; Jouhaud, the most attached to his native Algeria, plodding uneasily about the apartment and resembling, one friend recalled, a sun-baked farmer who "watches the earth under the storm."

The final details were slapped together in considerable haste and unmilitary disorder. There was a dearth of time. After hesitating too long, Challe was now in too much of a hurry. When Argoud and Broizat suggested preliminary staff work, they were told it could wait. Broizat himself only thought of notifying Gardes twenty-four hours before the target date, and the former chief of the Algiers Cinquième Bureau joined the plot without knowing what was expected of him or what the plan of action was; still more typically, this did not deter him. The colonels confided in some officers who could not be trusted, while activist officers, who were sympathetic and could have helped, were kept in the dark. When Challe announced that there was no reason to worry about logistic support from abroad, that the problem had been looked after, no one asked further questions, the colonels were ready to let him command. However, Broizat was stunned when Challe suggested running the putsch by remote control from Paris. Even in uncritical military circles, this idea proved hard to swallow. From Algiers, Degueldre, who had gone underground, coldly sent word that he would do nothing to raise the 1er REP, in fact, would prevent it from rising, until Challe, or whoever led the putsch, was present on Algerian soil. The message left no doubt about Degueldre's meaning—he wanted a superior officer as a hostage, to forestall any last-minute wavering resembling the Army's vacillation in December. And by now, Degueldre was becoming known as the most formidable plotter among the junior officers, a giant of a man, with uncommon fixity of purpose, who implacably did what he threatened to do. So Challe's suggestion, absurd in the first place, was hastily scrapped.

On other major decisions, however, Challe got his way. Until he judged it expedient, armored units in France and West Germany, and civilian commandos in the provinces, would make no move. The putsch was to be exclusively a military affair, led, organized and carried out by the Army, without civilian participation to sully it with politics. Challe abhorred the prospect of back-room deals and uncontrollable street demonstrations. His strategic objective was dangerously simple: he wanted to score a lightning military victory over the FLN in three months, then allow the politicians to take over a healthy situation. He was setting out, Jacques Fauvet later observed, to "finish what two regimes, four commanders in chief and seven governments were unable to finish in seven years."

Brusquely, in that final helter-skelter week, the civilian plotters at Rue Vavin and elsewhere in Paris found themselves cut off from last-minute arrangements; there was a blackout of information.

The colonels, by contrast, were kept busy. Godard was informed, to his relief, that Challe, with whom he had clashed during Barricades Week, wanted him in Algiers. Lacheroy was already in Algeria, to coordinate details of a psychological-action campaign justifying the putsch. Argoud and Broizat were putting final touches on the proclamation to be read by Challe.

On April 17, and again on April 18, the colonels met in Lacheroy's office at the École Militaire. The target date of April 20 was confirmed.

Sergent, privy to these preparations, impatient and intense, went down a mental check list of conspirators—Jouhaud, Zeller, Argoud, Broizat, Godard—and concluded that Challe was setting out with as capable a staff as any general could desire.

Michel de la Bigne informed his wife that he was leaving on maneuvers and boarded an Air Force plane for Algiers with regular travel orders procured through a fellow officer. As he left for the putsch, his overnight bag contained pajamas, two paperback novels and a missal.

The rendezvous was in the early afternoon at the Porte de Pantin, on the eastern edge of Paris. Zeller arrived late: at the last moment, realizing that he was short of cash, he had called at his bank. Broizat and a small group of waiting civilians perceived with dismay the approaching figure in dark glasses, hat pulled low over forehead; one eyewitness remarked, "Zeller looked nothing so much as a military man trying to avoid being recognized."

They drove out in a three-car convoy led by an Algérie Française deputy who was entitled to an official tricolor sticker on the windshield of his vehicle, which would be useful if they ran into police checkpoints. In the second car sat Zeller, Broizat and several civilians. It was already five o'clock. As they maneuvered through dense traffic, Broizat, who had come up to the capital with leave papers issued for Annecy, estimated that they enjoyed a fifty percent chance of succeeding. "He thought we had to go through with it anyway," recalled one civilian. The third car was occupied by a young woman, the civilian's wife, to whom had been entrusted Challe's proclamation; her orders were to turn back at once if the preceding cars were stopped.

Their destination was Creil, a small military airfield thirty miles north of the city. They arrived without a hitch. Before flying back to Algiers on his own, Jouhaud had made arrangements for their unauthorized flight through two top-level contacts, Air Force Major General Jean-Louis Nicot, in Paris, and General Pierre-Marie Bigot, commanding the 5th Air Region in Algeria. Zeller and Broizat expected to find Challe on the field. He was nowhere in sight, so the convoy prudently left the base and waited on a nearby road. Almost at once, two motorcycle policemen roared up and stopped. Zeller was so rattled that, without a word to the others, he slipped behind the wheel of the second car and drove off at full speed. The two off-duty policemen watched the retreating car, looked at the others, and then went off into the woods to urinate. About a half hour later, long after the incurious policemen had disappeared, Zeller rejoined the others.

For the previous two hours Challe had been driving in circles around the countryside of the Oise department. He did not know the exact location of Creil; he had failed to procure a road map before leaving Paris, and he did not dare ask anyone for directions. Finally he found the way and arrived at the field.

Four hours behind schedule, the twin-motor Nord 2500 took off with three clandestine passengers. It was now eight o'clock in the evening. They must arrive at Blida, south of Algiers, before 11 P.M., to carry out the putsch that night. Past 11 P.M. it would be impossible for the 1er REP to move out of its encampment and invest the city under cover of dark.

Godard obtained compassionate leave to visit his sick mother in Toulouse. The colonel drove that morning to Paris, left his car at the Orly airfield parking lot (where it was subsequently found by police), and met General Gardy, who had returned from Madrid and Bayonne. With airline employees' complicity, the two men hid in a food-delivery van, got past ticket and visa control, then boarded an Air Algérie plane. The two stewardesses knew that someone of special interest would be on the flight. After the takeoff, one girl recognized Godard and whispered to him, "You're crazy."

But Godard is an attractive man, and upon landing the same girl volunteered to drive him to a street-corner rendezvous in Algiers, outside an apartment building, where he expected to find Lacheroy.

At the prearranged meeting place, there was no sign of the colonel. Worried, Godard got out, reconnoitered the vicinity, then left with the girl. It was only as they arrived at Villa des Tagarins, in Hydra, on the heights of Algiers, that he realized with concern that he had set down his briefcase, containing his passport, outside the building. If police leafed through the passport and suspected his presence in the city, it could presumably jeopardize the entire putsch.

The girl, this time alone, drove back and retrieved the briefcase just as neighbors were on the point of reporting the suspicious object at the door—for this was Algiers in 1961, when *plastiquages* were commonplace.

Safe for the moment at Villa des Tagarins, which paratroop-commando officers used as a rest center while on leave in Algiers, the colonel took stock of the situation. It was the first time he had set foot in the city in a year.

Godard is a roughhewn, compact man in his early fifties, with an elastic, muscular stride and ferocious smile, who exudes a tigerish vitality. He is a product of two diametrically opposed traditions: the white-gloved formality of St.-Cyr and the spartan improvisation of *maquis* battles in the Savoie Alps during the Occupation. He is one of the few French officers in whom these two backgrounds wed with no apparent strain.

For five years after the war, in Indochina, he had commanded the crack 11ème Bataillon de Choc, running secret operations behind enemy lines. Then, in Algiers, General Jacques Massu picked him to track down FLN terrorists based in the Casbah. To do the job, Godard received unprecedented civilian and military powers, which he employed with cunning and flair. A spider's web of subterfuge, invisible but clinging, grew around the energetic colonel at Sûreté headquarters. Algiers' multiracial underworld—petty thieves and pimps, corruptible police officials, women go-betweens, and Moslem informers—became his private fief. His knowledge of the city was unexcelled, but it was the specialized knowledge of a master spy.

Godard's satisfaction at being back in the seaport that afternoon proved short-lived. To his dismay he learned that officers and men of the 1er REP were unaware of the impending putsch, or of their role, on which everything hinged. It was one more illustration of the extreme haste with which Challe had embarked upon the venture. And as the evening wore on, there was still no sign of Challe himself.

Challe carried three important documents in his briefcase. The first was the proclamation on which Broizat and others had labored until past midnight the night before. It denounced de Gaulle for his readiness to sacrifice part of the nation's territory for his personal glory, noted that the January referendum was unconstitutional, and declared the government illegitimate. It proclaimed France's policy to be "Mediterranean, European and Atlantic." As a sop to external opinion, it promised to maintain France in NATO and to support British entry into the Common Market. Above all, it pledged to settle the Algerian affair "in a matter of weeks."*

The second document was a shorter version, prepared for use in the eventuality that the first proclamation could not be read at length. The second said merely that France would continue to respect its commitments to the population in Algeria, that the rebellion could be quickly terminated, allowing a pacified "province" to re-

---

* The draft text of this proclamation is given as an appendix in Henri Azeau's *Révolte militaire*. Ex-Captain Pierre Sergent also quotes from it in his book, *Ma Peau au bout de mes idées*.

sume its place within the French Community. This version contained no direct attack on the Gaullist government. The conspirators' understanding was that Challe would, if the putsch succeeded in its initial phase, read out the longer proclamation.

A third document consisted of the names of fifty liberals who were to be arrested on sight, given a speedy trial for "treasonable contacts with the FLN," and presumably shot. The Paris activists, mindful of past vacillation, specifically wanted to create what they called *une situation irréversible,* persuade the fainthearted of the putsch's seriousness, and deny Army officers the temptation of a backward look. But aboard the plane that night, Challe himself gave no indication of what he planned to do or what he thought of this plan for summary justice.

The plane touched down two and a half hours later at Boufarik Air Base outside Algiers. Air Police immediately came aboard the craft, their flashlights probing the darkened interior. Challe, Zeller and Broizat, alerted by the pilot, squatted out of sight behind seats at the far end of the cabin until the police went away, their cursory search completed. It was a clear, starry night. With the complicity of the control tower, the Nord 2500 had landed undetected in the midst of a squadron of fighter planes. Now finally, after another delay, it was being cleared to continue its journey to Blida.

Blida is only a half hour's flight from Boufarik, but when the Nord 2500 arrived it was 1 A.M. Broizat hurried from the plane to call Degueldre and assure him that Challe was on Algerian soil. However, Broizat knew by this time that the putsch would have to be postponed for twenty-four hours.

In Paris and the provinces, small groups of men and women listened carefully at their radio sets for a news bulletin and a coded message; finally, hearing nothing exceptional as broadcasting ceased for the night, they went off to bed baffled. In Madrid, Salan feared that Challe was maneuvering to carry out the putsch without him.

Challe arose late next morning at the Villa des Tagarins and buckled down to the task of allotting duties. Zeller would handle finances; Jouhaud, administrative and organizational questions. Argoud had arrived in eastern Algeria on his own and was preparing to rally the Constantine Army Corps commander, General Marie-Michel Gouraud. Godard drew up a final list of twenty-four military targets in Algiers itself; the list included combined staff headquarters at Quartier Rignot, Army Corps headquarters at Caserne Pélissier, *gendarmerie* headquarters at Fort de l'Empereur, the Admiralty, the Town Hall, the Prefecture, and—since the putschists were aware of the impact of communications on a modern population—the studios and relay stations of the state-run radio and television network. The plans laid for the December 1960 riots would now stand in good stead.

That same morning, however, Major Élie Denoix de St.-Marc, acting commanding officer of the 1er REP,* responded unenthusiastically when Degueldre sounded him out about rising against the government. "Would you do it if Challe asked you to?" inquired Degueldre. In the afternoon, the major—an idealistic and highly esteemed career officer, a survivor of Buchenwald and a veteran of Indochina—arrived at the villa, conferred with Challe, and after being assured the putsch would have no "racist" or "fascist" overtones, agreed to issue the necessary marching orders. Having made his decision, he returned to the regimental encampment at Zeralda, ten miles east of Algiers, and waited for evening to come.

Certain members of the government in Paris had been aware for weeks of trouble of an unspecified sort brewing within and without the Army.† Louis Joxe, Minister for Algerian Affairs, had heard rumors in early March about the rebellious intentions of some generals; he was concerned, but felt still greater concern that he could find only a few colleagues to share his worry. Most argued that putsches were distinctly not a tradition in the French Army; the

* The commanding officer was in France on leave.
† The first tip-off came from Barthélemy Rossello, a photographer and member of the Gaullist MPC (Mouvement pour la Communauté) living in Algiers. Acting on his own initiative, Rossello managed to infiltrate the newly formed OAS, attended meetings at Zatarra's house and learned of imprecise plans for a putsch. Suspicious, the OAS gave him a *plastiquage* mission, which he muffed. He was held, interrogated and shot; police fished his discolored body out of a river ten days later. His warning, communicated to friends in the MPC, went disregarded by the government. Rossello can be considered the first *barbouze*.

way of the French general was to grouse and plot politically, hand in glove with the eternal civilian malcontents, but Bonapartism was not fashionable, nor were South American pronunciamentos. The consensus within the cabinet was that Jouhaud was an obscure general with some audience among the *pieds noirs* but no following in the Army; Zeller merely an angry old man; and Salan too immersed in right-wing politics to recruit substantial support among a cross section of officers on active duty. This estimate, fundamentally, was correct; however, it did not take Challe into account. Challe was not regarded as an activist.

Joxe alerted Jean Morin, the Delegate General, to the eventuality of trouble, but there was nothing definite to go upon. The Vincennes Committee on April 18 held a seminar, where hints circulated about a forthcoming putsch; one participant passed on this intangible bit of information to the government. The Paris police already knew a good deal about the secret meetings at Rue Vavin and elsewhere, including civilians' names, addresses, political affiliations and contacts. As April 20 approached, attendance at these meetings grew—and the overconfident core of activists forgot a useful maxim: "In a secret society comprising ten members, the tenth member is always a police spy." At a final rendezvous, the apartment of one plotter, Bernard Sabouret Garat de Nedde, head of the transportation division of Électricité de France, overflowed with people—too many people. Still, the details known by the police remained fragmentary.

Then on Friday, April 21, the threat became more precise. In Tizi-Ouzou, the capital of Kabylia, Captain Georges Oudinot, a tenacious partisan of French Algeria, told a small group of fellow officers that a putsch was imminent and that he planned to seize military and civil power, on behalf of the putschists, by occupying the local prefecture, the post office and the headquarters of the zone commander, General Jean Simon. One of those confided in by Oudinot was a young *pied noir*, Lieutenant Savary. Oudinot saw no reason to mistrust him, but—either because he lost his nerve or because, as he later claimed, the putsch appeared foredoomed—Savary immediately informed Simon.

The latter called in Oudinot.

"Oudinot are you connected with an activist organization?"

"No, *mon général.*"

"Are you thinking of making off for Algiers?"

"No, *mon général.*"

"Would you lift a hand against me?"

"*Mon général! Je suis un soldat.*"

"I thought, Oudinot, that you might do something foolish tonight."

"If you think that, *mon général,* keep me here with you."

The general accepted the reply, but, being no fool, put Oudinot under watch overnight and then alerted Military Security in Algiers.

Morin duly received the information and called Premier Michel Debré, who had just canceled a trip to Cherbourg because of a sore throat. By this time, the Premier's office was getting similar reports from other sources in contact with the Paris activists. The authorities took a few precautionary measures—in Algeria, roadblocks were set up at strategic points on roads leading into Algiers; in France, the bodyguard around de Gaulle was reinforced. The Armed Forces Ministry recalled several armored units from West Germany, and instructed the commander in chief, General Jean Crepin, to remain vigilant.* But there is a limit to the steps a government can take to thwart a problematical putsch, especially if it has not identified the ringleaders; and there is still less it can do to cope with a disaffected army. Paris had full and justified confidence in the recently appointed commander in chief in Algeria, General Fernand Gambiez. Many members of the government retired without apprehension. Few recalled that Gambiez, appointed to his post two months before, had lacked time to hand-pick a trusted staff.

That evening, the President of the Republic accompanied a state visitor and friend, President-Poet Léopold Senghor of Senegal, to the Comédie Française, on the last night of a three-day official visit. De Gaulle haughtily discounted the Army's potential for trouble-making as foreseeably ineffectual; he wanted to let the ferment come to a head, then lance it once and for all. With Senghor he sat in the presidential box and listened to the imperial alexandrines of Racine's *Britannicus,* including lines that were not inappropriate to the situation and are familiar to many literate Frenchmen:

"*. . . De quel nom cependant pouvons-nous appeler*
L'attentat que le jour vient de nous révéler?"

---

* French forces in West Germany comprised several motorized divisions and some 60,000 men, including many activist officers transferred out of Algeria. In general, the FFA (*Forces françaises d'Allemagne*) were shot through with pro-Algérie Française sympathies.

But it was still more than six hours to daybreak.

At about the same time, Dominique Zattara, member of the Algiers OAS, was piecing together bits of information he had received during the day from various sources. He knew that something was in the wind, but had no substantial details and was far from suspecting Challe's presence in the city. The day before, indeed, Zattara and other OAS chieftains had sent a mission to Paris to urge immediate action, noting that they could not elude police raids indefinitely.

Like the groups in Paris and Madrid, they had waited up all Thursday night in vain.

Friday evening, they gathered hopefully again at Zattara's villa. The group included thirty-eight-year-old René Villars, an employee at the Délégation Générale, and authoritarian head of the nationalist France-Résurrection movement; and Charles Isselin, Susini's hand-picked successor as president of the Algiers Students Association.

At eight o'clock, Degueldre arrived, took Zattara aside, and told him that a coup would occur during the night; exactly how, where or when, he refused to specify. He was under strict instructions to furnish no further details.

Shortly afterward he left, and so, in a different direction, did Villars, without saying where he was bound.

Zattara is a burly, exuberant organizer of some warmth and gusto, with a *pied noir*'s knack for cultivating friendships and extending trust. He was bitterly chagrined when the truth sank in that the OAS was being excluded from the putsch. This did not square at all with the directives and exhortations the FAF secret branch had received in February urging mutual cooperation and promising joint civilian-military action.

At eleven o'clock, a talkative *pied noir* police inspector dropped in with rumors of sudden activity within the 1er REP at Zeralda; but now Zattara and Isselin found themselves prevented by the ten-o'clock curfew from venturing abroad to check the reports. At Rue des Pins, they waited in mounting frustration.

While the OAS was being passed over, without Zattara's knowledge Villars and France-Résurrection had been assigned a role in the putsch. Drawing its membership from prosperous, middle-class shopkeepers in Oran, and to a lesser extent in Algiers, the movement passed for a simon-pure extreme-Right organization. It was considered more compact, less vulnerable to penetration, than the already sprawling OAS. Challe had agreed to the smaller group's participation not through sudden liking for its policies or its members, but—at Jouhaud's urging—to give the *pieds noirs* a token role in the coup. Led by Villars, forty-eight members of France-Résurrection now waited at street corners to guide the paratroopers in the dark to the targets chosen by Godard—two guides for each target.

About midnight, the colonel received word from sympathizers at Army Corps headquarters at Caserne Pélissier. They reported that a first wave of uneasiness was beginning to seep through official Algiers—at Quartier Rignot, where General Gambiez was vainly seeking to determine whether any troops had moved without authorization from Zeralda; at the Palais d'Été, where a bridge game between Morin, Coup de Fréjac and two aides was interrupted by calls from nervous officials in Oran and Paris. Godard stepped out on the terrace of the Villa des Tagarins, and felt a surge of optimism; he had received a simple but formidable directive—to secure all key targets in Algiers, so that Challe could sit down at his former desk in Quartier Rignot by 5 A.M.—that was about to be carried out with textbook dispatch.

In Algiers, Denoix de St.-Marc broke away unusually early from a dinner given by his superior, General Bernard St.-Hillier, commanding the 10th Paratroop Division; as soon as the major reached Zeralda he issued march orders. No one now, not Gambiez nor Morin nor St.-Hillier nor Challe himself, could call off the putsch. The trucks of the 507th Transport Group, attached to the 1er REP, were driving out of the encampment and thundering down the highway at suicidal speed, some overtaking others on the right, headlights on full, in the direction of Algiers.

5

The Challenge

EARLY RISERS in Algiers suspected nothing amiss. On their way to work Saturday morning, a few observed the presence of Air Force commandos, unshaven and in rumpled leopard battle dress as though they had missed a night's sleep, deployed before Quartier Rignot, where infantry soldiers normally stood guard. But the *Algérois* were used to sudden influxes of commando units before and after anti-*fellaga* operations, and thought nothing more of the matter. In homes throughout the city, France V broadcast pop tunes and a disk jockey's purr of accompaniment. The spring day gave promise of being warm.

The first indication of something untoward occurred at seven o'clock. An anonymous male voice broke into a news program and announced: "The Army has assumed control of Algeria and the Sahara. The operation proceeded according to plan, in orderly fashion, without a shot being fired." Then the tone rose stridently: "French Algeria is not dead. . . . There is not—there never will be —an independent Algeria. Long live French Algeria so that France may live!" A military march followed. Another speaker declared that Radio Algiers was changing its name to "Radio France"—the implication being that henceforth it alone spoke for France.

The unhoped-for news in a matter of minutes set off a din of car horns sounding the three long beats and the two short ones, *Al-gé-rie fran-çaise!* with which Algiers in those days automatically reacted to developments. As a truckful of paratroopers rolled into view, European passers-by broke into applause. Tricolor flags reappeared at balconies and shop fronts. Yet, uncharacteristically, the *pieds noirs* were flustered; *their* way of forcibly bringing change about, of "making a revolution," as they said, was straightforward and vociferous; by entire neighborhoods, arms linked fraternally, they surged into the Forum, bellowing themselves hoarse, jostling, flinging paving stones at the gendarmes and frightening Paris with their number and fury. The Army, on the contrary, had struck soundlessly, with a total absence of breast-beating, during the night while the *pieds noirs* slept. The Army's way, in the *pieds noirs'* view, was more formidable; surely, less stirring. Radio France was now broadcasting one bulletin after another, but some indefinable emotion, an undercurrent of doubt, checked the crowd's readiness to celebrate. Salan, it appeared, was not physically present in the city. Challe's name boded little good, for he was associated with the Barricades' collapse; Zeller was utterly unknown. Jouhaud's participation reassured them somewhat; he was, after all, a native son. They milled hopefully about the streets, waiting, expecting a miraculous repetition of May 13. Some concluded that Challe's leadership of the putsch implied NATO backing.

The facts in the first radio bulletin were true—but deceptively so.* Shortly after 2 A.M., the 1er REP had entered Algiers and made contact with the guides of France-Résurrection. The targets designated by Godard were swiftly invested. The paratroopers ran into virtually no resistance by paramilitary security forces deployed behind hastily erected sandbags to protect government installations. At the port, CRS troops put up no fight and indeed helped commandeer Moslem fishing boats to get fish for the invaders' breakfast. Lieutenant Michel de la Bigne drove straight up to a group of gendarmes manning a command post near the Hotel St. Georges, and persuaded them with little difficulty to share a champagne toast. Some of his men clambered aboard the gendarmes' command car to drink. The putsch, almost everybody agreed, represented a turn for the better.

---

* The bulletin erred, however, in stating that not a single shot had been fired. The coup claimed one casualty, a sergeant-major shot to death while a group of paratroopers occupied the television relay station outside the city at Ouled-Fayat.

There had been isolated resistance by a few high-ranking officers. The diminutive commander in chief, General Fernand Gambiez, ordered his jeep, pennant flying, driven before the Délégation Générale in an attempt to prevent paratroopers from storming the gates. He was arrested for his pains by a rebellious lieutenant, at whom he roared:

"When I was in the Legion, lieutenants did not arrest generals."

"Generals in those days did not liquidate empires," the lieutenant snapped—a retort that subsequently earned him a two-year prison term.

Long before dawn, the city was in the putschists' hands. Nonetheless, they had committed mistakes.

One detachment of commandos made straight for the Palais d'Été, a priority target, and placed the occupants under house arrest: Morin; Sûreté chief Jacques Aubert; and an unexpected capture, Public Works Minister Robert Buron, who had just flown into Algiers. But within an hour, Morin managed to elude the paratroopers' surveillance, ring up Paris and inform Premier Debré of what was happening: Debré then issued the first government communiqué, noting pertinently that the insurgents controlled only the city, "the rest of Algeria is calm." Morin had made the call through an auxiliary communications center installed in a concrete bunker on the Palais grounds. The paratroopers learned of the center's existence only several hours later.

Morin also called Vice-Admiral Jean-Marie Querville, commander in chief of French naval forces in the Mediterranean, and Maritime Prefect of Algiers. Learning that a coup was underway, Querville, a stanch Gaullist, slipped into civilian clothes and fled into the garden of his villa just as a detachment of paratroopers turned up at the front door. They talked to the admiral's wife, briefly searched the house, and left empty-handed. An hour later, Querville reached his office at the Admiralty, in the port of Algiers. He called up Paris, proclaimed his loyalty to the government, then—as senior French officer still at liberty—announced that he was assuming command of forces in Algeria and forbade all further troop movements. By this time, however, communications facilities were blocked, Querville was isolated at the Admiralty, and his order remained a dead letter; but the putschists' failure to capture him subsequently weakened their position.

As soon as he heard France V's bulletin, Information Officer Jacques Coup de Fréjac drove back to his house, Villa des Oliviers, at El Biar. A former agent of the French Resistance, he remembered a number of wartime rules for eluding capture: a city crowd offers the best camouflage; remain near some form of communication, preferably a telephone; carry a substantial amount of cash; and finally, hide out if possible in a well-to-do home, where an extra guest's unannounced arrival attracts less attention and creates fewer material problems than in a modest household. He proceeded to apply these rules.

He rang up a friend and fellow member of the Resistance he had not seen in fifteen years. Although the conversation was vague, his friend understood immediately and volunteered to hide him. Coup de Fréjac arranged to have the Information Ministry in Paris notified of his arrest, knowing that the telegram would be intercepted and hoping that it would be taken at face value by police collaborating in the putsch. He backed his car, with its incriminating official license plate, into a parking lot reserved for paratrooper vehicles (where it remained, undamaged and well-protected, until the end of the insurrection). Then he set out on foot amid the excited crowd, occasionally shouted "Algérie française!" himself and safely reached his friend's apartment.

Radio producer Lucien Bitterlin was not so lucky.

He was aroused from deep sleep by a colleague, who broke the news. Bitterlin is a slight, sloe-eyed jet-haired Frenchman now in his late thirties who was acting, at the time, as secretary general of the Association pour le Soutien du Général de Gaulle in Algiers. He has only one good eye, the left one; as a boy, he lost the use of his right eye during a German bombing of the Paris suburb of La Garenne-Colombes. He harbors no liking for Rightists.

Bitterlin dressed hurriedly and went straight to the Télévision Française studios at Boulevard Bru. An activist journalist stood on a table and informed the staff that they were free to stay on and collaborate with the ruling junta or get out. Bitterlin got out. He went on foot to the nearby frequency-modulation-radio center at Rue Hoche. Here he listened to short-wave broadcasts of Europe Number One and Radio Monte Carlo on the Continent, and learned that the putsch was confined to Algiers. He felt deepening skepticism about its chances of success.

In one studio a disc jockey was playing military marches, one after another, under the watchful eye of a paratroop lieutenant, whose automatic pistol swung from a shoulder strap. Bitterlin considered at first sabotaging the modulation-control unit on the second floor, but gave up the idea after learning that stand-by equipment existed at Boulevard Bru. He advised one group of technicians to stop work in protest against the putsch. They listened to him noncommittally. "If Challe is in on this," one man said, "it must be for good."

Bitterlin went out into the street. It was late morning now, and quite hot. He saw Europeans applauding paratroopers, but he saw no Moslems participating in the applause. He bought *L'Écho d'Alger*. It had appeared too early to carry news of the putsch. Bitterlin had spent the entire week arranging for singer Richard Anthony to come to Algiers to star in a rock-and-roll festival, and now that it no longer mattered, he discovered a story publicizing the show in the newspaper.

He walked steadily uphill and came before the Palais d'Été. At the sight of paratroopers occupying the Moorish-style compound, he spat on the sidewalk. A chunky lieutenant seized him, smacked him twice across the face, knocking off his sun-glasses. Another soldier came up and hit him hard just under his good, left eye. He wiped blood from his mouth. He was driven in a jeep to Caserne Pélissier, then to the Central Police Commissariat. He learned that Colonel Godard would interrogate him personally later in the day. He was being held on two charges—as a prominent Gaullist, and for having eyed the duty lieutenant "in a mocking manner." When Bitterlin asked how his mocking expression was visible through dark glasses, he received no reply.

The courtyard of the Central Commissariat was littered with beer bottles, loaves of bread and empty ammunition boxes. German-speaking Legionnaires came and went. A policeman with keys to the cell doors waited to lock up newly arrested suspects. A police officer gave orders to put Bitterlin in one of the cells, then the order was countermanded and he was left seated on a bench with two other civilians taken into custody. What worried Bitterlin, however, was not the prospect of incarceration so much as the growing number of teen-age Europeans in the courtyard. They carried submachine guns, ammunition belts were slung militia-style over their shoulders, and they belonged to the OAS.

The corridors of Quartier Rignot were thronged with officers of every political leaning—some firmly in favor of the putsch, some loyal to the government, a notable percentage uncommitted and determined to wait and see. There were officers with field commands in the Algiers-Sahel sector who had abandoned their posts and driven pell-mell into the city to gauge the situation for themselves. There were staff officers, politicking zealously, seeking to sway or being swayed. The confusion at combined staff headquarters was extreme. Telephones rang, Telex machines clattered, motorcycle estafettes roared up. Lieutenants shouldered aside majors.

Challe was very busy. With Jouhaud he had just proclaimed a state of siege; Article 5 of the proclamation threatened to bring before special courts "all individuals who had conspired to abandon French Algeria." He dealt with another problem—what to do with his important prisoners Morin, Buron and Gambiez—by deporting them to In-Salah, hundreds of miles south in the Sahara. He had also worked out a curious compromise with Querville, still at bay in the Admiralty: the Navy would play no part in the putsch, but would maintain normal operational activity, which meant air and sea surveillance, under the "de facto" authorities. Challe received a call from Zeller, who reported that only three weeks' stocks of medical supplies and milk and olive oil were available; rationing might become necessary. The coffers of the Banque de France contained twelve million dollars, but less than a million in gold and foreign currencies, the rest having been removed to Paris shortly before the outbreak of the putsch. Zeller was already concerned about financial "asphyxiation."

Godard called, and proposed rounding up all officers in the huge courtyard of the Police School at Hussein Dey, where Challe would address them, and give each an opportunity to make an unequivocal choice on the spot. Godard's objective was to put an end to the officers' hesitation, to get them out of Algiers, where they were of little use, and back to their units, where they belonged.

One must attempt for a moment to imagine the situation through Challe's eyes. His plan was to seize Algeria, pacify it rapidly and appease French public opinion by shipping the conscripts home— he was confident that he could crush the *wilayas* in three months with the Operational Reserve. If the ALN on the frontier proved troublesome, he intended to order a division into Tunisia. Challe was prepared to fly to Tunis to give President Bourguiba a pledge that the Tunisian Army was not the target.

With the professional Army of Algeria supporting the putsch, public opinion disarmed by the return of the conscripts, and political opposition on the Right and Left rising in concert against the President, Challe expected de Gaulle to be paralyzed. But if he proved belligerent, Challe was ready—once French home opinion was softened up, but not before—to drop paratroopers on Paris.

All this was very well in theory, but it remained to be done. For a disastrous misunderstanding existed: Challe had arrived in Algiers believing that everything was ready, that he could count on twelve elite regiments totaling 40,000 men, even that the putsch would be underway as he landed; artlessly he visualized it as a parade-ground operation that required his presence only as a capstone. In reality, however, nothing was ready and Challe commanded no more than three regiments and several Air Force commandos—10,000 men at most. He could hardly occupy Algeria, much less menace France, with this force; the bulk of the Army still had to be rallied. And time was crucial. The second phase of an insurrection—consolidating power—is less spectacular but more subtle, more demanding and more dangerous than the first phase; the threat of a backlash always exists.

So on Saturday morning Challe already found himself hard pressed. He is very bitter to this day about the "vileness" of "tens of thousands of French officers who did nothing." It is true that officers showed a marked reluctance to fire on other officers, Frenchmen on Frenchmen—and Foreign Legion regimental commanders were still less willing to order foreign troops to fire on French soldiers. Henri Azeau compared the putsch to a "Laotian conflict, where no one fires unless he is absolutely forced to—and even then, no one fired." But Challe's own behavior was irresolute. He rejected one proposal after another—for investing the massive naval base of Mers el Kébir, at Oran; for seizing Blida Air Base, where loyal troops were in control; and even Godard's idea for separating activist from progovernment officers. Challe wanted, he says, to avoid civil war.

He spent the day reasoning by telephone with the Army Corps commanders on his flanks, General Marie-Michel Gouraud in Constantine and General Henri de Pouilly in Oran, and the zone commanders. He issued no orders and made no threats; they were being given a choice, and time to consider. It was an unprecedented way of conducting a coup.

The response at first was encouraging; in the dawn of Challe's apparent success, some field officers made oral commitments. The news of their shift of allegiance was promptly aired on Radio France.

The telephones on Challe's desk kept ringing.

At dawn that day, immediately after the lifting of the curfew, Dominique Zattara slipped out of his house and drove about the streets to see for himself what was happening. At strategic intersections and on rooftops, Zattara saw paratroopers manning heavy machine guns; but the half-tracks of the *gardes mobiles* were also everywhere in place, and visibly no tension existed between the two forces. It did not seem to Zattara as if a putsch had occurred at all. Zattara went round to awaken a fellow schoolteacher and activist, Georges Moureau. Then he drove quietly past the Délégation Générale, and ran into Gabriel Conessa, a photographer of *Paris-Match*, who assured him that the putsch had indeed taken place. Zattara is a prudent man. He made no attempt to draw attention to himself; he turned the car about and went off to alert the other leaders of the OAS. He still had some doubts.

At 8 A.M. he was summoned by Jouhaud to Quartier Rignot. Challe, who was in the same office, pointed out on a wall map the location of the units which at that moment were rallying to his cause. When Zattara urged the immediate mobilization of 50,000 *pieds noirs,* Challe told him dryly that he had no need of civilian reinforcements.

From Quartier Rignot, Zattara went to see Godard at Caserne Pélissier. Here some of his dissatisfaction with the way things were going—the passing-over of his group in favor of France-Résurrection, the Army's lack of trust in the civilians, and above all, the OAS's exclusion from any voice in the decisions being taken—all his resentment burst out. Godard conceded that it was regrettable, promised to give the civilians a role, and issued orders to put office space in the Mairie at the OAS's disposal. The colonel was simultaneously attempting, with incomplete success, to obtain a commitment of support from a fellow colonel commanding a CRS regiment. Godard struck Zattara as being immersed in tactical problems that required immediate attention. There was no time to reflect on the over-all situation. As Zattara left the barracks he came upon Degueldre. The tall, solemn ex-lieutenant, back in leopard dress, said simply: "It's hopeless; this is not a revolution." He was more pessimistic than usual and predicted that the putsch would be a fiasco.

By the time Zattara reached Boulevard Laferrière, an OAS recruiting office had been set up on the second floor of the Mairie. European men of all ages crowded the stairway, eager to join, in an atmosphere Zattara found strongly reminiscent of the overnight popularity of the Resistance after the Allied landings on D day and the first signs of German collapse. Hundreds of *pied noir* youths, tricolor patches hastily sewn to their shirts, roamed the streets in packs, beating up any Moslems and European liberals they could lay their hands on. One band kept busy painting enormous white Celtic crosses on paving stones, while another raced from house to house, pressuring occupants to show the flag. For better or worse, the Organization was now out of the shadows, enjoying a sort of semiofficial status under the distrait sponsorship of the Army.

Other activist movements were abroad too—France-Résurrection and Susini's Mouvement Nationaliste des Étudiants. The most excitable of the lot, Jeune Nation, headed unerringly for the arsenal at the Central Police Commissariat. When he spotted the approaching teen-agers, the police superintendent in charge at the sprawling building on Boulevard Baudin ordered the front gates shut and bolted. He repeated the order three times. Ignoring him, *pied noir* policemen stood by as the mob burst in and began to help itself to 400 machine guns and boxes of ammunition. These were the adolescents whom Bitterlin saw later in the day parading about with automatic weapons they were obviously impatient to try out.

In Paris, telephones rang at dawn in the homes of certain civilians and officers, who lifted their receivers and heard the word "Arnat." On the strength of this, Colonel Roland Vaudrey left his Montparnasse lodging and crossed the river to the apartment of Captain Philippe de St.-Rémy on Avenue Kléber. Here he met two majors. Simultaneously, Captain de St.-Rémy set out for Major Philippe Bléhaut's apartment on Avenue Niel, where General Faure was waiting.

The two groups were just settling down to a review of last-minute tactical arrangements when the police arrived. The putsch in Paris was over before it had begun.

One of the few who escaped was Bernard Sabouret Garat de Nedde. As he arrived at the Avenue Niel rendezvous he saw police; he turned back without being hailed, and walked rapidly away.

The members of the Vincennes Committee listened to Challe's declaration on the radio. They expected him to announce that the Army, in its role as guardian of "the higher interests of the nation," refused to obey a government that had acted illegitimately. Challe was expected to say that de Gaulle had no constitutional right to give away Algeria through negotiations. Above all, they waited for him to say that the putsch would continue until the Gaullist government in Paris was replaced.

What Challe said was far different; the direct challenge embodied in the draft proclamation was sidestepped. By Saturday morning, Marc Lauriol and other Rightist deputies concluded that they had been misled. Jacques Soustelle already viewed the putsch as a failure.

Since long before daybreak, the President of the Republic had been kept informed of developments by Debré. De Gaulle's first action was to dispatch two men he could trust—Algerian Affairs Minister Louis Joxe and General Jean Olié, chief of general staff—on a reconnaissance mission to Algeria, with orders to land wherever they could; otherwise he saw few advisers and kept his own counsel.

Throughout the morning telegrams of support for the Fifth Republic poured in from leaders of the French Community in Africa —Mamadou Dia in Senegal, Fulbert Youlou of the Congo Republic, Mauritania's President Moktar Ould Daddah. Late that afternoon, de Gaulle called an emergency cabinet meeting at the Élysée Palace. "The serious thing about this business," he told the unhappy ministers, "is its lack of seriousness."

It was his first outward reaction of any sort; and, up to a point, it represented a measured assessment of the men challenging him in Algiers. He did not discount their capacity for making trouble, but he did not rate their strategic and political ability very highly.

The government nonetheless was badly off balance. Overconfident, it had minimized the Army's readiness to participate in a new coup.

Misinformed, it had suspected all the generals but Challe. It had no contingency plans to speak of. The putsch, moreover, came at an awkward time: the ailing Interior Minister, Pierre Chastenet, had just been replaced by Roger Frey, and Armed Forces Minister Pierre Messmer was away at Rabat. And one minister was now in the insurgents' hands.

No one in the French government could be certain that the generals' prime target was not—as it had been in 1958—France itself. The existence of anti-Gaullist networks throughout the country was a fact. The attitude of the home-based Army and French troops in West Germany could shift in hours from precarious neutrality to hostility.

Paris Police Prefect Maurice Papon thought that if the paratroopers had struck before dawn, the seizure of the capital would have been, in his words, *une balade,* a walkover. He spent the next four days and nights at his office on Boulevard du Palais planning a three-stage defense of the city. He proceeded on the assumption that some of the veiled threats Radio France was uttering might be executed; he could not tell for sure, because no one had a precise idea of the putschists' strength or intentions. Papon's plan called for blocking airfield runways, concentrating security forces at bridges leading into Paris, then falling back on an inner defense zone, the *Polygone sacré,* containing key ministries.

That Saturday evening, two platoons of Navy commandos, of unquestioned allegiance, took up positions around the Élysée Palace.* The government had at its disposal twenty companies of CRS totaling some 3,000 men, thirty squadrons of *gendarmerie,* and the 10,000-man police of Paris. These forces were presumed loyal. It could count on approximately three hours' advance warning from Navy radar-equipped picket boats on alert far out in the Mediterranean, in the event that airborne units from Algeria were sighted heading north toward Paris.

Orléans, some seventy miles south of Paris, is a staid provincial center renowned historically because during the Hundred Years'

---

* According to several sources, de Gaulle spent Saturday night away from the Élysée Palace. Some Gaullist officials showed extreme nervousness, arranged for their families to be in safe places, but remained on the job. A few cases bordered on panic.

War its siege was lifted by Joan of Arc, and in more recent years for its annual fair and flower show. On this Saturday it was a magnet for hundreds of French youths, who converged on the city.

Orléans' annual fair was being held over the weekend, but the youths bypassed the fairground and milled about the barracks of the 2d Regiment of Hussars, a former cavalry unit converted to armor. The influx did not, of course, go unnoticed, but local authorities remained curiously oblivious to the youths' presence. As the day wore on, they dispersed into cafés and cinemas.

Among themselves, they had a password, "Arnat." They planned next morning to seize the tank regiment and march on Paris. The would-be insurrectionists comprised young reserve officers, ex-paratroopers, members of Jeune Nation. They were high-spirited and itching to show their mettle.

When Salan heard about the putsch he said laconically, "It looks all right." His composure cracked only later in the day.

It was Susini who, voice tense with excitement, rang up the Princesa early Saturday morning and broke the news. Almost at the same moment, Serrano Suñer called. He reported that the police had learned of the developments in Algeria and would be arriving at the hotel at any moment. Serrano Suñer urgently advised Salan and Ferrandi to clear out.

Two *guardias civiles* at the side door failed to challenge the silver-haired elderly man and his companion who hurriedly walked out to a waiting car just before 8 A.M. Plainclothesmen and early-rising newsmen continued their vigil in the pleasantly cool gardens of the Princesa, unaware that their quarry had fled.

Salan and Ferrandi spent that day in the apartment of the Duchess of Abrantes, a friend and political ally of Serrano Suñer. At noon, Franco's brother-in-law arrived with bad news: the Spanish government had banned all flights, and the police had thrown a dragnet around Madrid to prevent all French activists from leaving the country. He had sought to have the flight ban relaxed, but was told that Spain would honor its commitments and cooperate fully with de Gaulle's government. Serrano Suñer left the apartment, promising that he was working on an alternate scheme to get them to Algiers.

At five in the afternoon he returned. Everything was in order; they would be able to depart the following morning. He had made arrangements through a prominent Falangist, Dr. Narciso Perales, who had found a pilot, who in turn had found a plane. The charter cost three thousand dollars, and final details were being elaborated to take off without official interference. When Salan learned that not more than three could go aboard, he decided without hesitation that Susini and Ferrandi would accompany him, while Lagaillarde and Ronda remained in Madrid. In view of the interdependent relationship that had sprung up between the general and Susini, the choice was not surprising.

That night, while the government in Paris concealed its nervousness and the *pieds noirs* triumphed noisily in Algiers, Salan and Ferrandi slipped off to still another hiding place, the suburban flat of a Madrid music critic. Salan betrayed some emotion; he feared that Serrano Suñer's plan would fall through, that the police would somehow get wind of it; he told Ferrandi that if it miscarried, they would make off across the Portuguese frontier and fly from Lisbon. Susini joined them in the apartment, they stayed awake late and listened to the radio bulletins. That morning Susini had rated the putsch's chances of success at one hundred percent: twelve hours later, his initial enthusiasm was alloyed by Radio Algiers's silence about the revolutionary reforms he expected and the paratroop drop he thought essential. He had understood that two regiments, the 2ème REP and the 2ème RCP, would take Paris by complete surprise on Friday night; he could not account for Challe's failure to act.

Each man realized that the departure from Spain represented a leap into the dark. Nothing forced them to go. Challe visibly was in no hurry to see them arrive. Presently, Salan fell asleep on a sofa, the others dozed as best they could in the critic's armchairs.

The next morning they drove to Barajas, hid disguised as workmen on the floor of a pickup truck, and got out at the far end of the airfield. Serrano Suñer saw them off. After listening to Radio Algiers, his own impression was unfavorable. The succession of bulletins and messages gave no sense of drama, of an implacable test of wills and violent change. Recalling the outbreak of the Spanish Civil War, he said to Susini sadly: "You French are too civilized to carry out a putsch."

The Aviaco Convair chartered through Dr. Perales had special permission to carry an emergency case—a doctor and his stretcher-borne patient—to Rome. It was the only authorized flight that Sunday morning from Barajas. They watched the plane taxi down the runway and come to an unscheduled stop near where they were standing. The doctor and his patient quickly stepped out, and Salan, Ferrandi and Susini went aboard. Carlos Texidor, the pilot, set his course on Palma, then Algiers.*

At Challe's headquarters, a certain optimism prevailed on Sunday morning. More regiments had thrown in their lot with the putsch, Greater Algiers' thirty-eight municipal councilors and thirty general councilors had signed a declaration of loyalty to the junta. General Zeller, meanwhile, flew to Constantine to rally General Gouraud, whose prolonged hesitation Challe was beginning to find unacceptable. For the occasion, Zeller adopted tough tactics, and mercilessly bullied the unhappy Army Corps commander—the one eyewitness present at the meeting, Lieutentant de la Bigne, later described it as "painful." In the end, Gouraud wilted and made a halfhearted commitment; in the putschists' view, it sufficed.

Sergent, diligently hovering about Quartier Rignot, maintained his own morale and that of other junior officers by repeating that Challe was proceeding slowly, step by step, without spectacular announcements, to give the plotters in Paris a chance to rise. But Sergent admitted that the insurrection was, at this stage, as "unstable as a tightrope act."

For there had been some ominous developments. Oran, Algeria's second city, was in the putschists' hands—but not the city's military and civilian chiefs. After failing to win over the Army Corps commander, General de Pouilly, Colonel Argoud had authorized him to leave with his staff and the prefect of Oran for nearby Tlemcen. It turned out to be a major psychological blunder, for de Pouilly promptly became, not entirely as he planned, an example of resistance to the Algiers junta.

A far more disturbing development was, in a sense, invisible. Field commanders who had replied favorably to Challe on Saturday, on Sunday experienced second thoughts. Confronted by a choice between loyalty and revolt, they chose neither—and stalled for time. Some summoned their staffs, and instructed junior officers to act as

* The Spanish police arrested Texidor as soon as he returned to Madrid. It also cracked down on Lagaillarde and other activists, and effectively prevented them from leaving Spain. But charges against Texidor were later quietly dropped, which partially bears out claims that Franco's government winked at Salan's flight as a form of insurance on the future.

they saw fit. Some rigidly followed Army discipline, obeying orders of superiors and letting *them* decide. A great number of officers went on sick call.*

They remained uncommitted for numberless reasons—because the putsch struck some as poorly organized and feebly led; others succumbed to pressure by progovernment fellow officers and enlisted men. Many, a great many, feared the consequences of open revolt for their careers.

Whatever the reasons, officers at divisional, regimental, battalion and company levels, in towns and douars, at airfields and in barracks, in outposts throughout the immense breadth of Algeria, hung back. And the putsch began to falter.

As soon as they landed, the atmosphere struck them as unpromising. The weather had changed, a gritty south wind blew dust across the field. At Maison Blanche airport, although it was Sunday, few *pieds noirs* were assembled. (Salan and Susini later discovered that Challe had ordered their arrival downgraded on Radio Algiers.) Entering the city, they crossed truckloads of conscripts, who shouted antiputsch slogans.

While Salan went straight to Villa Dominique, where he put on his summer uniform and his medals, Susini sought out the clandestine activist leaders. He found them gathered in a garage near the port—Zattara, Capeau, Isselin, Villars, Jean-Marie Zagamé of Jeune Nation, and a tough-talking doctor from Bab el Oued, Jean-Claude Perez, released the day before on Godard's order from the internment camp of Tefeschoun.

To a man, they were a sour and frustrated group. Challe had refused to see them and was dragging his feet on all their demands. They were smarting under an Army-inspired directive which forbade civilians to go about with arms and emphasized that maintenance of order was purely a military responsibility. Radio France was in the civilians' hands, but European listeners were apathetic from a surfeit of military marches, and still more exasperating, word

---

* Jean-Louis Guillaud, an information aide on Coup de Fréjac's staff in Algiers, has estimated that 15 percent of the French officers in Algeria supported the putsch; 15 percent opposed de Gaulle's Algerian policy without favoring the putsch, and all the rest remained uncommitted. (*La Nef*, special issue, *Soldats perdus*, October 1962–January 1963.)

had arrived from Quartier Rignot prohibiting any outright verbal attacks on de Gaulle over the air.

Disenchantment was setting in, and some activist leaders already threatened to return underground—it was not worth running risks, they argued, for an insurrection that was going to fail.

The one point of agreement was disillusionment with Challe. They were cheered up a bit now by the news of Salan's arrival.

A short distance away, the Casbah remained realistically calm. The inhabitants made no secret of their hope that, in this struggle between Europeans, de Gaulle would emerge the victor, if only so that cease-fire negotiations could begin; but the insurgents were entrenched in Algiers, and it was impossible to display open defiance without incurring reprisals. The Casbah limited its show of displeasure to a few scrawled signs that said stubbornly: *"Le FLN vaincra."*

In Tunis, Information Minister M'hamed Yazid declared: "The Europeans of Algeria must refuse to be the unconscious tools once again of colonialist and Fascist interests condemned by history." It was a grandiloquent declaration, but privately, the GPRA feared that Challe might carry his offensive into Tunisia, to make good his pledge of crushing the rebellion. And if he did, the rebellion was vulnerable. A number of ALN battalions were presently at rest in the so-called "duck's bill," along the Medjerda river north of Souk-Ahras, where Tunisian territory describes a wedge into Algeria. The area, lightly patrolled by Tunisian forces, could appear a tempting target to a general in quest of a swift knockout blow.

From Tunis that Sunday, orders went out to the ALN to cease operations until the situation became clearer. For the same reason, within Algeria, in the *djebels,* the *ferkas* (guerrilla platoons) lay low. There would be no provocation to make matters easier for Challe.

Parisians scanned the skies—casually for the most part, not fearfully—for paratroopers. They saw none. The emergency interfered with no weekend plans. Thousands drove off to enjoy the raw spring sunshine in the countryside. The bland assumption was that de Gaulle would master the situation.

In Orléans, the insurrectionists massed at the caserne of the 2nd Regiment of Hussars discovered with humiliation that the password *Arnat* could not get them past the sentries. Particularly galling was the realization that duty officers were not ill-disposed, but had no idea what *Arnat* meant. Furthermore, it was clear that activist elements within the barracks had not risen as planned. Garat de Nedde, fresh from his escape in Paris, arrived and briefly saw the Hussars' commander—who asked him to come back some other day. All this raised serious questions about the efficiency of the Paris plotters.

Then, with the disconcerting news that General Faure had been arrested, it began to rain—a relentless downpour. The crowd outside the barracks scattered. One youth persuaded the potential putschists to disperse into the countryside. He announced that at the appropriate moment they would be picked up in trucks and reassembled in Orléans.

The wet revolutionaries waited in the houses of sympathetic but bewildered farmers. Presently, word arrived that the tank-borne march on Paris had been canceled. The threat to the capital from this quarter, if it had ever seriously existed, was over.

Debré was in charge of hour-by-hour operations. His primary concern remained the danger of a coordinated airborne assault, and as one step to forestall it, he ordered the paratroop training center at Pau guarded by local CRS troops and ten Nord 2501s transferred to Toulouse. Later in the day he gave orders to Air Force Major General Jean-Louis Nicot to open fire on unidentified and unauthorized aircraft approaching the capital; but here he ran into trouble getting his orders obeyed.* He was not yet aware of Nicot's role in Challe's departure for Algiers.

Debré was almost as much concerned by the public's indifferent attitude, and it prompted him to suggest that the General address the country at large. Eventually de Gaulle agreed; and since he seldom, if ever, speaks wholly extemporaneously, he spent most of Sunday afternoon closeted in his study at the Élysée Palace composing, polishing and memorizing his text.

---

* Nicot delayed issuing the order to Air Force operations headquarters until early next morning.

The putsch directly challenged his authority as President of the Republica—as the Barricades of 1960 had not. This was no street defiance by the civilian small fry of Algiers, by Ortiz and Lagaillarde and their rabble of followers. The fact that fellow generals would mutiny outraged de Gaulle; there was no tradition in the French Army of revolt *between* generals. (His own disobedience of Pétain's orders in 1940 he considered in another light.) His shock found voice in the triple-hammer-blow exclamation that would become famous in the dead center of the speech, *"Hélas . . . hélas . . . hélas!"*

The day-old insurrection showed no sign of abating, but as he totted up the balance-sheet, de Gaulle could enumerate some assets. There was the intangible reaction of loyalty which, in a fluid situation, could be relied on to maintain some officers and units and some of the civil administration on his side through sheer force of habit and discipline. There was also the undeniable fact that French public opinion did not favor a pronunciamento against the Republic addressed from Algiers; this meant that the paras, if they landed, would not swim like fish among the population. The Navy would probably remain loyal—not through any special liking for him, but out of a traditional desire to bypass politics and keep its ships and crews intact. However, such support, he well knew, would count for little if the insurrection spread and engulfed the entire Army of Algeria. De Gaulle has always tempered his response to circumstances and personalities. To this particular challenge he responded like a gamecock. He set out to mobilize opinion actively around himself; he set out to convince the rebellious generals that if they persevered, civil war was inevitable. Challe, he had long ago concluded, was no Franco, and had little stomach for bloody confrontation.

He put on his general's uniform and recorded his speech; at 8 P.M., the dinner hour, when Frenchmen had returned from their Sunday outing, he appeared on the television screens of the nation.

The speech was short, eloquent and to the point. De Gaulle aired it with forceful persuasiveness in a voice occasionally breaking with an old man's anger. However unconcerned with the putsch's outcome Frenchmen were, he was not; on the small home screens, the looming figure allied his audience brusquely with great issues; he denounced the quadrumvirate of generals as usurpers, lashed out at the colonels in the wings, and predicted that their venture could lead only to a national disaster. "The state is flouted, the nation defied, our power degraded, our international prestige lowered, our role and our place in Africa jeopardized"—rolling French prose of this order was calculated to make a mark. He forbade all Frenchmen to obey the insurgent generals, ordered the use of "all means"—which meant firepower—to put them down, and served notice that he would resort to special powers under Article 16 of the French Constitution. Shrewdly, he called on Frenchmen and Frenchwomen to help him restore order. He displayed not the slightest inclination to yield an inch.

It was superb use of television as a means of mass persuasion. De Gaulle turned the arm of psychological warfare against its foremost military advocates, and on this score he was unbeatable; the generals in Algiers had no television at their disposal, and there is no reason to think that they would have been adept at exploiting it.

Unlike the appeal of June 18, 1940, the April 23 speech at a critical moment set in motion forces that would utterly reverse the trend of events. With it, de Gaulle outfoxed the quartet of generals in Algiers, and gave his own badly jolted entourage a lesson in astute tactics and iron will power. The speech thus ranks as one of the most momentous in his career, and in the Algerian putsch it was a watershed.

Three and a half hours after de Gaulle's appearance on television, Debré, sallow and unshaven after two days and nights on the job, brusquely decided to address the Parisians. Reports had arrived of paratroopers boarding requisitioned Air Algérie planes, but whether their target was Tunis or Paris it was impossible to tell. In doubt, the Premier, like Papon, decided that he could not afford to run the risk of scoffing at the eventuality of a move against the capital. Because it would take too long to set up recording equipment at the Hotel Matignon, he drove to the Télévision Française studios on Rue Cognacq-Jay.

Warning listeners of an imminent para drop, he exhorted the population to mass at Paris airfields "on foot or by car" and talk the invaders out of their error. Frenchmen, who had listened with constrained solemnity to de Gaulle's appeal, gave vent to their irritation by subjecting the luckless Debré to a barrage of Parisian ridicule. The reference to cars was jeered at as a middle-class reflex; yet, by dramatizing the danger, the midnight address had considerable effect and crystallized the response of the powerful trade-unions and Leftist and Center political parties.

The Interior Ministry, whose information had led to Debré's appeal, was in a state of disarray. The atmosphere in that nerve center was a bizarre mixture of panic and resolution. The tapestried salons were thick with cigarette smoke and flustered officials. All sorts of sensational rumors were afloat in Paris, and irresistibly they converged at Place Beauveau.

When Interior Minister Frey received word about midnight that troop planes had been sighted over Sicily, he asked about the source of the news flash. "It's not Agence France-Presse, it's Reuters," he was told.

"Then it must be serious!" exclaimed Frey. But there still was no firm indication of an approaching airborne force.

It was to be a long, all-night vigil. Volunteer groups began to assemble in the Ministry courtyard. Communist cells in the industrial suburbs rang up and demanded arms. Gaullists, middle-of-the-road republicans, Socialists, liberals of various stripe turned out. The Ministry became the focal point of impromptu resistance to an anticipated Rightist coup.

Between three and five o'clock three trucks drove up with uniforms and arms. The Minister momentarily considered the formation of a popular militia. The Paris police's strong opposition, the evident risk of swinging from one extreme to the other, and above all de Gaulle's hostility led to quick rejection of the plan. A few weapons were handed out;* several packing cases were ripped open, and middle-aged men buckled combat boots on. Culture Minister André Malraux walked about, haranguing an impressed audience that remembered Teruel, Guadalajara, and the heroic moments of the Spanish Civil War.

It is facile to poke fun at the scene of not untypical Gallic confusion in the courtyard; but the expectation of attack, fed by rumors, self-interest and some genuine alarm, was real enough at the time.

As the night wore on, however, the government took steps to re-

* Two or three hundred weapons, according to a police estimate—but the police admit that an exact figure is unavailable. Members of the Gaullist MPC (Mouvement pour la Communauté) declined arms, for the good reason that they were already armed.

gain control of the situation. It relieved the lukewarm commander of the Paris Air Region. General Bernard Challe, who had instructed his men to fire warning shots close to unidentified airrcaft instead of downing them. It tardily arrested General Nicot and replaced General Bigot. André Malraux changed his mind about the threat and described reports of an imminent drop as "intoxication"— though, in fact, "self-intoxication" would have been a more accurate term. The government meanwhile gingerly backed away from any tactical alliance with the Left that could be construed as a resurrection of the Popular Front of the Thirties. It banned an antiputsch demonstration called by the Communist party and the Communist-dominated CGT (Confédération Générale du Travail). It forbade the formation of a workers' militia at the nationalized Renault auto works. The scare, in a sense, had produced the desired result: it had aroused some of the population from political apathy, but it had gone almost too far for the government's taste.

As the night wore on—for reasons that had little to do with developments in Paris, but much with General Maurice Challe's faint leadership—not a single parachute blossomed over the capital. By this time, squadrons of Mystère fighters loyal to the government were patrolling the valley of the Rhone, the natural approach for aircraft arriving from the south.

6

The Collapse

CHALLE WAS in deepening trouble on Monday morning, and he knew it. Strategically he had failed to carry the attack to the homeland— because, he said, he lacked air transport for two paratroop regiments and at any rate could not spare the regiments;* because it would take motorized divisions in West Germany two days to cross the Rhine and cover the four hundred miles to Paris, assuming that they ran into no organized resistance; and primarily because he felt that most of France—at least the working class—opposed a military putsch. This, for Challe, was the most damaging admission of all to have to make.

He had likewise failed to constitute a government or secure a tangible promise of outside aid; all this, he reasoned, could wait until the essential business of rendering himself "master of Algeria" was accomplished. He had been particularly optimistic about the leverage that control of Algeria's oil wells would give him: "Once you own oil fields," he swore, "you acquire a lot of friends."†

* Henri Azeau, in *Révolte militaire*, disputes this argument, and notes that Challe had available at various airfields 45 Noratlases, 16 Douglas DC-4s, 3 Douglas DC-3s, 5 Caravelles, etc., in short, enough carriers to transport two regiments.

† Challe categorically denies receiving firm offers of American aid before the putsch, or meeting personally with any Americans during the four days. There is no evidence of *active* CIA planning or backing of the revolt. The au-

But now his hope of victory in forty-eight hours was eroding relentlessly under pressure of developments beyond his control. Militarily, his position was unpromising. Both flanks were weak; Gouraud's loyalty appeared doubtful, and the situation in Oran remained precarious. Gardy had failed to rally the Foreign Legion; a band marched into Oran, bugles blaring, to public acclamation, but neither battles nor insurrections are permanently won by parades, and except for one company the Legion infantry remained neutral in its spacious headquarters at Sidi bel Abbès. Months before, Colonel Albert Brothier, commanding officer of the crucial 1st Foreign Legion Infantry Regiment, had received a secret message from Salan, Jouhaud and Gardy qurying him about his reaction if asked to march on Oran by the chiefs of a military rising. In response, Brothier made four points: he said he would do nothing detrimental to the Legion's unity (a statement open to misinterpretation); he thought it a serious error to ask a regiment composed of foreigners to initiate a revolt; he expressed doubt about the chances of success of a movement cut off from the homeland; and he stated that French opinion would not tolerate a military dictatorship.

Oddly, the generals paid no heed whatever to this negative reaction.

At first indifferent, the Air Force was now hostile to the putsch—sixteen planes had taken off in defiance of the junta's orders grounding them, and this in spite of Challe and Jouhaud being Air Force

---

thor has been told that CIA made contact with Challe while he was at Fontainebleau, and it was certainly aware of revolt brewing within the French Army. U.S. Army officers assigned to NATO shared many of Challe's reservations about de Gaulle's global strategy and undoubtedly led him to believe that he could count on U.S. support *after* the putsch succeeded. President Kennedy immediately sent a personal message through U.S. Ambassador to Paris James Gavin to de Gaulle, not so much to offer positive aid, as reported at the time, as to bring reassurances that CIA was not involved in the revolt. The staff of Algerian Affairs Minister Louis Joxe evaluated rumors of CIA backing as baseless (*sans valeur*). On May 5, Foreign Affairs Minister Maurice Couve de Murville told the National Assembly that the French government considered the incident "closed." There are, however, persistent stories by eyewitnesses, interviewed by the author, of two U.S. colonels in uniform at Challe's side on Saturday, April 22—this is, of course, in complete contradiction to Challe's version of events. The colonels remained through midday, then vanished, never to be seen again in Algiers. It is said they understood by noon that the putsch was doomed. It is also possible that they were summarily recalled when and if the White House learned of Pentagon involvement, but this remains conjecture.

As for the oil wells, they continued to function through the four days.

generals. Blida Air Base was barricaded to prevent paratroopers from gaining access to the field.

As for the Navy, it showed no disposition to intercept ships sailing for France without clearance from Quartier Rignot. One passenger ship, the *Sidi Ferruch*, specifically ordered to remain in port, had lifted anchor and, without tugs, gained the open sea, unchallenged by any of the patrol boats in the roadstead.

At noon, Jouhaud brought news that the French Mediterranean squadron at Toulon, consisting of the aircraft carrier *Arromanches*, the cruiser *Colbert* and four escort vessels, was under orders to get up steam for Algiers. Challe ruled out any idea of a clash with the fleet. By now, he was confronted with a potentially far more ominous problem.

The conscripts of the Army of Algeria—several hundred thousand strong, making up two thirds of the ground forces, patriotic but homesick, uninterested in nationalist dreams of a greater France extending "from Dunkirk to Tamranset," and hostile to the whole notion of *Algérie française* as reflected in the *pieds noirs'* patronizing attitude toward Metropolitan Frenchmen—the conscripts revolted against Challe's authority on Monday. At first, scattered cases of defiance occurred, in units separated from one another by immense distances. A private went from platoon to platoon, canvassing signatures for a petition expressing loyalty to de Gaulle. Enlisted men held an open-air meeting without asking leave of their commanding officer and chanted, *"Non au fascisme!"* Then quickly resistance became coordinated: a group of draftees called in a body on their officers and urged them to side with the government. Signal Corps men transmitted instructions over Army field lines to carry on passive resistance and refuse orders from insurrectionist officers. In a few cases, sabotage of communications was undertaken, and mail was deliberately misrouted.

Transistor radios had partly done the trick. In mess halls and orderly rooms and under tents, the conscripts had listened to de Gaulle's Sunday evening speech, broadcast to Algeria on static-ridden short-wave by Radio Monte Carlo. They heard the President of the Republic order them in the clearest possible language to follow loyal officers only, and they heeded the order. De Gaulle's address not only appealed to their sense of obedience but surprised them by its unusualness. Paul-Marie de la Gorce has written that "without doubt it was the first time in French military history that a chief of state appealed to troops over the heads of their rebellious superiors."

There was little Challe could do to counter this. He was discovering that de Gaulle's description of the Algiers junta as usurpers was literally true: being retired, they commanded nothing and must seize everything. But the Signal Corps network remained in loyal hands, and even if it had not, it was impossible to prevent contact with France via pocket transistors. "In communications," Challe has observed dryly, "everything is two-way. You cannot cut everything. Even in the occupied countries during World War II, the Germans never managed to block signals from London."

There was another reason for the conscripts' revolt. They wanted no part of a putsch that might prolong the war, even if the future of French Algeria could be assured into the bargain. But the generals had paid as little attention to their men as to the Moslems in their plans. "*L'officier dine, le sous-off' mange, et le soldat bouffe*"*—this sentence expressed as well as any the time-encrusted relationship of the three castes within the French Army. When the draftees, who consisted of students, trade-unionists and office employees as well as unskilled manual workers and farm hands, displayed an ability and will to think for themselves, it upset the generals' calculations.

However, the importance of the conscripts' reaction should not be exaggerated. They made their opinion felt; it did not go much beyond this. There was no major breakdown of discipline in the Army of Algeria. A mutinous condition temporarily developed in one unit only, the 14ème Bataillon de Chasseurs Alpins at Bône, where conscripts locked up putschist officers. The enlisted men's aversion to the putsch often grew in direct proportion to their officers' backing of it; this was the case in the 9ème Régiment de Chasseurs Parachutistes. There was also a natural temptation to take advantage of circumstances to run wild a bit. Defiance did not always succeed; some soldiers were promptly transferred or punished. What is clear is that one major consequence of the conscripts' resistance was to provide wavering souls in the officer corps with an unhoped-for pretext for sitting the putsch out.

---

* "An officer dines, a noncom eats, and a soldier gobbles."

The regimental commanders who had so roundly assured Argoud that they could be counted upon when the time came, had made the commitment with the serenity of men inwardly persuaded that the time was far off in the hazy future and perhaps would never materialize. When they were invited to honor their commitments, it proved to be another matter, all the more so when it became apparent that one could refuse to rally to the putsch without fear of losing one's life. This, of course, makes a difference in any uprising.

The officers' unheroic wavering came as a bitter shock to Challe. He had thought that he could carry out the revolt without the conscripts, but the officers' shapeless hesitation was too much for him. "I would have won," he declared later, "but there was no enemy to fight—it was like fighting an eiderdown quilt."

One must not fall into the error of taking Challe as seriously as he took himself. If he was "brilliant when discussing military strategy," as one French journalist commented, "he was utterly ineffectual at directing a revolution." The officers' studied inertia, in a sense, matched his own indecision, and at any rate he should not have been surprised. "Wait-and-see" was not a new phenomenon in the French Army; it had flourished in November 1942, during the North African landings, and surely on May 13, not to mention the spectacular lack of response to de Gaulle's appeal of June 1940.

As matters worsened, Challe remained unruffled, sucking on his pipe, never becoming angry or issuing an ultimatum; his composure concealed not iron determination but an unreadiness to strike out into deeper waters, although this was what was needed to make the putsch a success.

At Quartier Rignot on Monday morning, he found himself quite alone, without even an efficient staff officer. Not a single zone commander had rallied to his cause. The 20,000-man *gendarmerie* remained loyal to the government. "I needed," he mourned, "fifteen Zellers and Jouhauds." Instead, he felt the colonels imperceptibly but surely shifting their allegiance away from him, while his headquarters was thronged by unhelpful young paratroop lieutenants eager for the "honor" of being the first to drop on Paris. To get rid of them, he sent them off on fictitious missions across the breadth of Algeria.

In the crooked streets of Algiers the OAS seemed suddenly to be everywhere. Its volunteers joined the local police in their piebald

Renault patrol cars, swooped down on *pied noir* neighborhoods, distributed tracts and collected funds from shopkeepers. Claude Capeau enthusiastically put on his paratrooper uniform and raced about the city in a jeep; he was convinced that the Army had won. The OAS declared war on "liberals," and proceeded to make life miserable for them. Young activists invaded Lycée Gauthier in the heart of town, arrested a dozen teachers on charges of being FLN sympathizers, and removed them to the Beni-Messous internment center. Marcel Bucaille, the liberal mayor of nearby Guyotville, was held; and so for good measure was the police commissioner, who happened to be present when a commando arrived. The OAS helped "enforce order." It provided local activist politicians with bodyguards. Its men were running Radio France and seeing to it that only bulletins of the most reassuring sort were aired. OAS recruiting offices were now functioning at three different locations: the main office on Boulevard Laferrière, and two suboffices at the Town Hall and in a driving school at El Biar.

For most of the European population, OAS had been a name vaguely identified with tracts and fence signs; now its members were out in the open, in paramilitary uniform, haphazardly armed but better disciplined and led than the old FAF formations.

In spite of this superficial triumph, the OAS leaders were more and more perturbed. They correctly sensed something wrong with the whole setup. De Gaulle's speech had underscored his firm intention of forcing an issue, at the cost of civil war if necessary, a confrontation that Challe obviously shrank from. The OAS was also worried by the increasing turbulence of Jeune Nation's teen-agers, who, brandishing automatic weapons pilfered from the Commissariat Central and occupying public buildings, were visibly trying to gain control of the putsch for their own ends. Finally, there was the disturbing reaction of Algiers' civil servants, who refused to cooperate in any way with the junta, or "Conseil Supérieur de l'Algérie," as it was now called.

Zattara, Capeau and the others gathered at the Délégation Générale for a working session under Colonel Gardes; Degueldre and one of Sergent's aides, Lieutenant Daniel Godot, attended. The purpose was to decide what to do next to give the stationary putsch further thrust. If Challe was downhearted, they were impatient. Their allegiance to him, never very intense, crumbled. A hitherto unspoken thought was now out in the open: to save the putsch, stage a putsch; surround Quartier Rignot with paratroopers, take Challe prisoner, put Salan in charge, and create a new Public Safety Committee composed of activists and colonels to deal with Paris. A nostalgic yearning for the victory of May 1958 was uppermost in their minds, and once again in this scheme the critical factor was Salan.

Salan was at Villa Dominique. Like Challe, but for different reasons, he wanted to avoid a drastic move as long as possible. He was not ready to stage a second putsch. He listened carefully to proposals in this vein by Perez and appeals by Sergent, but turned them down and declared that Challe was managing satisfactorily. Then he called in Susini. This was on Sunday evening, and the basis for Salan's sanguine behavior is interesting; objectively, there were few facts to justify it. The truth is that Salan realized clearly by this time that Challe was heading straight for disaster and said as much to Susini.

But Le Chinois thought developments would force Challe to change his methods, at which point he (Salan) would be able to influence him and swerve the putsch in a different direction. It apparently did not occur to him that time for this subtle wearing-down of Challe might not be available. At any rate, he was not going to act against a fellow general—because it was repugnant to him, and because he knew that he had still less control over the Army than Challe did. It more than bore out Susini's contention that Le Chinois, by instinct, did not create circumstances but exploited them.

What Salan proceeded to do instead was typical. On Monday he moved into the Délégation Générale and assumed all civilian powers, which Challe had neither given nor refused him. Then he formed a skeleton cabinet. The choice of counselors was both curious and hasty, and reflected a woeful lack of talent on which to draw. Ferrandi and Susini received nominally important duties and occupied offices flanking Salan's; but the key position of Political Affairs Director was filled by an aging garrulous nonentity, Marcel Lavest *alias* Marc Laffont, a former airline employee with no qualifications whatever for the task. No one else of much ability or experience joined. It all smacked of improvisation and, worse, superficiality. If this was the best the supposedly politically minded Salan could manage, it augured poorly for the putsch's future.

By Monday afternoon, the situation had still further deteriorated, and at Susini's urging the OAS called a mass meeting at the Forum—another of those panaceas for curing political ills inherited from May 1958. Susini argued that a show of popular support was more important than ever to counterbalance the lack of Army support. Salan agreed to address the crowd. Challe, who is not eloquent in private, and even less so before larger groups, at first balked—"I don't want to make a clown of myself," he muttered to his former chief of staff, Colonel Georges de Boissieu—but then he accepted. He had an idea of what his fellow activists were up to, and one reason for showing himself in public was certainly to forestall a takeover by the civilians.* At this point, he was still assuring Rightist Algerian Deputy Marc Lauriol of his determination to see the struggle through no matter how hopeless it became.

That evening the four generals stood at attention on the balcony of the Délégation Générale before a plaza alive with *pieds noirs*—some 100,000, according to Radio France, although the figure was no doubt exaggerated. The setting sun left the square flushed with the last of the day's subsiding heat and light. The enormous crowd was receptive though puzzled. It had been waiting vainly for the announcement of important decisions; Radio France's endless replaying of military marches was beginning to pall. It was a measure of their readiness to grasp at any straw that the *pieds noirs* still flocked upon short notice to the Forum, to that colossal and spurious stage setting from which so many misleading, disappointing pronouncements in the city's history had already been made, including de Gaulle's *"Je vous ai compris"* and Salan's own *"Vive de Gaulle!"*

The four generals cut intrepid figures as seen from below—tough, united and durable; reassuring stereotypes for a mass audience—but they said little of consequence. "We have come with you to fight," cried Challe, telling the *pieds noirs* what they wanted to hear, "to suffer and to die if necessary so that Algeria remains French." Salan was more restrained. "We will stay with you to the end, to the victory

---

* Challe also arranged to broadcast the false news that Lagaillarde and Ronda had arrived from Spain and were serving in the Army under his orders. He admitted at his trial that he "resorted to this trick" to neutralize the two civilians in advance. Challe considered Lagaillarde a smart aleck (*un petit rigolo*), and feared that his arrival would have a disastrous effect on the Moslems. In fact, the two men never budged from Madrid.

you have been promised, and this time we'll do it," he said. Zeller remained a remote and rather uninteresting silhouette. Jouhaud paid "solemn homage to the clandestine comrades who fought, ran enormous risks and mounted the magnificent organization which has enabled us to succeed." This was adroit, but in fact, it had not occurred to him to praise his fellow activists until Georges Ras, an ultra journalist, plucked at his sleeve and beseeched him to say something. This led to his tribute to the OAS and FAF.

Each time one of the generals paused, the *pieds noirs* roared approval and encouragement. However, though Challe was in charge, though Jouhaud was a *pied noir* and predicted success, the roar grew loudest when Le Chinois, chesty and deliberate, smallish of stature, secretly horror-struck by the seething mass at his feet, stepped up to the microphone: then the roar swelled into a hoarse and frantic *"Vive Salan!"*

"Salan au poteau! [Salan to the gallows!]" shouted striking workers in France, where demonstrations of a very different nature took place that Monday. To protest the putsch, the Communist CGT trade-union, together with the CFTC and FEN,* ordered a one-hour work stoppage; Force Ouvrière, although spurning an outright alliance with the Communists, advised its members to participate as they saw fit. Factory hands, rail and dock workers, students and teachers assembled in the streets, in spite of a government ban on mass meetings, and thundered their hostiilty to a Rightist military coup. For the moment—it would last only through the emergency— there existed superficial unity among the Left.

The strike was significant because it demonstrated that Challe and his paratroopers could no longer hope to take Paris without a battle. The government and its temporary allies on the Left could, at the very least, count on 15,000 cadres culled from the Communist party and the no-less-aggressive Parti Socialiste Unifié; 2,000 CFTC militants; some 2,000–3,000 volunteers from Gaullist party neighborhood clubs and federations; and numerous Free French veterans.† Loyal paramilitary security troops and the Paris police were on the

---

* The Confédération Française des Travailleurs Chrétiens and the Fédération de l'Éducation Nationale.

† According to an estimate by Jacques Fauvet and Jean Planchais, in *La Fronde des généraux.*

alert. The walkover Police Prefect Maurice Papon had feared was now out of the question.

Hope died hard.

Throughout southern France, in towns of Provence and Languedoc and Béarn, anti-Gaullist networks had waited for the signal from Paris. They had been waiting for four days, since Thursday, delaying action to avoid a premature rising. Communication with confederates in the capital was spotty. The emergency numbers they called no longer answered.

Over the radio they learned that Morin, Buron and General Gambiez had not been shot out of hand but had been transferred to the Sahara. It was not the drastic action the plotters had expected.

It took some time for the truth to sink in. When it did, they were very bitter.

The Paris Bourse staged a sharp rally on Tuesday, there was heavy trading, and those who had bought during the dip the day before made a profit on the putsch.

It was a notable sign of the turning tide, and the government now counterattacked. Armed Forces Minister Messmer ordered all planes in Algeria to fly back to the Métropole. Some forty did, leaving Challe with no aviation to speak of.

This was followed up by the issuance of arrest warrants for the four dissident generals and their cohort of colonels.

De Gaulle himself was now governing under Article 16 of the French Constitution, which gives the President of the Republic exceptional powers—it authorizes him to decree a state of emergency, and it empowers the police to hold suspects in custody without preferring charges for fifteen days instead of the usual five. Notably, it enables the government to intern anyone who participates in "a subversive enterprise directed against the Republic, or who encourages it." To justify his recourse to these sweeping powers, de Gaulle sent a message to the National Assembly.

Debré on his own predicted bloodshed if the military directorate failed to capitulate.

This calls for a word of explanation. Throughout Saturday, Algiers had indulged in a war of nerves, implying over Radio France that a para drop on Paris was imminent. But now the government was aware that Challe's will was cracking and that the putsch was doomed—consequently, the prospect of civil war had receded. By implying exactly the contrary, Debré set out to give the psychological warriors at Quartier Rignot a taste of their own medicine and sap their morale still further.

The same afternoon Salan finished lunch with his family at Villa Dominique and prepared to return to the Délégation Générale. At the last moment, however, he drove to Quartier Rignot. He was halfway there when Sergent, pale and anguished, intercepted him with fateful news: Challe had decided to surrender.

"*Mon général*," blurted Sergent, "you must do something."

Challe's decision did not take Salan entirely by surprise—it was the logical culmination of developments during the past seventy-two hours—but his immediate, instinctive reaction was to try to keep the insurrection alive.

He hurried to combined staff headquarters, where he found Susini and the generals in a state of utter dismay.

Challe no longer sought to conceal his gloom. "I hope that I'll be the only one shot," he declared pessimistically.

The immediate reason behind his decision was the defection of a crack unit, the 1st Foreign Legion Cavalry Regiment. Colonel Charles de la Chapelle, the regiment's commanding officer, an Indochina veteran promoted from the ranks and a friend of Argoud, had concluded that Challe's prestige was manifestly insufficient to win over the bulk of the Army. Confronted by the vision of civil war, de la Chapelle recoiled from setting German Legionnaires under his command against French conscripts, and had just issued orders for the regiment to withdraw from Algiers.

This defection loomed large in Challe's mind; but so did a trifling detail—not a single sentry, he claimed plaintively, was available to stand guard outside his office. He had reviewed his position at length with Colonel de Boissieu, who urged him to terminate the revolt before it degenerated into a full-scale rout. The only honorable way out, de Boissieu contended, was to accept entire responsibility for the putsch's miscarriage. Challe concurred, and the colonel flew off to inform Paris.

The others reacted to Challe's announcement in characteristic ways—Zeller in a burst of red-faced, spluttering anger; Jouhaud, with heavy disapprobation; as for Sergent, he flew like a fierce cock about headquarters, loudly threatening to put a bullet in Challe's head. When he was icily reprimanded—a colonel told him that "one does not shoot General Challe"—his murderous ardor quickly subsided.

Susini's eloquence now came to the fore. He requested that he be left alone with Challe, and for the next forty-five minutes he did his utmost, employing his considerable talent for persuasion to change the general's mind. Above all, Susini argued for immediate mobilization—within the day—of all able-bodied European youths and men into the regular Army; he also demanded the immediate establishment of summary courts, to try uncooperative civil servants on a half hour's notice. On these two conditions alone he saw some hope of still saving the situation. His ideas about the use of civilians were precise and went well beyond the vague street demonstrations Salan prescribed. Susini wanted to put Algeria on a total war footing and involve the mass of civilians politically in the putsch's outcome. This meant calling them up for military duty, putting them in uniform and stationing them in barracks, away from their families as long as the emergency lasted; Susini wanted a good deal more than a part-time Home Guard that returned home and relaxed every evening. He had a point. Susini had flown from Madrid buoyed up by Faure's assurances about civilian commitment, but in the past forty-eight hours he had witnessed the failure to utilize the *pieds noirs* as either a disciplined street force or a paramilitary reserve—or, in fact, to keep them properly informed of what was occurring.*

Perhaps impressed, at any rate ready to clutch at expedients, Challe agreed to postpone his surrender, provided that the regiments he had counted on remained in Algiers; but on this score he was hardly confident. "Don't count on the Army," he told Susini prophetically, "but personally I'll stay." He then asked Susini to repeat his arguments to the other generals and colonels.

---

* Whether Susini's plan would have actually worked is open to question. Army sources point out that mobilization of the *pieds noirs* to allow the war to be prosecuted without conscripts did not take into account the need for skilled technicians who handle radar, telecommunications, maintenance and repair of armor, electronic equipment, etc. A call-up of the Unités Territoriales would have substituted for these technicians some 20,000 summarily trained men. It would also have meant a crippling interruption of normal economic life in Algeria.

It is to be noted that they listened to him with attention and respect. Both encounters—alone with Challe, then with the junta as a body—were unusual; here was a profane reenactment of the Biblical scene of the gifted youth astounding his elders; the confrontation speaks worlds about Susini's ability to adapt to a rapidly evolving situation, but even more about the generals' intellectual impoverishment.

Susini's eloquence was wasted, however. Prompt, decisive action was indispensable—but impossible to obtain. Salan, for example, ordered the 1er REP to invest the nearby Caserne d'Orléans, disarm the garrison of zouaves, and distribute 70,000 arms within to the civilian-recruited Unités Territoriales. In terms of his own aims this made sense, but discipline was breaking down badly, hour by hour, on the putschists' side, and the order was never executed—perhaps luckily for Salan, because Challe, when he heard about it, reacted violently, interpreting it as a maneuver to turn the civilians loose. Colonel de la Chapelle, for his part, was so outraged that he briefly considered arresting Le Chinois.

The most active of the insurrectionists that evening was Susini. From Quartier Rignot he raced back under jeep escort to the Délégation Générale, where he sat down to draft the mobilization order on which he had set his sights from the start. It provided for the recall of eight classes of Europeans and simultaneous demobilization of soldiers with eighteen months' military service, that is, the conscripts. He then got Challe to sign it and Jouhaud to voice it over Radio France. But by this time other regiments, in addition to de la Chapelle's 1st Cavalry, were packing up in disgust and entrucking for their distant bases. As the 1er Régiment de Chasseurs Parachutistes quit the city, it came upon a company of conscripts, whom it blamed, wrongly, for sabotaging the putsch; the retreating truckborne paratroopers fired in fury over the draftees' heads, and had the consolation of seeing them dive for cover into roadside ditches.

At the OAS command post on Boulevard Leferrière, the activist commandos who had enjoyed the run of the streets began to disperse. Secret files were removed. The Organization smelled defeat in the air and was returning underground.

It was withdrawing in good order. Its leaders, with the exception of Capeau, had managed to shun the limelight; Zattara, with his instinct for working in the dark, had steadfastly avoided claiming membership in the OAS and justified his presence at the Mairie through his rank as municipal councilor—identification of such men later would prove difficult.

But before dispersing, the Organization's leaders were arranging to put up a fight.

As evening fell, matters were beyond the control of Susini or any of the generals. Oran was back in government hands. A relief column led by Argoud was stalled indefinitely at Blida. Reports began circulating of the approach of *gendarmerie* armored units on Algiers. Then Challe changed his mind once more. He considered trying to hold an area from the port to the Délégation Générale—Get shot in Paris or die here; it's all the same, he thought. Susini and Perez assured him that they could raise a militia of 1,500 armed civilians, but there was no means of mustering additional men or weapons, and the advancing *gardes mobiles*, who might be expected to shy at a clash with paratroopers, would not be similarly daunted by a people's militia. And Challe doubted that he could do much with the relief column even if it arrived; as it was, Argoud the legendary walker, who always moved fast on a given objective, was proceeding at a snail's pace.

By ten o'clock, the 1er REP remained alone guarding the floodlit Forum. The insurrection was now practically confined to the huge Délégation Générale, where lights shone starkly in the columned hall and the second-story executive salons. This seat of civilian authority was where Challe, for all his aversion to nonmilitary affairs, chose to pass the last hours of the putsch.

Gloom, silence and studied self-control marked the atmosphere in Morin's office, where the generals were gathered. There were no open recriminations against Challe—they were all too disciplined for that. Challe puffed steadily on his pipe. Salan was more impassive than ever. The junta had drawn up no master plan to disperse, seek cover and regroup in case of defeat; the swiftness and completeness of the collapse had caught them unprepared. Each was left stranded high and dry in the ebb with the burden of making a decision. Even the perennially skeptical Salan had overlooked the possibility of total failure.

Breaking the silence, Zeller curtly announced his intention of carrying on. Jouhaud echoed him, and so did Godard and Broizat, the colonel who had accompanied the generals to Algiers. Sergent assured Zeller that he was ready to continue to the bitter end, then obtained authorization to broadcast an appeal to young officers to disregard rank from this moment on and follow their consciences; it was the next-to-last broadcast on Radio France. Salan appeared undecided; with one ear he listened to Susini's promptings to continue the struggle, but finally he decided—at least so thought Susini —to surrender with Challe.

It was all very haphazard. The putsch was unraveling as casually as it had taken shape. Challe made no attempt to impose a decision, but of course his stock with the others had dropped.* He had staked a career on a throw of the dice and lost all in four days' time.

To escape the unbearable atmosphere, Godard slipped out into the corridor and came upon two old friends, novelist Jean Larteguy and *Figaro* correspondent Jean François Chauvel. At this point, his nerves snapped. He exclaimed bitterly: "All you two know how to do is peddle your prose and close in for the kill." When they took the outburst to heart, Godard was dumbfounded and chastened; a few minutes later he offered to stand them drinks. Then he stalked back into the office, gathered together his officer's identity card and his cravat of Commander of the Legion of Honor, and angrily discarded both symbols of his military career behind a radiator. "I may as well shoot myself," he lamented.

In the midst of this, Challe mused about his surrender. There were several other courses of action open to him. He could flee and try to reach another country; but, he said, he did not want to go abroad. As for the other course . . . Patting his ample midsection, he turned to Broizat and said, "Can you see me going underground?"

He roused himself when civilians brought word of the advance of a *gardes mobiles* column on the Forum. He quickly overruled Salan, who wanted to open fire on the lead tanks. Government forces were moving up with Challe's knowledge and approval, to occupy public buildings and allow the 1er REP to pull back in good order. There would be no bloody clash, no vacuum, no last-moment civilian takeover of the putsch; on this, Challe was intransigent; this was why, in fact, he now delayed leaving the Délégation Générale. He planned to leave only after power had been transferred in an

---

* Challe said at his trial that Salan and Jouhaud fled instead of surrendering "with his complete agreement." He repeated this in a letter from prison, dated July 8, 1961.

orderly way from one side to the other. He did not entirely trust Salan.

The extremists of Jeune Nation had made their own plans. At a fourth-floor window one small group lurked in the dark, preparing a desperate ambush. Informed of their presence, Major Denoix de St.-Marc, the 1er REP's commanding officer, hastened upstairs and managed—but only by dint of great insistence—to persuade them to give up the project. Another youth had raced to the radio studios at Rue Hoche. Suddenly, his tense voice was heard on sets throughout Algiers: "We have been betrayed. Treason! Everybody to the Forum!"

The effect on the *pieds noirs* was galvanic. The apprehensions of the past forty-eight hours abruptly converged, grew urgent and audible. Several thousand people reassembled in the plaza. But the famed balcony remained dark, the recognizable silhouettes of the four generals, when they emerged in response to the uproar without, quite helpless; and when Challe attempted to speak—one wonders what he could have found to say—the microphone at which he fumbled remained dead. The current was cut.

Presently the disappointed population turned away from the Forum, this time without hope. But most still had no inkling that the tanks were so close. In some cases, paratroopers and gendarmes stood only fifty yards distant from each other.

One squadron of *gardes mobiles* and a detachment of the 7th Regiment of Zouaves were cautiously moving up toward the Forum when the first shots rang out along the ramp between the Hotel Aletti and the main post office. The gendarmes fell back for cover into the hotel lobby. OAS commandos were firing at them with semiautomatic weapons from nearby rooftops. Youths screamed insults at the uniformed shadows in the Aletti's gardens. At this moment moviegoers came out of the adjoining Colisée cinema, where the feature film had just ended. As the gendarmes returned fire, regrouped and pressed forward again, the rooftop commandos came out into the street, mixing with the panicky crowd of moviegoers. Some firing continued desultorily. One civilian was dead, three gendarmes were wounded in the gunfight. The diversion had enabled activist chiefs to pass through *gardes mobiles* lines, and scatter, far away from the center of the city.

Later, the tanks moved up slowly and surrounded the command post at Boulevard Laferrière. There was no resistance; the occupants came out, hands up, young, defiant, sallow in the headlights' glare, and unremarkable; the leaders were gone.

Zeller was the first to depart. He disappeared into an adjoining office, changed into civilian clothes, a nondescript coat and hat, then he bade the others goodbye and struck off into the anonymous crowd leaving the Forum—an unexceptional figure on whom no gendarme's eye would light. Godard put on a sport jacket lent him by a sympathetic police inspector over khaki shirt and trousers, and wandered out. His men in Algeria had thought him overprudent, "ready to act at 12:15 when action is slated at 11:45," but the energetic colonel was embarking upon clandestine life without "even a toothbrush." He had absolutely no idea where to go until he saw Marie-Elbe in the corridor.

Marie-Elbe is the pen-name of Jeannine Plantié, a dark-haired, shapely *pied-noir* journalist and novelist of arresting exotic appearance. She knew Godard well and liked him. She had called his office that morning to obtain information for an article, and from their conversation she deduced that the putsch was in danger of imminent collapse. That evening she hurried to the Délégation Générale. When Godard emerged on the landing, she drew him aside and held out her hand. Drawn in the palm, an arrow and some rough lines showed the nearby location of her apartment. She had moved in just the week before—there was no risk of the police searching for fugitives there. Godard studied her hand attentively and understood. Without being observed, he left at once.

Marie-Elbe was still standing in the corridor when Degueldre strode out, a gaunt and combative figure in leopard battle dress. He exhibited disgust with the generals but no sign of surrender. "When you lose, you pay," he said to her vaguely; then the darkness swallowed him up too.

Challe had still not come out. He did not relish the idea of being "kicked and slapped around by blockheads"—that is, the gendarmes. When Major Denoix de St.-Marc proposed taking him back to Zeralda, he readily agreed; from the encampment he could drive incognito around the outskirts of Algiers to Maison Blanche airport, and board a plane for Paris—and eventual judgment at de Gaulle's hands.

Susini remained with Salan to the end, trotting briskly beside him down the pillared staircase and into the Forum. Eyewitnesses like Marie-Elbe were unpleasantly struck by the "terrible exultant expression" on Susini's features, as though he "already foresaw the situation playing into his hands." Perhaps—but, for the moment, this wan, fanatic young apostle of street violence had the immediate future to worry about. Several of Robert Martel's men were waiting in the dark, and offered Salan refuge at their leader's farmhouse in the Mitidja. He promptly accepted the offer. Mme. Salan wrapped a scarf about her husband's throat against the night chill. A journalist asked whether he planned to give himself up. Le Chinois half turned and replied with a grim smile, "No."

Susini watched him climb stiffly aboard a waiting truck of the 1er REP alongside Jouhaud and Challe. When Susini approached the vehicle, a young lieutenant objected that he could accommodate only the leaders; but Susini had no desire to be part of the group, his own intention was not to surrender.

The truck drove off at once in the direction of Zeralda, from where it had come just four days before.

It was 2 A.M.

The hunted had ceased being hunted for some time now.

On the first day of the putsch, Jacques Coup de Fréjac had heard Radio France jubilantly broadcast the news of his arrest; although he seemed out of danger, he remained prudently in hiding for the next two days. His host set to work to get him out of the city. Coup de Fréjac was offered a ride in a well-guarded auto convoy of prostitutes leaving for Oran under command of a local band of pimps; and arrangements were made for him to join an overland FLN guerrilla column that after several weeks' grueling march would eventually arrive at the Tunisian frontier. He also procured a false American passport that could be used to book an airplane seat for Paris without questions, provided that flights resumed. These opportunities for escape were relatively foolproof; but after weighing the advantages of each, Coup de Fréjac decided not to leave Algiers at all. By Tuesday, it was obvious the putsch was in serious trouble;

all he need do, he reasoned, was steer clear of roving OAS commandos and wait out the inevitable denouement.

His principal worry was that in a final vengeful gesture before withdrawing, the activists would blow up the television and radio studios at Boulevard Bru. That evening, with a small group of loyal sailors and Moslems, he set out to reoccupy the premises. *Gardes mobiles* were advancing through the adjoining streets. By coincidence, he arrived on the heels of the young Jeune Nation extremist who had cried "Treason!" over the air a short while before from Rue Hoche. After a brief scuffle, Coup de Fréjac overpowered the boy and handcuffed him to the heating pipes in a studio. A few minutes later, Coup de Fréjac spoke via a newly restored two-way radio circuit with Alexandre Sanguinetti, one of Interior Minister Roger Frey's top aides in Paris, and informed him that Boulevard Bru was back in government hands.

As the senior loyal official present—and the first to reenter into radio communication with Metropolitan France—Coup de Fréjac was instructed to reoccupy his office at the Délégation Générale and resume his normal duties. He went to the Forum and found the huge building plunged in darkness and invested by black-helmeted gendarmes and CRS. Outside, the guns of armored cars pointed up at the balcony and upper stories. The generals had vanished, but in the offices where they briefly had governed there were signs everywhere of their tenancy—cigarette butts, wastepaper baskets overflowing with captured files; small-arms ammunition left behind on a table; a photograph of de Gaulle ripped out of its frame; and Morin's safe, singed by a blowtorch, yawning open, pilfered of $34,-000 set aside for current administrative expenses and secret operations. Presently, François Coulet, the political counselor, turned up unscathed; as he outranked Coup de Fréjac, he assumed temporary charge. Soon lights began coming on again throughout the structure.

Lucien Bitterlin had spent Sunday in a cell at the Central Commissariat. A plump Arab girl (whom he later married) visited him and brought fresh fruit and chocolate. He was not easy in mind about his immediate future, but his paratroop captors made no further mention of Colonel Godard.

From the Legionnaires' hectic orders and counterorders, Bitterlin sensed that the outcome of the putsch, as he had expected, was still far from certain. Presently the cell door grated open, and a para-troop captain advised him, without explanation, to make himself scarce.

He left at once, returned on foot to his apartment, locked the door, and being tired and grimy and bothered by his puffed-up eye, he slipped into bed. Nothing he had seen in the street had per-suaded him that the putsch was a success.

Early the next morning, a friend rang up and counseled him to remain out of sight. Bitterlin had the impression that if he man-aged to stay at liberty another day or two, his troubles would be over. He fell asleep again.

An insistent banging and man's voice awoke him. Bitterlin re-signedly padded to the door and pulled back the latch—it seemed foolish to be re-arrested at this late date. The man on the landing was, in fact, his landlord, who, in the midst of the insurrection, had crossed the city and come to claim the month's rent due that day.

The next morning, a small plane from the Sahara touched down at Maison Blanche airport. Back from their short desert captivity, Morin, Buron and General Gambiez drove in official cars to the Délégation Générale, where an honor guard of draftees presented arms. The putsch was over.

Despair gripped the *pieds noirs*. The swift transition from over-night triumph to blank defeat had occurred too abruptly—in just ninety-six hours—and it left them unnerved, plunged in consterna-tion and gloom. Caught unprepared when Challe took power, they were equally unprepared when he lost it.

Three times in a row, they had placed their trust in the regiments —at the Barricades, in December 1960, and during the astonishing weekend just elapsed—only to see the regiments waver each time at a critical moment. The *pieds noirs* emerged from the putsch pros-trated by the idea that they had tried everything and nothing had succeeded. It was on Wednesday that a European settler announced at the Hotel St.-Georges, more prophetically than he imagined, "From this point on, there is no valid solution"—by which he meant no solution the *pieds noirs* could impose through force; and in their eyes, no other solution was feasible.

Across the Mediterranean, de Gaulle loomed all-powerful. On the defensive knowing that the bulk of the French had been unsympathetic to the putsch, the Europeans buckled down to await reprisals for an insurrection which they had approved, but in which they had played almost no role. They were terribly discouraged yet a flicker of defiance continued to burn, feeble and undetected, fed more by tenacity than logic.

That Wednesday, Minister of State Louis Joxe appeared on Algerian television, looking weary, and said, "The law has been upheld, the law will be upheld."

But would it?

Within hours a bomb exploded in the center of Algiers—the work of European terrorists. Then two days later, *pieds noirs* found a tract slipped into their letterboxes. It laid the blame for the putsch's failure on "certain Army leaders who did not know how to make use of the potential we represent. . . . We are returning underground, but our action against treason will continue." And it spoke of the need to create a "psychosis of fear" among Gaullist underlings. The tract was signed "The Monocle."

7

The Missing Generals

"I INTEND," de Gaulle declared coldly at a cabinet meeting on the same Wednesday, April 26, "to draw short- and long-term conclusions from a crisis that threatened the state." It was his only epitaph for what he called the "odious and stupid putsch." His contained wrath derived from the fact that he was "more impressed than he wanted to seem" (according to Public Works Minister Robert Buron)—indeed, badly shaken up—by the four-day revolt. The timing had caught him off balance; worse, the only thing that had saved de Gaulle was de Gaulle himself; the government, and the French as a whole, had relied on his unflinching will, and that alone, to right the situation. As a bulwark against insurrection, the government—the rigidly centralized, conservative administrative machinery run by so many ducal ministers—had shown itself vulnerable and anything but sure-handed in the first critical hours. The lesson was plain. He could ignore Army discontent further only at his own peril; he would have to remove its cause, which involved a modification of his entire Algerian policy, or root the discontent out.

Few were surprised by the choice he made.

All officers of the 1er REP formally constituted themselves prisoners as of 10 A.M., April 27, at Zeralda. Colonel Guiraud, their commanding officer, who had been absent during the putsch, informed the eight hundred Legionnaires that they would be transferred within twenty-four hours to Thiersville, near Mascara in southern Algeria; the rebellious unit would be dissolved, and officers would stand trial in France.

One must imagine the effect this produced not only on the regiment but on the *pieds noirs*.

The 1er REP had been formed five and a half years earlier—on September 1, 1955—out of the remnants of the 1st Foreign Legion Paratroop Battalion, a unit badly mauled at Dien Bien Phu, where, of 650 Legionnaires, only about a hundred survived the siege and straggled through the Viet-Minh–infested hills to their own lines. During the 1956 Suez War, the new regiment dropped on Port Said, then occupied a part of the canal. The following year it arrived in Algeria. Almost at the outset it was committed to the Battle of Algiers, and for this reason and because of numerous marriages with *pied-noir* girls, its men became emotionally identified with the *Algérie française* cause. The 1er REP fought the *fellaga* in 1960 and in the spring of 1961 until the putsch. Its officers, noncoms and men garnered more than three thousand citations; with pardonable swagger, they fancied themselves as the "number-one shock regiment of the French Army." De Gaulle's action was as upsetting as though an American President had disbanded the crack 82nd Airborne Division—all the more so since the clear implication was that the future of the Foreign Legion as a whole was at stake.

On the morning of April 28, the regiment's sand-colored jeeps and trucks were drawn up in the compound at Zeralda for the last time. Tanks ringed the camp. At the gates stood women, immobile, faces set and emotionless, some holding bouquets of flowers. The 1er REP came to attention under the cloudy burning Algerian sky as a bugler blew and the regimental flag with five palms was carefully struck and folded. Then, as men hoisted their gear into place aboard the trucks, throaty shouts of *"Vive la Légion!"* and *"Vive l'Algérie française!"* broke out. A camp storehouse containing surplus ammunition was blown up. Men fired off their last rounds into the air. Then the trucks and jeeps lumbered off past Europeans massed on the sidewalks, who cried hopefully, *"Au revoir."* This time the convoy was moving in the opposite direction from the pitfalls of *Alger la Blanche*. To avoid further temptation, it was split up into several sections, each under an officer set at temporary liberty. The Legionnaires roared in full-bodied farewell the words of Édith Piaf's song: *"Ah non! je* *ne regrette rien . . ."* It was a moment of some emotion. In a cloud of dust the convoy rolled away across the well-irrigated Sahel countryside, flanked by a loyal motorized infantry escort; *gendarmerie* helicopters hovered overhead on the watch for the first sign of rebellion. But there was none.*

The same fate overtook two other paratroop regiments (the 14ème and 18ème RCP) and four air commandos of the Operational Reserve. Elements of the dissolved units were transferred to a newly formed light division and three *brigades d'intervention,* which also comprised infantry and paratroop units from Metropolitan France, presumably less infected by the political contagion that had raged so virulently in Algeria.

A full-scale purge struck the Army. Special commissions were set up at each Army Corps headquarters to seek out participants in the putsch and recommend disciplinary action. A secret order by Armed Forces Minister Messmer dated April 30 prescribed carrying out the investigation "discreetly," but without loss of time; personnel files under review were to be forwarded to Army Corps by May 9. The investigation embraced Army units in Metropolitan France and West Germany as well. In one important respect, however, Messmer pulled his punches. His order specified that all ranks who wanted to volunteer information must transmit it through channels; anyone with the slightest insight into the military mentality knew what this meant. The effect, inevitably, was to cripple the investigation at the outset. Officers were loath to inform upon fellow officers, even those with whose political opinions they disagreed; there was a distinct, and probably justified, fear that once resorted to, informing could become a permanent and dangerous habit within the Army. Enlisted men were not eager to draw down officers' displeasure and vengeance upon their heads. The commissions got practically no help.†

* Formally disbanded on April 30, 1961, the 1er REP has never been reconstituted.

† The *malaise* was aggravated by the spread of alarmist tales about enlisted men's kangaroo courts and "Soviets" being set up within a decomposing Army. There was no truth in the stories, which betrayed a few panic-prone officers' latent fears. What did happen was that many groups of conscripts, including trade-unionists, decided to keep a closer eye on activist officers and, if necessary, report them to higher-ups. In a few cases, during the putsch enlisted men roughed up officers, in the Constantinois area.

Nonetheless, the purge affected perhaps a thousand officers. The government understandably minimized the humiliating extent of disaffection within the Army, and it withheld most statistics. It has been estimated, however, that six or seven hundred officers were punished in one way or another—fourteen were cashiered, one hundred were hauled up before special and military courts, many were retired on various pretexts; others were placed under fortress or house arrest and transferred. In some cases, suspect officers escaped punishment, but their promotion was held up. Moreover, hundreds resigned their commissions in disgust, anger or irritation. *

For a majority, the four-day insurrection had provided a disconcerting glimpse, as *Le Monde* put it, of the "abyss" into which Challe had fallen and into which they could all tumble, and they recoiled from this vision. The officers' messes in Algeria underwent a transformation: exasperation ran as high as ever—some officers were, if anything, more wrought up—but the outbursts against de Gaulle's perfidy bore a new edge of caution and were followed by fewer of the clannish, conspiratorial gatherings that had mushroomed in the early spring. Activism was no longer countenanced in many units. The most restless of the officers were no longer ready to enter into open revolt.

It was, in fact, a sorely tried Army victimized by its own reliance on psychological warfare, shot through with self-division, but still bent on maintaining a threadbare semblance of unity. The internal stresses and strains became painfully obvious at Challe's trial.

Challe, an Air Force jacket thrown over his shoulders and suitcase in hand, stepped off the plane that brought him back to Villacoublay airport, and stumbled; a policeman had to help him to his feet. To add to his humiliation, a horde of photographers was on hand to record the curiously symbolic misstep.

He was driven not to see de Gaulle, but direct to the grime-caked Santé Prison on Paris' Left Bank.

The government, mindful of the procrastination of the Barricades Trial, which had created an impression of official impotence at best, and tolerance at worst, this time accelerated the judicial machinery.

* Estimates are based on figures quoted by Henri Azeau (*Révolte Militaire*), Albert-Paul Lentin (*Le Dernier Quart d'Heure*), and Axel Nicol (*La Bataille de l'OAS*).

Two days after the putsch, applying Article 16, it established a special court, the Haut Tribunal Militaire, to try the ringleaders without delay.*

On May 29, the trial opened in the sooty Palace of Justice. By this time Zeller was also in the government's hands. That perpetually irate general had—in a moment of resignation and pique, it seemed, after hiding with a relative in Algiers—simply given up and walked straight into the office of Police Prefect René Jannin.

Both generals appeared in mufti. They stood accused of usurpation of military command, leading an insurrectional movement, arresting and sequestering legitimate authorities, and constituting stockpiles of arms. This was misleading, in a way: Challe, the principal defendant, was made to appear as a general bent on grabbing power for his own gross ambitions, like some Latin American strongman; the arid terms of the Penal Code provided no hint whatever of the complex, subtle struggle being waged over the continuance of French rule in Algeria.

Challe, for once, was not chary of words, and spoke comprehensively, if at times evasively. He reminded the court of the government's promise not to abandon Algeria, and invoked the sacredness of an officer's word for the men under his command. De Gaulle's press conference of November 4, 1960, he said, had convinced him that French Algeria was going to be lost for good; this marked the moment when he had entered into moral, if not yet open, dissidence. About the mechanism of the putsch itself, however, a subject on which he could have been endlessly interesting, he revealed little— except to maintain that, apart from Admiral Querville and two generals, all the senior officers he had sounded out had remained indecisive, which was to say that, from his standpoint, they had been no more eager to support de Gaulle than Challe. This was hardly earthshaking news. The most telling exchange occurred when, asked about his reaction to Salan's arrival in Algiers, Challe said grimly, "I prefer not to answer."

Zeller also testified, but he was under great strain; he suffered from a weak heart. Twice his lawyers requested a suspension of the hearings to allow him to recover. To the end he appeared an old man destined to shake his fist furiously but unavailingly at history.

A sense of incompleteness, of things left unsaid and others muted,

* A second court, the so-called Petit Tribunal Militaire, was set up to try lesser figures.

of a shapeless but persistent conflict pervaded the courtroom. The nine judges, in a way, set the tone from the bench. They addressed the main defendant as "Monsieur Challe"; if the rank was missing, the respect for his person was audible for all to hear and mark. Witnesses called to the stand demonstrated the same ambiguity. One of France's top generals, Maurice Valluy, explained that although militarily he did not condone Challe's action, emotionally he stood with him. One junior officer of the 1er REP, Lieutenant Jacques Favreau, spoke with force about his fellow officers' feeling of despair at Algeria's drift toward independence. This, he said, was the prime motivation that had driven Challe to act, before still rasher acts were committed—by the civilians of Algiers, he implied. "I am convinced that we owe it to Challe to be able to appear in court with our hands clean," he concluded. When the lieutenant stepped down from the stand, he turned toward the dock, brought his heels together and saluted the two generals. Once again, it was a moment of high if misdirected idealism.

As the trial progressed, Public Prosecutor Antonin Bresson received a significant communication from Justice Minister Edmond Michelet. He conceded that Challe had shown moderation during the putsch, refraining from an appeal to the mob; he showed less indulgence for Zeller, whom he described as bent on overthrowing republican institutions. But he advised Bresson to demand the death penalty for both generals. Michelet argued that both had committed potentially disastrous acts of sedition, which could have destroyed the state. He argued also—this was his letter's entire purpose—that the trial was the first to come before the Haut Tribunal Militaire; the judgment handed down here would affect subsequent verdicts in the case of lesser plotters; in brief, a lenient verdict now would make it doubly difficult for the government to demand stern application of the law later.*

The presiding judge, Maurice Patin, received an equally revelatory letter from a group of officers. They accused "Mister de Gaulle" of sowing discord among the French and betraying the West, because in "handing over Algeria to FLN killers" he was preparing the way for Communist subversion of all Europe. The unsigned letter accused Patin of staging a parody of justice, and warned that he would pay for his misdeeds.

---

* Michelet's letter is quoted by J. R. Tournoux, *L'Histoire Secrète*.

Major trials seldom resolve the great issues that are at their inception. The issues become distorted or oversimplified in court; they cannot easily be encompassed within a particular case. The trial of the two generals bore out the rule. Bresson did not heed Michelet's letter, and forbore from requesting the death penalty. Both prosecution and defense avoided embarrassing questions throughout: the forthcoming Évian negotiations were scarcely mentioned; the troubling Si Salah affair, not at all, although more than any other single development it was said to have influenced Challe's revolt. The presiding judge at one point went out of his way to tell Challe: "I am not asking you for names." As for Algeria, the Army, the FLN, they remained enormous vague shadows in the panoramic background.

After twenty hours of hearings, the court found both generals guilty and sentenced each to a term of fifteen years' imprisonment. In view of what had been attempted, it was too little or too much; but the sentence was not surprising in political terms, at a time when the government was trying to bring the Army round to a former concept of duty, yet revive negotiations with the FLN.

These negotiations were at a standstill. Nothing had happened since the FLN's postponement of the Évian meeting on March 31. Contrary to expectations, the dangers which the putsch had so clearly revealed—"lightning in a storm suddenly illuminates objects shrouded in shadow," de Gaulle put it—did not spur either side to the bargaining table at once.

Fearing that French terms for a cease-fire would be raised now the emergency was past, the Algerian nationalists ended their temporary support of de Gaulle and waited for Paris to make the next move. But it was not until May 8 that de Gaulle again addressed himself publicly to the problem, and then it was only to express hope, but no certitude, that talks would enable Algerians to vote on their own future.

There is no convincing explanation why further precious weeks were lost, but one reason was, of course, that de Gaulle, Debré and the others were trying to put their own house in order.

Meanwhile, a wave of optimism spread through Paris, encouraged by official reports from Algiers, which concluded that the badly jarred civilian activists were on the run, disbanded and a threat no longer. Newspaper stories went so far as to claim that agitation was limited to some five hundred hotheads, and subversion would be over within weeks.

If all this were true, it was undoubtedly a propitious moment for de Gaulle to issue a firm statement about Algeria's future, aimed at *pied noir* opinion, to dispel any lingering illusions. But no such statement was issued, and in the event, silence proved to be the wrong policy. A writer as favorable to Gaullism as Paul-Marie de la Gorce has concluded that, had the government exploited the opportunities available in the last days of April, a desperate, final convulsion would have taken place among the *pieds noirs*, but it would have been "shorter and far less serious" than what did follow.

So the advantages that flowed from the putsch's collapse were frittered away.

With astonishing rapidity the *pieds noirs* took heart again.

Le Monocle's tract set the new, aggressive, self-confident tone by making Challe the highly conspicuous scapegoat for the putsch's failure (although some sympathized with his impotence before de Gaulle's superhuman cunning). Whoever Le Monocle was, he promised that the OAS stood ready to resume the struggle, and this promise fell on receptive ears. When the *pieds noirs* took stock of the situation, they realized with satisfaction that indeed the OAS leaders had not been arrested and the Organization had not been dismantled. Thus the promise appeared based on hard fact as well as sheer hopefulness. Nightly *plastiquages* had recommenced. Zeller's surrender was interpreted as a noble sacrifice to allow the other generals to escape.

In time, a new tract appeared, announcing the formation of "a great army of the *maquis*." Europeans were advised: "Hold on to your arms; shoot anybody who tries to arrest you; pay no heed to the state-run radio's lies; kill all traitors." The handbill promised that the new army would "fight to the death." And—as leaders of innumerable earlier causes had found expedient—it prophesied: "God will come to our side." Soon, Algiers was persuaded that some 25,000 resistants were concentrated in the countryside.

A myth was being sedulously cultivated—that of the putsch's nearsuccess, which justified a fresh effort, the insinuation being that where the Army had held back and bungled, this time a determined handful of underground leaders, awaiting the opportune moment to strike, would succeed.

Every evening, a growing number of *pieds noirs,* the courageous at their balconies in the tepid peacock dusk, the less valiant behind shuttered windows in stifling apartments, banged kitchen pots and pans together, beating out the hopeful measure of *"Al-gé-rie fran-çaise."*

On the first weekend after the putsch, Monseigneur Léon-Étienne Duval, the city's ascetic, liberal archbishop, who made no secret of his condemnation of the activists, dispatched a pastoral letter to be read throughout the diocese the next day. Quoting from Isaiah, he renewed a warning against "false prophets"; the ultras were reproved as "those who have strayed." But before going to Mass, Europeans found another tract in their letterboxes that accused the archbishop of tainting religion with politics. It added that since he could not be refuted in a holy place, Catholics would do best to stay away from church altogether—"God will pardon you," it guaranteed. The faithful did not heed the counsel, but they arrived in a belligerent mood. At St. Elizabeth's loud fits of coughing broke out when the pastoral missive was read; at St. Joseph's in Bab el Oued, men left the pews noisily and banged doors. At St. Augustine's, the priest refused to read the letter at all.

Fifteen hundred automatic and semi-automatic weapons stolen from government arsenals during the putsch were stockpiled in the city—this much Morin and his staff at the Délégation Générale knew for sure. Salan, Jouhaud and Gardy remained elusive, as did the battlesome colonels; after the final confused night at the Forum, they had vanished and not been heard from again—and Algeria's spaces are not the easiest place to track down a few isolated men; but whether they lay up somewhere in the city, biding their time, or camped in open country constituting a *maquis* of desperadoes, as rumors insinuated, no one in authority knew.

To deal with this potentially dangerous mixture of activists and arms, the government in the last days of April launched the biggest security drive Algiers had known since the 1957 battle against FLN terrorists. Nine companies of CRS were transferred from France to reinforce gendarmes, zouaves and dragoons. This was made necessary because locally recruited police, after openly sympathizing with the putsch, were useless for the task. General Bernard Cherasse, the newly appointed commander of *gendarmerie* forces in Algeria, estimated that of his 20,000 men, thirty percent—all the *pieds noirs,* in a word—were unreliable. The antisubversive operation thus was turned over to inexperienced soldiers and CRS troops freshly arrived from France, who were too unfamiliar with the terrain and the situation to do much good. This factor contributed to its ultimate failure.

A radio appeal to the population to register arms provoked an outburst of angry sarcasm: Europeans duly formed lines outside police stations, and indeed turned in some two thousand weapons—consisting of antiquated shotguns and other rusty, dismantled weapons. The machine guns and automatic pistols taken from the Central Commissariat were not surrendered.

Meanwhile, the manhunt swept methodically through places where the fugitives might logically have found shelter; through the officers' club at El Kattani, the Police Prefecture and the university, the Hotel St.-Georges, the villas of El Biar and Hydra—in a word, Algiers' entire residential-administrative complex, where *Algérie française* was an unchallenged article of faith and search parties seldom intruded. General Massu's paratroopers had carried out similar raids before, but in the Casbah, not in the European quarter. To the *pieds noirs,* this upsetting of the traditional alliance of forces appeared the clearest sign yet of coming abandonment; their outcry was loud and genuine. As rumors about the missing generals' whereabouts proliferated, the dragnet was extended to garbage trucks, the morgue, the holds of ships, a church, even the apartment of the outraged Spanish consul—all to no avail.

On May 6, the Délégation Générale published the results of the city-wide crackdown—some 9,000 apartments searched, 400 persons detained, of whom 310 were under arrest.* The figures were meant to impress, but they could scarcely conceal the fact that few arms had been retrieved and none of the missing generals had been apprehended.

---

* Simultaneously, other security measures were enforced. Curfew was moved up from ten to nine o'clock in the evening; three out of four of Algiers' daily newspapers, including Alain de Serigny's biased and outspoken *Écho d'Alger,* were indefinitely suspended; and the municipal council, which had rallied with alacrity to Challe, was dissolved.

The government continued to function in May as though all were back to normal, but the limits on its powers were there for everyone to observe. A notable psychological transformation had occurred: the *pieds noirs* no longer looked to the Army or to the Délégation Générale—or to Paris—for deliverance from their life-or-death predicament.

A political vacuum existed—into which would soon step the OAS.

PART TWO

In a war of counterrevolutionary nature, there is no place for guerrilla hostilities. Because guerrilla warfare basically derives from the masses and is supported by them, it can neither exist nor flourish if it separates itself from their sympathies and cooperation.

—MAO TSE-TUNG,
  Yu Chi Chan (Guerrilla Warfare)

8

Operation Survival

THE FARMHOUSE, the property of an aging Frenchwoman who lived alone, lay in stark sunlight throughout the stunning African heat of the day. In May it is already very hot in the Algerian interior. It was only at dusk, when the Arab farmhands vanished into their own quarters, that Susini felt safe and emerged from the confinement of his room to draw a breath of air. He later described, in surprisingly sensuous prose, his stay in this hiding place of calm and plenty, a relic of comfortable colonial days where no gendarme thought of searching for a fugitive from French law:

". . . It rose like a white mausoleum in the middle of a clearing, its two stories flanked by watchtowers and encircled by a long balcony. Below, a flight of stone steps cracked by drought led to a row of empty and dusty rooms. . . . Crossing the veranda, I went to sit on the balcony's hot stones. A magnificent rose garden embalmed the evening air. Roundabout, tall palms mounted guard and wove a crown of drooping fronds. I waited, like the sun to go down aflame, for a stork to fly past. Deserting its nest in the palms as darkness approached, wings outspread, it glided obliquely over the rose garden and disappeared beyond the hilltops in silent flight."

Susini had fled here from the misfortunes of Algiers.

Within forty-eight hours of the putsch's collapse he had tracked down Ferrandi. Salan's aide-de-camp was hiding—on the realistic theory that the closer one is to the enemy, the safer—at the Hotel St.-Georges, the imitation Moorish palace where Algiers officialdom met. Ferrandi gave him ten thousand dollars from the funds purloined in Morin's safe; on this meager capital, Susini later said, the OAS was relaunched. With the money and OAS secret files removed from Boulevard Laferrière, and a suitcase of official records seized at the Délégation Générale on the last night of the putsch, Susini skipped nimbly during the next few days from one hiding place to another. He expected at any moment to be arrested. He dyed his scant hair lustrous black, grew a mustache, wore eyeglasses, and sallied forth in a priest's cassock or a paratrooper's uniform—until it was borne in on him that real security hinged on the people he saw and the places where he slept. Eventually he came to rest in an isolated farm on the Mitidja plain. Here, finding no safe repository, he burned most of the OAS files.

He had few callers. Ferrandi came to see him once with news of the three missing generals. Friends paid brief visits with messages of encouragement. But as in Madrid there was endless time to analyze the situation. The main lesson Susini drew from the putsch was that "one is not necessarily wrong because one is beaten." His reasons for persevering were personal, sentimental, political. De Gaulle's policy was evil, because it meant scrapping the birthright of a million *pieds noirs* and the probable totalitarian enslavement of millions of Moslems. French rule could still be preserved in Algeria, Susini concluded, but it was, he admitted, a "thin, fragile hope."

He brooded about Algeria; the irrigated fertile plain that stretched out to the heat-dazed, silvered horizon of olive groves and cork-oak forests symbolized, in his eyes, France's future. But he also brooded about the *pieds noirs*, to whom he belonged, and their political shallowness, and wondered whether they were worth fighting for. Finally he brooded about the self-defeating intelligence of the French—"this tool which other people use constructively and which so often, in our hands, boomerangs."

There was nothing to be gained, he decided, from a "moribund" French Army or France itself. France and Algeria were not attuned; for French Algeria, sheer survival was a question of months, a proposition to which Metropolitan Frenchmen could or would not adjust. The *pieds noirs* must rely on themselves through a civilian army of 100,000 men mobilized secretly and prepared to fight and die to defend their land. Susini thought in terms of an Algerian

Haganah, composed of civilian-soldiers exchanging plows and brief-cases for rifles, and instinctive dependence on the French Army for self-protection. And, as he later told this writer, he already foresaw the possibility that this force could be committed against the French Army. If the latter could be won over, so much the better; otherwise it would be treated as an enemy.

The Organization behind this secret army must be ready to carry out profound changes. Foreseeing land reform, nationalization, an enhanced role for Moslems, he wrote enthusiastically: "The revolution could be French. Socialism need not necessarily be Arab, Russian or Chinese"—and he meant every word of it. Given the fact that his allies in such a struggle were conservatives, upholders of a rigid status quo, the prospects for social reform and revitalization were slight, but this did not daunt him. This odd, fanatical young Frenchman, whose talent was for calculated efficiency, believed that French Algeria's salvation might come about through an "accident, a chain of circumstances."

At bottom, he wanted to do something. Isolated in the country-side, ignorant of the others' exact whereabouts, he read, began laboriously to patch up a network, and waited impatiently for a chance to return to Algiers. Quick action was indispensable: time, after all, hal defeated the putsch. Of all the activist leaders, Susini was the most painfully aware that, if the Évian talks succeeded, the coming summer would be Algeria's last under French rule. Nasser has been defined as a hero who roamed the Arab world in search of a cause. In mid-spring of 1961, Susini saw French Algeria as a virtually abandoned cause at a loss for a hero—and he was not averse to eventually filling the role.

Salan was also hiding on the Mitidja plain, but in wholly different circumstances—a complaisant hostage of Martel, who held him incommunicado at various farms in the Boufarik area, intercepted his correspondence and turned away messengers. His singular host's purpose was to wean him away from impure associations, which, in Martel's overheated mind, meant almost all those involved in the putsch; Ferrandi, in particular, was darkly suspected of Freemasonry. Salan offered no resistance; he was dejected, adrift, reeling from misadventure, and at one point close to suicide. Days slipped past. He seldom saw his wife.* When Ferrandi and other alarmed emissaries finally located him, he showed no haste to be pried loose from Martel's poisonous jeremiads. His sole suggestion was to organize a new *coup de force* on the anniversary of May 13, to be staged by civilian groups seizing strategic points in Algiers—an unlikely feat, given their present weakness. Clearly, for the moment, Le Chinois was out of touch, and visibly he did not share Susini's compelling sense of time.

One day, a *gendarmerie* helicopter whirred over the farm. Before landing it hovered overhead a half hour, affording Salan ample time to scamper off to another cache on Martel's extensive grounds. The pattern was repeated subsequently. The gendarmes probably were not aware of Salan's identity, at any rate, they made no serious attempt to capture him; meanwhile, however, Martel would not release him.

The others eluded capture in various ways. Jouhaud disappeared into his native Oranie region, where numerous lifelong friends sheltered him. Gardes, the militant Catholic, stayed in an Algiers rectory, recovering from nervous exhaustion. Broizat, who laid special stress on security, spent weeks in an apartment located opposite a police precinct; the sympathetic police knew it and made sure the lodging was not raided. A while after the putsch, Godard moved out of Marie-Elbe's flat into a drab room in Hydra which, he discovered, had been used by Spanish girls from the Fantasio nightclub near the Hotel Aletti to entertain men clients. Two of the colonels cleared out of the city for good: Lacheroy, disguised as a monk, reached Bône, then stowed away aboard a tanker bound for Genoa, and eventually arrived in Spain; Argoud, utterly demoralized, hung about Algiers briefly, irritated by the *pieds noirs'* banging of pots and pans and the nightly plastique bombings, both of which he found ridiculous, and in early May he managed to get to Paris, where he settled down in the Seine-side weekend house of a *pied noir* industrialist named Maurice Gingembre. The colonel on the run considered migrating to South

---

* She had fled with their daughter from Villa Dominique on the final night of the putsch, principally to prevent police from obtaining a lead to her husband. During the spring she hid with French families she had met while working in a charity organization, l'Association de Solidarité Franco-Musulmane, when Salan was commander in chief in Algeria.

America, where engineers were needed. Activism at this point struck him as an unsatisfactory vocation.

As the immediate danger of capture receded, the putsch survivors cautiously emerged from their hiding places and, through letter drops and liaison agents, reestablished contact.

On May 4, Zattara asked an aunt for the use of her apartment in a housing development at the Champ de Manoeuvre on the heights of Algiers. Seven men arrived inconspicuously next morning and stayed all day—Godard, Susini, Gardy, Degueldre, Perez, Sergent and Zattara. The principal purpose of the meeting was to determine what to do next. Gardy was the senior in age, and as far as the mili- tary were concerned, in rank; but just as he had voluntarily taken or- ders from Argoud at Oran, he accepted a secondary role now. By default Godard assumed temporary command. His practical knowl- edge of guerrilla warfare—which Degueldre alone shared with him —made this development almost inevitable; besides, he was a born organizer, whose quick temper and notorious silences had bowled over a great many men. "No one ever knew what he thought," re- called a French diplomat. "He spoke little; what he said was per- haps not brilliant, but it was always well thought out and *to the point*. He was courageous. He was by far the most dangerous of the colonels." Susini, who had returned to Algiers after obtaining a set of false identity papers, viewed Godard's rise without pleasure, but there was little he could do about it as long as Salan remained in the Mitidja.

In a way, the putsch had cleared the air; the advocates of subver- sive war would no longer be hampered by the timorousness of gen- erals like Challe. They would proceed with the original idea elabo- rated at the Torre de Madrid of joint civilian-military action. Each was powerless on his own; united, they formed a hard core of re- sistance. They were aware that the population's mood had changed too: the putsch was viewed as a temporary setback that had come close to success; what had failed once—through Army mishandling— would not necessarily fail again under bolder leadership.

Several days later they reconvened in the same apartment, and this time Godard brought a table of organization. He distributed six copies, drafted in his neat military hand; he had not dared type among the flimsy walls of his disreputable hideout.

In brief, Godard proposed dividing the new organization into three main branches: Organisation des Masses (O.M.), whose purpose would be to mobilize the entire European population; Action Psychologique et Politique (A.P.P.), to carry on information and propaganda activities and elaborate the movement's doctrine and political goals; and Organisation-Renseignements-Opérations (O.R.O.), to practice "direct action" (a euphemism for terrorist attacks ranging from relatively mild shakedowns to plastique bombings and murder).

To gain public attention, they would adopt the same methods as the enemy—and in fact, this table of organization owed everything to the FLN, whose command structure Godard had carefully studied during the 1956 Battle of Algiers.*

The underground war was to be carried on from Algiers—on this point, Godard was adamant. The movement's first objective, he insisted, must be to gain a secure foothold in the city; then resistance would spread throughout Algeria. He had received a letter from Argoud in Paris urging him to return to France and await a better opportunity to strike against the Gaullist government, because the *pieds noirs* as such were not worth further sacrifice. Godard had retorted furiously that the fight must be carried on from Algiers, or not at all.

The table of organization was adopted—it was clear and uncluttered, and no one had proposed a better one. However, it was essentially a tool; as Susini, who did not attend the second meeting, pointed out critically, it did not define the uses to which the tool would be put, or priority targets, or a broad strategy, or the movement's ultimate objectives. And as it turned out, these were never fully defined. Godard noted sarcastically that if they attempted to solve all their problems first, French Algeria would be liquidated before they accomplished anything. In fact, they were all possessed by a feverish desire to act; the consequences of action could be embodied into a doctrine later, they thought. In this they did not differ from many other protest and pseudorevolutionary movements.

Perez, the doctor from Bab el Oued, asked for command of O.R.O. Godard hesitated; he later claimed it was his intention to give Gardes the assignment. However, the colonel was absent and personnel was short. So Godard set aside O.M. for Gardes and with a

---

* Godard boasted that he "knew more about the FLN than did Yacef Saadi"—a statement that came close to the truth. Saadi, a soccer player and former baker's assistant, was one of the chief Moslem terrorists in Algiers.

flicker of misgiving agreed to turn over the key operational branch, O.R.O., to Perez.

Gardy was assigned charge of A.P.P., with Susini as his deputy.

Curiously, Godard's own role remained vague: he assumed over-all responsibility for Intelligence, at which he had experience, but no operational command; administratively he acted as Salan's deputy, but only for the Algiers area.

There was no leader. By common consent Salan was to fill the role, but the problem of his stay with Martel had become acute. Flitting from one farmhouse to another in the Mitidja, Salan was kept informed of developments. Susini, however, wanted him back in Algiers as soon as possible, if only to counter Godard's growing influence. Godard made it plain that, while ready to recognize Le Chinois's authority, he did not plan to wait for his return to begin operations. Gardy was outraged by insinuations appearing in *La Voix du maquis*, Martel's newspaper, about the motives of OAS leaders. The Organization, in general, viewed Martel's farms as the worst hiding place Salan could have chosen. There was talk of paying a call in force on the "Rasputin of the Mitidja" if he refused to give up his guest—but it was to take all summer to work him free.

The group began meeting regularly now, often at night, always in the anonymous center of the city, never twice in the same apartment, choosing among various lodgings provided by *pied noir* doctors, lawyers and even a magistrate. Others in hiding joined them: Gardes; René Villars, the chief of France-Résurrection; Jacques Achard, Salan's civilian aide. In the new movement, only two *pieds noirs*—Susini and Perez—occupied key posts. Local activists, men like Zattara and Capeau, accused of narrow horizons, lost influence, their places preempted by outsiders, for the most part ex-soldiers from Metropolitan France. The alliance of civilians and soldiers was opportunistic, an outgrowth of sheer necessity. The OAS, they fully realized, represented a last chance. If it failed, there would be no further opportunities. But offsetting this was the realization—as they met on spring evenings in apartments overlooking the city spread out in concentric white tiers below—that for the moment nothing was irredeemably lost; they were at liberty, the network of militants and sympathizers remained virtually intact, they enjoyed a whole population's fervent hopes for their success. It was to be, as they saw it, a patriotic movement—"the beginning of a dark and tena-cious Resistance," Susini wrote, "conducted by a handful of men and supported by all the French of Algeria." The set of letters remained unchanged—OAS—but it was a new start.

As the soft, odorous dark fell, Algiers became a mountain of light, a beacon on the Mediterranean shore scintillating with energy, one of Africa's largest cities and France's second-biggest seaport. Navy destroyer-escorts, a huge passenger steamer from Marseilles, cargo ships, fishing smacks and troop ships rode at anchor under a translucent moon within the protection of the breakwater. Beyond loomed illuminated cliffs inhabited by Europeans, and darker, poorer patches on the bluffs occupied by Moslems. Past the visible city lay the great moonlit hinterland climbing and dropping off in successive mountainous waves toward the gas- and oil-rich Sahara. This, in Godard's view, was the stake, the prize.

Only a year before—in 1960—French writer Jules Roy had depicted Algiers in the following terms: "The city is a French city, humming with business, bursting at every seam. Blocks of fifteen-story apartment houses terrace its hills, and new suburbs are sprouting all around the perimeter. New docks are under construction; new factory sites stretch as far as Cape Matifou. Hotels are always full. Jets arrive from Paris in two hours."[*]

Roy wrote at a time when the government in Paris—publicly, at least—was pledged to maintain French economic interests and encouraged private investment.

In 1961, the offshore nighttime impression of prosperity and fulfillment was deceptive. For, when night fell, a change came over the city. The *pieds noirs'* sullen irritation with the way things were going grew audible. It began after dinnertime—after dishes had been dried and children tucked off to bed—with a *casserolade*: a banging of casseroles, skillets, pots and pans, and in fact, any noise-making instrument on which a family could rap out the three long and two short beats of *"Al-gé-rie fran-çaise!"* The refrain was taken up next door, and soon the din became neighborhood-wide. It was harmless, it eased smoldering dissatisfaction, thought Paris; it marked the first modest step in mobilizing the masses, thought the OAS. Shortly after the *casserolades* died down, plastique explosions thudded nearby, at irregular intervals, acrid smoke poured thickly into the streets, and then came the wailing of police cars. The *plas-*

* Jules Roy, *The War in Algeria*.

tiquages ripped apart doorjambs, shattered windows, loosened pipes; sometimes passers-by were injured, but the blasts at this stage almost never killed—they were not intended to; they were given as warnings to European liberals and Moslems collaborating with the FLN. Still, the nightly number of explosions crept upward: from two or three, they rose in June to five and six.

And when day rose, the city found itself a little grimier than before, coated with plaster dust, and discovered its true nature—sundered into two antagonistic communities tensely noting each other's every movement. Instictive reflexes persisted from the past. Moslems arrived for work every morning in the European quarter, at the docks, around the market place. Europeans still came on a variety of errands to the Moslem neighborhoods of Climat de France and Belcourt. But patience was wearing thin on both sides.

Alger la blanche, the white city, shimmered and pulsed in the driven desiccating heat. At the Place du Gouvernement, gateway to the Casbah, the air smelled immemorially of cooking oil and dried-out dung and roasting coffee far more than of the placid sea; bare-soled shoeshine boys darted through the limp, murmurous Arab street crowd. Ten minutes' walk away, in the shadow of steel office buildings, *pieds noirs* sat down to heavy lunches at flowered café terraces and contemplated scenes as unexotic as those in Lyons and Bordeaux. The colonial contrast was as stark as ever.

The city was thronged with helmeted, armed troops in narrow congested thoroughfares. Exasperated and unresigned, the *pieds noirs* took refuge in dim, cavernous cafés, cursed the *pathos,* swore oaths to remain French, and drew comfort from extravagant rumors. They were persuaded that Salan was traveling about the Mitidja at will in a flag-bedecked car protected by a convoy of three half-tracks and well-armed Foreign Legion deserters. Perhaps not all *pieds noirs* put stock in these tall tales, but they firmly believed that the missing generals and colonels were awaiting an opportune moment to regain the upper hand. At the Délégation Générale, Coup de Fréjac compared Salan's convoy to the Loch Ness monster—many claimed to have seen the apparition, but who could prove it?

The fate of the city and the entire country was being discussed almost a thousand miles away, at the Hôtel du Parc in Évian, on the southern shore of the Lake of Geneva. The French lodged in a group of chalets less than a mile outside Évian; the FLN in a twenty-five-room villa on the northern, Swiss shore, from which they shuttled ten miles across the lake by helicopter, or in bad weather by motorboat.

On the day cease-fire talks had opened—May 20—Paris had announced the release of six thousand FLN internees, the transfer of five FLN chiefs including Ben Bella* from the Île d'Aix to more comfortable quarters at the Château de Turquant, near Saumur, and the immediate unilateral suspension of all offensive operations throughout Algeria. These were major concessions, but they were insufficient to overcome years of accumulated distrust.

De Gaulle had instructed the French delegates to refrain from a handshake at the first meeting with their Algerian counterparts—a nod would do.

The Algerians arrived in a similar stiff mood, their suspicions enhanced, if anything, by the unilateral truce, which they promptly denounced as a trick to undermine fighting spirt among the *fellaga*. Convinced of French insincerity about ending the war, they refused to call a halt to their own operations.

So things began badly at the start. Philippe Thibault, the French information officer, found the atmosphere "courteous but tense and cold."

The first major stumbling block that arose was the Sahara. Aware of the FLN's minimum strength in the region, the French, under rigid orders from de Gaulle, declared that the Sahara was a problem in itself, independent of Algeria.† The FLN delegation retorted that it was an integral part of Algeria, where self-determination must be applied exactly as in the north; on this basis, they added that they would be willing to discuss joint exploitation of the desert's vast natural subsurface resources.

---

* With four other nationalist leaders—Hocine Ait Ahmed, Mohamed Khider, Rabah Bitat and Mohamed Boudiaf—Ben Bella had been arrested by the French on October 22, 1956, when the chartered plane on which he was flying from Rabat to Tunis was diverted by French Intelligence and landed at Algiers.

† Whether de Gaulle was really so rigid is doubtful: close collaborators believe that at this stage he already fully expected the Sahara to become independent with the rest of Algeria. But he was proceeding cautiously, to give public opinion in France time to adjust to the idea of losing the area. Keeping the Sahara, in de Gaulle's view, would have created an "abscess" in the center of Africa, bred continuing problems between France and Algeria, and compromised his entire African policy based on decolonialization.

The problem of the Europeans—referred to at Évian as the non-Moslem minority—revealed almost no common ground. The French demanded formal recognition of the *pieds noirs'* special interests. The FLN delegates adopted the position that they intended to make no discrimination between European and Moslem; they would have the same rights and same duties. They proposed offering guarantees to individuals, but not to the *pieds noirs* as a body. This was entirely logical; but, given the existing mood in Algeria's cities, it was entirely unacceptable.

The arid discussions dragged on for more than three weeks—thirteen sessions in twenty-four days. They were led by Algerian Affairs Minister Louis Joxe and the GPRA's Vice-President, Belkacem Krim, a tubby, balding guerrilla chief. The French press mordantly recalled the *mot* of former premier Félix Gaillard: "It is hard to keep Algeria, harder to lose it, and still harder to give it away." Finally, on June 13, Joxe asked for a suspension of talks.

In retrospect, the negotiation failed because each side believed that time was on its side. Paris considered the military battle won and was prepared to outwait the Algerians.* For the FLN, the prospect of further delay after years of waiting was acceptable as long as independence on its terms could be wrested in the long run.

Meanwhile, *El Moudjahid*, the FLN official organ, noted that European masses in the cities were being taken in hand by a new movement. It minimized the OAS as the desperate last thrashing-about of splinter activist groups, and officially dismissed them as an internal French problem. Privately, a split within the French camp was viewed as a not unwelcome development.

The breakdown of talks delighted Susini. From this point on, OAS propaganda referred to the French lakeside city as *Évian la Honte* ("the Shameful Évian").

---

* The French Army estimated that out of 120 *katibas* (companies) operating in the Algerian countryside in 1958, only a dozen remained by 1961. Similarly it claimed that out of a force of 30,000 troops on the Moroccan and Tunisian frontiers, only 300 had got past the electrified border fences into Algeria. Even with due allowance for official exaggeration, it seems certain that the nationalists were in bad straits militarily. But the serious *Revue Militaire Suisse* noted that the military picture was incidental; the Algerian question would be resolved not by arms but through a political deal.

9

The Gunmen

By 1961, *Algérie française* in its strict sense was an outdated slogan, a lost cause that no longer corresponded to French government policy. Among the *pieds noirs,* the upper middle class, a minority within a minority, recognized grudgingly this unpalatable truth; but among the *petits blancs,* the poor whites, for whom a little was a lot, it was a different matter.

For what they possessed was immeasurably more than they could expect to own in France or, if the master-servant relationship were overturned, in an independent Algeria. They were mortally afraid of being cut adrift from the mother country.

Inevitably they began to join the OAS.

Fifty thousand *petits blancs* were crammed into the low-income neighborhood of Bab el Oued, one of Algiers' oldest districts, cramped between the Casbah and the sea. There were other neighborhoods where pro–*Algérie-française* feeling ran as high, but Bab el Oued became a symbol of resistance to change.

The quarter had developed around a rubbish-littered stream that emptied into the Mediterranean, hence its name, which in Arabic means "The Water's Gate." It had been settled shortly after the 1830 conquest by an inpouring of Frenchmen, Spaniards, southern Italians, Maltese, Sephardic Jews and Corsicans, many unskilled, almost all ignorant, turbulent, vain, pious, lusty and credulous. They had

found their way into trade, uncompetitive small businesses, the undemanding lower grades of the civil service, into the police and occasional, ill-organized crime.

A maze of dingy streets and rusty stained fountains in tiny haphazard squares, Bab el Oued possessed charm of a slatternly sort.
The apartment houses had seen better days, but the interiors were
clean and displayed surprising comfort—refrigerators and shower
stalls were a necessity in this heat. The inhabitants stayed up till all
hours in the cafés, drinking amid a litter of peanut shells and al-
mond husks, the sound of radio and records blared from open windows as in any Arab *souk,* swart men, ample mothers and their
daughters in flowered skirts peopled the streets, pets roamed at will.
At dusk, between six-thirty and seven-thirty, boys and girls walked
in opposite directions in the evening cool, appraising one another,
from the Place des Trois Horloges with its three red clocks, down
to the Lycée Bugeaud and back.

There was de facto integration of a sort in Bab el Oued. So the
petits blancs were sincerely outraged when Americans accused them
of racism. It was not like the Deep South, they protested. Day-to-
day interpenetration between poor Europeans and poor Moslems
here was thorough if limited. They worked together, played on the
same teams together, ate together and often attended the same
schools; however, there was no question of intermarriage, they did
not worship alike, and almost invariably pay scales differed in
the Europeans' favor. The *petit blanc*'s attitude to the Moslem, composed of liking, contempt, superiority, curiosity, suspicion, gener-
osity and undeclared but dead-serious competitiveness, in fact, remarkably resembled the ineradicable attitude of the American Deep
South's rednecks to the blacks. The same social and economic factors bred the same response.

In Paris the government prosecuted scores of officers implicated in
the putsch. Colonels, captains, lieutenants, a sprinkling of noncoms
and civilians, appeared with monotonous regularity before the Petit
Tribunal Militaire, which sat throughout the summer. The public's
initial curiosity had subsided; an eloquent, spruce colonel in the
dock still attracted feminine spectators, but few turned out for a
mere insubordinate major. A pattern with hazardous consequences for
the future emerged from this series of trials: the ringleaders were

sternly punished, the others were let off relatively lightly—so it appeared, at least, from the great number of suspended sentences. Leniency often backfired: a number of convicted officers set at liberty immediately seized the opportunity to desert and join the OAS.* In fairness, it must be added that the courts found the hardest thing to prove was premeditation: many officers asserted truthfully that they had had no inkling of the putsch beforehand, then found themselves dealing with a *fait accompli*. But some circles within the Armed Forces continued to be more concerned with the harm done to its sacrosanct if mythical "unity" than with the threat of new revolt. Officers called to the stand as prosecution witnesses tempered their testimony, stressing extenuating circumstances and seeking excuses for the accused, so that in the end they acted as defense witnesses. Vice-Admiral Querville, for example, praised Navy Lieutenant Pierre Guillaume, who detested him and sought to oust him during the putsch, as an "energetic and courageous officer for whom I have considerable esteem"—this, in spite of the fact that Guillaume, a small, intense redhead from an extreme-Right milieu, testified at his trial, "The only thing I regret is that we have temporarily failed," and professed "a deep admiration for Salan."† A partial explanation of the Army's (and the Navy's) protective attitude toward its own was furnished by the long-resident, perspicacious Paris correspondent of *The New Yorker*, Janet Flanner, who referred illuminatingly to the Army as "the biggest emotional cult, next to the Church, in France."

As seen from official desks in Paris, the Algerian problem appeared relatively unalarming. A poll, taken before the breakdown of talks, showed public opinion running strongly in favor of de Gaulle's policy of a negotiated settlement; in reply to the question, "What is the most important problem for France at this moment?" 78 percent had said "Peace in Algeria"; and in answer to the question, "Do you have confidence in de Gaulle to solve the Algerian problem?" 84 per-

---

* Two notorious cases were Captain Guy Branca and Captain Pierre Montagnon, Foreign Legion officers who subsequently played an important role in the Organization. Both received one-year suspended sentences in July 1961 for their attitude during the putsch.

† Cited by Yves-Frédéric Jaffre, *Les Tribunaux d'Exception*. Lieutenant Colonel Pierre Darmuzai was one of the rare officers who in a report recommended judicial proceedings against officers under his command. He said his unit, the 2nd Foreign Legion Paratroop Regiment, did "not merit to survive."

cent had said Yes and only 9 percent No. The Police Prefecture counted fifteen right-wing organizations it considered subversive in the Paris area—political movements, war veterans' associations and student groups—but noted that only about one tenth of the membership posed a real danger. Reports from the Délégation Générale in Algiers claimed that a few hundred hotheads in hiding would soon be captured, and subversion would be over in a matter of weeks. Since the OAS was doing little else than setting off plastique bombs at this stage, there was some temptation to write it off as a band of crackpots. The *Courrier du Parlement* wrote in early June: "The OAS in France has no cohesion . . . it isn't the same in Algeria, where it has grouped together a number of disparate elements under several officers who participated in the putsch. But its action is limited to *plastiquages.*"

The optimism was not all-pervasive. At least three high officials drafted pessimistic reports. Public Works Minister Robert Buron was worried following conversations with liberal parish priests in Algiers, who reported that while in the past activist parishioners had kept them reasonably well informed of what was being planned, the link was now severed and the *pieds noirs* had totally withdrawn into themselves. Jacques Aubert, head of Algiers' Sûreté Nationale, warned that Algiers and Oran could pose problems of outright revolt. Jacques Coup de Fréjac saw all hope destroyed of using liberal elements in the European community as a lever. A movement aimed at combating OAS propaganda, Organisation de l'Algérie fraternelle (OAF), had quickly sputtered out for lack of support and funds, and it would soon be worth a European's life to advertise support of de Gaulle.

To forestall the new threat, Debré's government took a number of measures. Making use of special powers approved by the National Assembly, it clapped a first lot of twenty-four activists into "administrative internment" (the term was a euphemism for indefinite detainment at the government's pleasure) at a camp in the Ain department, in central France. On June 7, it promoted General Charles Ailleret, a stanch Gaullist who had served as zone commander in eastern Algeria during the putsch, to the four-star rank of *général de corps d'armée* and made him the new commander in chief in Algeria, replacing the unfortunate Gambiez. Ailleret's task would be to keep the Army politically neutral. Then Debré ordered a long-delayed reform of the functions of Military Security. Within the Army, Sécurité Militaire had played a modest role,* concentrating on identifying and weeding out Communist elements among enlisted men and reserve officers; career officers were generally considered above suspicion—and so they were, if the danger of infiltration and subversion was assumed to exist only on the Left. The fragility of this point of view came to light when it developed that the officer entrusted with military security matters in the 1er REP was none other than Major Denoix de St.-Marc, who had ordered his troops to seize Algiers for Challe. From June onward, Sécurité Militaire began to concentrate increasingly on the identification of disloyal, pro-OAS elements within the Army; and its staff grew.

However, all these measures were timid and fell short of their intended mark.

At about this time, Nobel Prize winner François Mauriac, novelist, polemicist and ardent defender of Gaullist policy, told an interviewer: "De Gaulle did not say all that should have been said to the *pieds noirs*, but the question is, did he do all that could be done?" Mauriac thought that he had. However, the writer predicted that troubles were not over in Algeria. "The history of France," he added with his usual acerbity, "is a long civil war."

At first, the OAS was feeble and bedeviled by a thousand difficulties. Godard and Degueldre were almost captured on their way to a meeting with Salan at Martel's farm the first time they drove out of the city. At a checkpoint in suburban Birmandreis, police ordered them to turn back to headquarters for further questioning when it developed that their driver's papers were not in order. A gendarme assigned to escort them entered the car, and sat down beside the driver on a pile of papers. Among them was the table of organization Godard was carrying to the meeting. Godard and Degueldre claimed they were late for a business appointment, and obtained the gendarme's permission to get out of the car and allow the driver to fend for himself. The ex-colonel and the ex-lieutenant turned down a side street and vanished.

Susini narrowly escaped capture one night while sleeping in a beach shack outside Algiers used by a *pied noir* for extramarital

---

* In the U.S. Army the corresponding branch is C.I.C. (Counterintelligence Corps), which, however, has other duties as well.

affairs. The police arrested the *pied noir* in town, as a suspected activist, but only searched the shack the following day, by which time Susini had cleared out.

Zattara enjoyed less luck. While he was hiding in a schoolteacher's apartment a neighbor called the police. The activist showed the inspectors identity papers in the name of Fabiani, and they were about to leave, when one of them asked to see his wedding band. It bore on the inside the engraved initials D. Z. Zattara was arrested, tried, and sentenced to four years' imprisonment.

Apart from the basic need to remain at liberty, the Organization's leaders faced almost insurmountable practical problems of recruitment, communications and financing. It would be excessive to tax the reader's patience with a comprehensive account of these difficulties, which resembled those of underground groups everywhere, but some details will shed light on what ensued.

The OAS was implanted in Algiers, a foothold existed in Oran, but in eastern Algeria, where the European population was scanty, and throughout most of the countryside, from the Mitidja plain to the Hauts Plateaux, it boasted a skeletal organization at best, and more often than not, none at all. Greater Algiers was now theoretically divided into six sectors, each headed by a sector chief in accordance with Godard's table of organization; Jacques Achard was in charge of the Orléans-Marine district, which included the port, but there was a serious dearth of cadres, and for months the five other sectors would go leaderless. All together, the OAS did not amount to more than several hundred militants, although hundreds more helped on a part-time, sporadic basis. Runners were used to deliver important messages, but as more troops evacuated the hinterland and crowded into the city for anti-OAS operations, the danger of interception leaped, so the leaders clustered together in disregard of elementary security precautions. Sometimes, Susini noted, the entire OAS command was in hiding on the same street, Boulevard du Télémly, on Algiers' heights.*

The most urgent problem was the lack of funds. Without money, the handful of men running the Organization could not procure arms, carry on propaganda, meet the living expenses of deserters who enrolled in the movement, or, for that matter, subsist very long themselves.

In June, after rejoining the others and assuming command of

* Cited in *Histoire de l'OAS*.

O.M., Gardes settled down to the thankless task of secret fund raising. He sent out rank-and-file members under the authorities' noses to canvass the city both horizontally and vertically. They solicited in the European quarters on a door-to-door basis and contacted banks, insurance companies, business firms, factories, trade-unions, professional associations and municipal services. Families were taxed two dollars a month, small shopkeepers ten; but industrial concerns were expected to contribute a substantial percentage of their profits toward a patriotic cause. Very soon, Gardes ran into difficulties. The odor of money attracted unwanted attention. Fund raisers scoured neighborhoods ostensibly on behalf of the OAS, then made off with the proceeds. During these early, lean months the Organization had trouble honoring its pledge to provide for militants' families. Cash was misplaced or unaccounted for; operational costs were excessive—especially for cars and gas—and receipts were meaningless. From his hiding place Gardes dispatched one piteous letter after another to Gardy, Godard and the others, threatening to quit unless his directives were obeyed, repeating that he would not stand being made a fool of. The letters are a study in frustration; the chronic problem of finances was never mastered. But Gardes's own invincible idealism stood in the way of a solution; he felt some reluctance about approaching Algiers businessmen for aid, and advised Susini that it would be a proof of the movement's purity if they all subsisted "as lean as wolves." Susini was unimpressed. He felt priority should be given to raising money with little quibbling over how it was obtained—in a life-or-death struggle, winning was all that mattered; defeat would not be justified by a simon-pure attitude. He bitterly resented the niggardly attitude of European capital in Algiers. "The Algerian wine industry had just netted 140 million dollars in annual profits," he wrote. "Of this, they charitably gave us one thousand dollars."

Susini contrasted this inability to see where one's own interest lay with successful FLN fund raising among Moslems in France and in the Algerian interior, and the help it received from both the Communist bloc and oil-rich Arab countries.

As the deputy chief of A.P.P., he wanted funds to set up an intelligence and information station in Switzerland. He also considered paying monthly bribes to journalists on *Le Monde* and other widely read newspapers in France, reasoning that the FLN had attempted the same method of influencing opinion. Whether Susini's brash schemes would have succeeded is questionable; but in the event, they were never undertaken, for lack of capital.

In the midst of these difficulties, Sergent abruptly cleared out for France with a fellow deserter from the 1er REP, Lieutenant Daniel Godot. Sergent found Algiers' political atmosphere unendurable, but Godard had hoped, nonetheless, to dissuade him from leaving by assigning him a key position as sector chief. As far as could be ascertained, the two men had packed up and departed without precise orders from Salan or anybody else. It was understood they would seek to contact activist networks in France, although for the moment the OAS remained without word of their whereabouts. The incident illustrated the glaring lack of discipline in the Organization.*

As summer began, the OAS was at a standstill. It was on the defensive, many *pieds noirs* still regarded it as a myth rather than a real movement. Susini's vision of street revolution remained as far out of reach as Godard's ideal of city-wide resistance. Measurable headway was being made in one branch alone—O.R.O. The tangible results reflected the strong, though dissimilar, personalities of the two men directly associated with it, Perez and Degueldre.

Assigned the responsibility of the OAS's special branch for sabotage, intimidation, murder and mayhem, Jean-Claude Perez was, to a certain degree, type-cast.

He was thirty-three years old. He had been born into a Catholic, traditionalist-minded family in Bab el Oued. He studied medicine. On November 1, 1954, the day the Algerian rebellion broke out, he became engaged to a daughter of the Limanina family, distillers of anisette in a country where drinks with an anisette base are gulped more casually than water. The next day, he reported for military service with an Algerian *tirailleur* regiment. During his tour of duty he became passionately involved in the war's ideological issues.

A year later, demobilized, he set up as a general practitioner in his native quarter. He was popular—olive-skinned, strapping, voluble, fiery-tempered, a lover of hearty food, something of a brag-

---

* Broizat also thought of leaving Algiers in discouragement, but was talked out of it by Susini. The former seminarian struck a curious bargain: he would oversee propaganda for the OAS without formally belonging to the movement. He stuck to this compromise to the very end.

gart, and a playboy. He was one of the *petits blancs,* but just a notch above them. Marriage into a wealthy family had made things easier for him; he treated a great many poor, Europeans and Arabs alike, without charge. But he was "far more interested in politics than in medicine." What money he earned went into nationalist political agitation.

He made no secret of his ideas. He saw the struggle in Algiers as part of a "cosmic dialectical battle" between Christianity and Communism; this fascinated him far more than the primitive motivations of home and country, which he dismissed as simple-minded. He recruited a counterterrorist group to deal vigilante justice on suspected FLN collaborators—it foreshadowed what was to come six years later in the form of the Delta commandos. The local police winked at Perez's terrorist expeditions, but he eventually drew a two-month jail term for "constitution of an illegal society."

During his imprisonment chalk signs appeared on walls in Bab el Oued: *"Délivrez le docteur des pauvres."* So was born the legend of the Saint Vincent de Paul of Algiers' poor quarters. In jail he met café owner Joseph Ortiz, joined his Front National Français, and sallied forth with the FNF insignia stuck into his lapel. He was a competent organizer. When Georges Bidault harangued the *pieds noirs* at St.-Eugène stadium in December 1959, the former premier was closely flanked by the FNF "protection service"—roughnecks in armbands and khaki shirts recruited by Perez. It was reminiscent of the Brown Shirts.

That year Perez and Susini haunted working-class cafés of Bab el Oued, making speeches and drumming up membership in the FNF. Each considered himself as Ortiz's eventual successor. But while Susini promised revolution, Perez promised hangings. Some elements of the audience undoubtedly preferred to hear the latter.

After Barricades Week he was indicted and put on trial. Thus this fervent advocate of French rule gained his first glimpse of France from a cell window at Paris' Santé Prison. He told the judge his political program in one sentence: "Ferhat Abbas must never be allowed to sit down at the same table as a French general." Acquitted, he was slapped into Tefeschoun internment camp outside Algiers. Godard, who knew him, ordered his release on the first day of the putsch, instructed him to refrain from any nonsense, then in early May agreed to let him head up O.R.O. Perez threw himself into the task with enthusiasm and conscientiousness; he knew the topography of Algiers, and he found recruits easily among former acquaintances in Bab el Oued and members of his earlier counterterrorist group. Godard soon assigned him a deputy. The deputy was Degueldre.

He was tough. Photographs show a big, somber, grimly resolute man with a long horse face, prominent, even teeth, and a dangerous mouth. Photographs can mislead, but there is the testimony of survivors, who unanimously use the words "brute force," "harsh," and over and over again, "hard" to characterize him. He was a Northerner, born near the Belgian frontier, a heavy-moving six-footer of fierce black humor and undoubted courage. According to his friends, he was forthright, all of one piece, foul-spoken, but free of pretense. *L'Express*, which had no use for him, compared him to a great Dane, to "an animal with a tremendous underjaw."

Inside and outside the Army, he was a born leader who dominated other men through sheer physical drive, the sort of lieutenant company commanders dream about and seldom find for night patrols into enemy territory. Yet all his life Degueldre was a lone wolf.

At seventeen, he joined the Communist-led Francs-Tireurs et Partisans in occupied northern France; at the Liberation he enlisted in the regular Army; but less than a year later, as the war ended, he reenlisted, under an assumed name, in the Foreign Legion. The facts here are obscure and contradictory. A persistent story claims that he was not French at all, but Belgian, lived during the war in Brussels, served in the ranks of the collaborationist SS brigade Wallonie on the Russian front in 1943, then participated in war crimes at Charleroi, Belgium, in 1944, for which he was condemned to death. According to the story, this is why he fled Belgium and took refuge in the Foreign Legion. The story has never been confirmed by official French or Belgian sources; friends of Degueldre deny it, insist he was born at Louvroil in the Nord department of France, and say he was confused with Léon Degrelle, head of the Belgian collaborationist Rexists. According to this version, Degueldre, a Frenchman, underwent a turnabout of political convictions during the last stages of the war, and joined the Legion to escape the consequences of his open sympathy for the Rexist movement. Degueldre himself steadfastly denied being Belgian or ever having belonged to the Rexists. But he gave evasive answers about his reasons for becoming a Legionnaire.

He served in Indochina, was wounded at Dien Bien Phu, then in 1958 he was commissioned from the ranks and resumed his real name. His emotional involvement in the battle against the Viet Minh acquired a new dimension in the battle against the FLN; it transcended duty and obedience and became obsessive. In a much-quoted retort to his superior officers after Barricades Week, he declared: "You have taken an oath to keep Algeria French. I have taken this oath with you. As far as I am concerned, the oath will be kept. I'll go the limit."

His odd, gradual desertion by stages from the 1er REP and his role in the putsch have already been recounted. In May, bridges burned, he had no intention of surrendering; he was available for a suicidal assignment. The OAS gave him one.

Godard and Perez put him in charge of the Bureau d'Action Opérationelle, a branch of O.R.O. As its name implied, it dealt in action; and in OAS terms, action meant terrorism. Degueldre recruited deserters—Frenchmen and foreigners, noncoms and junior officers, from paratroop and Foreign Legion regiments; young *pied noir* toughs from Bab el Oued, a sprinkling of underworld ruffians, even a few Moslems,* and grouped them into small, mobile, heavily armed commandos. In the French Army Signal Corps radio and telephone alphabet, the letter *D* is known as "Delta"; so, Degueldre adopted "Delta" as his code name, and the commandos became known as Deltas. He signed all orders to his underlings, including orders to kill, with the Greek letter delta (Δ).

He wanted two hundred men, but he had trouble at first recruiting even one hundred. Algiers swarmed with embittered Europeans itching to bait Moslems and brawl with security forces in street

---

* Moslem participation in the OAS, though hard to believe, has been personally confirmed to this writer by such varied sources as Susini, Perez and Belkacem Krim. The Moslems in question were violently anti-FLN, and often opportunistic. They were grouped in a Bureau Musulman run by an Arab lawyer who reported direct to Susini. The Bureau consisted mostly of former Moslem officers in the French Army. No reliable figure is available, but Susini himself admits they were "not numerous." From the Organization's point of view, the security problem was enormous: it involved detecting possible double agents as well as protecting bona fide Moslem militants from FLN reprisals. It must be recalled that in this early stage the OAS still professed to defend the Moslems, and had not yet begun indiscriminate attacks against them. But even afterward, some Moslems fought with the OAS.

riots, but few had the stomach for hazardous individual assignments, much less cold-blooded murder. Among those who entered the Delta commandos, some backed out almost at once. Those who remained were in deadly earnest. They became OAS gunmen not primarily for easy money—they received little pay; it varied from $80 to $100 a month—but out of warped patriotism, a streak of viciousness, ignorance, lawlessness, influenceability. The Deltas were intoxicated, it has been said, with *Algérie française* propaganda and anisette.

There was another reason: some were foreigners, Legionnaires completely at sea following the post-putsch arrest or transfer of their officers. They were not particularly interested in French politics or saving French Algeria, but they felt a strong sense of loyalty to their immediate superiors. This motivated some desertions. Psychologically maladjusted to begin with, they ran amok when removed from regimental discipline and thrust into the political snake pit of Algiers. The first night on the run, a deserter was provided with a girl in bed, $200 spending money, and some plastique in a suitcase. Told to go and blow up a building, he readily did so, then returned and heard himself praised as a patriot—and the cycle started anew. A tradition existed among *pieds noirs* of softening up newcomers to Algiers—bureaucrats and police officials—with bribes and girls, to win them over to the *pied noir* cause. Degueldre was simply adapting an old technique to a new situation.

He cracked the whip mercilessly over his recruits to maintain a semblance of Foreign Legion discipline. He was brutal and ready to use a knife or a bomb to do away with traitors. Few chose to cross him.

He became totally immersed in his assignment—an intense figure speeding about Algiers, frowning and preoccupied, concerned with immediate problems of weapons and ammunition and hideouts and cars, so absorbed in detail that it left him loftily indifferent to the possibility of arrest and imprisonment. Several times, *pied noir* policemen recognized him at street corners and cautioned him against running foolish risks.

He was obsessed by what he had heard of the 1956 Budapest uprising; his entire effort was bent toward preparing for a similar insurrection, when the embattled *pieds noirs* of Algiers would wage stubborn, house-to-house resistance, from doorways and rooftops, fighting for their city and their freedom against an invading juggernaut. In Degueldre's simplistic view, the FLN and the French Army merged into a common, totalitarian enemy. His predilection for street action impressed Susini, who hailed him as a "magnificent revolutionary." Gardy, who felt some concern for this former Legionnaire, was sure that the police would pick him up in a matter of days. Susini feared that the striking figure of the lieutenant was fated to be swept away in revolutionary turmoil. Others concluded that, subconsciously, he was seeking a hero's death.

The Deltas began to kill in late May. The Socialist mayor of suburban Fort de l'Eau, a member of the Algerian Communist party, a dope peddler employed by the police as an anti-OAS informer were ambushed and shot.

But the Deltas' first important victim was Police Inspector Roger Gavoury, and the assassination pointed up Degueldre's methods and mistakes. He had already tried to apprehend the police inspector during the putsch, with the intention of liquidating him, but Gavoury was absent in France. After the insurrection Gavoury had returned to Algiers and set about purging the Central Commissariat of local police favorable to the OAS. What irked the Organization was the suspicion that he was doing a zealous job out of personal ambitiousness, without particular political convictions. For the movement to spread without interference, Gavoury had to be removed; from this point on, he became a priority target on the Deltas' blacklist.

Degueldre confided the *opération ponctuelle** to Sergeant Albert Dovecar, a dreamy, mustachioed Austrian of Yugoslav descent who had deserted from the 1er REP at the time of its disbanding and wandered into the Delta commandos. Dovecar showed no curiosity about the identity of the man he was told to kill, or the reason. He borrowed a revolver with a silencer from a *pied noir* insurance agent, Claude Piegts, and enlisted the cooperation of two other Foreign Legion deserters, Claude Tenne and Herbert Pietri. All three, if they stopped at all to think about what they were doing, would have argued that they were following an officer's orders. Subsequently, at their trial, a prosecution witness testified that one characteristic of Legionnaires was a "dog's faithfulness" to their officers —"They had no critical sense. They were men without country. They gave their officers the sum of attachment and affection of

* OAS leaders used this term to designate executions; they shied away from the word *assassination*.

which they were capable. They were ready to accept anything from their officers."

On the night of May 31, the three Deltas slipped into an apartment building at 4 Rue du Docteur Trolard, where Gavoury was temporarily staying. They waited until the front door had been locked, then entered with a key supplied by Jacques Malmassori, a *pied noir* student who lived next door to Gavoury. Malmassori was away, and they set up the ambush in his room. For security reasons Dovecar had decided at the last moment against the use of the gun. The three Legionnaires had received close-combat commando training in the Army; each was armed with a knife.

Gavoury dined that night with Madeleine Vanuxem, a young secretary at the Central Commissariat, who lived in the same building. He escorted her back to her ground-floor apartment, she made coffee, then he walked up alone to his fourth-floor studio. It was close to midnight. The men on the landing watched him unlock the door, then pressed in for the kill.

Downstairs, the girl heard cries for help, but they were indistinct and appeared to come from outside the building.

When Gavoury failed to turn up next morning to drive her to work as usual, she went upstairs. She found him sprawled on the carpet, messily dead, stabbed repeatedly.

There was a wealth of clues for the police. The door of the adjoining apartment was open, electric lights inside were still burning, and cigarette butts were strewn on the floor. Investigators learned that Malmassori had not returned home during the night; when he eventually turned up, he was taken into custody and interrogated. He proved to be relatively simple-minded. He admitted that three Legionnaires had borrowed his apartment, and he furnished police with their description, but claimed that he had been unaware of their purpose. There the investigation stopped, although the police, who were not happy about the death of a fellow policeman, were determined to pursue it.

Several days later, an Italian deserter roaming through downtown Algiers ran into a fellow Legionnaire who boasted of having taken part in a murder, and gave his friend the address of his hideout. The Italian went straight to the police with the information. That night gendarmes raided a villa in suburban La Bouzareah belonging to a seventy-six-year-old Frenchwoman, Mme. Yvonne Gauthier-Saliège, and her son, a doctor, both known for their activist sympathies. The gendarmes arrived minutes late; in a garden shed they found four cots that had been slept in recently; the occupants had fled with the caretaker who had hidden them.

But two days later police arrived in force at another villa belonging to Pierre Paul Lung, a wine dealer related to the Gauthier-Saliège family. As they approached the house, a submachine gun spattered from a ground-floor window. Returning fire, the gendarmes moved in to surround the villa. The barricaded occupants kept up a hail of small-arms and machine-gun fire. Dovecar, who was in the house, vaulted over a back wall and disappeared. Minutes later, one gendarme scored a direct hit on the door lock, which flew apart. Storming the house, the gendarmes collared two of the gang and found one man, Claude Tenne, bleeding on the floor.*

Flags flew at half-mast at Algiers police headquarters for Gavoury's funeral. Upon interrogation, the Deltas testified that, when they learned from the newspapers that they had killed a policeman, they had shared a good laugh about it.

---

* With Pietri, he drew a life sentence. He escaped from the maximum-security prison on Île de Ré, off the French coast, in November 1967, and was the object of a nationwide manhunt. He managed, with the help of surviving networks, to reach Rome.

10

The Return

TERRORISM CAME late to Oran.

Albert Camus described his city as "turning its back to the sea." Topographically this was correct, but spiritually, Oran, the capital of western Algeria, looked across the Mediterranean to Majorca, Alicante and the Levant. The municipal telephone directory listed countless Gomezes, Martinezes, whose forebears had emigrated during decades of want at home. Oran lived on a Spanish timetable: the siesta benumbed it on hot, breathless afternoons, when the only sound outdoors was the steady plashing of fountains in empty somnolent parks; the European population stirred abroad at twilight, dined late, and retired still later, as sea breezes rose through the faintly lighted center of the city.

When the Algerian war broke out in the Aurès mountains, five hundred miles away, at the other end of the country, the *Oranais* expressed outrage but no alarm. The raids, ambushes, massacres were remote; and even when Algiers, its rival and sister city only some 280 miles distant, fell prey to FLN terrorist attacks, daily life in Oran did not suffer. The two racial groups here were of nearly equal numerical importance—some 210,000 Europeans and 190,000 Moslems—and coexisted warily but, on the whole, pacifically.

Unlike Algiers, Oran's geographical layout discouraged intermingling. To be sure, the thickly populated Moslem quarter, Ville Nouvelle, or *"Village Nègre"* as it was locally known, Oran's Casbah, drove like a dagger into the European heart of the city; but the other Moslem quarters—Lamur, Lyautey, Medioni—all lay near the perimeter, and the danger of day-to-day friction was thus reduced. The FLN regarded Oran and the entire Oran region—*Wilaya* 5—as an unofficial rest-and-rehabilitation center for terrorists fleeing the police and the Army in Algiers. European residents of other parts of Algeria came to Oran for a night's fun, uncomplicated by an early curfew. As late as 1961, the Théâtre de Verdure, with a seating capacity of ten thousand, staged open-air variety shows with Parisian music-hall stars like Gilbert Bécaud.

Oran's complacency was due first and foremost to the bulking presence, only three miles away, of the huge naval fortress of Mers el Kébir. Even if the French government evacuated all the rest of Algeria—reasoned the *pieds noirs*—it could never afford to abandon Mers el Kébir, because of its prime strategic importance guarding the western Mediterranean. The base was the *Oranais'* trump card.

The April putsch made little impact on the city. Oran's prefect learned of troop movements in Algiers in the very early hours of Saturday morning, and called Roger Coignard, the young acting mayor.

"*Monsieur le maire, il y a encore un putsch.*"

"*Merde!*"

The local Army corps commander, General Henri de Pouilly, whose reaction Challe had so dreaded, was, in fact, torn between two attitudes: doubt about the putsch's chances of success and a desire to smooth things over; but when a local roughneck tactlessly stuck a gun in his stomach, and gave him the choice of backing the insurrection or being shot, the general lost his temper. The civilian's mistake was immeasurably aggravated by Argoud, who allowed de Pouilly to leave with his staff for the nearby city of Tlemcen, where he constituted a core of legitimate authority.

During the next three days, the local OAS accomplished next to nothing.

With the putsch's collapse, it returned underground. A few days' run of the city had revealed it to be an ineffectual, self-divided group; it was in the hands of small businessmen, a number of doctors, a few deserters, and it received financial aid from several local factory owners. It was woefully short of the minimum political talent which Algiers' OAS commanded. Finally, Oran had no full-fledged university, thus there was no volatile student mass on which to draw.

During the next few weeks the Oran OAS limited its activity to setting off plastique, until abruptly, in mid-May, the situation took a turn for the worse. Moslem terrorism flared: incidents of Arabs stoning cars and hurling Molotov cocktails at gas stations multiplied; residents of Ville Nouvelle opened fire without warning on a gendarme patrol. A young Frenchman just demobilized made the mistake of venturing into the Moslem quarter; a gang of youths stabbed him, clubbed him with a plank, then finished him off with a butcher knife. Another European was attacked with hatchets. There was no immediate cause for the outburst of violence; but in retaliation Europeans tossed grenades into a Moorish café, set fire to several Moslem grocery stores whose owners were suspected of being FLN fund raisers, then shortly afterward, for good measure, burned down the San Remo restaurant in downtown Oran, a gathering place of Free French veterans of World War II. For two grim days in a row, Oran was the scene of *ratonnades*—manhunts organized by European street gangs, who beat to death the first hapless Moslem they found.

At this point, Pierre Laffont, publisher of the moderate *L'Écho d'Oran* and one of the city's responsible civic leaders, announced that he was giving up his deputy's seat in the National Assembly and ceasing all journalistic activity. "Only extremists on both sides can now find an audience," remarked Laffont; few shared this clairvoyance.

On July 4 a confidential report from Police Prefect Jules Plettner to the Delegate General, Jean Morin, outlined the situation in gloomy terms. Plettner noted that Oran's eight hundred European policemen were *"Oranais* first, policemen second." They thought nothing, he added, of conniving with *plastiqueurs,* sheltering deserters, and allowing demonstrators the run of the streets. The report said that the attitude of the force's plainclothesmen was no different; some eighty inspectors detailed to the Renseignements Généraux and 120 Sûreté inspectors had adopted a position of "prudent neutrality": between them, not a single case involving a European activist had been prosecuted. Security forces were overworked, on edge, and might be obliged to use firearms to enforce the law. Plettner concluded by calling for reinforcements to deal with what he plainly regarded as a tinderbox.

Still, a relative calm prevailed early in the summer. Many European families were away on holiday, at nearby beaches or inland, or in Spain, where they made nuisances of themselves sounding the five-beat *"Algérie française"* rallying cry whenever two cars with Algerian plates met on the open highway.* An incongruous respect for law and order survived: the police noted, for example, that activists scurried to set off their plastique before the curfew hour.

This was the situation when Pierre Le Thiais, the new police prefect, arrived, in July.

He flew from Paris with a threefold assignment: maintain order, prevent a second putsch, avoid a head-on collision between Europeans and Moslems.

Stopping over at Algiers, he ran into pessimism. Jacques Aubert, the Sûreté director, foresaw the possibility of the government being forced to fight on two fronts, against terrorists in both camps.

In downtown Oran, Le Thiais found his future headquarters, the three-story police prefecture, guarded by sandbags, barbed wire and zouave and infantry units. A door blew up as he arrived.

Le Thiais, a heavy-set unruffled man in his early fifties who had been serving in the farming department of the Creuse, felt a certain sympathy for the Europeans and pride in French accomplishments in Algeria, but he was first and foremost a loyal civil servant. He settled down to his assignment with no illusions. Conditions were such that he had left his family behind in France. He quickly discovered that no office was safe from spying or pilfering; one secret report left unattended for ten minutes was found photostated during a raid of an OAS apartment two days later. Of the entire police force for a city of 400,000, he estimated that he could rely on perhaps a half dozen officers—his immediate aide, the first secretary of the prefecture, and a few inspectors from France. The chauffeur assigned him was a *pied noir;* Le Thiais kept him since replacing him entailed hiring another *pied noir,* but he adopted the habit of never telling the driver where they were bound until the last moment. In this way he survived.

* The OAS felt strong enough to warn all Europeans in Algeria against leaving on holiday, except for reasons of health. A tract issued in Oran on June 29 said: "The OAS will have a list of all those having left by ship or plane, and the apartments of vacation-goers will be blown up. . . . It would be inacceptable that while some remain and eventually fight on behalf of French Algeria, others go off on trips. . ." Few *pieds noirs* heeded the threat. In July, 33 *plastiquages* punished those in Algiers who had violated the order.

Le Thiais held a daily morning meeting at nine o'clock with police inspectors and Army liaison officers. On the basis of available information, he estimated the Oran OAS included about one hundred killers abetted by a considerably larger number of militants available for part-time missions. Thus the Organization had reached the same stage of development here as in Algiers. The FLN, he concluded, possessed about an equal number of killers.

The FLN killed in the morning, generally between five and nine o'clock, to catch victims on their way to work; the OAS killed in the afternoon, after closing hours, when its victims were returning from work.

In July, police work in Oran was limited to preventing attacks; it was tacitly recognized that investigating and solving them and punishing the perpetrators were out of the question.

Le Thiais took several stopgap measures. He moved up the local curfew from midnight to nine o'clock, and a strict eight-o'clock curfew was imposed for all under eighteen. He cracked down on unauthorized billposting. He recruited local informers to penetrate the Organization. Mixed patrols of soldiers and police began circulating at night in battle dress, and mobile checkpoints were increased to trip up the activists.

For the moment, Oran struck him as a battlefield over which reigned a superficial and misleading calm. Both Europeans and Moslems knew that the police were shorthanded. Le Thiais thought that with reinforcements the situation could still be mastered; but reinforcements were urgently needed in Algiers, which had a priority claim. Under the circumstances, he foresaw that matters would get worse.

That summer Joxe and Krim met again. For a week, at the Château de Lugrin rented expressly for the purpose two miles from Évian, they made a new stab at ending hostilities.

At the outset, Joxe was disconcerted by Krim's mood. The chief FLN delegate appeared torn between two attitudes—he wanted a cease-fire, but, unsure of political backing in Tunis, he recoiled from concessions that could render him vulnerable to charges of softness. And the major stumbling block remained the same—the Sahara's future status.

Getting wind of an impending breakoff, Joxe hastened to Krim's residence for an hour-long private meeting in a last-minute attempt to bring him round. It was unsuccessful. On July 28, this time at the FLN's urgent behest, the two delegations announced the adjournment of cease-fire talks "sine die."

In Paris, gloom pervaded the government after the double failure of Évian and Lugrin. Joxe was discouraged: the FLN walkout had caused some surprise; there was no really clear idea why it had happened. At his office on Rue St.-Dominique, Bernard Tricot, de Gaulle's chief adviser on Algerian policy, hoped, in a variation on the old French maxim *"Jamais deux sans trois,"* that new negotiations would eventually be pursued. But in the meanwhile, precious time had been lost.

In late June, Susini told a visiting French journalist that the OAS's aim was simple—popular insurrection. Susini spoke for himself; at this point, the colonels' more modest hope was resistance . . . until the Army would tip its weight in their favor. Godard boasted that he had fifteen tons of plastique accumulated in various caches and all the counterfeit identity papers he could use; he needed nothing else—outside Algeria, the Organization should confine itself to one major objective: assassinate *la grande Zora.** Gardes, whose artless idealism made him the least plausible counterrevolutionary in French history, attained the height of nonsense when he claimed that world opinion would be impressed by the extent and depth of *pied noir* resistance even if it consisted only of old ladies flinging flowerpots from their terraces at gendarmes' heads.

For the moment, the Organization busied itself storing arms, establishing letter drops and hideouts, pilfering ammunition and explosives from Army dumps, recruiting, and penetrating the civilian and military administration in Algeria. Perez talked of shipping all women and children out of Algeirs to clear the decks for action.

Mao Tse-tung's famed handbook, *Yu Chi Chan,* which French officers of the Cinquième Bureau revered so much and so arduously misapplied, divides guerrilla warfare into three phases: organization, direct action, and destruction of the enemy. During the first phase, volunteers are trained and indoctrinated; agitators are sent

* The OAS's contemptuous term for de Gaulle, *le grand Charles;* many Moslem charwomen bore the first name Zora.

forth to persuade and rally the countryside. The aim is to enroll the people, who form a mass. From this mass, a militia is raised.

As the torrid summer of 1961 progressed, the OAS carried out Phase One.

Susini himself was busy forming an autonomous group within the OAS, the Front Nationaliste. To head it up, he turned to a thirty-five-year-old oil-well driller, Michel Leroy, who had been active during Barricades Week and whom Susini regarded as the only level-headed member of the extreme-right-wing movement, Jeune Nation. Leroy was an affable Metropolitan Frenchman engaged in raising a family of three in Algeria and studying for an engineering degree. When he showed no interest in resuming political activity, Susini went to considerable lengths to wear down his arguments. He faked medical certificates and arranged with a manager of Repal, the oil firm that employed Leroy, to grant him extended sick leave—a minor example of industry's collusion with the OAS. Finally Leroy accepted, and became Gardes's deputy. The arrangement involved one unusual advantage: because of Leroy's long period of inactivity, no arrest warrant had been issued for him after the putsch; the police were unaware of his contacts, and throughout the summer and fall he remained above ground, one of the few OAS members who could travel freely whenever he pleased to Paris. It would lead to his death.

Recruiting principally among former members of Ortiz's FNF and France-Résurrection and activist students of Algiers and Oran, the Front Nationaliste rapidly attracted a thousand young militants. Students, in particular, flocked to it, for unlike the inarticulate OAS, the Front was a thoroughly indoctrinated, intellectual group with dogmatic nationalist, not to say neofascist, ideas. René Villars, the former chief of France-Résurrection, became active in it, and so did Jean-Marie Zagamé, of Jeune Nation, and Jean Sarradet, a tense, thin young *pied noir* university student.

Sarradet assumed command of the Front's "Z Commandos"—units of 125 students trained for defensive operations to begin with, then offensive missions when Susini's long-awaited mass uprising would take place, notably occupation of public buildings and attacks on gendarmes. Gardes enthusiastically referred to the Z Commandos as the "spearhead of the OAS"; but the students were neither as tough nor as ruthless as the deserters and hoodlums in Degueldre's Deltas.

Susini justified the Front's creation by saying that he could bring a thousand armed students into the streets within an hour. This was hardly candid. His basic though unavowed purpose was to establish his own power base, which he had lacked from the start and needed now more than ever. Perez had his own vociferous followers in Bab el Oued; the colonels wielded influence within the Organization by virtue of their rank; but as long as Salan remained absent, Susini's basic position was weak. He did not view Perez or Gardes as serious political rivals. With Godard, however, it was a different matter.

And predictably, within weeks, warning against "a state within a state," Godard flatly demanded the Front's integration into the OAS. Susini stalled for time. For the moment, in spite of his overpowering personality, the colonel failed to get his way.

The two men disagreed on practically everything. To Godard's insistence on an Algiers foothold, Susini retorted: "The OAS cannot hold one city without holding the country." Godard's way of building an intelligence network was to exploit his widespread friendships with senior officers in the police, Army and SDECE.* They provided him with detailed, and sometimes remarkably recent, information about FLN agents and sympathizers, which he turned over to Perez and Degueldre. Susini carped that Godard was behaving as though he were still at the Sûreté, and "as though the only enemy were the FLN." The Gaullist government and the French Army were equally dangerous, argued Susini. As much as he dared, at secret meeting after meeting, he implied that against both forces Godard was pulling his punches—which was one way of undercutting him. Godard sneered at the "bloodthirsty errand boy" and threatened, if Salan remained in the Mitidja, to replace him with the first willing general he could find. This only heightened Susini's hostility.

---

* SDECE (Service de Documentation et de Contre-espionnage), the French CIA. Operating abroad, it was extremely active during the Algerian War in neighboring Tunisia and Morocco; theoretically its field did not include French Algeria, but in fact it was equally active there under the cover name of CCI (Centre de Coordination Inter-armes). CCI included a high percentage of pro-*Algérie française* officers, but also some Gaullist elements; SDECE's main worry, according to well-informed sources, was to protect its own personnel and interests during a difficult period. Godard's link with SDECE went back to Indochina, where he had commanded the 11ème Bataillon de Choc on special missions. He remained in touch with some of its officers in Algeria. The battalion, which by this time had become a demibrigade, was riddled with pro-OAS sentiment, but as a unit it remained loyal.

Sûreté deputy director Louis Grassien, whose previous experience had been mostly with professional criminals, thought that he had seldom met people so willing to talk. Dozens of Army deserters roamed Algiers' streets, and each time one was picked up for questioning he felt a compulsive need to brag, and meanwhile spilled everything that he knew about the OAS. The information triggered raids, which in turn led to the discovery of the movement's voluminous correspondence—reports, messages, orders, appeals for funds. The documents were coded, but childishly easy to decode. Grassien already knew that "Soleil" was Salan, "Guy" was Gardy, "Pauline" was Perez, and "Jeannine" was Jean-Jacques Susini.* Subordinates' names, moreover, were often left *en clair*.

Grassien now had a special team working solely on anti-OAS operations. For all Algeria it consisted of eight men—six French police inspectors and two Moslems. Like his colleagues in Oran, Grassien had asked for reinforcements, but thirty inspectors sent from France lacked familiarity with Algiers and proved of little use. So Grassien purposely kept his task force down to its small size and felt he accomplished as much. The two Moslems on his staff were especially useful in obtaining information about activists from sources in the Casbah.

Yet in spite of Moslem cooperation and code cracking and city-wide dragnets, arrests turned up only small fry, while the OAS chiefs remained free.

Grassien, accordingly, proceeded to set a trap for the biggest quarry of all—Salan. The bait was dope—several hundred grams of cocaine, which he turned over to André Palacio, an Algiers pimp and gangster occasionally employed by the police. Grassien assumed that the general must be encountering trouble obtaining cocaine in the Mitidja.

Palacio aroused no suspicion at first when he made it known in activist nightclubs and bars that he wanted to contact Soleil. The Algiers underworld passed for emphatically pro-OAS, if only through fear of unemployment under an Arab socialist state. The trail led to a lawyer closely connected with Salan. When Palacio received word that a meeting would be arranged within a week, Grassien had high hopes of smashing the Organization then and there; but, un-

* See Appendix for full list of code names.

known to him, Godard had simultaneously learned about the scheduled meeting and had decided to take no chances. The Deltas were alerted. Several days later, as Palacio left a restaurant on Rue Berthezène, near the Forum, Dovecar—the deserter who had killed Gavoury—stepped from behind a tree and fired twice. Palacio fired back, then collapsed and was rushed, shot in both lungs, to a nearby clinic. An hour later, Grassien's headquarters received an urgent call from the doctor in charge, who had been informed that Dovecar planned to come to the sickroom to finish his victim off. Palacio was rapidly evacuated to a hospital in Blida, then to France, where he survived.

Unwittingly Salan had sidestepped the trap, and Grassien remained in the dark about his whereabouts.

Somewhere in Algiers—in all likelihood only a few blocks from his office, Grassien was aware—the underground leaders hid and met with impunity. Godard knew as well as the police, if not better, how to burrow into the city's life and strike out by surprise.

In the strange undeclared war that was raging, the two sides had at one time trained and fought together; each knew the other's weak points and techniques intimately.

It was a lethal version of the childhood game of *gendarmes et voleurs* ("cops and robbers"), where roles are interchangeable.

The point was driven home unpleasantly when an Italian-born agent of Military Security, who had penetrated the Deltas, contacted Grassien with the news that he had been assigned to kill him. Grassien thought of stage-managing a simulated attack on an empty car to build up the agent's cover. However, before he could do so, Degueldre took the assignment away from the Italian.

This was bad news for Grassien, who now had to worry about a killer in dead earnest.

Colonel Antoine Charles Argoud was expected at one time to become Chief of Staff of the French Army. He was a little coil-spring of a man, whip-smart, annoyingly sure of himself, conceited, essentially humorless, a tiger for work, an ascetic. He was slight and bony, with a long, thin face and a dry, cutting voice. But he was not as inhuman as this sounds, for he also wooed the former wife of an Iranian diplomat and married her.

He had a legendary fondness for striking out on foot, stick in hand, across the flinty Algerian *djebels,* tramping uphill and down-hill for miles, burning up energy and wearing out his subordinates.

He was a product of the École Polytechnique, which shapes some of the most uncompromisingly mathematical minds in France. He put his to work following graduation, organizing the prototype of a streamlined armored brigade for commitment in atomic warfare. This drew him to the attention of the State Secretary for War, Jacques Chevallier, a liberal *pied noir,* who assigned him to his staff.

Argoud in consequence was one of the few top-rated French offi-cers who saw no service in Indochina. He participated in the Suez War, then arrived in Algeria, where he was assigned command of the Arba sector, some thirty miles south of Algiers. His methods here quickly became controversial.

From the start, he set out to cauterize FLN terrorism through deliberate terror and summary justice. An interrogation center was set up where treatment of Moslem suspects vied with the third-degree practiced by paratroopers in Algiers villas; Argoud, more-over, ordered an indeterminate number of *fellaga* shot publicly and their bodies exhibited in town squares. He was not the first or last to resort to these means of repression. What was more revealing, perhaps, was his method of dealing with the European settlers in his area. He ordered files kept on all civilians, their movements checked and their opinions recorded, to identify and weed out all elements who did not unreservedly back his pacification program—a program he described, with little effort at concealment of its true nature, as "Protection-Commitment-Control." His confidence in the *pieds noirs,* visibly, was not much greater than in the Moslems.

Argoud claimed that his methods "pacified" the countryside in the space of five months. The authors of *Histoire de l'Organisation de l'Armée secrète*—a book violently hostile to the OAS—claim that the sector, before Argoud's arrival, was fairly free of FLN attacks, then quickly became a hazardous area wherein an armed escort was nec-essary to move about—and desertions to the FLN soared.

Recalled to Paris, he returned to Algeria in 1959 as Massu's chief of staff. In this post he met daily with two other Algérie Française colonels, Broizat and Gardes; among the three there arose a dan-gerous assumption of infallibility. When Premier Debré flew into

---

* *Histoire de l'Organisation de l'Armée secrète,* by Morland, Barangé and Martinez, the pseudonyms of three police inspectors, who wrote the book with the active cooperation of the French Interior Ministry.

Algiers after Barricades Week to sound out the Army's temper, Argoud notified him—during a stormy meeting that remained legendary—that de Gaulle must either mend his self-determination policy or bow out in favor of Challe. This ultimatum by proxy to de Gaulle on the part of a colonel would have got him into serious trouble in another army. Paris, however, again erred on the side of leniency and merely transferred him to a staff post in Metz. From this comfortable assignment he exercised pressure on Challe to lead the putsch. On April 21 the colonel deserted. Expecting to return to France in triumph within a week, he flew to Algeria.

After the putsch's collapse, as has been described, he arrived in Paris, a demoralized fugitive. Here he learned from Colonel Hervé de Blignères, the principal coordinator of pre-putsch civilian and military conspiracies in the capital, that Sergent and Godot had begun organizing an OAS network in France; de Blignères told him that the Army was undeterred by the putsch's failure and might throw its weight behind a new attempt to block Algerian independence. To what extent these shreds of gossip and conjecture corresponded to a yearning on Argoud's part to persevere, it is hard to state; but, in any case, he gave up the notion of emigrating to South America. Instead, he bought a counterfeit passport through the aid of an activist priest at the church of St.-Pierre de Chaillot, and with de Blignère's blessing left for Spain.

He arrived in Madrid in early July. The activists in the Spanish capital were preparing to form their own organization.

There was Lagaillarde and soft-spoken Dr. Bernard Lefèvre, one of Algiers' leading pre-May 1958 ultras, and Lacheroy, and de La Bigne, who had made his way to the capital from Spanish Morocco, and the efficient, unpretentious Ronda. And there were others, less important.

Lagaillarde's seesawing career was on the rise again. After being jettisoned by Salan, and finding himself out in the cold with the Spanish too, he had worked his way back into the good graces of Serrano Suñer. For what it was worth, Lagaillarde trumpeted his claim as the sole founder of the original OAS; he was just one step, friends thought, from considering Salan, Susini and the others in Algiers as usurpers. But he was grateful nonetheless for reinforcements, and when Argoud turned up, Lagaillarde tacitly divided the leadership of the small Madrid colony of activists with him. This made sense: the two men complemented one another; Lagaillarde, when he bestirred himself, was the doer, Argoud the planner. Argoud had come to Spain believing that his rank and prestige would enable him to impose his ideas on the exiles. It proved to be an accurate calculation.

Lagaillarde had long since moved out of the Torre de Madrid. Serrano Suñer had provided him with a modest apartment at 10 Calle Concha Espina, and now, under the alias "Leroy," he set up headquarters with Argoud in three similar, sparsely furnished apartments near the huge Santiago Bernabeu stadium in Chamartín. Chamartín is one of the capital's fastest-growing residential districts, on Madrid's northern rim, where the Avenida del Generalissimo runs out among sandy mounds, where cows were tethered not so long ago and air-conditioned ministries are now rising. Many foreigners live in the neighborhood—a feature that appealed to Lagaillarde in choosing it. He had suddenly discovered the advantages of anonymity.

The apartments attracted a swarm of hot-eyed, self-styled revolutionaries and "freedom-lovers." Dr. Lefèvre described the hectic atmosphere as "romantic and disorderly . . . resembling France Libre offices abroad during World War II." It was tinged with an unquestionable addiction to intrigue for intrigue's sake. There was endless coming and going of couriers and liaison agents from Paris and Algiers. There were self-important declarations, denials, rectifications. Jean Gauvin depicted the Madrid activists as "rising at midday, gathering around a pool, sitting down to a late, Spanish lunch . . . the true workday began at four in the afternoon, broke off for dinner at eleven, then continued through two or three in the morning."* In the midst of this high disorder, Lagaillarde, who was incapable of sustained staff work, relied on spur-of-the-moment inspiration and did a lot of declaiming: he talked of training camps for OAS guerrillas in the Spanish countryside and anti-Gaullist short-wave broadcasts from Portugal. The heady talk usually occurred late at night, between two highballs, at his favorite nightclubs, l'Elefante Blanco and Parsifal; next morning, Spanish journalists who drank whisky at his expense discounted what they had heard.

Argoud meanwhile labored to define the OAS's political philos-

* Jean Gauvin, *Le Procès Vanuxem.*

ophy in a brochure he entitled "Algerian Problem—French Solution."

A secretariat was set up. The first pamphlets it issued hammered away at the idea that the struggle in Algeria would be meaningless unless accompanied by the overthrow of the Gaullist government at home—one of Argoud's pet theories.

This outpouring of energy was intended to establish Madrid as the Organization's capital-in-exile. Neither Argoud nor Lagaillarde showed enthusiasm for returning to Algeria to participate in a local battle; they wanted Salan to join them in Spain, where he would become a sort of counterpart of Ferhat Abbas in Tunis, presiding openly, without fear of arrest and away from the pressure of daily operations, over a vast politico-military effort. Argoud began writing in this vein to Algiers in August. With utmost seriousness he cited the example of Lenin, who had ". . . prepared the Russian revolution while living in France, Poland and Switzerland."

One can easily imagine Susini's uneasy reaction to this. It was bad enough for Salan to be off in the Mitidja, but to have him fly back to Madrid where he would come under Argoud's and Lagaillarde's influence was unthinkable. Perez and Gardy emphatically shared this view. Salan himself—apparently after some hesitation— decided against a new sojourn in Madrid, noting that he could not count automatically on the Spanish government's support. Salan spoke out of experience.

Franco was, in fact, still offering the activists superficial cooperation only. He was far from ready to allow them to establish a government-in-exile on Spanish soil; good ties with de Gaulle were far more important. Serrano Suñer alone remained faithful; he arranged for *ABC,* one of the capital's leading newspapers, to run favorable biographies of the activist leaders, and did what he could to offset hostility within the cabinet toward the Frenchmen. But their situation remained precarious.

And meanwhile a sterile tug of war was developing with Algiers.

With sublime self-confidence, Lagaillarde grandly ordered his former confederates in Algeria to submit an accounting of the Organization's finances and send him funds. He complained that he had been deliberately excluded from the OAS during the putsch. Although some money, surprisingly, was sent *le barbu,* to tide him over, the correspondence quickly developed an acrimonious undertone. Godard announced curtly that Lagaillarde was welcome to come and fight in Algiers, otherwise his complaints were of no interest. Susini derided him as a man building castles in Spain, blinded by the illusion that he could exercise power at a distance; but Susini also wrote a letter addressed to *"mon cher Pierre,"* carefully advising him to stay put in Madrid—there was no need to have still another rival in Algiers. Susini also contemptuously dismissed Argoud's brochure when it came out, and poured sarcasm on the author as a little man "perched on skinny legs like a falcon," more interested in theoretical ideas than their application.

To try to patch up some of these misunderstandings, Argoud in early August introduced to Lagaillarde the man who had hidden him outside Paris, Maurice Gingembre. The son of a wealthy family settled in Algeria for five generations, Gingembre had worked his way, at the age of thirty-five, to the vice-presidency of one family holding, the Djebel-Onk mines in eastern Algeria, which control the largest phosphate deposits in the world. Impressed with his own social standing, Gingembre was seized by an itch to plot that seems to have overtaken a marked number of French bourgeois as soon as their interests were threatened.

When Argoud and Lagaillarde asked him to handle top-level liaison between the three centers of conspiracy—Madrid, Algiers and Paris—and manage the Organization's finances, he was delighted, and agreed. In the next few weeks he traveled assiduously to Paris and Algiers. He carried secret reports and directives, but above all, in his suitcases he transported banknotes—funds contributed to the cause by his friends and social connections, right-wing French politicians and businessmen.

Algiers greeted the "Treasurer of the OAS" with mingled irritation and incredulity. They had had no voice in selecting him. Susini inwardly cursed Madrid for its frivolous choice—Gingembre was tall, glib and polished, with a marked taste for gossip—and the meeting between the two men, one burning with impatience to launch revolutionary mass action, the other dedicated to the preservation of solid bourgeois economic interests, was a classic case of incompatibility. Susini told his visitor nothing. Gingembre sought to tell him everything. They got nowhere.

Others, however, confided in Gingembre, if only because of the suitcases bulging with bundles of francs and pesetas. In this way, he learned a lot—with consequences that were disastrous.

Following his departure from Algiers in the spring, Sergent had set out to contact the various minuscule activist "*maquis*" and "networks" and "commandos" springing up throughout France. The next step, as he conceived it, was to impose his authority over them, in Salan's name. But in the southwest Sergent ran into trouble: the biggest local group, Maquis Résurrection-Patrie, formed of ex-Poujadist tradesmen, balked at taking orders from an outsider, and Sergent's inflexible parade-ground manner did not ease relations. Shopkeepers and Legionnaires made an unsatisfactory mix. The attempted takeover proved so heavy-handed that it drew the police's attention—so charged the angry leaders of Résurrection-Patrie; in one month's time, at any rate, several cells were identified and destroyed.[*]

Shortly afterward, Sergent announced that he was acting as "chief of staff of the Metropolitan OAS." The announcement caused consternation in Algiers. Sergent was thought of as a capable junior officer who could be useful in a subordinate role as a sector chief but was obviously out of his depth as Salan's personal representative in France. For that role, Salan and the others were seeking a man who possessed toplevel military and political contacts and no open affiliation with the far Right. As for Sergent, Salan faced the choice of disowning him, which meant negative publicity for the Organization, or living with his pronouncements. He chose the latter course.

Promoting oneself is one of the advantages of serving in an underground army.

At La Boisserie, his country house near Chaumont, de Gaulle that summer was not optimistic. The Algerian situation was stalemated. After Lugrin, official contact had been lost with the FLN, and there

---

[*] Résurrection-Patrie sprang up during the putsch, then spread through small and medium-sized towns of southwestern France. A triumvirate headed it: Marcel Bouyer, an ex-Poujade deputy and pastry cook who corresponded to the trite image of a jolly French *pâtissier;* Dr. Bernard Lefèvre, who established residence in Madrid; and Jacques Roy, a Navy reserve lieutenant. In June and July 1961, Bouyer, Lefèvre and Roy toured the area in a car, somewhat like an itinerant circus troupe, stopping where their fancy dictated and political sympathizers were reported present. Their arsenal consisted of the car, a typewriter, a radio transmitter, and a duplicating machine for turning out tracts. They had no real idea what to do with the transmitter.

Their tactical objective was to set up a redoubt in the Basque country, from which networks could spread across the rest of the country.

was no certainty that the Algerians wanted to maintain unpublicized, indirect links through the Swiss.

Almost daily de Gaulle threatened to regroup the European population around Algiers and Oran and evacuate the hinterland. "Once that's done," he told a group of deputies, "we may have a new crack at negotiations." This was de Gaulle at his most characteristic—obstinate with regard to the ultimate goal, but tacking and shifting to attain it, finding his way pragmatically, appearing to confide but in fact admitting no one into his full confidence. Bernard Tricot, his closely heeded adviser and one of the most intelligent men in the Gaullist government, knew that the president conceived of regrouping as the worst possible solution, but Tricot had no idea whether, if the stalemate persisted, he was prepared to apply it. And, he adds, neither did anyone else.

The explanation of the Lugrin failure came several weeks later. After meeting at Tripoli, Libya, in strict secrecy, the National Council of the Algerian Revolution, the seventy-two-man supreme body to which Krim and the other delegates were responsible, announced a major reshuffle: Ferhat Abbas was out as president of the Provisional Government, replaced by forty-one-year-old Ben Youssef Ben Khedda. A long-simmering struggle for power within the FLN had finally boiled over.

The French viewed the change with uneasiness. Ben Khedda, organizer of the terrorist networks of the Casbah, was reported cold and intransigent. In a bleak moment, de Gaulle wondered whether even if he gave way on the Sahara it would be enough to reach agreement with a suddenly tougher-seeming adversary. What de Gaulle did not realize at the time was that Ben Khedda had been grudgingly elected with a six-months' deadline to conclude peace. The FLN too was beginning to find that hostilities were dragging on unconscionably.

Chiefly, however, de Gaulle feared that the international situation might render his plans theoretical. In Vienna, Khrushchev had threatened to settle the Berlin problem one way or another before the close of the year; de Gaulle took the threat at face value, and told his entourage that a menace to world peace was developing—all the more so since the Soviet premier had informed Sir Frank Roberts, the British ambassador in Moscow, that six H-bombs would suffice to destroy the United Kingdom, and nine to annihilate France.

Other Frenchmen had other concerns.

Paris-Match polled its readers and discovered that they were interested in Berlin and Algeria, but almost equally in Brigitte Bardot and the recent marriage of Johann of Hohenzollern and Birgitta of Sweden. The magazine advertised a set of floating chairs for a host eager to serve guests cocktails in his swimming pool.

It was summer in Europe.

That summer afternoon—August 5—a burst of static on television sets throughout Algiers interrupted the one-o'clock news broadcast. As viewers stared, the picture faded from the screen, then after a minute's disconcerting silence a man's deep voice proclaimed: "This is Radio France . . . *l'OAS vous parle.*" It was reminiscent of the putsch. Military music followed. The screen remained dark. The same voice ordered: "Open your windows. Turn up your sets as loud as possible."

Pieds noirs came out on balconies, calling to one another, then hurried back in to listen.

Another man identified as General Gardy said something, apparently an appeal to the Army, but he was hardly audible.

The first man spoke again, clearly as though he were quite near. He enumerated the number of *plastiquages* carried out by the OAS in one month—380 in Algeria, a score in France—then he bragged of the execution of several traitors to French Algeria. The program ended with the "Marseillaise." The interruption had lasted a quarter hour.

The surprise was total, and the effect enormous. Europeans flocked into the streets, persuaded that Salan had seized power in a new putsch. Young officers lunching in the pleasant courtyard of their club in the old Janissaries barracks were urgently ordered by loudspeaker back to their posts. Police cars arrived sirens wailing at the radio studios at Rue Hoche. Tanks drove up around the Palais d'Été.

It was some time before regular broadcasting resumed.

An investigation revealed that saboteurs had blown up power lines that supplied the state-run TV and radio network; then broadcast on the television sound channel. The geography of Algiers spread around the half-moon bay permitted ideal reception. The Signal Corps Detection Service traced the broadcast to an illegal transmitter somewhere on the heights of El Biar, but there the trail ended.

Few in Algiers had actually heard the pirate broadcast, but within an hour the city was talking of nothing else. The government had been made a laughingstock: Joxe, the Algerian Affairs minister, had been sitting down to lunch with Délégation Générale officials when the interruption occurred. Next day, censors mishandled the pirate broadcast by forbidding any mention of it in Algiers' only remaining newspaper—which heightened the incident's importance in *pieds noirs'* eyes.

At very little risk, the OAS had scored a major psychological coup. Susini's Action Psychologique et Politique was off to a brilliant start.

Aided by Georges Ras, a former correspondent of *La Voix du Nord,* Susini followed up this exploit by issuing the first copy of *Appel de France,* the "newspaper of the OAS," a mimeographed sheet that exhorted its readers to "remain French on French soil." Susini laid down the editorial line; Ras grappled with the innumerable material problems of printing. Five thousand copies of *Appel* were run off; students dropped it free into letterboxes, sector captains distributed it among shopkeepers, and the newspaper was smuggled by train and truck into Oran.

Concurrently, the first issue of *Les Centurions* appeared—a four-page leaflet edited by Broizat and addressed to the Army. The unconcealed aim was to sow disobedience within the officer corps. From the authorities' point of view, the appearance of *Les Centurions* seemed less disturbing than the disclosure that military postal channels were being used to distribute it.

At the same time, Algiers was flooded by a tide of tracts, stickers, handbills, brochures and posters. At first Ras used a mimeograph machine concealed in a washhouse, then four offset machines which could be easily moved from one hideout to another; much later, what he referred to as his "heavy artillery," a 2,500-pound printing press. The essential purpose was to keep the three letters *O A S,* which still did not represent a program of action, a coordinated political force or an underground army, alive in the public eye.

The single most ambitious effort of this press campaign was a seventeen-page tract entitled "Who is Salan?" It purported to describe Salan's career, his motivations for giving up security and comfort for the hardships of clandestine opposition, and his ideas for the future. But for once, Susini and Ras's generally skillful touch deserted them altogether. The result was page upon page of fawning nonsense in which "Soleil" was depicted as a superhuman paragon of insight, depth and determination ("Salan knows more about the Algerian problem than any other man in the world. . . . Salan's patriotism is absolute.") Susini's ostensible purpose was to prove that his hero was superior to de Gaulle—a challenging proposition under the best of circumstances—but, in fact, "Who is Salan?" was a public-relations gesture aimed at identifying Salan with the OAS. Susini had a vital stake in getting this idea accepted. The tract was dispatched to newspaper officers in France, where it ended up in wastepaper baskets.

But if home opinion remained impervious to the OAS's shadowy leader, the *pieds noirs* increasingly threw their support behind a man they had decried, distrusted and at one time tried to liquidate. Up to a point, one can sympathize with their plight. Nearly seven years of warfare, terrorism, profiteering and brainwashing, a succession of dizzying turn-abouts in government policy, Army shilly-shallying had left them dazed. Whenever de Gaulle spoke, it gave them a fresh case of nerves.

Word spread that the OAS would stage a second putsch on August 15. The Feast of the Assumption, a holiday in French Algeria, fell that year on a Tuesday; another long weekend was in store, and every weekend was thought to be a propitious moment for Salan to come out of the Mitidja to the Europeans' rescue. Army headquarters nervously ordered several regiments' transportation taken away from them.

August 15 came and went without incident. The Organization had, in fact, never contemplated a putsch—it was still too weak for that; but it noted that the weekend scare was taken quite seriously.

Susini, Gardy, Godard and the others concluded that it was now imperative for Salan to return to Algiers. During his absence the OAS had taken root—it was raising funds, enlarging its ranks and developing professional propaganda; plastique explosions were soaring; and OAS signs were appearing for the first time on French highways. Among *pieds noirs* and even Moslems, the Organization was acquiring a reputation for toughness and purposefulness. The Délégation Générale appeared incapable of damming it.

The appearance, however, belied the reality. The OAS still possessed no coherent political platform, and its elaboration seemed less certain with each passing day. In the vacuum of leadership, Susini, Godard and Perez jockeyed for position. The movement threatened to break up into rival autonomous factions. No large-scale action could be undertaken until a recognized leader asserted his authority.

In early September they obtained satisfaction. Salan brusquely returned to Algiers. He did so because he was restive with the indolence, the isolation and the insecurity of his stay in the Mitidja. He was anxious to rejoin his family, whom he had seen only three times during the summer. And of course, word had drifted even into those remote farms of the OAS's growing force.

He returned, a good many pounds heavier, his silver hair unrecognizably darkened, sporting a thick coal-black mustache and a loud tie worthy, Susini said, "of a Mitidja farmer." It was a gross but effective disguise. Susini faltered at their first reunion in Ferrandi's apartment on Rue Auber, not sure that the flashily dressed, bullnecked man *was* Salan.

The most pressing requirement was to take the chaotic movement in hand. Salan bestirred himself for once with uncharacteristic speed. From a villa in El Biar, which was to be his hideout that fall, he issued Special Instruction No. 1, a confidential, six-page memorandum in which he laid down some basic guidelines.

"There must be only one and the same Organization for all of France and Algeria," he ordered. "It will be under my command and divided into two major branches: OAS/Métropole and OAS/Algeria-Sahara."

The memorandum dealt briskly with the Madrid group: ". . . I insist once again that Lagaillarde and Argoud find their place within the Organization, either in Algeria or in France. If they decide not to accept my offer, the same attitude must be adopted toward them as toward other isolated groups." He had already recommended ostracizing activist movements that failed to rally to the OAS banner.

Salan's Special Instruction No. 1, in a sense, betrayed more than he intended. By calling for a monolithic bloc and "unity of doctrine," he tacitly recognized that these objectives had not been attained. The memorandum's chief significance, however, lay in the terse announcement that he was forming an underground staff in France led by "Verdun," a general, and "Raphaël," a civilian. It meant that after the long summer interlude "Soleil" had revised his strategy and, in addition to resuming active leadership of the OAS in Algeria, was preparing to carry the fight to France.

11

A Hole in the Road

THE RED drapes parted, and he stepped out onto the podium, blinking owlishly. Seven hundred journalists rose to attention in the room, then resumed their seats amid a scraping of chairs. De Gaulle wore a navy-blue double-breasted suit. His hair was freshly cut and combed.

"I think we have some things to talk about," he said, his voice hoarse. Some thought he looked weary and disillusioned—it had been a trying summer.

The old-fashioned chandeliers flashed in the Salle des Fêtes, the ornate and fusty setting for presidential press conferences at the Élysée Palace.

He spoke about Berlin and Bizerte, but the statement that made news dealt with the Sahara. "If an Algerian state were constituted," rumbled de Gaulle, "the great majority of the Saharan population would want to belong to it. . . . Our line of conduct," he noted with the frankness only a very self-confident chief of state can afford, "is that which safeguards our interests and takes realities into account." He spelled out what these interests and realities were in the desert: oil and gas royalties, air bases and transit rights for French commercial flights to Black Africa. "The question of the sovereignty of the Sahara," droned de Gaulle, slightly hunching into the table microphone before him, "does not need to be considered, or at least it should not be considered by force." He could not altogether refrain from sarcasm: he referred to the passionate interest people "other than nomads, cave explorers and passing tourists" were suddenly showing in the Sahara since the discovery of oil.

The journalists seated on their precarious chairs took notes in utter stillness.

No matter how one cut it, de Gaulle's statement represented a sharp retreat from Lugrin. It was, thought Jean Mauriac, the long-time Agence France-Presse correspondent at the Élysée Palace, an "extraordinary chapter" in the Algerian denouement. At the time of the first Évian talks in May, de Gaulle had felt the Sahara could be negotiated separately, since the FLN was not implanted in depth in the desert. By September his view had changed; the FLN showed unexpected stubbornness about asserting its rights over the area, motivated by the prospect of oil royalties. But for the desert to bloom, thought de Gaulle, "we must invest much more in it"—and he was unwilling to do so.*

The rest of his remarks at the September 5 press conference contained very little balm for open wounds. He noted that the situation in Algeria, such as it was, could not last forever; but for the discomfited Europeans the only chill prospect he held out was regrouping and repatriation.

The Right reacted with tremendous indignation. At one stroke, almost casually, de Gaulle had abandoned France's claim to a vast area of prime strategic and mineral value. The Sahara was the last line of defense in preserving French Algeria, and it was crumbling virtually without opposition. The Rightist minority alone could do nothing to stop de Gaulle, and other parties showed no readiness to mount a parliamentary motion of censure.

Among activist networks, de Gaulle's apparent intention of resuming talks with the FLN appeared as a point of no return.

Three days later, two black Citroëns avoided the main gate of the Élysée Palace and drove out through a side exit on Avenue Marigny. There was no honor guard. The cars bore no special markings.

It was eight o'clock on a Friday evening.

---

* De Gaulle considered two other solutions for the Sahara: a Franco-Algerian "coprosperity sphere," rejected as a "brilliant but impractical idea"; and a Republic of the Sahara under Tuareg leadership, but it would have been defenseless and unviable.

The unobtrusive convoy was stopped frequently by weekend traffic and only picked up speed as it left the city behind and headed into open country.

The two cars drove east through Brie-Comte-Robert and toward Provins. They maintained a uniform speed of seventy-five miles an hour, the second car keeping some forty yards behind the first.

De Gaulle, bound for his country house at Colombey-les-Deux-Églises in the Haute-Marne department, sat in the first Citroën DS with Mme. de Gaulle and an aide-de-camp. Four men occupied the second limousine—two bodyguards, a young doctor doing a tour of military duty, and André Ducret, the head of Sécurité Présidentielle, the French Secret Service. The second car kept in intermittent radio contact with the Interior Ministry and *gendarmerie* posts in eastern France.

Beyond Nogent-sur-Seine the fields are flat and open, but here and there woods rise near the road's edge in dense array and delimit the tidy countryside.

By nine o'clock darkness fell.

A man stood at the woodside beside a car parked in a dirt road. He checked his watch, studied the highway two hundred fifty yards away through infra-red Navy field glasses, and waited, as he had waited every weekend during the past month, for the signal.

Ducret reflected, not for the first time, on the security problems that arose whenever *le patron* spent the weekend at Colombey-les-Deux-Églises. Ducret was not overly concerned about traffic jams between the Élysée Palace and the city limits. A would-be assassin could easily approach the car, to be sure, when it was stopped in rush-hour congestion—as it just had been—but if he made a threatening move, the chances were great of his being mowed down on the spot; and there were few kamikazes among the activists. Ducret worried more, once they found themselves on the open road. De Gaulle had ruled out a protective escort of more than one car on unofficial trips, and an ambush was always possible. It would have been a relatively easy matter to place the General in a different make of car each time but for his declared liking for the Citroën DS's hydraulic suspension. So Ducret, who was conscientious, fulfilled his responsibilities by sending decoy DS limousines along other roads, shuffling the seating arrangement inside the General's car and deciding upon the itinerary at the last moment. This time they were taking the most direct route, Nationale 19. Normally it was little more than a two-hour run to La Boisserie.

Ahead, the highway curved. On the right, a slight rise led to a wood whose outline Ducret made out indistinctly in the night.

Just off Route Nationale 19 stood a Highway Department sand pile deposited for use when roads are glazed with ice in fall and winter. Undetected, electric wires led from the sand pile across a field to the wood. The wire terminals were attached to four battries and a bell button.

The man peered nearsightedly through his field glasses. The headlights of a Peugeot parked out of sight behind a farmhouse near the curve in the road flashed twice. Immediately the man, with a slight sound of satisfaction, pressed down on the button.

The occupants of the second car saw a sudden, immense sheet of flame as high as the lowest tree branches bordering the road. The sheet abruptly shot across the entire width of the highway. Ducret in fascinated horror watched the red tail lights of the DS ahead vanish into the inferno. For a split second he thought the car's gas tank had blown up—he was sure de Gaulle was dead. His own car screamed to a lurching halt. After the first second's numbness, convinced now that it was a trap, he leaped out, ready to spray the road with his automatic pistol. The two bodyguards stood next to him. It only occurred to Ducret later that silhouetted against the white surging glow they made perfect targets for killers lying in ambush at the roadside. But except for the hissing flames, there was no sound at all—no sound of an explosion in the empty dark. In this eerie silence he realized that the first Citroën probably had emerged unscathed from the conflagration and streaked off at full speed to avoid a new attack.

There was a tremendous smoking crater in the center of the road.

Ducret shouted to his chauffeur to drive as fast as he could. They sped down the dark road without coming upon any sign of life. By radiotelephone Ducret ordered roadblocks set up throughout the Haute-Marne department. Twelve miles further on, in the village of

Romilly, they still saw no trace of the first car. But outside the village they spotted it parked before *gendarmerie* barracks, its right headlight smashed, scorched by smoke stains, windshield splattered with sand and gravel. The occupants, however, were uninjured. As Ducret rushed up, de Gaulle growled from the rear: "They didn't use perfume."

The man in the wood was in trouble. He had driven off without lights to avoid attracting attention, and his car was bogged down in a muddy ditch. Now he heard the faint sputter of an approaching motorbike.

The President's convoy was speeding to make up for lost time. As the lights of La Boisserie came into view, Ducret noted that they were only fifteen minutes behind schedule.

Daniel Pillet helped the stranger back his car out of the ditch. Then they went together to nearby Pont-sur-Seine. Pillet, a farm hand who had been returning home, found the other man somewhat overeager to thank him. A short while later, sipping his beer at the Café Degas, he listened to the excitement of other patrons who had just heard a special news bulletin. After a few minutes' thought Pillet slipped off to find the nearest gendarmes.

Weekend guests at La Boisserie—Lieutenant Philippe de Gaulle, the general's son, and his wife and three children—learned of the attack through the same radio flash. De Gaulle had not breathed a word of it upon his arrival.

When police later reconstituted the assassination attempt, they discovered what had gone wrong. The would-be assassins weeks before had concealed a five-gallon jerry-can of gas and a butane cylinder stuffed with eighty pounds of plastique under the sand pile. Electric wires connected to both containers led to a firing device in the woods. The gang had expected the car's occupants to plunge to their death in the huge crater torn out of the road surface by the exploding plastique but as an added precaution they had set the gas afire so that the car would be engulfed in flames. The planning was thorough: there was enough plastique, police said, to blow up the Pont de Tancarville, France's biggest suspension bridge. Each weekend the assassins had waited in vain; the convoy always chose another route; at the end of each weekend, to avoid detection, they transported the cylinder and the jerry-can back to Paris on the top of their Peugeot. In the process the plastique had settled. On the night of the attack, they hid the butane cylinder under the sand pile without realizing that it was no longer solidly packed, a layer of air had formed between the contents and the cylinder wall. When the spark was fired, the plastique did not explode but was hurtled in chunks across the highway. The chauffeur of de Gaulle's Citroën was driving fast enough to miss foundering in the hole in the road, and in the second before the gas ignited he sped out of danger.

Within an hour of the *attentat,* on the strength of Pillet's tip, police arrested the nearsighted man, a former radio announcer and intractable anti-Gaullist named Martial de Villemandy. Under questioning he identified the ringleader of the commando, Henry Manoury, and four other men. They turned out to be very small fry indeed—a used-car salesman, an electrician, an obscure airline employee, and a thug. All had carried out a number of earlier *plastiquages* and boasted of belonging to the OAS.

From Algiers, incongruously, came a prompt disclaimer. The OAS was not responsible for the attack and had no link with its perpetrators, Salan wrote stiffly to the editor in chief of *Le Monde,* adding with sour sarcasm: "I am not a regicide." Gardes issued a similar denial, foolishly bragging that the Organization had nothing to do with the attempt or it would have succeeded. Extreme Rightists in France launched a whispering campaign questioning the miraculous way in which the Citroën and its occupants had emerged intact from the fire, and insinuating it was all a sham engineered by the Élysée Palace to block a possible vote of no confidence over the Sahara. Some suggested that there were, in fact, two plots that converged: one a put-up affair in which French counterespionage agents maneuvered Villemandy, probably without his knowledge, and the other, an authentic attempt.

The contention that it was a hoax was raised at Manoury's and

Villemandy's trials.* Top government intelligence officials—Jacques Foccart, Alexandre Sanguinetti, and Colonel Pierre Fourcaud of SDECE—testified and denied it. The defense failed to prove its point. Setting off eighty pounds of plastique is a risky proposition; driving a car through a sheet of flame, still riskier—under the circumstances, no explosives expert could have guaranteed the car's safety. There seems no reason to credit these charges.

But, by the same token, no evidence was ever turned up to prove that the assassination order came from Algiers. Salan had received offers from would-be assassins eager to kill de Gaulle, but to all he said no; to do him justice, he was horrified by the idea—besides, he was seeking to win political allies who would be squeamish about outright murder. The colonels (with the exception of Godard) opposed the idea because they feared making a martyr of de Gaulle. Eight years later Sûreté officials are convinced the *attentat* was the work of a tiny group of activists operating autonomously in France, convinced they were striving for the same objectives as the OAS high command.

The Pont-sur-Seine attack nonetheless brutally focused France's attention on the OAS. It was the first criminal attempt on a French president's life since a Russian anarchist had assassinated Paul Doumer in May 1932. De Gaulle, who had taken little interest in the OAS except to prescribe more vigilance, revised his estimate of his enemies; it was plain that some activists were desperate enough to murder him to prevent Algerian independence. And, he told some ministers, if he disappeared France would be plunged into civil war between two extremes, Communism and neofascism. In the French press, the muffed assassination attempt led to a flurry of hostile editorials which pinned the blame on Salan and the colonels. Newspapers made the point that never before had France seen high-ranking officers ready to murder one of their own, a companion of St.-Cyr days. One could disagree as much as one wanted to with de Gaulle, the editorialists from Left to moderate Right concluded, but to try to kill him was something else again.

Thus, due to a crime it had probably not perpetrated, the OAS overnight became a national front-page problem.

* Tried a year later, Manoury was condemned to twenty years' imprisonment, the others received lesser sentences. Two other men took part in the plot, apparently serving as lookouts who alerted the commando to the convoy's departure from the Élysée Palace—they were identified in court simply as "Germain" and "Aubry," and are alleged to have participated in the later attack against de Gaulle at Petit-Clamart in August 1962.

12

The Order of the Day

GINGEMBRE WAS arrested that month. His arrest followed a curious blunder by Godard, the professional intelligence officer who seldom blundered.

In early September Algiers police during a routine search came upon some of Gardes's correspondence; this discovery led them to raid the apartment of a young Frenchwoman demobilized from the Army, Captain Noëlle Luchetti, Salan's former secretary in Indochina, who was living in the suburb of St.-Eugène under the name Paschetti and acting as a liaison agent and letter drop. Here police found more OAS documents, including a message from Godard; in one passage he mentioned—for some reason—Gingembre by name. The police promptly set out to exploit this break.

The "treasurer of the OAS" was in Paris, preparing a new trip to Algiers. He saw de Blignères and Sergent, who gave him letters for Salan; then on September 7, a courier brought additional confidential documents which Gingembre stuffed into his briefcase just a few hours before flight time. By now, the Paris police had picked up his trail. They planned to shadow him to Algiers in the hope that he would meet a high-ranking member of the Organization, hopefully Salan himself. In this they were not far from the mark, for this was precisely Gingembre's intention. But at the very start the plan misfired: at Orly, an unwitting airport inspector overzealously checked

Gingembre's baggage and aroused his suspicions. Realizing that he would now try to give them the slip, the police canceled their original arrangements and alerted *gendarmerie* Colonel Jean Debrosse, who through coincidence was traveling on the same Air Algérie flight.

As soon as the Caravelle was airborne, Gingembre—by this time decidedly on edge—sought out a crew member he knew, appealed to his "patriotism," and tried to conceal his briefcase in the forward cabin. Seeing what was going on, Debrosse stepped in, confiscated the hand baggage, and as the plane touched down at Maison Blanche airport arrested the industrialist. Gingembre shouted to several acquaintances on the field that he was being illegally held, that he was loyal to the OAS . . . His intention apparently was to give the alarm; waiting police cut short the tirade, and drove him blindfolded to *gendarmerie* headquarters at the Caserne des Tagarins.

Word of Gingembre's arrest immediately reached the Organization's leaders, among whom the first reaction was one of almost positive relief. "He can do less harm inside prison than out," observed Susini. In this he proved wrong.

To begin with, the documents in Gingembre's possession listed names and addresses of letter drops in the Paris area; they also included secret instructions from Madrid. One report, "Coordination III," dealt with Godard's tactic of waging subversive war primarily in Algiers. All this was of considerable interest to the police. During the summer they had possessed only fragmentary—and often inaccurate—information about the new movement. The material in Gingembre's briefcase afforded police their first real insight into the Organization's strength, intentions and inner rivalries.

Meanwhile, in the hands of experienced police interrogators, the "treasurer of the OAS" talked—and talked.

He began by informing nonplused inspectors: "I don't mind answering your questions. In three months' time you'll be in my place and I'll be in yours." His captors refrained from arguing the point, and jotted down everything he said. It developed that he had a good deal to say; and as a result of his disclosures, a wave of arrests occurred within forty-eight hours in Paris. At dawn police broke into the apartment of the former deputy commander in chief of French forces in Germany, General Paul Vanuxem, and charged him with being Salan's personal military representative in France—

the mysterious "Verdun." Simultaneously they apprehended General Jean-Marie de Crèvecoeur, a former infantry division commander erroneously thought to be "Raphaël"* De Blignères, accused of being "Balance," the OAS's chief of staff in the capital, was likewise arrested.

In the next two weeks, Debrosse pressed home the first major anti-OAS offensive in Algeria. Noëlle Luchetti was arrested, and Ferrandi, who lived in a room on the same landing, narrowly escaped capture. Godard almost came to grief while hiding in the clothes closet of an apartment on Rue Michelet during a raid: as gendarmes rummaged among the clothes, a police dog sniffed tobacco in the air and sneezed, but somehow, the colonel was not caught. Networks in western Algeria—in Orléansville, Mostaganem, Tiaret and Vialar—were smashed. Several hundred suspects were detained. Comparing the crackdown to an "earthquake," Susini later wrote: "The OAS general staff as a whole was almost arrested. Liaison was broken off; some of our agents abruptly disappeared; for two weeks the wheels of the Resistance stopped turning. We barely escaped total disaster."

Friends subsequently argued that Gingembre, far from cracking, did a masterful job of stalling for time, withholding crucial information and revealing only what the police already knew. Up to a point this was true. Susini himself, who could hardly be accused of indulgence toward Gingembre, laid blame for the crackdown essentially on overconfidence and a relaxation of security measures, which had permitted double agents to penetrate the Organization. But Gingembre's disclosures were catastrophic enough; the repercussions were especially marked in France.

Vanuxem, an articulate and chubby general known for his *Algérie française* views, energetically denied that he was Verdun. He told the police that he had never belonged to or led a clandestine network, that he had entertained no direct dealings with Salan although sympathizing with his ideas. To be Verdun, according to Vanuxem, would have implied three things: a firm offer, an acceptance on his part, and a plan of action. None of the three, he said, existed. In time, the Cour de Sûreté de l'État acquitted him of the charge, and to this day Vanuxem denies that he was Verdun. But the fact remains that, following his arrest, further reference to Verdun in OAS

---

* He was freed at the end of the month. "Raphaël" was later identified as a high Finance Ministry official, but was never prosecuted.

correspondence ceased, and no other general was ever identified under the pseudonym.*

Salan's first serious attempt to set up a parallel underground structure in France had collapsed before fairly getting underway. From this point on, the OAS in France lagged far behind Algiers and was left temporarily at Sergent's mercies. Gingembre's arrest also destroyed one major link between Algiers and Madrid.†

The question that persists is, Why did Godard leave Gingembre's name *en clair*? According to Gingembre, Godard's message contained detailed biographical information about the "treasurer of the OAS," and was in seven copies; there was thus a reasonable chance that one copy would find its way into official hands. Godard, Susini and Perez were seeking at this moment to prevent Salan's departure for Spain, and Gingembre's ties with the Madrid group may have struck them as dangerous. Susini, moreover, considered him a hopeless amateur conspirator and a security threat. Godard himself later explained that he attached little importance to Gingembre's activities; but this scarcely explains why he flouted minimum security precautions.

In Algiers, the offensive petered out. Liaison was quickly reestablished. The Organization realized that, in fact, not a single one of its leaders was in prison, and the network was secure. The receding threat prepared the way psychologically for a new effort.

From mid-September, although nothing went wholly right, the OAS gained strength every day. Its impetus was too great, thought Godard, who said to Salan: "We're going up like a balloon; we may get shot down." Salan did not reply.

Godard had carved up Algeria into three major regions corresponding to Army Corps areas, Constantinois, Algérois and Oranie; Algiers itself, as has been noted, into six sectors. The sectors, in turn, were divided into subsectors, quarters and blocks—the latter entrusted to a block leader (*chef d'îlot*), a militant who was made responsible for overseeing all inhabitants and reporting back to the Organization; it was an ideal totalitarian tool for intelligence-gather-

---

* Shortly after Vanuxem's acquittal in September 1963, a letter by Argoud strongly hinted that he belonged to the OAS; in another letter, Sergent categorically stated that Vanuxem was "Verdun."

† Two years, to the day, after his arrest, Gingembre was sentenced to ten years' imprisonment.

ing, intimidation and plain snooping.* It gives some idea of the OAS's expansion that by late September one militant, Axel Nicol, estimated that the work of organizing the lower-class neighborhoods was "sixty percent complete"—which meant that the Organization exercised some sort of control over three out of five *pieds noirs* in a building, a street, a block.

Before World War II, Bab el Oued had voted Communist, while Belcourt was considered a Socialist stronghold; but in the fall of 1961 traditional political and social ties were repudiated in an atmosphere of panic as the late-dawning realization sank in that the unthinkable, independence, *could* happen. Arrests showed that the Organization was most virulent in former extreme-Left districts. There was nothing fundamentally inconsistent about this; the *petits blancs* were afraid—generally afraid of being forced to choose between "a suitcase and a coffin," as FLN propaganda reiterated, and specifically afraid of expropriation, rape and disembowelment in the event of a Moslem takeover. And so they rallied behind a Rightist standard as the fearful lower classes of Germany did to the Nazi party for protection from the Bolshevik ogre. The bourgeoisie showed less enthusiasm; they dutifully paid dues to the OAS, signed petitions and distributed subversive leaflets; but that was all. Few became Deltas. The flight of subterranean capital went on uninterrupted.† There was a world of difference between being actively of the OAS (*"il est de l'OAS"*) and simply pro-OAS (*"il est OAS"*).

The OAS was not a political party in the open: no one joined it formally; some contributed to it; some carried explosives; most

* The idea derived from the Nazi party's system of *Kreisleiter, Ortsgruppenleiter* and *Blockleiter*. The French Fourth Republic had recklessly instituted more or less the same system during the Battle of Algiers and dubbed it "DPU" —Dispositif de Protection Urbaine. Godard had played a role in setting it up.

† An OAS tract was issued forbidding this flight of capital. As happens in these cases, modest-income groups took the prohibition seriously; its effect on the wealthy was to incite them to put their money where it would be reasonably safe, that is, outside Algeria. The OAS would have found it difficult to exercise effective control over this movement of funds. The Constantine Plan provided for transfer of profits back to the mainland. It was extremely difficult to determine whether a company was transferring funds for its own use or that of its principal officers. The Banque Française du Commerce Extérieur was often used for these transfers; so, too, the Banque d'Algérie, in spite of the well-known OAS sympathies of some of its directors.

Revealingly, many modest-income *pieds noirs* knew what was happening and approved, saying they would have done the same with their own money if they had any. This to the fury of some OAS chiefs like Susini, who regarded the bourgeoisie's self-seeking attitude as just short of treason.

worked for it only as actively as they saw fit. Since there was no political program, each read into it what he wanted; the sole common denominator was the will to preserve French rule. The *pieds noirs* put their faith in the Organization because it was run by officers, it possessed arms and it boasted of its willingness to fight to the last man; because it existed and no other movement did; because they thought it could do something and hoped that it would gain world attention by using the same terrorist methods as the FLN. There is nothing quite as impervious to common sense as wishful thinking.

Pirate broadcasts were now a weekly feature of Algiers life. *Gendarmerie* helicopters hovered over the city, unsuccessfully attempting to pinpoint the exact site of the transmitter. The broadcasts themselves showed more skill; they featured jazz, patriotic airs, and a gong striking out *"Algérie française"* to mark important announcements. On September 21, an anonymous speaker called on the *pieds noirs* to demonstrate on four different days to show their support of the Organization.

The first such demonstration, a night-long casserole concert, was a success. The *pieds noirs* made an enormous din, shouting, screaming, klaxoning, thumping tables and exploding firecrackers. A visitor might have thought that the grimy downtown districts near the port were celebrating. In fact, they were letting off steam. The uproar lasted until midnight. In the Moslem quarters there was utter silence.

A fortnight later, the *pieds noirs* with equal enthusiasm followed instructions to create monster traffic jams at noon in the heart of the city; a general-strike call was likewise obeyed. But it was a different matter when the Organization ordered Europeans to show the new OAS flag, a black-and-white affair emblazoned with a Celtic cross-within-a-circle. On the scheduled day, September 25, many *pieds noirs,* particularly in bourgeois neighborhoods, put out only the legally permissible tricolor.

It could be concluded that when the danger of individual reprisals existed, the *pieds noirs* showed little stomach for defiance. Still, the psychological campaign was considered a marked success, it had united the Europeans and the OAS more closely than ever.

A *pied noir* mother in Algiers was principally conscious of "hatred in the air." . . . She saw women standing in the street half crazy, shouting insults at soldiers and sobbing. In Bab el Oued, Europeans booed night patrols advancing up the street, shining searchlights on the balconies. And at posthumuous ceremonies for a young lieutenant killed by an FLN mine, an officer began: *"Au nom du président de la République,"* and got no further, drowned out by catcalls. The radio was on everywhere, all the time, she wrote in her diary;[*] the *pieds noirs* pretended not to listen to the state-run radio, but in fact they did, eagerly awaiting bulletins. The windows were open all night as they waited for something important to happen that would change the course of events.

In early October, with mingled relief and forboding, they heard a familiar, slow-speaking, Midi-warmed voice announce during a pirate broadcast: ". . . all Algerians are or will be mobilized. By the end of the year, an army of one hundred thousand men will exist. Victory is certain!"

It was Salan.

Salan no longer believed in an immediate popular insurrection, which was likely foredoomed—or, for that matter, in *Algérie française* as such. He had quietly dropped this concept in favor of a "Federated Algeria" which would enjoy some autonomy but would retain links with the French Republic. As the situation evolved, so did his objectives. He favored continuous harassment of the enemy, attrition that would wear down the Gaullist government instead of the seizure of vital centers, until some of the Army—the Foreign Legion and the paratroopers—shifted its weight in the *pieds noirs'* favor. It would require time; but since the breakdown of cease-fire negotiations he thought time was working for the OAS. It was to be a major miscalculation.

Wrote one French correspondent: "The OAS's ambition was not so much to win clandestine war through effective counterterrorism as to bring round a lukewarm, purged and broken-up Army to its side . . . in the name of a program in which the Army no longer believed —integration."[†] This was true enough. In addition, Salan wanted to gain the support of anti-Gaullist political parties at home.

This reflected Susini's thinking. Susini emphasized that he was ready to make common cause "even with the devil"—he meant the

[*] The material in this paragraph is taken from Francine Dessaigne, "Journal d'une mère de famille pied-noir," *Écrits de Paris*, March, 1962.

[†] Gilles Mermoz in *Écrits de Paris*, October–November 1962.

Communists—to save French Algeria. More practically, he thought in terms of a broad spectrum of opposition ranging from the Socialists to the OAS. So, as part of a full-fledged political offensive, Salan dispatched appeals to the opinion makers of France—its influential prefects, deputies, mayors, municipal councilors and bishops. Poor Salan! There was something grotesque about this elderly general on the run firing off one missive after another from his whitewashed villa hideout in El Biar, in the hope of creating a countercurrent of opinion. Letters were bound to be no more effective than Challe's plaintive telephone calls to the regimental commanders, but from the battlefield of Algiers, as a fugitive from the police, Salan's possibilities of legitimate political action were, to say the least, limited. Godard insisted that the General needed a representative in France, but that project had already failed. And there was his unquenchable need to communicate with the legally vested authorities of France —he could not lightly overcome his career-long training to work through republican institutions. Becoming a revolutionary at sixty is not simple.

The tone of the letters was studiously moderate. Salan—or rather Susini, who authored most of them—tailored the message to the audience. The Church was told that the OAS's prime purpose was the defense of Christian values against the Marxist threat; the mayors, that the defense of "fundamental freedoms" (whatever this meant) was at stake. In Algeria itself, appeals were directed to the Moslems in Arabic, and to the Jewish minority. The underlying aim was to reassure—to present the Organization as a selfless and patriotic movement committed to the victory of a higher cause.

"The OAS is not a party," Salan wrote, noting that his purpose was neither to set up a de facto provisional government in Algeria nor to impose a government by force on the mainland. There was, after all, a Constitution . . . He was all the keener on making these points after the embarrassment of the Pont-sur-Seine *attentat*. What, then, was the OAS? "One belongs to the OAS," the letter concluded tersely, "as one belonged to the Resistance."

This was to be the leitmotif for the coming months—the deliberate parallel with the underground struggle of the French against a wartime occupation force. It arbitrarily overlooked the fact that, in one case, the force was foreign and, in the other, not, nonetheless it would pose a touchy emotional challenge for de Gaulle's government.

Perez's clandestine headquarters were in Robertsau, near the Pont du Télémly, a middle-class *pied noir* residential district; Degueldre's command post, a scant hundred yards away in L'Algérie, an office building on Boulevard Saint-Saëns. Each morning, one man or the other struck out on foot past police checkpoints to reach the other's hideout. Perez swaggered through these streets without much fear—in this neighborhood he was virtually unknown; it was not like Bab el Oued, where Arabs and Europeans alike recognized him. Degueldre, totally committed, went abroad armed, equipped with counterfeit identity papers, unconcerned about arrest—a tough, leathery, grimly intent blue-eyed figure whom, for some reason, no gendarme stopped. The two men remained together in a sunny room three and four hours at a time, discussing tactics of a special sort.

O.R.O.'s job was to identify the Organization's enemies, obtain tactical information about their movements and habits, seek them out and murder them. However, gathering such information about the city's Moslems and European liberals and Gaullists within the police and Army—which was what the job amounted to—was a staggering undertaking only a professional intelligence service could effectively cope with. O.R.O. was a makeshift creation. It possessed neither sufficient time nor expertise, as Perez realized, to attempt classic espionage; there was no question, for instance, of recruiting a network for long-term penetration of the Délégation Générale. O.R.O. opportunistically gathered facts from employees "in place" who happened to sympathize with the Organization's goals; the *pied noir* mistress of a Sûreté official was a case in point. Strongly pro-OAS in her views, she proved to be a knowledgeable source about every aspect of the department's activities and passed on all she knew. However, she was an exception. Postmen, gas and electricity inspectors, telephone linesmen and switchboard operators volunteered tidbits; their efforts were well-meaning but amateurish. A secret group within the Army provided news of transfers and troop movements, as well as leads about "traitor" officers engaged on anti-OAS missions. Perez's files bulged with information—most of it, by his own admission, uncorrelated.

He turned all this material over to Degueldre for action. Punitive sorties by Delta commandos generally followed.

Each Delta commando consisted of six or seven men—in OAS

jargon, *opérationnels*. A twisted pride came into play here. A man who carried out assassination, sabotage, armed attacks on road-blocks would call himself an *opérationnel;* a fund raiser did not. An *opérationnel* prided himself on killing only on the basis of written orders from Degueldre (orders generally being hastily type-written scraps of paper). Theoretically, thirty Delta commandos were available; in fact, at the height of the OAS's power, twenty-three existed, of which Degueldre's hand-picked favorite was Delta One—the team that had killed Gavoury.

Degueldre ruled over this dangerous force by dint of concentra-tion, threats and personal example. He arranged hideouts and dis-tributed assignments, organized a motor pool, even procured one or two military vehicles (forging double sets of license tags and regis-tration papers to confuse the police), but above all he furnished ammunition and arms—revolvers, submachine guns, automatic pistols and bazookas pilfered from Army stores.

In all this he persevered with a certain illogical grim single-mindedness. He felt no particular liking or esteem for the *pieds noirs;* like Susini, he wanted to make revolutionaries out of them and swiftly discovered that it was impossible. Out of touch for days with any OAS leaders but Perez (whom he resented), darkly suspecting that he was being left out of the bigger picture (which he was), Degueldre went through periods of black gloom. He demanded a different, more responsible role in the Organization; but Susini, his only real ally, was in no position to obtain it for him over Godard's objections. The colonel cited Degueldre's troublesome pre-Foreign Legion background and his reputation for extremist politics, both of which could be an embarrassment to the Organization, and con-cluded that he could not be entrusted with broader responsibilities. (There was always some subjective distrust on Godard's part to-ward anyone who hit it off too well with Susini.) So, from first to last, Degueldre's thankless task would be to handle the dirty work —the execution of enemies.

By September, the commandos were operational. And terrorism spurted.

In Belcourt, a Moslem boy lingered a second too long at a street corner with friends. A car passed and slowed down, drove off, turned and came back. The boy realized that the *pieds noirs* inside were taking their time to decide which Moslem group—his or one across the street—presented a better target. As the thought occurred to him, the car opened fire on the first group. The boy was hit six times, but survived.

Police Inspector Alexey Goldenberg drove back from the Délégation Générale through the Tunnel des Facultés in rush-hour traffic. A motorcycle with two men roared up alongside his small car. The man on the back seat slipped a gun out of his jacket and fired point-blank. Goldenberg slumped at the wheel, dead, and the car crashed into a wall of the tunnel.

In September the OAS killed fifteen and wounded 144. Salan was saying one thing in his letters to France and doing quite another.

Fall comes far differently to the Île de France than, for example, to the East Coast of America. There is no Indian summer, no riot of color heralding brilliant winters. Northern France's exemplary season is spring; autumn is lackluster, decay gnaws at the somber countryside, melancholy rains seep into Paris.

It was on these overcast October days that the OAS made inroads into Parisians' daily life. Businessmen received the visit of fund raisers, who "taxed" them up to $20,000 to share the burden of the struggle in Algeria; in most cases the businessmen paid. The three talismanic letters O A S dripped black paint on school walls. Night drew down swiftly, and Parisians learned to recognize the dull *whoosh* of plastique blasts after dark. One night a black OAS flag was surreptitiously hoisted atop one of Notre Dame's bell towers, and created a scandal next morning since it flew in full view of the neighboring police prefecture.

The Left clamored for the government to take action. At a Socialist party national congress in suburban Puteaux on September 28, Marseilles' mayor Gaston Deferre, a politician never noted for restraint, thundered: "The OAS has acted with impunity . . . the only way to subdue them is to kill them—hang or shoot them. . . . Our duty is to combat them with a maximum of violence." The outburst, surprisingly enough among these peace-loving Socialists, drew prolonged applause.

As the OAS moved closer home, the Left could draw cold comfort from the fact that, long before the government, it had denounced the danger.

The government *was* taking action, but of a limited and cautionary nature. It had cracked down on anti-Gaullist networks in southwestern France and rounded up the Pont-sur-Seine gang. A general housecleaning of Algiers' police force began in earnest; 157 policemen were stricken from the rolls or suspended from duty, and in the lot were a dozen criminal inspectors. Anyone who knows the stability of employment in the French bureaucracy and the years of service it takes to attain the rank of inspector can appreciate the scope of these sanctions. The purge, however, obviously did not strike deep enough. Except at the top, the police in France—the criminal police, the Renseignements Généraux, the DST* charged with combating internal espionage—remained stubbornly sympathetic to the cause of *Algérie française* and, in consequence, the OAS.

This was not surprising: for the past six years many police officers had concentrated entirely on anti-FLN operations; moreover, Moslem terrorist attacks on police stations in Paris had not endeared the cause of Algerian independence to the police. A total turnabout in its attitude could not be hoped for at once. As a result, OAS militants taken under arrest were sometimes astounded by the favored treatment or outright complicity they encountered: contacts with lawyers were facilitated, they were given help in dictating statements as unincriminating as possible, and they received tactful offers of assistance in escaping. Worse, some police steadily leaked information to Sergent's expanding network.

While the Left criticized the government for not acting firmly enough against the OAS, the Right charged no action was being taken against FLN killers in France. This was far from true; the government held an estimated nine thousand Algerians in prison, half of them for political offenses; but it was equally true that Moslem terrorism was a cruel and widespread problem. The FLN since the start of the year had killed perhaps five hundred and wounded seven hundred in Metropolitan France, mostly attacking uncooperative fellow Moslems, who were found shot and strangled in sacks; but it also murdered French soldiers and policemen.

* Défense et Surveillance du Territoire.

The government, in the last analysis, was attempting to steer a careful course between what it considered two perils. De Gaulle himself remained as suspicious of the Left's effort to exploit the OAS threat as he did of the Right's perennial plotting. In this situation the major question mark, once again, was the Army's attitude and intentions.

The Army of Algeria's new commander in chief, General Charles Ailleret, correctly estimated upon assuming his command in the summer of 1961 that the military battle against the FLN was won. The reason for the Army's strong presence in Algeria had been to fight the FLN in the field; this had been done. The political problem of Algeria's future, he reasoned, did not concern the Army.

Upon proclamation of the unilateral truce, two divisions were withdrawn from the countryside. Ailleret's boss, National Defense Minister Pierre Messmer—whom the OAS mocked as the Minister of National Debacle—issued a nervous communiqué: "The new combat in Algeria is a peaceful combat. It supposes total discipline, which will demand of cadres abstraction of their personal feelings. . . ."

This was asking a good deal in the Army's present disgruntled mood. Unlike Ailleret, many officers saw the war as far from over—and the divisions' recall as a disastrous opportunity for the *fellaga* to enjoy a breathing spell and regroup. The recrudescence of Moslem terrorism seemed to bear out this argument.

The Army of Algeria's hostility to a cease-fire was far from being wholly idealistic. The Foreign Legion equated Algerian independence with its own demise as a fighting unit; it looked without relish upon the prospect of being transferred to vest-pocket colonies like French Somaliland. The elite paratroop units were in danger of losing their privileged status, higher pay, better equipment and distinctive uniforms. Throughout the military establishment a lively worry existed that upon termination of the war quick promotions and other advantages would suffer; in a new, nuclear-minded service, the deadwood risked being eliminated drastically.

By September, Military Security estimated that twenty percent of the officer corps were sympathetic to the OAS, between eight and ten percent firmly opposed to it, and an overwhelming seventy percent neutral. The Army in its vast majority, however, was loath to condemn former fellow officers and emphatically unwilling to smash the Organization.* This attitude permeated even the Armed Forces Ministry in Paris, which considered its task limited to transferring unreliable officers out of Algeria (usually to West Germany) and, through appeals to their sense of honor and loyalty, preventing others from deserting. The Army maintained that the OAS, as such, and its civilian leaders constituted a criminal problem for the Interior Ministry.

Ailleret's main preoccupation at this moment was to pull back an army scattered in five thousand outposts throughout Algeria, assure frontier defenses until a political settlement was reached, and maintain order. For the moment, the last of these responsibilities was confined largely to the 20,000-man *gendarmerie*, whose principal function it was anyway.† Field troops were neither equipped nor psychologically trained to cope with street riots and urban terrorism; Ailleret's policy was to keep them in reserve, outside the cities wherever possible, to avoid incidents. The real danger, he judged, lay not in the OAS's military power, which was nil, but in its psychological grip on the European population. If the trend continued, the Organization could call infuriated *pieds noirs* into the streets and stage a mass uprising, in which event the Army would be forced to intervene. Lieutenant Bernard Ridard, a young officer serving on Ailleret's staff, has recalled that at messes in the fall of 1961, over and over again the same blunt question was asked: "If a column of French armor is ordered into Algiers to quell a European insurrection, will the lead tank fire?" There was no convincing answer.

But the government's policy hinged necessarily on the answer. To provide one, Ailleret issued an order of the day on September 20

* The exception, in the ranks, was the underground OCC (Organisation Clandestine du Contingent), a loose-knit conglomeration of trade-unionists, Catholic Youth militants and a sprinkling of Communists that sprang into being after the putsch. As its name indicates, it recruited mostly among draftees; cells made use of civilian, not military, channels to communicate with each other. The OCC stressed surveillance of activist officers, and planned to neutralize them in the event of another putsch. The OAS jeered at the OCC as the "Organisation Communiste du Contingent." It claimed to have seventy secret cells in the French Army.

† The *gendarmerie* in France is a paramilitary force under the Armed Forces Ministry. It breaks down into stationary and mobile units—the latter possess their own transport including helicopters, scout cars and light tanks, and are trained to carry on both police and military duties in cities and open country. They stand halfway between urban police and army regiments. General Bernard Cherasse in Algeria had 8,000 stationary gendarmes, 4,000 auxiliaries (mostly Moslems), and 8,000 *gendarmes mobiles* at his disposal—the last he considered his operational spearhead.

committing the French Army alongside the police to fight the "so-called OAS." The commander in chief castigated the movement as a subversive group seeking to overthrow republican institutions through terrorism and civil war.

Ailleret's order of the day marked a turning point. It left no room for further convenient areas of ambiguity in officers' attitude. This was its underlying purpose—remove military complicity, Ailleret reasoned, and the OAS would stall. It is interesting to note that the government and the Organization were not far apart in their views. Salan recognized the Army's prime importance to his schemes, and so did Ailleret.

The order of the day caught many regimental and divisional headquarters by surprise. It hardly changed any officers' ideas, but it put the vast majority on notice that they could no longer indulge in the luxury of biting the hand that fed them: if they continued henceforth to aid the Organization, they knew they were going against specific orders; if they remained neutral, their careers might conceivably suffer from their lukewarm attitude. It was an argument that carried considerable weight.

The OAS reacted violently. Susini's propaganda service reviled the order of the day as "a monument of bad faith" and a "proclamation of civil war." Two days later, a bomb blew up in the doorway of Algiers' downtown Hotel Oasis, where numerous Army Corps personnel habitually stayed, killing a major—the first French officer in uniform to fall victim to that other, underground army.

13

A Farewell to Algiers

SPAIN'S FOREIGN MINISTER Fernando Maria Castiella noted with mounting exasperation that suddenly Madrid had become a haven for French activists of every stripe—for far too many, he concluded. After meeting with some and seeing them at work, he was convinced that they enjoyed no chance of winning their impassioned but unrealistic struggle against de Gaulle. Moreover, they were a nuisance; after the abortive Pont-sur-Seine attempt, another OAS commando had left Madrid with the intention of killing de Gaulle and had been intercepted at the frontier. The effect on Franco-Spanish relations was deplorable.

Certainly Spain could hope to gain more from the government in Paris than from a group of illegal and mercurial activists. Specifically, a trade agreement which it regarded as highly profitable was about to be signed. At a bimonthly cabinet meeting on Friday, October 6, Castiella boiled it down to a choice: the arrest of the Madrid group's leaders, or his resignation.

It would be an exaggeration to state that the fate of the exiles around the Bernabeu stadium became a hotly debated issue at the cabinet meeting. Argoud, Lagaillarde and the others simply did not seem that important. The Spanish Army, secret service and police, all of whom had facilitated Salan's departure during the putsch, still showed interest in the activists' ideas. The Falange certainly favored their goals—but the Falange itself was out of favor with

Franco. Serrano Suñer's influence bordered on the negligible. Many key positions in the government were in the hands of *Opus Dei* members, liberal Catholics who were hostile to the OAS. And Franco's influential deputy, Captain-General Muñoz Grande, had no special liking for the movement.

Whether Castiella really meant to resign is beside the point; the cabinet deferred without much trouble to his point of view.

At eleven o'clock that night (cabinet meetings, like meals, begin and end late in Spain), the police received orders to submit a full report at once on the exiles' activities. The order reached the euphemistically named Social Brigade, which was entrusted with surveillance of the group. The chief of the Brigade, who maintained extremely cordial relations with the Frenchmen, assumed that the request was a routine administrative measure. He had no reason to believe any unusual action was contemplated.

At midnight, he received a rude jolt when further orders came to round up the activists and place them under arrest within the next half hour.

That they were conspicuous was undeniable. Sympathizers and volunteers had flooded into the capital during the late summer, making no attempt to conceal their comings and goings, and hinting broadly at the subversive missions for which the four apartments served as an operational base. Dr. Lefèvre himself felt that everybody showed far too little discretion—"Another month," he recalled later, "and our name would have appeared in the phone book like any other business firm."

The exiles were aware of a remarkable procession of cars passing and parking in Calle Concha Espina, and they knew their movements were being filmed, and not only by the Spanish police. French counterespionage agents blandly made little attempt to conceal their interest.*

* French agents were dispatched to Madrid and coordinated anti-OAS action directly with the Spanish Interior Ministry, bypassing the French Embassy. They received instructions when necessary through the French consulate, a customary tactic in such cases and not confined to the French alone.

In its search for good relations with Paris, the Spanish government had closed down an FLN office in 1957. In 1961, more or less openly, the FLN maintained a two-man office inside the Tunisian Embassy in Madrid. OAS and FLN agents stalked and killed one another in Algiers, but ignored each other in neutral Madrid.

The group did not take alarm. From pro-OAS employees within the French Embassy, Lagaillarde and Argoud learned in the fall that some sort of police crackdown was imminent. They took no action to protect themselves, partly because the Embassy had cried wolf too often, partly, it would appear, through overconfidence in the Spanish government's laziness and reluctance to make an issue over their presence in the capital. Lagaillarde continued to overrate Serrano Suñer's influence. The group went ahead with plans to concentrate all its operations in the four apartments.

One of the few who took the Embassy tip to heart was Lefèvre. The day before moving into Calle Conche Espina, he received a fresh warning from Spanish Falangist friends. He heeded it and remained in the inconspicuous household where he had been living.

The Social Brigade made a near-clean sweep that night. They found Lagaillarde in a neighborhood nightclub, and Argoud at home. Ortiz, who arrived by chance in Madrid a few days before, was picked up in a hotel near the Puerta del Sol. In all, seventeen French activists were arrested. Argoud bitterly assailed the chief of the Brigade, recalling that they had dined together and treated each other as friends. The unhappy official carried out his duty, but six months later resigned from the force.

The activists were hustled off to police barracks at Canillejas, outside Madrid. Police sealed the apartments in Calle Conche Espina.

As soon as the arrests were made public, they were interpreted by Spanish opinion as a sign that Franco saw no further hope for French Algeria. Perhaps—in fact, he was under strong pressure from the French government, which reasoned that if the growing Organization could not be rooted out in Algeria, it could be checked decisively in Spain—with the Caudillo's cooperation. To help him make up his mind, de Gaulle took a number of steps. French police abruptly arrested that legendary old Loyalist figure of the Spanish civil war, General Valentín Gonzáles, "El Campesino," who had been living for years in undisturbed exile in France, charged him with illegal traffic of arms and hauled him up before a court at St.-Brieuc; simultaneously, the French withdrew permission for Spanish refugee leaders in Toulouse to publish and distribute anti-Franco tracts. Official sources in Madrid disclaimed any link between the two governments' actions, but the message from Paris was as clear as any promissory note.

Following the crackdown, the OAS in Algiers said nothing during four days, then declared in a pirate broadcast that none of the activists detained in Madrid had played a role in the Organization.

To the seventeen men held incommunicado at Canillejas, the broadcast came as a mortifying blow and appeared the epitome of betrayal. They compared notes and concluded that Salan had conspired through connections in Madrid to bring about their arrest. Lagaillarde was especially bitter.

There is no evidence to confirm their suspicions. Although Salan— and to a considerably greater degree, Susini, Perez and Godard— were surely not unhappy at the rival organization's misfortune, it is hard to believe that from their hiding places in Algiers they wielded sufficient power or prestige to influence events in Spain. The broadcast's prime purpose was to reassure the easily rattled *pieds noirs* by minimizing the crackdown's significance. In addition, naturally, Susini exploited an opportunity to belittle the dissidents.

Three weeks later, Franco's government announced plans to transfer four of the activists—Argoud, Lagaillarde, Lacheroy and Ortiz— to Santa Cruz de la Palma, a tiny speck at the western limit of the Canary Islands, almost eight hundred miles from the mainland.

Before they emplaned for La Palma, the quartet formed an Executive Directory under Argoud's presidency to carry on resistance to de Gaulle.* It was a desperate, last-minute maneuver to preserve the Madrid organization's independence of both the Algiers and the Paris OAS. It appeared a remarkably quixotic gesture on the part of men leaving for indefinite confinement on the smallest of the Canaries in the midst of the Atlantic Ocean.

In Madrid, Dr. Lefèvre—benign, careful, measured—lay low, still at liberty, and hoped for the best. He had refused to join the Directory; he thought that the OAS in Spain was virtually washed up.

Being a prefect in France—one of the country's top career civil servants—supposes a solid education in political science and law, an ability to pick up information and get things done, a talent for administration and, naturally, loyalty to the Republic. Jean Morin

* The Directory included a fifth man, Marcel Bouyer, head of Maquis Résurrection-Patrie, whom the Spanish police were holding in León as a suspect foreigner, without, however, realizing his true identity.

possessed these qualifications. None of them helped him much in Algiers in the late fall of 1961.

When, in 1960, he had been tapped to replace Paul Delouvrier as Delegate General, Morin displayed scant enthusiasm about the proposed new assignment. He was unsure of de Gaulle's ultimate aims in Algeria, and when he was eventually reassured on this point, he foresaw only trouble and increasing misunderstanding before the distant objective of a cease-fire could be achieved. Summoned to the Élysée Palace, he lunched first with an old friend at one of their favorite Left Bank restaurants, La Méditerranée, and unburdened himself of his doubts. The friend listened sympathetically, but was only partially surprised to learn that evening that Morin had accepted; few French civil servants could resist the Olympian prodding and gruff encouragement which de Gaulle employed when he chose to impress a subordinate.

A year later, Morin was trying, not very successfully, to maintain a semblance of authority in a city dominated by the shadow government of the OAS and the steady encroachments of the FLN.

Morin is a tense, brusque, sallow-skinned man. He is descended from a family of *hauts fonctionnaires,* and enjoys a reputation as one of France's best bridge players. During World War II he worked with Georges Bidault on the Conseil National de la Résistance, then when Bidault became premier, as his private secretary. Later, the two men remained friends although Bidault's attacks on Gaullist policy intensified, while Morin steadfastly served the Fifth Republic.

He was forty-four. As the top-ranking civilian authority in Algeria, he had been taken prisoner during the April putsch and held in the Sahara—an experience most other civil servants were spared and which perhaps influenced his present attitude. He feared a second putsch, and his assumption was that this time it would be bloody.

Morin is a man of courage, and friends praise him as a troubleshooter. But on the strength of testimony by his colleagues during this period, he showed some tendency in Algiers' spectral, coldly antagonistic atmosphere to treat the OAS as an invincible steamroller—he became, in brief, a significant victim to Susini's psychological war of nerves. Some think that Morin specially dreaded losing a communications link with Paris and being confronted with a foaming street mob. At any rate, beginning in October, he undertook partial evacuation of the Délégation Générale's services to Rocher Noir, the recently completed fortified administrative enclave east of Algiers. This move was interpreted by the *pieds noirs* as a flight. The OAS assiduously spread the word that if the Delegate General were assigned elsewhere he would accept with alacrity, and one hostile critic in Paris compared him to a "champagne cork bobbing on unruly seas."

In fact, Morin was prepared to fight the Organization; but to complicate matters, he was at odds with the government in Paris and the commander in chief in Algeria about the best way to do so.

The disagreement with Ailleret sprang from a basic personality clash. Morin suspected the Army of doing less than it could or should to combat the OAS—and said so. He resented Ailleret's imperturbability about civilian casualties, including police, which contrasted sharply with his outrage at an OAS attack on an officer. In the course of the fall, Morin persuaded himself that CCI commandos were ready to revolt and invest Rocher Noir. Accordingly he made detailed emergency arrangements to evacuate his staff aboard the *Laita,* a French Navy communications vessel standing offshore.

At La Reghaia, the Army of Algeria's headquarters, Ailleret minimized Morin's fears. The commander in chief dismissed OAS terrorism as "soap bubbles" and refused to dispatch more troops into the cities. A starchy little general, military to the core, he found Morin's nervousness distasteful and was not prepared necessarily to defer to the ideas of a civilian. Ailleret's over-all estimate of the situation undoubtedly was sound; but he did not have the responsibility of keeping Europeans and Moslems from each other's throats, and he was living in a different psychological climate than Morin.

As a result of steady friction between the two men, anti-OAS action lagged.

Morin's troubles with Paris were of another sort. The Delegate General had available three thousand CRS troops, in addition to those of the Army, to help maintain order in Algiers; but only eight companies were from Metropolitan France, sixteen were locally recruited and hence deemed unreliable. In response to Morin's urgings, the government agreed to replace at least two local companies with home units. This struck Morin as far from sufficient. He flew to Paris to ask for more reinforcements; and to make the point stick, he announced that without fresh strength he could not guarantee order in Algiers. The request was turned down.

The reason for this was simple, although obscured in the Byzantine mysteries of compartmentalization, interservice rivalry and distrust that hamstring all bureaucracies. Morin's immediate superior was Algerian Affairs Minister Joxe, who was not unsympathetic to Morin's point of view; but, to obtain reinforcements, Joxe had to apply to Interior Minister Roger Frey. Frey's deputy, Alexandre Sanguinetti, who supervised the anti-OAS struggle in France on a day-to-day basis, opposed Morin's attempts to procure reinforcements and expel all suspect *pieds noirs,* which, Sanguinetti said, would result in "all the police being in Algeria and all the OAS in France." Frey concurred. It was significant of the concern that was being felt (though not openly voiced) by the government, that Frey, Sanguinetti and others stressed the need of safeguarding France first. "Algeria by this time," recalls one official, "was regarded as a gangrenous limb which sooner or later must be cut off." But six months earlier there had been no suggestion that France itself, as distinct from Algeria, was in danger from the activists.

It could be a mortal mistake, Sanguinetti argued at government strategy sessions, to adopt Godard's way of thinking and fight him on his terrain. The decisive struggle must be fought in France, where the OAS was at a disadvantage. He won this point. However, to appease Morin, the Interior Ministry for the first time raised the possibility of organizing a "special service" to combat the OAS on Algerian soil. Nothing happened for the moment, but the germ of a dangerous idea was sown.

"Algeria is waiting for action by Paris, which is waiting for action by Algiers," tartly commented *Le Monde.* This about summed the situation up. Constantin Melnik, a close collaborator of Michel Debré for police affairs, thought that Frey and Sanguinetti's decision to maintain CRS reserves in France made a certain amount of overall sense—noting, however, that in the short term it favored OAS growth in Algeria. The government, in other words, was accepting a calculated risk; and for the moment the only unit Morin had to challenge the Organization was Grassien's anti-OAS brigade, or, as Godard, who loathed its members, called it, the "red brigade."

Throughout that fall, in one form or another, privately and publicly, at press conferences and on trips throughout the provinces, de Gaulle drummed away at the threat of Algerian partition. At one cabinet meeting he exploded: "Our policy—and I'm surprised that people insist on not understanding it—is to get out. . . . To get out with honor, we're ready to do business with the other side if it wants to. If not, we'll regroup and let them all go to the devil!"*

Alain Peyrefitte, a rising young Gaullist deputy of the Seine-et-Marne department, had written a series of four articles which appeared in *Le Monde* under the title "Pour Sortir de l'impasse algérienne"; and these drew wide attention, because they were reportedly a faithful echo of the General's thinking. Peyrefitte compared the advantages and drawbacks of outright French withdrawal from Algeria with a division of the country into two racial zones, like India and Pakistan. The latter course, he wrote, would enable France to retain a toehold in Algeria; eventually hatred between Europeans and Moslems might die down and economic cooperation might begin—it was up to the FLN to decide. This visibly represented a high-level effort to prod the FLN back to the bargaining table. Peyrefitte and de Gaulle fully realized that the Algerians could never accept partition as such, but likewise dreaded the abrupt cessation of French assistance.

Privately de Gaulle admitted that permanent partition was impractical in view of the interwoven economic activities of the Moslems and *pieds noirs.* "Two Algerias are a fantasy," he told moderate-Rightist Valéry Giscard d'Estaing, but he pointed out that as a temporary measure regrouping merited consideration. He was profoundly anxious to attack other problems, French constitutional reform and the carrying out of his grand foreign-policy design, but he was stalled by the Algerian problem.

Under its taciturn new president, Ben Youssef Ben Khedda, the Algerian Provisional Government maintained unnerving silence. No diplomatic initiative came from Tunis; no sign of which way its leaders planned to go—toward an accommodation with Paris or increased dependence upon financial and military aid from the Communist countries.

In reality, Ben Khedda was far from being as powerful as the Western press depicted him. The image of a tough, lower-middle-class, pro-Communist revolutionary far more difficult to negotiate with than his predecessor, the bourgeois nationalist Ferhat Abbas,

* Cited by Robert Buron, *Carnets politiques de la Guerre d'Algérie.*

was a newspaper invention. Behind the dark glasses he perpetually wore, Ben Khedda masked nothing more alarming than myopia and a desire to carry out moderate social reforms in Algeria.

His silence at this point was partly attributable to a pressing need to shore up his own position, for his election had by no means put an end to internal dissension within the FLN. Moreover, he remained skeptical, even after de Gaulle's September press conference, about the General's stand on the Sahara.

The same haziness permeated Tunis's attitude toward the OAS. The members of the Algerian Provisional Government at times suspected the French of the worst—of sparing the outlaw movement, in order to brandish it as a scarecrow when negotiations eventually resumed. At any rate, until a cease-fire was signed, they would continue to view the various factions on the French side as one and indivisible. Considerable opportunism entered into this attitude. By pretending to see in the OAS a veiled desire of the Gaullist government to maintain a death grip on Algeria, the GPRA simultaneously made propaganda capital and ignored the problem.

In October, Information Minister M'hamed Yazid still referred to the "insignificant OAS." *El Moudjahid*, the FLN's official organ, published a significant commentary. The OAS, it forecast, would in no wise hinder the Algerian people's march toward independence, but it could dangerously "compromise the future of the European minority in Algeria." What apparently cut the FLN to the quick was the equation in some quarters of the OAS with the FLN as armed revolutionary movements. Nationalist spokesmen hastened to point out the differences between the two. They accused the French press of magnifying the Organization's importance and belittled reports of OAS capability to partition the country by force. But, above all, they stressed the OAS's total lack of support abroad, except in Franco's Spain.

This was the limit of Tunis's anti-OAS action. It must be added in fairness that, apart from editorializing, the GPRA could do little: it feared that a Moslem riposte against the OAS might make matters worse by triggering large-scale bloody clashes between the two racial communities. The Algerian nationalists abroad, Belkacem Krim declared, realized that independence would be a costly, painful process; this did not imply that they accepted OAS attacks on fellow Moslems in the interior with equanimity.

The point remains, the Algerians for three months—from August to October—emulated the Gaullist government and ran the calculated risk of allowing the situation inside Algeria to deteriorate before it improved. The period coincided with the OAS's growth.

Then from Tunis Ben Khedda finally broke the GPRA's silence and declared on October 24 that self-determination was no longer an issue, that the only remaining matter to be threshed out was the new state's accession to independence and its future relations with Paris; he was asking France, in effect, to turn over the country to the FLN without offering the population another choice. This ultimatum flew in the face of the sole condition on which de Gaulle had always insisted. It was obviously inacceptable—as Joxe lost no time making clear at a press conference in Paris three days later. Joxe declared that self-determination remained a prerequisite.

The outlook for further peace talks appeared darker than ever.

The legitimate political parties of France, with the exception of the Communists, were not completely unresponsive to Salan's campaign. The Left publicly decried the OAS in editorials, speeches and resolutions; but Guy Mollet, Robert Lacoste, and others to whom Salan wrote privately knew that the star of the OAS was rising in Algeria. There was a show of interest among groups representing almost the entire political spectrum in France. It ranged from the Independents and the conservative entourage of Valéry Giscard d'Estaing through the Poujadistes to the Socialists. It included student groups. Within the civil service, some prefects formerly posted in Algeria and reassigned to the Metropole were sympathetic; so, as has been described, were elements in the police and the Army.

The grand finale to Salan's political offensive came on November 8 and 9. During a debate in the National Assembly on the military budget, deputies including Georges Bidault and Jean Le Pen rose and hailed the OAS as a "legitimate movement" enjoying the backing of the vast majority of *pieds noirs*. Thus, for the first time, the Organization in spite of its terror tactics gained open public support at the highest parliamentary level in France—not, to be sure, without some scandalized hooting and banging of tables from benches on the Left. Nonetheless, this represented remarkable progress for an outlaw faction which, only seven months before, was disbanded, on the run and virtually unknown by home opinion. It seemed to prove Salan's strategy eminently correct.

The next day, the extreme Right gathered its forces for an all-out effort. A deputy from the Charente department, Jean Valentin, introduced an amendment to the military budget which provided for the reduction of universal military service to eighteen months and the drafting of eight classes in Algeria to make up the loss of manpower. This amounted to nothing other than a recouching in parliamentary language of Jouhaud's last rebellious order on the final evening of the putsch. The amendment's transparent purpose was to give the OAS control over the Army of Algeria by decreasing the number of draftees and increasing the number of *pieds noirs* in uniform.

The maneuver was so obvious that the Assembly promptly dubbed the rider the "Salan amendment." The extreme-Right parliamentary group, Unité de la République, backed it, as did twenty-five Independents, a few center-of-the-road MRP deputies, and a lone Gaullist—a Moslem deputy from Algeria. During the debate, amid cries and insults, Armed Forces Minister Messmer rose flushed with anger to urge the amendment's rejection, and shouted: "To vote for it is a crime!" Inevitably, in view of the Gaullist majority, it went down to defeat on the same day, by 383 to 80 votes. Susini, in Algiers, thought the effort ill-advised, since the public backing of far-Right deputies confirmed the popular impression of the OAS as a neofascist movement. On the other hand, the Organization had mustered a not inconsiderable bloc within the Assembly and could claim a psychological victory of sorts.

Emboldened by this result, the Vincennes Committee met exactly one week later at the Left Bank Salle de la Mutualité. Theoretically it was a private gathering, but an estimated three thousand persons attended. The huge hall was filled with French activists conscious of new-found strength. The atmosphere crackled with aggressiveness. One after another, stalwarts of *Algérie française* rose to extol the expanding OAS. Bidault declared: "The Army of the New Resistance is forming, its ranks are growing—a *coup d'état* cannot be excluded. . . ." Léon Delbecque, a former Gaullist, exclaimed: "The only effective power in Algeria is the OAS." The most outspoken orator was a former police inspector and far-Right deputy, Jean Dides. Dides hailed the putschist generals in prison and cried, "Glory to General Salan, who will restore France's grandeur and freedom!" According to some, he also cried, "Death to the felonious General!"—meaning de Gaulle.

The government's reaction to these developments was curiously halting.

The basic strategy question of whether the Organization constituted a police or a political problem remained unresolved. The most lucid Gaullists argued that it was both—a political problem in Algeria, a police problem in France. Bernard Tricot considered the OAS a serious political problem in France itself: but after the roll call on the Salan amendment he changed his mind and decided that, while the Organization could still inflict extensive damage, it did not have the breadth to sway a significant number of voters.

In the wake of the uproarious meeting at the Mutualité, the government ordered the Vincennes Committee dissolved and Dides arrested. A judge swiftly set the ex-police inspector at temporary liberty, since some doubt existed about whether the alleged death-threat to de Gaulle had really been uttered; so the government, with a certain lack of coherence, moved to hold him without a trial as an "administrative internee." Dides, when he heard of this, refused to leave his cell at the Santé Prison. Other inmates staged a tumultuous three-hour demonstration; a fire broke out in one wing; journalists alerted by Rightist lawyers gathered at the gates; three squadrons of *gardes mobiles* were finally brought up to subdue the rioters, and drag Dides from his cell to a waiting van under an avalanche of protests and cries of *"Algérie française!"*

It was the sort of behavior the government could not safely tolerate and yet expect to maintain order. De Gaulle himself had repeatedly told the cabinet that he wanted the anti-OAS battle stepped up.* Now, by dint of constant prodding, he got satisfaction on several points. On December 6 the cabinet tardily pronounced the dissolution of the "de facto organization known as the OAS," basing its action on a 1936 law against factious groups. It also opened an investigation, for what this was worth, into the movement's origins, membership and backing. Messmer repeated and extended the scope of Ailleret's order of the day, and called upon the entire French Army inside and outside Algeria to put down seditious elements.

* A French writer closely linked to the Gaullist government noted: "Each time measures were discussed to crush subversion, de Gaulle always tended toward extreme rigorousness." Paul-Marie de la Gorce, *De Gaulle et deux mondes.*

Foreign correspondents received a warning from the Interior Ministry that interviews with OAS chieftains would lead to immediate expulsion; the aim naturally was to cut down the publicity being given the movement.*

Toward mid-December de Gaulle took a sufficiently serious view of what the OAS might do in Algiers to summon his top advisers to a secret meeting at the Élysée Palace, where he proceeded to give them a personal lesson in military tactics. The general's plan was, in the event of a new putsch in Algiers, to evacuate all official services from the city (as General de Pouilly had done at Oran in April), then retake it in force. De Gaulle based his tactical demonstration on the premise that Morin and his subordinates could retrench in stoutly defended Rocher Noir and La Reghaia during the time it took to mount the necessary forces for a counterassault. The impromptu *Kriegspiel* must have been arresting. Objectivity requires one to note that several French officials who attended found de Gaulle's concepts impractical and outdated, inspired by World War II tactics for employing armored columns to liberate an occupied city. The professionals in charge of the anti-OAS struggle claim they did not take the lecture seriously; but it can be assumed that no one voiced much open disagreement.

The record at this stage does not bear out the Right's accusation that a rubber-stamp cabinet and parliamentary majority carried out every wish of de Gaulle's unquestioningly. In reality, he encountered some trouble getting his orders obeyed; his directives were constantly being modified, diluted, blunted, and by the time they reached an implementation level they often reflected the opposite of the original intention. Debré strove loyally to fulfill the official twin-pronged policy of negotiations with the FLN and destruction of the OAS, but he could scarcely conceal his distaste for dealing with Ben Khedda. There persisted leaks to the OAS of security measures discussed at the Élysée Palace. While no cabinet member was personally suspect, high-ranking staff aides with access to cabinet memoranda were believed to be aiding the Organization.

A trial in Riom, in central France, at this time epitomized the government's difficulties. At Debré's urging, proceedings against nine *plastiqueurs* were speeded up, and prison sentences handed down; but during three days of hearings the court did not once refer to the OAS by name, and showed so much partiality toward the

* There is no record of any journalist being expelled for this reason.

accused that anti-activist opinion was scandalized throughout the country.

The press noted sarcastically that while the government still sought a liberal third force as an intermediary between *pieds noirs* and Moslems in Algeria, the OAS had become a third force of a very different type. One newspaper, *Est-Éclair*, said that three forces were indeed present, but two—the FLN and OAS—shared real power, while the government's authority was only "a façade." In the meanwhile, it added, the Army's war had lost "all meaning."

In early November, de Gaulle made a speaking tour of Corsica and southern France. It was far from being an unqualified success. In Marseilles he ran into heckling by Socialist dock workers and Rightist shipping families alike; at the prefecture, under sunny skies, hostile shouts of *"Algérie française!"* and *"Paix en Algérie!"* mingled. At the port the din was so great that loudspeakers were inaudible as the official party cruised in a municipal launch. The crowd has an animal instinct for smelling weakness, and it sensed de Gaulle's temporary disarray before the concerted challenge on both flanks. Asked about the OAS, he replied stonily, "I don't know it"; and he added, somewhat insufficiently, that he placed his trust in French common sense to triumph. Like the FLN, he chose to ignore the Organization, on the assumption that lofty contempt would lessen its significance. It was a dangerous decision, given the movement's spurt of popularity in the Algerian cities. Parts of the French press raised a howl of protest, charging that the government's "quasi silence" had enabled the OAS, which had been only a band of rebels to begin with, to expand its influence. And they accused everybody from the President down of simultaneously misunderstanding and underestimating the problem. In Tunis, Ferhat Abbas sardonically noted: "De Gaulle must put an end to the Algerian War, or it will put an end to de Gaulle."

The fall of 1961, in short, was a period when de Gaulle uncharacteristically faltered, unsure of what to do next, encouraging, by his very indecision, the other side's belligerence. If ever there was a moment during the final year of French Algeria when his enemies temporarily grasped the initiative from him, it was now.

On October 24, several of Grassien's inspectors were posted around the main square of El Biar watching two Europeans at breakfast in a café. It was eight o'clock in the morning, and high-school students were crossing the square under the palm trees. A third man—tall, thin, long-legged, dressed in civilian clothes but unmistakably military in his bearing—neared the café, when one *pied noir* burst out and gestured to him. The newcomer hesitated. Suddenly all three men fled down an alley, zigzagging, dodging between pedestrians and motor traffic. Before a Peugeot packed with more plainclothesmen, they pulled up short, wheeled, and scampered off in different directions.

The tall man darted down a side street and vanished. A Moslem on Grassien's brigade took careful aim at one of the *pieds noirs,* and fired but missed. The man fired back, also missing. As he reached Boulevard Jules Ferry and tried to sprint to the safety of a garden wall, another shot struck him in the left thigh and he tumbled to the ground, wounded but still alive.

The Moslem inspector ran up. "You tried to kill me," the *pied noir* at his feet exclaimed. The inspector shook his head—years before, they had played on the same Algiers soccer team.

On a tip, police had maintained surveillance of the café where a breakfast operational meeting of Deltas was scheduled to take place. The tall man who had escaped was Degueldre's deputy, ex-Lieutenant Pierre Delhomme, a deserter like his chief from the 1st Foreign Legion Paratroop Regiment. The second man was an anonymous Delta. Grassien's brigade identified the wounded man transported to Mustapha Hospital as Jean Sarradet, leader of the student Z Commandos. It was an important capture. Several hours after the gunfight, however, a tall young doctor and two stretcher-bearers arrived at the hospital, showed an official-looking release order to gendarmes, and removed the patient in a private ambulance. It was only an hour later that authorities discovered the order was fake. The bogus doctor was Delhomme. Sarradet vanished again into the city's underground.

One after another, the men trying to infiltrate the Organization were struck down. The most spectacular victim was Air Force Major René Post, a forty-year-old investigator for Military Security and former head of the pilot-training school at Marrakech, Morocco. In October Post set out to capture Susini through a Corsican night-club operator and member of the Algiers underworld, Dominique Fondacci.

Just as running a double agent is one of the most sensitive operations in Intelligence work, employing criminals in police investigations entails high risks.

Post's scheme was not foolish. Aware of the Organization's pressing need for arms, he instructed Fondacci to contact a thug named François Leca with an offer to sell three hundred submachine guns to the OAS. Leca pretended to show interest, and subsequently met Post, who pointed out that there was money to be made by a middleman in the transaction. Leca then went straight to Degueldre, and reported that he had been approached by Fondacci and an Army officer who obviously wanted to set some sort of trap. Degueldre took careful note of the information, then told Leca what he was to do.

When Grassien learned what Post was up to, he advised him to drop the whole matter, arguing that it was impossible to tell whom the Corsican gangsters of Algiers were really working for. They were sure to switch allegiance to whichever side offered them more money. Dealing with them could be a waste of time—and dangerous.

Post agreed. He did not drop the operation, but he made a point henceforth of informing one of Grassien's aides, Inspector André Bardoux, of his movements.

At seven o'clock on the morning of October 23, he received an urgent call from Leca asking him to come immediately to an address in the La Redoute neighborhood on the heights of Algiers, where he could meet Susini. This was exactly what Post had been waiting for. Bardoux was not yet at his office; and for some reason, Post did not or could not contact the inspector at home. He set out alone.

Leca was waiting alone in the hallway of an apartment building. Post made the mistake of momentarily turning his back to the man he believed he had duped. He paid for his mistake at once. There was a sharp report, and the major crumpled to the floor with a bullet in the back of his head. Leca fled in a waiting car.

This was not the end. Degueldre, who was anything but a sentimentalist, insisted that Leca completely prove his good faith by shooting Fondacci too—failing which, he would be shot himself. The same day Delta commandos drove the unhappy thug to Fondacci's apartment, then waited in the street.

Leca entered the apartment where Fondacci was sleeping and found the way barred by a police dog. It seemed a good reason to turn back. When he arrived downstairs, however, the Deltas pointed out that nothing prevented him from shooting both the dog and the man. So, reluctantly, Leca reentered the apartment and shot Fondacci dead. The dog made no attempt to interfere and hence was spared.

Post's murder attracted considerable attention. The Organization had struck down another French Army officer. Délégation Générale spokesmen deliberately publicized the attack, to shock home opinion with the OAS's murderousness. Because the assassination contained elements of a good mystery story—with a dimly perceived link to Algiers' underworld—the press gave it wide play.

This did not displease the Organization, for Post's killing was meant to serve as an example and intimidate others.

Terror breeds more terror. The men who bore ultimate responsibility for these deaths were totally and irreversibly committed. *Plastiquages* soared in November; the shooting of policemen became a weekly affair; European liberals—a doctor, a trade-unionist, a surgeon, a politician—were gunned down with monotonous implacability. Through the city roved Degueldre's commandos in search of Moslem victims: workers cycling home at dusk; a taxi driver trapped into taking the wrong, fatal turning; housewives shopping at a neighborhood grocery when a car slowed down and opened fire . . .

To try to understand the motives of the OAS leaders, one must examine briefly the conditions in which they were waging their struggle; for the conditions, to a certain extent, fashioned their outlook. They were men under sentence of death* who had sacrificed careers, shed families, even their identities. Salan ventured into the streets in his gross disguise as a Mitidja farmer, Susini traveled about in nondescript sweater and pants, describing himself with devastating accuracy as "a beatnik whom no one would trouble to bother"; a voluble publicity agent turned out to be Ferrandi. Broizat passed himself off without trouble as a Protestant evangelist. Godard grew a mustache and a heavy shock of tawny hair. Only Degueldre, with his fatalistic, obscure commitment to violence, refused to stoop to imposture, relying for his security on his counterfeit identity papers.

It is hard to reconstitute this period. No written record exists of

* The same court that judged Challe and Zeller had condemned the others to death *in absentia* on July 11, 1961.

how they lived and felt; they took care not to be photographed or to keep diaries, they preserved few documents. Each was alone a good part of the day, ignorant of the others' actions; sometimes a week went by without personal contact. Meetings required complex, careful arrangements; and when they met the chances of discovery and capture multiplied. These sessions were nerve-racking, tedious affairs. They lasted up to eight hours at a stretch in various hideouts, and were taken up unavoidably with immediate problems so that no time remained to thresh out the fundamental question of a political program.

When they met, furthermore, the absence of unity of purpose stood out—each was obsessed with his own theories and solutions. Susini wanted a mass uprising that would introduce social reforms under French rule; but Perez, influenced by nineteenth-century papal encyclicals, yearned after a genuine White counterrevolution. Gardes was preoccupied by the problem of integrating the Moslems, whom he cared about and so little understood. Godard thought of the struggle in almost purely military terms—he wanted to keep the pot boiling in Algeria, but to what ultimate political end he never made clear.

As for Salan, he struck those about him as deliberately refraining from having a platform, a program or a doctrine—for fear that it was premature and could cost him political support among various factions in France. So he remained purposely vague, and indeed went to some trouble to hide his opinions from his subordinates. Later, he bitterly complained that decisions were kept from him, but at the outset it was Gardy and Godard who protested at his own ambiguous directives.

To many observers it seemed as if the Organization was resisting for the mere sake of resisting and would decide later what it was fighting for. Meanwhile, in the taut unsparing atmosphere of underground life, nerves snapped and jealousies grew. Susini and Perez systematically sought to outflank each other. Degueldre grudgingly obeyed Perez, who took orders with reluctance from Godard. Godard distrusted and despised Susini. "We never had a chance to work out disagreements," Susini recalled, ". . . so they festered. Our only unity was in silence."

However, all these men believed fiercely in the rightness of French rule in Algeria; they brought to this cause more than mere personal ambition and opportunism. They were arrogant but dedicated. As time passed they could lay their hands on considerable sums, but for the most part the money was conscientiously spent on the Organization's needs, not on private requirements. (Gardes was a thoroughly honest officer, who exasperated the others with his insistence on almost monastic abnegation.) They were determined men, who were prepared to see the struggle through and did not easily give way to discouragement. In fact, one can say that the OAS suffered not from a lack of fortitude or self-sacrifice but from a desperate strategic situation, incurable jockeying for power and paralyzing confusion about what it was supposed to be.

"Halfway between the French Resistance and a secret-service network"—so Susini saw the OAS; and he criticized it for failing to be a revolutionary party. Another member compared it to the paramilitary secret societies in post-1918 Germany, which was close to the mark. But it also bore some resemblance to the Sinn Fein in Ireland, the Commune of Paris and, later, to the Jacobins during the Terror.

It was a very odd Organization, an uncooked pudding of conflicting freakish ideas and aspirations and principles. It had grown much too fast. What had happened, essentially, was that a small group of fugitive soldiers and civilians had set out to wage eleventh-hour resistance against the seemingly inevitable denouement of seven years' war; and suddenly and unexpectedly, this resistance struck a responsive chord among the Europeans. However, as the OAS spread, it became less secret and more vulnerable to informers; it was armed, but only incompletely; and its organization was fitful. Recruiting was haphazard. As one French writer noted, "the OAS was everybody . . . it was also anybody." By November, the men who ran it were virtually administering Algiers; but there were well-defined limits beyond which they dared not step. Salan remained uncomfortably aware that the Army's firepower was close by, and there existed a distinct suspicion that de Gaulle, if hard pressed, would not hesitate to use it. Thus, the OAS was in a paradoxical position: popular support for it had come soon, its very existence constituted a threat to Paris, yet the threat could not be carried out. A subversive organization must enjoy external support, but the Organization could count on no hope from abroad. Portugal, a likely ally, had received tanks from de Gaulle; Spain had an advantageous commercial treaty with France; South Africa saw the Algerian problem as remote and dissimilar to its own. The men behind the OAS were as isolated as though marooned on an ocean island. In this quandary they continued to base their hopes on a political change in France and—contrary to the lessons of December 1960 and the putsch, and fantastic as it now seems—on a change of heart within the Army.

The ranked evergreens stood stiff with frost in the icy wind. Electric lights were already looped through the heavy branches although Christmas was more than a month away. More than two thousand French officers and noncoms braced at attention in the freezing cold. Round about the square, civilians, Alsatians accustomed to an early winter, pressed forward to get a good glimpse of de Gaulle.

Bareheaded in a military greatcoat, flanked by cabinet ministers, and immensely self-assured, he dominated his audience. He had ordered a cross section of officers and men to Strasbourg ostensibly for the seventeenth anniversary of the city's liberation. But addressing himself as he seldom did in public to the Army, he spoke about World War II only long enough to remind them dryly that he had been right about the use of armor. The main thrust of his speech on November 22 was Algeria. He said that he understood some officers' hopes for a different solution there, but noted acidly the illusion of thinking that "one can make things be what one desires and the contrary of what they are." The Army's future, he observed, was not in the Aurès mountains, it was in Europe. He saved his most cutting lines for last. "At that moment when the state and the nation have chosen the way," he rumbled, "military duty is traced out once and for all. Outside these limits there can be only—there are only—lost soldiers."

The frostbitten ranks of officers listened unmoved. When de Gaulle, with his usual heavy-handed touch, attempted to lead them in singing the "Marseillaise," many remained mute.*

The phrase they resented most—"lost soldiers"—was sarcastically repeated; nonetheless it took wing. Later, back at their bases, in barracks and mess halls, during long hours of discussion, the officers

---

* The speech itself was violently attacked the following day in *Combat* by Professor Raoul Girardet, a pre-putsch conspirator in Paris who, since his release from custody, had been writing regularly on military affairs. "The need to contribute to the Free World's defense is extolled," he wrote, "but we are abandoning the only bastion which we can defend by ourselves"—a summing-up of the military case for French Algeria by one of its few intelligent defenders.

who had attended the Strasbourg ceremonies concluded that by recalling the Army's basic duty to obey, de Gaulle had somewhat cleared the air. He had not gained their confidence, but from this point on—unhappily for Salan and Godard and Susini—there was less chance than ever of their straying into the paths of revolt.

Grassien and his entire brigade were recalled in late October. They were credited in Paris with having done a competent job under trying circumstances; their withdrawal was no reflection on their efficiency, but a belated admission that the situation was deteriorating. Grassien noted wryly that there were no volunteers in the capital to take over his task.

On their final night in Algiers, November 9, the eight men of the anti-OAS brigade met for a drink at L'Universel, a bar on Boulevard Gallieni. Evening traffic outside was heavy. Grassien posted two of his inspectors at the terrace as a precaution. The others gathered at a table indoors. During a lull in traffic a car passed and sounded "Algérie française." Grassien's deputy, Inspector René Joubert, looked up and commented briefly: "They still believe in it."

It was the last thing he ever said.

A second car stopped before the bar. The two inspectors had just motioned the driver on, when a man alighted, whipped out an automatic pistol held under his raincoat, and fired a burst. Joubert slid to the floor. The car speeded off amid a hail of gunfire. Grassien leaped to his feet and found a neat ring of bullet holes drilled into the wall directly above his head. Joubert lay where he was, killed instantly by a bullet in his forehead.

For two days the brigade postponed its departure and pressed an angry, vengeful search for the killers. The search yielded no results. In Algiers, Degueldre's men were immune.

A number of men in Paris took grim note of the carefully planned attempt to wipe out Grassien's brigade, and concluded that the government had waited perilously long and shown dangerous softness about fighting back. They laid their own plans for tougher tactics. The shadow boxing was over. In place of the police would come secret agents—the *barbouzes*.

Pierre Lagaillarde and Jean-Jacques Susini (right), photographed during Algiers' Barricades Week (January 24–February 1, 1960), when Europeans' growing distrust of de Gaulle's self-determination policy exploded into open defiance. Tried in Paris for their participation in the uprising, Lagaillarde and Susini managed to flee to Madrid, where they joined forces with Salan.

Raoul Salan, who became head of the underground OAS (Organisation armée secrète), served with distinction in the French Army during World War II in Indochina and Algeria. As holder of the Croix de Guerre, Médaille Militaire, Distinguished Service Cross and other citations, he was France's most decorated general.

Colonel Jean Gardes was the only officer put on trial for involvement in Barricades Week. As chief of the French Army's Cinquième Bureau (Psychological Warfare) in Algiers, he encouraged European extremists. Acquitted, Gardes continued to meet with other Army officers determined at all costs to keep Algeria French.

Air Force general Maurice Challe (right) succeeded Salan as French commander in chief in Algeria, launched combined ground and air operations against FLN guerrillas, and was decorated with the Grand Cross of the Legion of Honor by de Gaulle in May 1960. Less than a year later, Challe flew to Algiers and joined the fight against de Gaulle.

The Arab population of the Casbah and other Moslem quarters of Algiers brandishing the outlawed green-and-white FLN flag on December 11, 1960. The unprecedented demonstration, which followed European-triggered riots the day before, shattered once and for all the illusion that Algeria's nine million Moslems would accept prolonged French rule.

The four generals who led the short-lived April 1961 putsch (from left to right): Edmond Jouhaud, a pied noir; *Salan; Challe; and Henri Zeller, former Chief of Staff of the Ground Forces and long-time supporter of* Algérie française.

The pieds noirs *assembled in the Forum, a traditional rallying point for Algiers street demonstrations. The mood of the European population changed from jubilation to concern during the four-day putsch as Challe and his fellow generals failed to invade France and numerous Army commanders in Algeria refused to back the revolt.*

Colonel Yves Godard, one of the moving spirits in re-forming the OAS in the wake of the putsch's collapse. An intelligence specialist, Godard claimed to know Algiers' political underworld, its spies and secret agents, as well as any FLN leader—and undoubtedly did.

Susini, Godard's chief rival for power within the OAS, was negotiator of the final truce with the FLN. He favored "revolutionary" mobilization of the European masses, while Godard advocated guerrilla-warfare tactics.

Jean-Claude Perez, the "doctor of the poor" in Bab el Oued, Algiers' working-class hotbed of dissension. Sharp-tempered and rough-tongued, Perez was nominally responsible for OAS terrorist operations against Moslems and European liberals.

Lieutenant Roger Degueldre, a deserter from the Foreign Legion. Admirers claimed that Degueldre, who recruited and led the notorious Delta commandos, "was the OAS."

Colonel Antoine Argoud was considered one of the most promising officers in the French Army. After participating in the putsch, he escaped to Spain, where he and Lagaillarde organized the "Madrid branch" of the OAS before being interned by Franco.

Colonel Henry Dufour. In early 1962, Dufour, a sympathizer with OAS objectives, reached Oran, where he played a key role in the city's last days under French rule.

OAS slogans on the walls of Algiers. The angered European population donated funds and supported Salan's movement as the only force prepared to fight in the streets to stave off independence.

Salan in hiding. The former commander in chief grew a mustache, dyed his hair black and escaped arrest for months. This picture was taken by a French photographer to whom Salan gave an interview in one of several hiding places he used—an apartment "somewhere in Algiers."

OAS mobilization order in French and Arabic, posted in Algiers shortly after New Year's Day, 1962. The order, signed by Salan, decreed the mobilization of all able-bodied men to counter de Gaulle's alleged sellout of French territory.

ORGANISATION DE L'ARMÉE SECRÈTE

مُنَظَّمَة الْجَيْش السِّرِّيّ

AVIS DE MOBILISATION

إعلان بالتَّعْبِئَة الْعَامَّة

La Constitution adoptée par le Peuple Français lors du Référendum du 28 septembre 1958 dispose :

PRÉAMBULE :

« Le Peuple Français proclame solennellement son attachement aux droits de l'Homme et aux principes de la souveraineté nationale tels qu'ils ont été définis par la Déclaration de 1789, confirmée et complétée par le préambule de la Constitution de 1946. »

ARTICLE 5 :

«...Le Président de la République est le garant de l'**INTÉGRITÉ DU TERRITOIRE**... »

En conséquence, moi, RAOUL SALAN, Général d'Armée, Commandant en Chef, décide la mobilisation de tous les Algériens pour faire face à l'action conjuguée du Pouvoir de fait et de la rebellion afin de conserver l'Algérie à la Mère-Patrie.

Vive la France.

The ruins of the Hotel Rajah, last headquarters of the *barbouzes*. Recruited on a haphazard basis and inadequately trained, they arrived in Algiers to combat OAS terrorism with counterterrorism. The Rajah was blown up by the OAS in March 1962, after the *barbouzes* had evacuated it.

A photograph taken just after a deadly OAS mortar attack on the Place du Gouvernement, in Algiers' center. The barrage occurred shortly after the announcement of the Évian cease-fire, and preceded by several days the ill-fated rising of Bab el Oued against the French Army.

A rare photograph of French barbouzes, anti-OAS secret agents whose existence the French government never officially acknowledged. The photograph was taken in the El Biar villa later blown to pieces by a booby-trapped grate. Jim Alcheik (right) was one of the more than a dozen men killed in the blast. Lucien Bitterlin is on the extreme left.

L'Écho d'Oran

DIRECTEUR GENERAL Pierre LAFFON

EDITION SPECIALE DE L'O.A.S.

L'O.A.S. VAINCRA!

A *pirate edition of* L'Écho d'Oran, *the most widely read newspaper in western Algeria's capital, where OAS sympathies ran high among Europeans.* L'OAS vaincra! (*The OAS will win*), *a subhead proclaimed as independence drew nearer.*

General Charles Ailleret, commander in chief of French forces in Algeria, arriving as a prosecution witness at Salan's trial. Ailleret bitterly upbraided Salan for his role in the OAS.

General Joseph Katz, one of the French Army's toughest officers, appointed by de Gaulle's government to command anti-OAS operations in Oran. The OAS attempted several times to assassinate him but never succeeded.

This photograph was taken just after an OAS gunman killed two Arabs in broad daylight on an Algiers street before an indifferent group of Europeans. The OAS attempted to justify the wave of indiscriminate murders by arguing that it was locked in a life-and-death struggle with FLN agents in the city.

British Petroleum oil tanks blazing in the port of Oran on June 25, 1962, as pieds noirs *watch curiously. The huge fire was part of systematic eleventh-hour destruction carried on by OAS desperadoes.*

The final departure. Beginning in May 1962, tens of thousands of fearful Europeans, realizing that the OAS was doomed, fled Algeria. The former French territory achieved independence on July 3, 1962.

PART THREE

Civil war is marked by complication, uncertainty, suspicion, anguish, a nervous wear-and-tear, a special sort of pain, which exist only to a much lesser degree in a national war, or do not exist at all.

—HENRY DE MONTHERLANT,
La Guerre civile

14

The Spooks

It all began when a dark-haired, soft-spoken young Frenchman named Jacques Dulac moved into a villa on Rue Fabre, a quiet residential street high above Algiers. Dulac was a salesman for a paint-supply firm and spoke vaguely of using the house as a sales office.

The white Villa Andrea gleamed in the midst of orange trees and bougainvillea in the crisp winter light. The premises suited Dulac's associates, and soon they acquired a second house, which overlooked winding Chemin Reynaud, not far from the Palais d'Été. Dar Likoulia, the second villa, was inconspicuously set within high protecting walls.

A secretary was hired; but after the first meeting with her fellow employees she quit. Secretaries, even in Algiers in those days, were choosy.

Shortly afterward the paint firm rented a third villa on nearby Chemin Beaurepaire. Within seventy-two hours the outraged landlady appeared at the door and threatened to summon the police if the tenants did not clear out immediately. She went so far as to volunteer to reimburse their deposit in full—an untypical action for a French landlady. The tenants packed up and left.

The proprietress was scandalized because she had unexpectedly come upon the paint salesmen practicing karate and oiling submachine guns in the cellar. Some of them were Vietnamese.

Jacques Dauer, leader of the Gaullist Mouvement pour la Communauté,* approached Louis Joxe in May 1961 with the idea of
forming a pro-French third force in Algeria, whose objective would
be to promote cooperation between Europeans and Moslems after
independence—his assumption being that independence in the near
future was a foregone conclusion.

Dauer proposed canvassing the countryside, where, he reasoned,
it would be logical to bring together Europeans and Moslems to
discuss agricultural matters of common interest, and then—only
when a minimum foundation of mutual confidence existed—politics.
He advised bypassing altogether the big coastal cities, where the atmosphere was already far too explosive.

Dauer, a hearty, convincing talker, an ex-paratrooper and owner
of a printing works in Paris, received some encouragement. The
government earmarked some funds. By October, the MPC—which
had altered its name to Mouvement pour la Coopération in Algiers,
to distinguish it from the parent body and give it local meaningful-
ness—was ready to undertake preliminary action in two departments,
Algiers and Orléansville. There was, however, a significant modification. The main effort would be made in the cities; two of Morin's
top aides at the Délégation Générale, Claude Vieillescazes and Louis
Verger, had insisted upon this from the start. If Dauer agreed to
this major shift of emphasis, it was because he concluded that was
the price he must pay for government backing. Still, he did so with
misgiving—all the more so after an initial $30,000 was supplied, not
by Paris, as he had requested to avoid coming under Algiers' control, but through the Délégation Générale, which clearly meant to
retain a guiding hand over the operation.

* Founded in the spring of 1959 with members drawn chiefly from the
wartime Resistance and the subsequent Rassemblement du Peuple Français,
the MPC in Dauer's own apt phrase consisted of the "orphans of Gaullism"—
Leftist-leaning Gaullists who had conspired to bring de Gaulle back to power a
year before, in May 1958, then found themselves out in the cold.

The MPC's modest, inconspicuous headquarters were in the Left Bank
apartment of a lady who sold fabrics and sympathized politically. In France
the MPC had about eight thousand members, in Algeria it numbered approximately one hundred militants, including some trade-unionists.

During the Generals' Putsch, a group of twenty MPC members gathered
under Dauer in the Interior Ministry courtyard to meet Challe's paratroopers
head on if they sought to land. Dauer says his group declined a government
offer of arms for the good reason that they were already armed.

Dauer's plan called for distribution of tracts and a newspaper, *Démocratie algérienne,* and above all, an ambitious poster campaign to counter OAS and FLN themes with the slogan "Neither suitcase nor coffin but cooperation." Dauer hoped to persuade at least some *pieds noirs* that a third, moderate solution existed for the future. He foresaw, however, that most Europeans' reaction to such interference—not to mention the OAS's—would be violent, and he decided the billposting must be carried out at night to hold down street brawls to a minimum. To move about freely after curfew, however, volunteers would need special passes. They would also need weapons for defending themselves in case of attack—a very real possibility at this point. With suspiciously little urging, Vieillescazes and Verger agreed to issue both the passes and the guns. In Paris, Dauer, perhaps already suspicious, once again emphasized that the MPC would play solely a political role; but there was set in motion a process over which he would rapidly lose control.

The guns—7.65-mm. pistols—came from Military Security stores and were genuine. The tricolor passes were another matter. They were eminently worthless. They authorized the bearer to go about Algiers by day and night, called upon civil and military authorities to facilitate his mission (although the latter was not spelled out), listed two telephone numbers in case of emergency and bore the signature of Lieutenant Colonel Martin of Military Security—but in fact there was no Martin; this was an invention of Morin's staff, who could find no real official to lend his signature to the whole doubtful enterprise. Thus, from the start the operation was clouded in hocus-pocus: the passes were made out to aliases and signed by a nonexistent individual.

On November 13, under cover of dark, one hundred volunteers equipped with brushes and pots of glue ripped down OAS stickers and posted green MPC bills—green, the color of Islam and Algerian nationalism—on walls throughout Algiers. They enjoyed the advantage of total surprise.

Next morning infuriated *pieds noirs* complained to Morin, insisting that the whole procedure was inadmissible and charging that the MPC consisted of "thugs, Communists and FLN agents"—a sure gauge of the billposting's effectiveness.

In the next few days, a number of known activist cafés in Algiers blew up—first the Coq Hardi, Brasserie de Joinville, Le Petit Bonheur one night, and L'Otomatic, Le Viaduc, Le Cheval Blanc forty-eight hours later. The new terrorists, whomever they represented, were visibly in earnest; the force of the explosions, considerable even by Algiers' standards, blew several establishments' grillwork to smithereens and sent chunks of iron whistling across the street into parked cars. Police attributed the *plastiquages* to "unidentified anti-OAS elements."

In Paris, suspicions aroused, Dauer discovered without much difficulty that Military Security had organized the attacks with the help of three MPC members. It constituted the first unwarranted manipulation of his movement by Algiers authorities, in return for the guns and passes. Dauer sharply objected, but Morin's aides countered by pointing out that during the next few days there were no OAS *plastiquages*. Indeed, for the first time in months, the *pieds noirs*, upon hearing a blast, could no longer be smugly sure that the destruction was aimed at Moslems and liberals and not at themselves.

The young man's name was not Jacques Dulac, and the paint-supply firm was a fiction (although it was legally set up). Dulac was Lucien Bitterlin, the Gaullist radio producer arrested during the putsch, secretary-general of the MPC in Algeria and vice president of a coordinating committee for the MPC and the Association pour le Soutien du Général de Gaulle. He found it preferable to keep his real identity secret even when conferring with Délégation Générale officials during this period.

With funds supplied by Dauer, Bitterlin rented the three villas on the heights of Algiers with the intention of using them as the MPC's unpublicized headquarters for billposting and other anti-OAS operations. As has been described, he retained only two of the three houses. He did not need more. The MPC in Algiers was not numerous; the hard core consisted of several dozen of Dauer's followers in France, who volunteered for action in Algeria during short periods, whenever their regular work permitted. It was understood that engaging in war for the MPC was dangerous; like Bitterlin, the volunteers arrived in Algiers under assumed names.

Bitterlin's principal associate was an ex-Gaullist bodyguard named André Goulay, a large, barrel-chested man with the sinews and disposition of a wrestler, who owned a laundry at L'Arba. Bitterlin put Goulay in charge of Villa Andrea—"Villa A," as it became known—

and installed himself with his wife in "Villa B," the house on Chemin Reynaud.

From the start, the MPC's decision to set up headquarters in a European residential district of Algiers appeared to be a tactical error: the arrival of a group of athletic-looking young Frenchmen without regular business hours did not, in the city's hypersuspicious climate, pass unremarked (and this was before the Vietnamese turned up). The MPC would have been far safer in a Moslem quarter; as it was, sooner or later a counterattack could be expected. Bitterlin concluded in a report that if the MPC were to carry on, men who could handle arms expertly would be needed. In his phrase, the MPC did not want *des petites natures* ("milksops").

Dauer concurred and went one step further: since the OAS employed terror tactics, equally rough tactics would be inevitable for an opposition group to survive. But he drew a distinction between a militant who unmercifully punches someone in the face in anger and a sadistic cutthroat who kills as a matter of course.

In late November, Dauer flew to Algiers for a firsthand look at the MPC operation. Aboard the plane were Rightist deputy Robert Abdessalam, a police official named Michel Hacq, and a *France-Soir* veteran reporter, Lucien Bodard. Dauer spoke freely—too freely —to Abdessalam about the billposting. He saw no reason not to, since he considered it a wholly legitimate political undertaking; the deputy succinctly told him that he was mad. Hacq said little. Bodard listened carefully. Upon landing, he filed a three-column story, which appeared on November 29 in *France-Soir* and caused a sensation.

Bodard wrote that the government's intention was to concentrate the anti-OAS fight in Algeria "before the OAS could contaminate France." In view of the *pieds noirs'* mood, a general crackdown was considered impractical; the government accordingly had decided to make a fresh effort to capture the ten or more men at the head of the OAS by sending a special force of espionage, counterespionage and subversive-war experts to Algeria. With the leaders' capture, it was hoped the OAS might collapse like a pricked balloon.

Describing the new force as the government's "secret weapon," Bodard melodramatically stated: "It will be autonomous, not subject to normal authority, acting outside the Army and the police, with its own means of action. Absolutely secret, it will be used for the immediate running-down of tips. . . . We are going to see war between OAS networks and anti-OAS networks."

It was a creditable piece of journalism. Bodard's facts were, for the most part, correct and summarized government strategy at the end of November 1961. Strangely, however, they applied to *another, separate police operation.* For the truth was, in response to Morin's urgent appeals, and to fill the void created by the departure of Grassien's brigade, the Interior Ministry had just assigned the brawny, cigar-smoking chief of Criminal Police, Michel Hacq, to lead a hand-picked team of two hundred inspectors to coordinate anti-OAS operations in Algiers. The task force's official designation was "Mission C." Mission C would act in concert with the MPC militants but was different from them; it comprised trained police officers assigned through normal channels to Hacq, and although totally independent of the regular Sûreté it would use standard police methods of investigation.

Morin was beside himself when he heard of the leak. Dauer and Bitterlin were concerned at the unwanted publicity about secret agents. What they feared did, in fact, occur: the OAS, which had possessed only the vaguest sort of information about the MPC's status and aims, confused it with Mission C as a dangerous new challenger on its own territory. In the end, Bodard proved right at least in one respect: there was going to be street war between two underground forces.

If the *France-Soir* story was unfortunate and the location of the villas unwise, another, more worrisome error followed. By December Dauer needed replacements—some MPC militants were already back in Paris, because they were ill, or because they had volunteered in the first place only for a limited period of time. Bitterlin was manning the villas with a token force. Dauer mentioned his problem to members of the Gaullist Service d'Action Civique. He could have done no rasher thing.

SAC, as it was called, was a loose-knit but tough-minded and little-publicized association, derived from the old protection service of the Rassemblement du Peuple Français, that furnished the Gaullist party with bodyguards, bouncers at political rallies, armed watchmen at local party offices and headquarters.* De Gaulle's own skilled, heavy-set bodyguards—the famed *"gorilles"*—were generally drawn from and belonged to SAC. It was, in short, a private police force that was composed of fanatic Gaullists and operated on the fringes of power. Word of Dauer's request was promptly relayed through SAC to Dominique Ponchardier and Pierre Lemarchand.

The role of the two men in what ensued remains shadowy. Ponchardier had gained considerable fame during World War II as the organizer of "Operation Jericho"—a combined land-and-air assault by the Royal Air Force and the French Resistance upon Amiens Prison to liberate French patriots sentenced to death by the Germans. The operation succeeded, although at heavy cost. Subsequently Ponchardier was connected with SDECE, the French CIA, and wrote a series of best-selling adventure tales about a hefty, inarticulate undercover agent, The Gorilla, an overweight Gallic James Bond who battles foreign spies and evildoers around the globe. The brother of an admiral—and an affable sinewy man, not nearly as muscle-bound as his fictional hero—Ponchardier retained close connections with Interior Minister Frey and other members of the Gaullist government.

Lemarchand, a lawyer and a much younger man, represented the Yonne department for the Gaullist party in the National Assembly. In Paris he acquired a reputation as an ambitious politician. In the subsequent Ben Barka affair,† his name would crop up recurrently, linked to a procession of underworld figures—police tipsters, informers, part-time counterespionage agents and gangsters. Both Ponchardier and Lemarchand belonged informally to a special group centered around Frey and one of de Gaulle's aides at the Élysée Palace, Pierre Lefranc.

Dauer's request for reinforcements brought unusually swift ac-

* De Gaulle turned to SAC in his May 30, 1968, speech after two weeks of near-revolutionary disorders in France, to set up committees for the defense of the Republic, this time against a Leftist threat. De Gaulle left no doubt that he would back these committees in Paris and the provinces to the hilt in using harsh measures to put down an attempted overthrow of the government. Membership in SAC and the CDRs (Comités de Défense de la République) often proved interchangeable. Since de Gaulle quit office in April 1969, SAC's role has waned.

† A prominent Moroccan liberal, Ben Barka was kidnaped in broad daylight in Paris' St.-Germain-des-Prés neighborhood in 1965 and never seen again. He is presumed to have been murdered as a result of collusion between Moroccan secret police and contractual agents on the payroll of French counterespionage, but the charge was never proved.

tion. A score or more of volunteers were recruited for unspecified hazardous duty in Algiers. The recruits included a fifty-year-old former Foreign Legion officer and veteran of the International Brigade in Spain, Mario Lobianco; a Tunisian-born Frenchman who ran a judo school in Paris, Jim Alcheik; two Tunisians; a Vietnamese close-combat instructor and ex-paratrooper, Roger Bui-The; and three of his compatriots. There were also a tattooed young French paratrooper, Claude Veillard, and two of Goulay's hard-nosed friends, a trucker and former Gaullist party bodyguard named Marcel Pisano and a Korean War veteran, Pierre Le Cerf.

They were chosen primarily on the basis of brute strength and physical skill; they had no formal police or intelligence training, their political comprehension was, to be polite about it, shallow. Most were Gaullists with war records in Indochina; some were drawn to Algeria by the prospect of a knock-down-and-drag-out fight wth an anti-Gaullist enemy, others simply by money. These were the *barbouzes*—a slang word meaning "phony beards" and first applied to special police missions, and later very loosely used to connote everything from "gumshoe" to "spook." In France it has a strongly pejorative sense. Among themselves the *barbouzes* referred to their group as *"Le Talion,"* which refers to the Biblical "eye for an eye" and means "retaliation."

They received identity papers under assumed names, entry permits for Algeria and the Sahara, and weapons. They were promised relatively high salaries ranging up to $800 a month. Special $10,000 life-insurance policies were taken out on their account—the figure could not be more generous because insurance companies would not issue high-premium policies for more than this amount without a medical examination, which would have been impractical, since some recruits were already on their way to Algeria.

Dauer at this point was suspicious of SAC and should have looked more closely at the reinforcements he was getting; but enthusiasm ran high, and furthermore he was not always kept informed of who was being recruited or for what purpose. In Paris there was talk of recruiting two hundred agents, a figure that corresponded oddly to Hacq's task force. In the *barbouzes'* case the figure was never attained; throughout Algeria they would never exceed eighty men.

There were now three distinct anti-OAS operations in Algiers: Mission C, working quietly but within the law; Dauer's group, purportedly political; and the new recruits, acting outside the law. But the two latter groups merged and became virtually one. Moreover, Bitterlin and Goulay did not share Dauer's scruples about overclose collaboration with SAC and resort to unorthodox, extralegal methods. In defense of the MPC's conversion, Bitterlin noted that for the past year no one had taken the movement seriously; the few remaining Gaullists and liberals in Algeria were to all intents and purposes abandoned by the mother party in France, and cooperation was written off as a lost cause. The Association pour le Soutien du Général de Gaulle had practically ceased activity during the summer. Now, equipped with arms and money, militant Gaullists suddenly had to be reckoned with again. Goulay, his deputy, took the same belligerent view.

Upon arrival in Algiers, the *barbouzes* settled into Villas A and B. Goulay's enthusiasm was so great at the presence of a Gaullist force in the hostile city that he advocated hoisting a tricolor flag emblazoned with the Cross of Lorraine over Villa A. In view of what ensued, it was just as well that he did not.

Dauer got his first clear idea on December 11 of what was happening to the MPC in Algiers, including the unusual fact that his movement now boasted a number of Vietnamese members. Again he objected; but it was too late. The Mouvement pour la Coopération had radically changed character in one week's time. "Once something like this gets going," Dauer observes simply these days, "it is almost impossible to stop."

The men who had recruited the Vietnamese acknowledged that it would be difficult to keep their presence in Algiers secret for long, but contended that they could be isolated and used to train others in judo and karate. It was a wholly insincere argument, and from this point onward, interference became flagrant. The MPC's original plan of action had been taken over midway without apologies by men who felt a compulsion to serve de Gaulle in the way they knew best—in the shadows, without rules.

It must be added, however, that it had become impossible to continue simply with billposting as an anti-OAS weapon: a choice presented itself between withdrawal pure and simple from Algiers or conversion into a secret "parallel" police. Dauer wanted the former; but he was at a disadvantage, for men who had access to government funds wanted the latter.

A good deal more money suddenly became available. On a flying inspection trip to Villa A, Dauer was unpleasantly struck by the corrupting effect quick money in the form of unvouchered funds had in only a week's time; he found the atmosphere anything but austere.

It has since been suggested that the real number of *barbouzes* was padded to justify the outlay of substantial sums. The truth is impossible to get at; *barbouzes'* finances were handled irregularly, all transactions were handled in cash, there were no receipts and no records. According to some reports, $500,000 in government funds were eventually earmarked for the operation, and of this amount $300,000 were never convincingly accounted for.

The government officially denied and redenied their existence (and to this day it has never admitted any link with them). But by the late fall the *barbouzes'* presence in Algiers was an open secret, a result partly of their own amateurishness. On one occasion, Bitterlin's men surprised an individual loitering about the villa on Rue Favre and forced him at gun-point inside. The man's wife alerted a neighbor, a smallish Air France employee, who, Bitterlin recalls, pounded repeatedly at the villa door, "barking like a mutt." He too was held for questioning. Soon, both men's wives were outside Villa A, loudly protesting. The entire street was presently in an uproar. Alerted, Military Security troops arrived with scout cars and freed the two men.

With all this, it was not surprising that the city got wind of the *barbouzes'* existence. The OAS reacted slowly. Through his Army network, Godard had received a tip about the recruiting of special agents in Paris, but that and the *France-Soir* story were all. He minimized the intruders' importance, just as he had minimized the chances of rallying the 11ème Bataillon de Choc to the OAS cause; an eternal realist, Godard thought all secret services were basically unreliable. Then, as more explicit information poured in through the *téléphone arabe*—the grapevine of gossip, conjecture and fact relayed Moslem-style mouth-to-mouth by the *pieds noirs*—and thanks to the *barbouzes'* own mistakes, Godard obtained a clearer idea of the enemy, who they were and where they were.

He transmitted this information to Degueldre, who decided, if only as a matter of prestige, to eliminate the *barbouzes*.

There had already been several false alerts at Villa A. Thus, Bitterlin and Goulay paid no special attention that evening—December 11—when they noticed several telephone linesmen lingering outside the house and two cars occupied by embracing couples parked farther down the street.

The next morning, Bitterlin's wife and an MPC member left the house early to attend an operations meeting in another part of El Biar. Bitterlin and Goulay planned to follow them in a second car, a Mercedes. A half hour later they stepped outside, and Goulay backed the car into a dead end. Two streets led uphill from the corner on which the villa was located; these were the only ways to leave the neighborhood. A car stood parked a short distance away in each street. Goulay quickly understood the danger, but as he shouted and slammed into forward gear trying to build up enough speed to break out of the trap, the occupants of both cars opened fire with submachine guns. Bitterlin rolled out on the sidewalk. Goulay, wounded in the chest, slumped onto the adjoining seat. The car stalled. The Deltas tossed a concussion grenade, which exploded at about thirty feet from the Mercedes, then the two attacking cars turned about and roared off.

Miraculously, neither Goulay nor Bitterlin was killed although police subsequently found *ninety* 9-mm. shells in the street. What had saved them was the heavy car's thick steel and the impatience of the gunmen, who had opened fire prematurely instead of raking the Mercedes broadside. Goulay was transported to Maillot Hospital and successfully operated upon; for official purposes he was identified as Guillot, a member of Military Security—the only way to obtain emergency treatment at the Army hospital. Bitterlin, alias Dulac, was bandaged up and released the same day. He was suffering from some shock.* The Délégation Générale arranged to keep the story out of the papers, but the attack meant that the OAS had identified and located its enemy.

Several days later Bitterlin drove with four bodyguards to Maillot Hospital. He assigned two Vietnamese to stand watch in the hos-

---

* Dauer believes that Bitterlin's shock and weakness after this first attack was exploited by Morin's staff to transform the MPC from a political to a police operation. He has suggested that if Goulay had not been hospitalized, he would have better withstood official pressure—this is not necessarily so, for Goulay too, as has been noted, favored tough tactics.

pital courtyard; the others went to Goulay's ward. Bitterlin was in the sickroom when he heard spaced bursts of gunfire. Rushing out, he found the men he had left on guard firing in vain at a fast-retreating blue Peugeot. The Peugeot had passed before the courtyard slowly, then—obviously on the basis of accurate information—sprayed the two cars from Villa A with automatic weapons. The guards' automatic pistols had momentarily jammed, then they had returned fire and driven off the attackers.

Attracted by the fusillade, a crowd stood just outside the hastily shut hospital gates. Some one shouted, "*Algérie française!*" and the cry was taken up, defiantly. The armed Vietnamese in civilian clothes were highly conspicuous. A murmur ran through the crowd. Several stones sailed through the air and landed at Bitterlin's feet.

Bitterlin and the guards began to move back from the gate.

The two Vietnamese held the growing *pied noir* crowd at bay, moving their automatic pistols carefully at waist level in a slow arc from left to right to cover the entrance. One Vietnamese was in a crouching stance, his pistol thrust far out, his thin finger fluttering very near the trigger. Bitterlin could feel as a distinct physical sensation the man's desire to start shooting. Bitterlin whispered to him to remain calm.

They were dimly conscious of another crowd forming in the hospital doorway behind; they heard exclamations and startled queries, but they dared not look around.

Bitterlin had no idea how to get away. The rear tires of both cars were deflated, punctured by bullets. It was midmorning, but not a policeman or military patrol was in sight. It was clear that the Deltas had followed them from the villa. Bitterlin was painfully aware that soon, alerted by the commotion, the Peugeot might return and, if no one came to the rescue, would wipe them out with the crowd's lusty approval. He was tempted to shoot his way out of the courtyard while there was still time.

Step by step they backed away and reached the relative security of the hospital. The other bodyguards were in the hall. An Army doctor, a colonel, strode out at the head of an indignant excited group—patients in dressing gowns, visitors, two soldiers in wheelchairs. Among them, thought Bitterlin, "there was not a friendly face." The colonel, speechless with anger, motioned to the Vietnamese to clear out. Bitterlin told them to stay where they were.

An hour passed. Bitterlin had called up the Délégation Générale and been advised to stay still and wait for reinforcements. The colonel had furiously called the police. Shortly after noon, a patrol car drove into the courtyard and blocked the entrance; the gates were then reclosed. The police chief of Bab el Oued stormed into the hall. "Who the hell are these people?" he roared with rage. Identifying himself as Dulac, Bitterlin explained that his men belonged to Military Security; on the strength of their desperate aspect and ragged discipline, it must have appeared a particularly unconvincing tale.

"We can't have this in a hospital. They'll have to surrender their arms and leave," the police chief ordered.

Bitterlin said flatly, "They need their arms to defend themselves."

While one Vietnamese covered the police chief, Bitterlin rang up Villa B for help.

At one o'clock, another car drove up to the locked gates. Bui-The, the ex-paratrooper, hopped out and peremptorily pointed his machine gun at the policeman on duty, while another Vietnamese slipped out of the car. The crowd hooted, whistled and cursed but backed off still further as the two *barbouzes* entered the hospital. The police chief was beside himself at Bui-The's behavior. "He pointed it at me! I'm responsible for law and order, and he pointed his gun at *me!*" Bitterlin thought the man was ready to break down.

Word of the *barbouzes'* plight by this time had reached Mission C, probably the only force in Algiers capable of dealing practically with the grim little standoff.

A half hour later, a detachment of CRS troops, policemen and detectives from Hussein Dey police school arrived at the hospital. An inspector of Mission C worriedly advised Bitterlin to try henceforth to keep his men under control. An alarm was out for the blue Peugeot, but the search was expected to yield no results. Presently, under heavy escort, an armor-plated police van containing the *barbouzes* moved slowly out of the courtyard. The convoy reached Hussein Dey without further incident.

Spotting unhoped-for propaganda opportunities, Susini and his staff launched a word-of-mouth campaign accusing the government of hiring "hundreds" of paid killers recruited among FLN terrorists under sentence of death, gangsters from the lower depths of Marseilles and Corsica, Vietnamese members of French military intelligence to hound and stalk the *pieds noirs*. Lurid tales were spread of the *barbouzes'* villas, car pool, short-wave radio link with Paris, and interrogation centers. Since these stories contained a grain of truth, the psychological effect on the Europeans was traumatic. They rapidly became convinced that hundreds of secret agents were on the loose, and claimed to see yellow-skinned interlopers at every street corner. The depradations of several Delta commandos had caused Morin to fear a howling bloodthirsty mob composed of thousands of OAS militants; the same mental process of magnification played havoc with the jittery *pieds noirs'* nerves.

In France itself, the Right thundered against the "parallel police," while the Left sneered at the Gaullist government as *la République des barbouzes*. Radical Socialist leader François Mitterand wrote, with considerable bias: "I don't think our country has ever known, as much as now, such a flowering of bureaucrats, parabureaucrats, and agents secret, semisecret and some not secret at all, whose only task is to guard the regime and the security of its leaders."* Some of these taunts undoubtedly stung, and behind the scenes official reaction to what was happening in Algeria was almost completely adverse. Debré registered strong displeasure, but temporarily held his hand. Ailleret, who had been given no opportunity to express an opinion about the advisabiliy of sending untrained secret agents into his area, predicted that they would do more harm than good.

This proved not wholly correct. The *barbouzes'* prime justification, in the eyes of the men who recruited them, was to collaborate with Mission C. Hacq's two hundred inspectors, newly arrived on December 1, needed time to become acquainted with local conditions; in the meanwhile, it was hoped the *barbouzes* could ferret out information and use strong-arm methods unemployable by the police to collar suspects and turn them over to regular authorities. And, in a sense, this was what they did.

From Moslem informants Bitterlin's men obtained detailed lists of OAS members with telephone and car-license numbers. They passed these lists on to Hacq, who was now installed in an office at Hussein Dey police school under the cover name of Professor Ermelin. Hacq screened the information for his task force's use, then relayed it to Paris, where it was matched against the early data obtained by Grassien's brigade.

The *barbouzes* also carried out an increasing number of counter-

---

* In *La Nef*, "La Police en France."

plastiquages, to give the OAS a taste of its own medicine. It was, however, typical of the confusion with which the entire episode was overlaid that their equipment proved inadequate to the task. On one occasion, Alcheik the Tunisian judo expert set out with plastique and a pencil fuse to blow up a café identified as an OAS hangout. He concealed the plastique in the washroom, and waited across the street for it to go off. It never did, for the supplier had failed to provide a detonator.

For Bitterlin it was a source of bitter irony that the OAS waged war with arms and equipment pilfered from military dumps, while the progovernment *barbouzes*, as time went by, could no longer draw on this source and had to rely on improvisation for logistical support.

Words like "counter-counterterrorism" are meaningless; they obfuscate reality.

From a *pied noir's* point of view, FLN agents were terrorists, OAS militants were counterterrorists; by this yardstick, the *barbouzes* were counter-counterterrorists. But from a Moslem's point of view, the opposite held true: the original terrorists belonged to right-wing European organizations, and when the FLN riposted, it was counterterrorism.

One must sum up matters in Algiers, as winter began, by saying that four or five semisecret forces, driven by duty, impassioned loyalty to a cause, despair and vindictiveness, were warring on one another—often for unclear tactical reasons—in a strange subterranean struggle where, as one OAS member remarked, "networks often resembled gangs." Ominously, the conflict aggravated racial tension. In the process, normal city life died.

During the dark the sign painters and bill posters went about their work anonymously. In the shadows, gunmen stalked their targets. Throughout that late fall fear came with the night.

Daybreak brought the return of a semblance of normality, if it could be called that. *Algérois* found MPC slogans on the walls, OAS flags streaming from trolley cables and OAS balloons floating over the city. The Prefecture hired Moslem volunteers to obliterate the OAS slogans with white paint; the police referred to them as the

"Rembrandt Brigade," but it was no laughing matter when the OAS killed some. Shopowners bombed during the predawn hours swept out the debris of glass into gutters before knots of curious onlookers. In an empty lot, workers came upon a man's body in a burlap sack, disfigured, throat cut and papers removed; they speculated whether the victim was a European set upon by the FLN or a Moslem who had fallen afoul of the OAS—it was impossible to tell.

In the midst of the spreading destruction, Algiers continued about its affairs although day by day administration and business faltered a bit more. Fewer customers bought in stores, fewer new buildings went up, bank managers noted fewer deposits and more withdrawals of accounts.*

The *pieds noirs* grew unaccustomedly taciturn. Occasionally the apathy gave way to bursts of sadistic anger. A crowd caught two Moslems on scooters in a narrow street and set them ablaze.

Children continued to play in the lukewarm sunlight of the Place des Trois Horloges at Bab el Oued: they had fashioned a makeshift rag doll in general's uniform, ungainly, tall, with a beak-nose and a swelling belly. Chanting nursery songs and urged on by their parents, they stood the effigy of de Gaulle upright and burned it.

---

* Axel Nicol, in *La Bataille de l'OAS*, described the economic situation toward the end of 1961 in these terms: "Building starts are stagnating, sales figures for cars have tumbled, merchandise is not being renewed, banks refuse credit, wholesalers and dealers in Metropolitan France insist on immediate payment . . . bills remain unpaid, and loan and credit corporations are nearly all bankrupt." Nicol said there were no further investments by French and foreign industrialists due to the fear of nationalization and confiscation by the FLN.

15

A New Year's Eve Celebration

THE INVOLVEMENT of the people of Oran in the movement took place gradually. Day by day a growing number of *pieds noirs* assumed mysterious airs, let it be understood that they were playing a role. There was naturally no open enrollment, no membership drive, but a spreading network of sympathy and complicity; small favors were requested and granted. A young blonde, Nicole Monier, was asked to deliver mail without asking questions. She accepted; without knowing it, she was serving as a letter drop for Jouhaud. Had she known, she would have been overjoyed.

It became virtually impossible to avoid running into a relative, a neighbor or an acquaintance on some sort of unusual mission. Nicole thought, It's easier to count up those who are against the OAS.

The European liberals had cleared out, or no longer dared express an opinion. A secretary at the prefecture who refused to join an OAS protest strike was found shot dead in her apartment.

Security forces were proving unwieldy in antiterrorist operations; gendarmes and CRS troops could seal off an entire quarter, but were slow at pursuing one or two youths who struck, then melted into street traffic.

By winter, the OAS commanded the active sympathy of personnel at the Banque de France and other banks, within the municipal administration, in trade-unions; among businessmen, parish priests and schoolteachers; from top to bottom of the social scale—a prominent foundry owner, a postal clerk, the Spanish fishermen of the port. Jewish shopkeepers mortally fearful of an Arab takeover rallied to the OAS and formed self-defense groups.

Charles Micheletti, president of the Social Security Fund for the Building Trades, a nervous suspicious middle-aged man, was the local Organization's driving force. Micheletti theorized a good deal about subversive warfare, though in fact his knowledge of it was rudimentary—as was that of the other OAS civilian chiefs, Daniel Brun, secretary general of the local trade committee, Tassou Georgopoulos, manager of Oran's Whisky à Gogo nightclub, Pancho Gonzalez, a gypsy who ran a driving school but derived most of his income from expedients. Together they formed a strong-arm gang determined to make life miserable and dangerous for anybody in the city who questioned their ideas or resisted their authority—it was as simple as that.

Theoretically they took orders from Jouhaud, who commanded all of western Algeria—Zone III—in Salan's name. After passing the summer in the hot interior among winegrowers and rural priests who sheltered him from the police, Jouhaud had come to Oran in early September and made a partially successful attempt to establish his authority over the city's four loosely knit activist groups.* Under a colorful array of code names—"Compagnon," "Soleil bis," and even "Yazid"—he flitted from one apartment hideout to another, enjoying a certain popularity as a native son. But his command was more apparent than real. Micheletti and the other civilian leaders thought of him as a useful figurehead who represented a stabilizing influence among the various hotheaded factions; but they deplored his reluctance to use "revolutionary tactics"—by which they meant political assassination.

The Moslems, wittingly or not, played into the OAS's hands. Whenever FLN terrorists attacked, the Organization's recruiting spurted. A car containing several Arabs ran down a forty-year-old European named Martin Agullo; as he lay helpless in the street, they jumped out, shot him in the head, poured gas over his body, set it afire, then drove off. It was Sunday afternoon in Oran; by Sunday evening there were *ratonnades*—manhunts organized against Arab victims.

---

* The OAS under Pancho Gonzalez; a militant group led by Georgopoulos; the so-called "Groupe Bonaparte," an equivalent of Degueldre's Deltas; and France-Résurrection.

Le Thiais, the police prefect, saw the city seesawing in a "balance of terror" between the FLN and OAS. In the same week his personal mail brought twin death threats, one, an OAS warning, scribbled on a post card showing a view of the Cathedral, the other, an FLN ultimatum to desist from further action, scrawled on a rough sheet of paper. The first was signed, *"Un pied noir qui vous reglera votre compte bien tôt."** The second said, in misspelled French, *"Bon corage, je fé de priair pour vous."*† If subsequently neither threat was executed, it was for lack of opportunity, not intent, Le Thiais was convinced.

At about this time, alarming stories began circulating in both communities about the hospitals. Some European doctors were accused of cold-bloodedly murdering Moslems in their care; *pieds noirs* brought to Moslem clinics were allegedly bled to death, and their blood transfused to wounded FLN guerrillas. The grisly tales, provoked by mounting distrust, were never proved; at worst, a doctor might refuse to treat a Moslem suspected of collaborating with the FLN even if critically wounded, which was bad enough, but even such cases were not documented.‡ But accidents could happen, and the hospitals of Oran were not safe.

Gaston Pernot, local head of the Association pour le Soutien du Général de Gaulle, had made the mistake of trying to note the license numbers of cars honking *"Algérie française"* during a street demonstration. A European mob had pursued him, broken his arm, beaten him bloody and tried to lynch him; when CRS troops res-

* "A *pied noir* who will soon settle your hash."
† Sarcastically, "Cheer up, I'm saying prayers for you."
‡ Dr. Bernard Laffy, a liberal *pied noir* who practiced in Algeria at the time, says there was a duality in the attitude of European doctors: they gave Moslems medical attention, but would not hesitate to set plastique at the apartments of the same Moslems once released from hospital. Oran's General Hospital boasted what amounted to an OAS ward run by a European doctor who contributed to the movement, faked medical certificates and facilitated the escape of wounded gunmen. The doctor was finally interned as a nuisance, but escaped—perhaps while officials looked the other way, for the government was more anxious to put an end to his activities than keep him under lock and key.
Conditions were no different in Algiers, where a crackdown was ordered at Mustapha Hospital after fifty-four OAS suspects escaped in a two-month period. Thereafter, visits were suspended; doctors were required to show papers upon entering and leaving; and a medical checkup was carried out to determine cases of malingering.

cued him he was dragged forcibly out of their jeep and thrown down on the street, on the side of his fractured arm.

Several days later he lay convalescing in a small private room of a seaside clinic. Without realizing it he was recuperating in an institution whose sympathies were strongly pro-OAS.

Pernot was drowsy with shock and did not pay much attention when a *pied noir* nurse entered the sickroom, flung open the window contrary to standing orders and immediately left. Across a narrow passageway stood several men studying him intently. Pernot saw an object sailing through the open window. It was a grenade. "You don't have much time to think. I was groggy and thought, It's a pebble," he said later. A bouquet of flowers on a table slightly deflected the grenade's trajectory, and instead of landing on the bed as intended, it rolled on the floor. Then it blew up. The underside of the bed absorbed some of the explosion. Pernot was still alive.

On de Gaulle's personal orders he was immediately evacuated to France. No attempt was made to prove criminal responsibility on the nurse's part.

The original impetus of the OAS had carried it very far, to a point where, in all but name, it ruled Algiers, did as it pleased in Oran, and extended its grip to a half dozen smaller cities with a high density of *pieds noirs*—Bône, Mostaganem, Tiaret, Cherchell.* A myth had taken root in the fall and flourished of an invincible, octopus-like Organization which "struck where it wanted, when it wanted," was commanded by a monolithic leadership and enjoyed surreptitious support in high places. The cease-fire had not been signed, pirate broadcasts tirelessly reminded the Europeans, and might never be signed. And as long as it was not signed there was hope.

Algiers by some was now referred to as "Salan's city." Thanks to Susini's assiduous efforts, the single word *Salan* was chalked everywhere on walls almost more frequently than O A S. A British correspondent reported that a questionnaire sent to the general through the central post office drew a reply within forty-eight hours.

Salan was behaving every day less like a renegade general, and more with the authority of a respectable rival for de Gaulle's power. He wrote an open letter to *gendarmerie* Colonel Jean Debrosse pro-

---

* The OAS made very imperfect progress in Constantine, the capital of eastern Algeria, where Moslems greatly outnumbered *pieds noirs*.

testing the arrest and torture of Captain Noëlle Luchetti.* He ordered the *pieds noirs* to remain calm on November 1, the seventh anniversary of the rebellion; congratulated the Moslems afterward for avoiding provocation, and promised to take the case of Algérie Française to the United Nations. The same month, he gave an interview "somewhere in Algeria" to a CBS correspondent and warned of the establishment of a Communist popular republic in North Africa in the wake of an FLN victory. To de Gaulle's notable displeasure the interview was aired in the United States, giving the movement further publicity abroad.†

The GPRA itself showed signs of treating the Organization seriously. From Tunis, Yazid served notice: "If the French authorities do not take necessary measures to put an end to murders and lynchings, the anger of our people will swoop down implacably." For all the GPRA's standard amount of huffing and puffing, this warning betrayed a new, tardy awareness of the OAS's force.

The Organization was at its zenith, at that critical point where a clandestine movement emerges as a semiovert fighting and political force. Did Salan realize the need to act decisively? Almost surely not. He was convinced that time was working for the OAS. His natural indolence encouraged this complacent outlook; but it was also due to the serious mistake of thinking that the OAS had the whole country behind it, and to the equally dangerous myth that as long as Debré continued as prime minister nothing could go seriously wrong and Algeria would at all cost remain French. Rightist Deputy Philippe Marçais called on Morin at this time, using Bidault as an introduction, and echoed Bidault's (and Salan's) confidence in an imminent collapse of the Gaullist government through its own inner contradictions. This wishful thinking permeated the OAS.

Salan's attention meanwhile was unproductively monopolized by the OAS's chronic problems—constant discord at the top, and a per-

* Arrested in September, Salan's ex-secretary was held for twenty-two days at the Caserne des Tagarins. The OAS charged that she was turned over for interrogation to Debrosse, who kept her in an "infamous room without air, light or water" and subjected her to threats and torture. She was eventually removed to France. Commenting on Salan's letter of protest, *Le Monde* noted on October 1: "It was under his proconsulate that torture developed, not to say was institutionalized, in Algeria . . ." This referrred to the 1957 Battle of Algiers.

† Salan's alarm left American public opinion unmoved, but he did receive autograph requests from several American admirers, and one minuscule group in New York formed a Committee for the Defense of French Algeria.

ilous absence of discipline. While most militants had made a conscientious effort in the early days of the Organization's development
to obey orders and practice caution, now, in the period of the OAS's
strength, they blabbed in cafés, bars and restaurants, ran wild and
committed frightful mistakes.

For two months a Delta commando had sought to execute William Levy, the Socialist party's secretary general in Algiers condemned to death on Degueldre's order for his open hostility to the
OAS; for various reasons the mission had aborted each time it was
undertaken. Then, on the evening of November 18, two Deltas roared
off on a motor scooter to get the job done on their own. By chance
they came upon Levy at a street corner near his house. The gunman
on the rear seat took careful aim, fired three times and dropped the
secretary general dead in his tracks. Before fleeing, they scattered
black cardboard triangles in the street to show that the murder was
the work of the Deltas.

When they returned to their hideout, they learned that the *opération ponctuelle* had been scratched a week before.

Salan learned of the assassination next morning through the papers. He went white with fury; no one had consulted him beforehand, and the attack came at an especially awkward time, in the
wake of the murder of two other Socialists, the mayors of Évian and
Fort de l'Eau.* Just as no crime affects a policeman more unpleasantly than the murder of another policeman, so the same may be
said of politicians, at least those who belong to the same party.
Mollet and the Socialists were unforgiving; Rightist deputies listened uncomfortably to their outraged recriminations and could do
little but weakly condemn the OAS's resort to murder. The emotional impact on the Socialists was all the greater since Levy's own
son had ben killed by the FLN; he could therefore hardly be taxed
with FLN sympathies. Then, two weeks later an OAS tract com-
pounded the blunder by blusteringly claiming credit for the slaying.
Salan brooded still another week in icy anger and finally wrote an
open letter to Mollet expressing "total disapproval" of the attack,
for which he blamed "extremist little groups" who were trying to

* An explosive charge set off by activists took the life of Camille Blanc,
mayor of Évian, on March 31, shortly before the Évian negotiations were to
begin. The OAS shot Dr. Schembri, mayor of Fort de l'Eau, on July 19.

destroy a political line he thought sound. This belated effort to patch matters up was unsuccessful. The Socialist Party Federation of the Seine organized a "William Levy Day," trade-union orators attacked the OAS, and even the moderate Right showed embarrassment. To all intents and purposes Salan's painstaking attempt to gain an alliance with respectable political forces in France was wrecked.

The affair revealed not only faulty communications within the Delta commandos, but—ominously—Salan's utter inability to control the deadliest elements within the Organization. For it was by no means certain that if he had forbidden the murder he would have been obeyed—"mistakes" occasionally happened, and in the secret army the commanding general had limited ways of enforcing discipline. As it was, his letter to Mollet nettled avowed Rightists like Perez and Degueldre and many *pieds noirs* who were already displeased by his effort to win over *Le Monde* and liberal opinion, and interpreted his latest gesture as a disavowal.

Susini's self-declared aim was to obtain for the OAS fifty thousand weapons that ranged from bazookas to machine guns and heavy mortars. In his opinion, this would give new stimulus to deserter officers already in the Organization, attract others, and permit equipping a clandestine army.

Susini's account of subsequent events is as follows:

In the late fall, using Salan's and Ferrandi's career-long contacts with United States intelligence services inside and outside NATO, the OAS leadership established contact with a three-man mission of Americans who arrived from Paris. They were connected in an unspecified way with the Embassy. It was understood the talks were technical and exploratory and could not engage the United States government.

The three men were well informed and matter-of-fact—they wanted to know what was needed, where it would be used, how many popular battalions the OAS could hope to muster. Susini quickly decided there was no reason to try to bluff, and spelled out the bleak truth: the OAS in Algiers amounted to several thousand militants and possessed no more than three hundred submachine guns; the situation was roughly the same in Oran.

Preliminary details were worked out to unload a clandestine arms shipment on the same beaches which the United States Army had used twenty years earlier when carrying out "Operation Torch," the North African landings against the Vichy French. At the time American officers had established close working contact with some *pieds noirs*, and their cooperation was to be sought again if the plan, which implied secret American support of the OAS's strategic aims, was approved and executed.

Susini stressed that time was short, and the three men agreed to give a quick reply. Shortly afterward they returned and said the United States government in the person of the State Department was uninterested in further contact. So the whole scheme was dropped there and then. The mission left and never came back.

Following this setback, the OAS made two further attempts to acquire weapons. First it turned to an international arms merchant in Monte Carlo, with the intention this time of carrying on strictly a cash-and-carry transaction with no political overtones. However, when Susini's emissaries admitted they had two million dollars at most, the businessman said he never dealt for less than ten million, and the negotiation was cut short. The same thing occurred in Italy.

Perez's budget alone was now running to one hundred thousand dollars a month. The money was needed for the Deltas, their families, and intelligence-gathering; the printing of *Appel de France* and equipment for pirate broadcasts simultaneously entailed heavy expenses for Susini's branch. Moreover, some attempt was being made to give rank-and-file militants enough money to cover one month's operational needs in the event they were cut off from the leadership during a new wave of government raids.

Fund raising and extortion* could not possibly meet these demands. A dangerous new course was traced out when an employee at the port of Algiers approached Gardes and told him that the

---

* The best-publicized victim of an extortion attempt was Brigitte Bardot. On November 30, she rceived a mimeographed letter asking for $10,000, based on an estimated proration of her annual movie earnings. The letter was signed by a certain J. Lenoir, "chief of the Financial Services of the OAS." She replied furiously that she would not give in (*"Je ne marche pas!"*) and turned over the letter to her lawyers. Police guarded her Paris apartment on Avenue Paul Doumer and the extortionist was not heard from again. Because of her strong anti-OAS opinions, Brigitte Bardot's films were temporarily boycotted by *pieds noirs* in Algeria.

Merchant Marine Retirement Fund payroll passed through his hands each month. The *pied noir* suggested turning over this money to Gardes as a patriotic gesture. Gardes refused on characteristically moral grounds, for he did not want to deprive retired seamen of their pensions.

When Perez learned of the refusal, he vehemently disagreed and argued that embezzlement was a military operation no more or less than pilfering arms from an arsenal. Furthermore, he said, the seamen would eventually be paid as the government was under an obligation to them.

In the end, the employee on his own brought $160,000 to the OAS. Subsequent press reports said $220,000 had disappeared; so the supposition arose that he had kept some of the money when he vanished from his office, or had already embezzled it at an earlier date and was covering up private dishonesty with an allegedly patriotic act. The sum constituted the OAS's first war chest.

As the need for money continued unabated, Perez's thoughts inevitably turned to another government-run institution—and shortly afterward Delta commandos attacked a Social Security office in Algiers. Later, Perez justified launching the Organization on this course: "Without holdups the OAS would quickly have smothered," he said. But he admitted that it attracted underworld figures, as well as mercenaries, tipsters, operators and opportunists who floated in the proximity of suspect sources of money. It presented an insuperable temptation—all the more so since holdups could often be carried out with practically no risk, thanks to the complicity of bank managers and other local "patriots."

Once again, the odd recurring duality between the OAS and FLN cropped up. For the methods were the same as thirteen years before, when a young Algerian nationalist named Ahmed Ben Bella held up the central post office in Oran for $60,000, which went into the treasury of the FLN's first terrorist group, the Organisation Spéciale.

Though on a much smaller scale than in Algeria, the malady of plastique was spreading in France. The explosions sometimes had almost a surrealistic character. A Jewish mathematics professor's study was bombed, and the keys of his piano were blown into the street. Paris' new American-style "Drugstore" was attacked, and through the broken plate glass a cloud of released perfume wafted onto the Champs Élysées. These were really circus stunts, as Sergent strove to make an impression on the public. He himself attached little importance to the attacks—"Plastique never hurt anybody," he commented blandly to a friend.

But his obvious deficiencies as the head of a revolutionary movement were increasingly difficult to overlook. His uncoordinated *plastiquages* had achieved the negative result of rendering the OAS odious in Paris, especially among those influential opinion molders, the concierges, and he was making no discernible headway in unifying the various activist networks throughout the rest of the country. The last straw came with the publication of another grandiloquent interview. On November 29, the Paris correspondent of the Stockholm newspaper *Aftonbladet,* Christina Liliesterna, was driven blindfolded to a suburban house, where she found Sergent, who described himself once again as "chief of general staff of the OAS in France," and declaimed: "France is the last rampart against Communism. . . . Salan is the supreme commander, and I am directly under his orders." This performance was followed by a similar interview for Radio Cologne.

Salan was convinced that his name was being used opportunistically. A few days later he dispatched a new and very different sort of man to France to coordinate civilian and military action in the Métropole.

The man he chose was André Canal. He was a small, muscular Frenchman from Niort who had settled in Algiers in 1940 and made a fortune in sanitary and heating equipment. He was a man who did nothing by halves; business associates said that he would take over any firm he was connected with. Godard introduced him to Salan as a "man of iron." During the late Fifties, Canal had plunged headlong into activist plots—equally motivated, it seemed, by a desire to protect his self-built empire and an addiction to cloak-and-dagger antics. He wore a black monocle in the socket of his left eye, lost as the result of an auto accident; the day after the putsch's collapse, he issued a tract that forecast further resistance, and he signed it, "Le Monocle." From this moment, he used his business cover, like Gingembre, to make frequent liaison trips to Paris; he generously contributed funds, and he obtained arms for the movement through industrial contacts. He was intelligent and slippery enough never to get caught. It must have struck Canal as only just—a recognition of past services—when Salan signed a handwritten letter entrusting him with the new assignment.

For Canal, Mission III* was a sort of apotheosis. In fact, it was true that Salan sorely needed someone in France with authority and shrewdness to represent his affairs; but Canal was also being sent abroad at the urging of Susini and others, who had begun to find his taste for melodramatic action a bit of a nuisance.

Canal arrived in Paris in mid-December. He recruited a number of activists at loose ends, and diligently divided Mission III into three branches—Action, Finance and Propaganda. This was all very well, but he had not reckoned with Sergent. The self-styled "chief of general staff of the OAS in France" swiftly resented the intruder, and when the two finally met in late December, Sergent balked at recognizing Canal's authority. Each thereafter set out to run his own underground organization.

Far from achieving unity, Salan's action had paved the way for permanent and bitter rivalry at the top, within the OAS in France.

December came and went. Some of the reasons why Salan did not try to deal a decisive blow have been examined; in view of his habitual secrecy, we may never know all of them.

The only spectacular action was the blowing up of the French Navy vessel *Laita,* crammed with electronic equipment for jamming pirate broadcasts, as she lay moored in Algiers harbor. *Plastiquages* dwindled; the OAS limited its agitation to tracts and broadcasts, and eventually ordered a Christmas Truce—*"une trêve de Dieu"*— from December 22 to 26, during which it called on Moslems, Jews and Christians to ask divine help for the triumph of a "just cause." The pledge to refrain from killing and bombing was observed— mainly, some said, to permit Europeans to attend midnight Mass. Before the new year began, the truce was over.

On the last night of the year, Degueldre's men crept up to the roof of a house overlooking the villa on Chemin Reynaud. They carried submachine guns, several makeshift bazookas fashioned out of lengths of tube, and a stock of French Army antitank rockets. It was eleven-thirty. They saw lights in the villa and the silhouettes

---

* Sergent's operation was designated as Mission II. Mission I consisted of an informal group of politicians and officers who studied ways of installing an Army-backed government before the April putsch.

of several men indoors. They heard the faint sound of glasses and radio music as the occupants celebrated New Year's Eve. Two sentries were on duty in the garden.

Things were not going well with the *barbouzes'* operation. After brooding for a week, Dauer had reminded Joxe on December 22 that his movement's task was primarily political, and that as the result of interference by "irresponsible elements"—he knew them but could not name them publicly—the MPC was calling off all further action in Algeria. Dauer believes this action saved him from arrest by an incensed Debré.

From the start, the Premier and his closest advisers had looked askance at the presence of a free corps of adventurers in Algiers that rendered the government vulnerable to attacks by both Right and Left. The *barbouzes'* own mistakes during their first month in North Africa had not lessened Debré's antipathy. Dauer was astute enough to foresee that the operation could jeopardize the MPC's future in France, to which he attached prime importance. Thus he decided to order all MPC militants home on December 29; it was the only sane course left, but his action, as he admits, was overdue.

He addressed a letter to Bitterlin in terms that were veiled but whose meaning was clear. The letter read: ". . . Confirming our conversation yesterday, all action must be suspended in Algeria, we'll resume our political struggle when the interference I spoke to you about ceases. I absolutely insist on all our friends being put out to pasture. There can be no exceptions. . . . I hope we can resume our activities, but for the moment the MPC will remain vigilant."

Some of the men in the two villas complied with Dauer's order; Bitterlin and a number of others, perhaps thirty, declined to return. Bitterlin argued by phone that the *barbouzes* were the only anti-OAS opposition to show their faces in Algeria, and by doing so had reinstilled confidence among remaining liberals, put a temporary end to OAS *plastiquages* and drawn offers of cooperation from OCC cells in the Army; moreover, the *barbouzes* were the only group providing Mission C with information. But even Bitterlin agreed that the overconspicuous Vietnamese should be recalled.

It took considerable courage to remain. One must make an effort to realize to just what extent the *barbouzes'* position was abnormal and fraught with hour-to-hour danger. It is hard to imagine secret agents who were so thoroughly like fish out of water. They were perpetually hunted and shunned, their movements spied upon by angry neighbors, local police and OAS informers. Military Security no longer accepted responsibility for their safety and had, they discovered, installed wire taps in the villas. The *barbouzes* purchased food in out-of-the-way Moslem groceries; traveled in threes and fours, always by car, a machine gun held ready in a raincoat, grenades in the glove compartment, and the safety slipped off their pistols. Yet in four days the OAS had put three of their cars out of commission, and Mission C bodyguards had opened fire by mistake on one vehicle when it approached Hussein Dey by night. The few wives present had been sent away for security's sake. As the year ended, the *barbouzes* were on their own.

At Villa B, one of the two guards turned his back and stepped indoors—and, as he did so, the attack began, the Deltas pouring concentrated machine-gun and bazooka fire into the lighted house. Several rockets went wild. Then one bazooka rocket scored a direct hit on a stockpile of grenades. There was a terrific roar and flames surged out of one room. The *barbouzes* made a stand from behind darkened windows. One Vietnamese poked the barrel of a submachine gun through a shattered window and began to rake the roof opposite. Within ten minutes the attack was over; Degueldre had timed it to allow the Deltas to slip off into homebound holiday traffic just before the curfew came into effect and the New Year began.

The OAS suffered no casualties. Later, Bitterlin claimed only one of his men was wounded and none killed in the attack. Other estimates ran much higher.

Elsewhere in Algiers that night, Perez and Broizat hid out in the same building, although in different apartments with different friends. They met and uncorked a bottle of champagne; each had spent a lonely Christmas. But Perez disapproved of Broizat's unwillingness to join the Organization outright; and the colonel refused to condone terrorism. They found they had little to say to one another.

16

The Executions

THREE DAYS after the New Year, tricolor-striped posters appeared on Algiers' walls ordering all European and Moslem males of military age into the ranks of the OAS. The posters bore Gardy's martial slogan, "One gun, one country," and crowds formed to read the stark black text with approval. The Organization compared the draft order to the call-up of the Israeli Army to defend the embattled homeland.

Pieds noirs and Paris officials leaped to the conclusion that Salan's draftcall foreshadowed the long-anticipated second putsch. The follow-up orders reinforced this belief. OAS pirate broadcasts advised housewives to stock two months' food supplies and withdraw all bank accounts. Each European family was requested, moreover, to convert available cash into louis d'or, to undermine the French franc (that this measure could only be self-destructive went unmentioned). The OAS in Oran broadcast advice that fell sweetly on *pieds noirs'* ears, to pay no more taxes to a government "that no longer governed"; and it warned tax collectors, process servers and marshals not to take legal action against citizens in default on their tax payments, on pain of execution. (The hand of the businessmen who ran the Oran Organization showed through clearly in this advice.) A clandestine transmitter nightly repeated the less-than-sibylline code message: "*Les orangers refleuriront bientôt* [The orange trees will blossom soon again]."

On January 11, Morin held an emergency meeting with police officials and the prefects of Algeria's thirteen departments to consider the growing threat. The mood was gloomy, and predictions abounded that soon the breakdown of order would resemble the chaos produced by the Belgian pull-out from the Congo the year before. Morin expected a *coup de force* on or before January 24, the anniversary of the activists' previous high-water mark at the Barricades; the OAS might have been vanquished, he thought, if Michel Hacq's Mission C had arrived the summer before; as it was, it seemed too late. From Oran he received a report that predicted there could be no further peaceful existence between the two racial communities. "It will be a long time before Oran operates as a normal town again," added Le Thiais prophetically.

By January 13, Algiers feared that a putsch would occur within forty-eight hours. The atmosphere at this point was peculiar; a visitor found Morin keeping confidential documents in his coat pocket rather than in his office safe. The Délégation Générale issued stringent new security measures: all motor traffic would be forbidden after nine o'clock in the evening; a car could be driven only by its owner and could circulate with two passengers at most; the reissue of all local license plates would be undertaken as a way of tracing the ownership of OAS vehicles.* In Oran, General Joseph Katz, the local commander, ordered a ban on street parking and authorized security forces to open fire, after a warning shot, on any person trying to evade an identity check. These orders were extended to Algiers.

When Morin learned at about this time that paratroop units had abruptly replaced gendarmes around the Rocher Noir complex, he spent a worried morning and made arrangements for the evacuation of key personnel by helicopter to French Navy vessels standing offshore. He also procured inflatable rubber rafts, a step that prompted sour merriment at his expense; but once again it must be recalled that Morin had lived through a putsch and was not eager to repeat the experience.

Ailleret himself, the commander in chief, now went about his fortified headquarters at La Reghaia outside Algiers protected by special troops and with a submachine gun constantly by his side; and when he drove to Rocher Noir in a bulletproof Citroën, the windows were kept rolled up in spite of the occasional terrific heat.

* This last idea was never carried out.

Ailleret, however, continued to believe that the Army—or a large part of it—would put down a putsch; after his Order of the Day, some officers had advised him they would do so, but gloomily anticipated that after firing on fellow Frenchmen the only honorable solution would be to shoot themselves. Morin feared that the OAS, with the complicity of a few units, would stage a coup and the Army would sit on its hands. On this crucial point Morin and Ailleret never managed clearly to communicate with one another. The misunderstanding between them persisted.

The government, for its part, no longer depreciated Morin's apprehensions. These winter days appeared to represent the ideal moment for the OAS to seize power openly in Algiers and Oran. The government expected a rising and braced for it. The Délégation Générale's political archives were already being evacuated to Paris, out of reach of both the OAS and the FLN. An order of priorities was set up: Rocher Noir must be defended at all cost, as the symbol of official French presence in the country; then Algiers; then Oran. The military plan was to send the Army under Ailleret to retake Algiers if it fell. No one doubted that it could be recaptured, but Debré and his staff thought that if the *pieds noirs* really defended the city and showed readiness to die, it would be difficult to muster enthusiasm in the Army for the task; and it would be necessary, moreover, to appease disturbed international opinion.

In the end, all these alarms came to nothing. No semblance of a putsch occurred either in Algiers or Oran. Why? Above all, it is clear, because Salan had no wish to carry out a *coup de force.** The reason was simple: Salan's trump card was the Army; the OAS's main, unchanged objective was to block a cease-fire agreement with the FLN, but it could not do this without the Army. However, in the event of a new putsch, Salan was by no means sure of the Army's support; the last thing in the world he wanted was a clash with this invaluable potential ally. In secret instructions drafted at the beginning of the month, he made this position clear. "The Army will

---

* Susini has categorically told this writer the OAS made no plans for an insurrection in January. The same has been stated by other former members of the Organization. Paul-Marie de la Gorce, a French writer who has studied the OAS's tactics in detail, believes that if Salan had gambled he could have taken Algiers that winter, then let the situation develop from there, but "he was too methodical, too prudent . . ." The government put itself in Salan's place, and decided that it was now or never; but Salan did not make this estimate of the situation.

not act on our behalf in Algeria," he wrote.* Pro-OAS officers, especially those who commanded conscripts, spoke only for themselves, he cautioned, and during a putsch might be neutralized by their own men; hence their practical use to the OAS was debatable. He had also been adversely impressed by the reaction to de Gaulle's year-end message announcing the recall of two divisions from Algeria: unlikely as it seemed to an activist general that the order would be executed without protest, not a single unit had deserted.

The OAS still could not be called an army in any conventional sense—it lacked troops and had no artillery, armor or aviation. Salan was convinced that a putsch was what the government wanted, to provide an opportunity to crush the Organization once and for all. And even if the OAS managed to seize and hold Algeria's major centers, he recalled the April disaster and stressed the problems the local economy would create "without outside aid"; and of this there was not the slightest hope. He also stressed that the aroused Moslem majority, "placed before a painful . . . situation," could signally aggravate the insurrectionists' position. Salan was one of the few military men in the Organization who ever appreciated that threat at its real value.

The OAS-inspired spate of rumors, urgent directives and cryptic radio messages was, therefore, merely another skirmish in the ceaseless war of nerves between Algiers and Paris, meant to intoxicate and soften up the population, to add to the breakdown of authority, to sow chaos and confusion, but not to prepare for immediate action. The mobilization order itself was an audacious move; but few heeded it who were not already fighting on behalf of the OAS. It is virtually impossible to call for widespread, overt mobilization from a clandestine base unless the appeal is accompanied by an armed uprising. Salan and the men about him knew this.

As the new year opened, only one major political formation in France, the right-wing Independents, still feigned to believe that Algeria should and could remain French. On January 12 a majority of its members approved an uncompromising motion that declared: "The FLN cannot be considered the sole representative of the entire Moslem population . . . the only solution is the maintenance of

* In Instructions of January 3 and 6.

Algeria and the Sahara within the framework of the French Republic."

This language was known to reflect Debré's views, and perhaps for this reason the influential periodical *Année Politique* noted in its year-end resumé of the domestic political situation that the Debré government now appeared cut off from most political parties and a large segment of public opinion. In effect, Debré still hoped against hope at this late date for the miraculous emergence of a Moslem third force that would bar the FLN's way to power, but de Gaulle did not share this hope, and throughout the country at large Frenchmen generally believed the war must end soon through direct negotiations with the enemy, Ben Khedda's exile government in Tunis.

About a third force that *did* exist in Algeria—the OAS—the Independents' motion did not whisper a word. This omission betrayed the acute embarrassment of the entire Right, which favored the Organization's aims but could not very well endorse its methods. In public, only a few prominent voices were raised in the OAS's defense, notably Jacques Soustelle's. Wandering in an uneasy state between freedom and the threat of imminent arrest, de Gaulle's erstwhile minister and collaborator, now a bitter foe of the government, held two press conferences at which he flatly denied belonging to the movement but declared the OAS was the real third force the government must reckon with and negotiate with to secure peace. He predicted there was no chance otherwise of stamping out underground resistance among an aroused people "who are defending their rights, their freedom and their homes." The outcome, he said, could only be a conflict of indefinite duration or bloody chaos; in this second prediction he was to prove tragically right. In private, Soustelle charged that the whole *pied noir* problem was being treated with extreme superficiality; he made the point that de Gaulle could draw on the past experience and counsel of five former Residents General who were alive and available and only too willing to proffer advice: Edmond Naegelen, Maurice Violette, Roger Léonard, Robert Lacoste and himself. What he omitted to mention was that the five were spokesmen for the same cause. With these last-ditch supporters of French Algeria, Soustelle foresaw (sometimes with manifest gratification) the deteriorating situation in Algeria as the first stage in what was destined to become a European civil war between the Christianized West and the Communistic East. From this point of view, the OAS's action quickly acquired the coloration of a divine crusade.

Most opposition parties more realistically viewed the Algerian problem that winter in terms of its effect on their own ambitions. While they paid lip service to *Algérie française*, to praise or damn it, both Right and Left kept an eye cocked on the Élysée Palace, the National Assembly and the electorate. The paramount question among Independents, Popular Republicans, Radicals and Socialists was whether the Gaullist government would survive. In Algiers, Susini with his usual distaste for French politics summed up their attitude sardonically: they hoped on the one hand to see the OAS overthrow de Gaulle, after which they planned to step in and enjoy the spoils; but on the other hand they hoped de Gaulle would survive long enough to rid them of the Algerian problem, which they could not solve.

Seven leaders of this opposition met one evening in mid-January at the Right Bank home of French banker Pierre Uri. Two former premiers attended—Guy Mollet, the Socialist, and Antoine Pinay, the Independent—as well as the Radicals' president, Maurice Faure. The *dîner de l'Alma*, as it became known in reference to the banker's address, was informal, and no firm commitments were made; the purpose, it was explained, was to discuss the situation in the event that de Gaulle stepped down or was forced to resign through the "gradual weakening" of his government. The gathering of forces nonetheless corresponded to the national union from Right to Left, excepting the Communists, which anti-Gaullists had preached almost since the start of the Fifth Republic, and which Soustelle and Salan favored. As such it excited considerable comment; it almost seemed as if something were in the wind that came close to an indirect alliance with the OAS. Mindful of criticism within his party, Mollet issued a disclaimer at a meeting of 250 Socialist mayors in Puteaux two weeks later. "The O in Mollet, the A in Pinay and the S in Salan do not necessarily stand for the OAS!" he said. But tantalizingly he added that if the Socialists *did* participate in a coalition government, it would be a transitional affair without a joint platform—which left the door open for incalculable politicking, perhaps even with extreme-Right elements.

Gaullists—who still constituted a majority—found that the Fifth Republic was being written off with unseemly haste. "The Alma dinner," one irked Gaullist snapped, "is the premature dabbling of politicians in *après-Gaullisme:* The king is dead. Long live the king. The trouble is, they *all* want to be king."

In fact, the King was still very much present, though he made no speeches that month, kept his own counsel and did not listen to Soustelle, Mollet or any of the other politicians. He was perturbed by the OAS's foothold in Algeria not because he considered it a direct threat to his own power, but for its effect on the FLN's willingness to return to the conference table. If he listened to anybody it was to two men on his private presidential staff, Bernard Tricot and Jacques Foccart, entrusted respectively with Algerian and African affairs. It has been said that Tricot made Algerian policy while Foccart found means of implementing it. This is an oversimplification; at most, they submitted proposals which de Gaulle adopted or rejected. The substance of Tricot's advice was to ignore the OAS in spite of all its inroads and to press on with the main objective, cease-fire negotiation. This advice de Gaulle heeded.

By winter Michel Leroy constituted a major problem for Susini.

Susini had created the Front Nationaliste in the first place to serve as a personal power base and a counterweight to the colonels in the Organization. It came, therefore, as a particularly unpleasant surprise when he perceived that Leroy, his hand-picked deputy, was emulating him and seeking to use the Front to personal advantage.

Just what Leroy intended, it is almost impossible to state in the absence of records, but there is no doubt he had growing reservations about the OAS's methods and objectives. The idea of partition —first outlined in Alain Peyrefitte's series of articles in *Le Monde*— had made a convert, not among the FLN but in Leroy, whom it struck as a valid way out of the political stalemate in Algeria. He was convinced the OAS had failed to tell the *pieds noirs* the full, uncomfortable truth about the situation. He wanted to detach the Front Nationaliste from the OAS, which he found too inefficient, rigid and dangerous, and he was all the unhappier since just the opposite had occurred; at Godard's urging, the Front had been dissolved and the bulk of its student members incorporated anonymously into the OAS. Leroy himself came under Gardes's orders. As weeks passed, he grew increasingly restive. On his own he flew to

Paris and began to expound his dissatisfaction in activist circles. Then—if Susini can be believed—he took it upon himself to transfer OAS funds without satisfactory explanation to the extreme-Rightist Jeune Nation group, whose archnationalist views he shared. Jeune Nation, however, was already suspect, in the OAS's eyes, of being manipulated by the French government; the suspicion now ricocheted on Leroy. Susini found it expedient to drop his protégé; he saw him less and less; the friendship finally petered out completely.

Leroy, however, was not alone in showing signs of revolt. Jean Sarradet, the Z Commando chieftain, was equally dissatisfied with the OAS. Recuperating on crutches after his run-in with Grassien's brigade at El Biar, he was cared for in an isolated seaside villa by a blonde young *pied noir* university student, Anne Loesch, with whom he carried on long, impassioned discussions about Algeria's future.

Sarradet railed against the Organization's "military mafia" for indulging in sterile terrorism and committing a major error by allowing the French government to become the priority enemy. He foresaw that *Algérie française* was doomed as a political concept; in its place he urged the establishment of a European coastal zone, an *Algérie pied noir*, which basically corresponded in spirit, if not in terminology, to Peyrefitte's ideas for partition. Sarradet, a tense, emaciated twenty-six-year-old, was not content to theorize. First, he sought a tactical alliance with Leroy. The two met in Sarradet's secluded hideout on a cliff overlooking the Mediterranean at Bainem, outside Algiers. Anne Loesch cooked dinner. She recalls that the all-night conversation was washed down with huge draughts of red wine and idealism.[*] Leroy would not agree to an outright pact, but promised to throw his weight behind any territorial settlement that Sarradet worked out with Paris and the FLN. Both men knew this scheme ran counter to the rigid OAS dogma of all or nothing—not a square foot of Algerian soil was to be abandoned to the detested FLN. But this did not deter them.

Sarradet then managed through a parish priest to enter into contact with a French government official at Rocher Noir, Jean Petitbon. Another secret meeting took place, this time at the Palais d'Été. Sarradet suggested nothing less, in return for government support of his ideas, than committing his Z Commandos to a purge

[*] She wrote a personal account of her experiences, *La Valise et le cercueil*, which relates the little-known story of opposition within the OAS. It is, by and large, an objective account.

of the entire OAS leadership.* Petitbon listened attentively but skeptically, and forbore from making any promises. The government's position was never to say no to any overtures that might put an end to the Organization; on the other hand, it regarded Sarradet's followers as a not-very-significant minority within the OAS. Finally Petitbon flew to Paris to submit the dissidents' plan to his superiors.

Unfortunately for Sarradet, he had been observed entering the Palais d'Été. Susini learned of it and concluded that the government was engaged in a grand-scale political maneuver, using both Leroy and Sarradet as willing pawns, to spark a revolt within the OAS and bring about its destruction. It was a situation that clearly could not be tolerated for long.

One must briefly see the problem from Susini's point of view: the students within the Front Nationaliste had tried to be helpful, and sometimes were, but they were dogmatic with the stubbornness of the young and inexperienced. They insisted—Sarradet in particular—on the importance of their ideas and solutions, and overlooked the danger of a flirtation with experienced politicians in Paris. In the eyes of the OAS, this represented a mortal peril.

Shortly afterward the Organization's official organ, *Appel de France*, printed a terse one-line statement: "We shall never accept an agreement leading to partition, much less abandonment." For Leroy and Sarradet, the warning could not be clearer.

While awaiting Paris' reply to his propositions, Sarradet committed a monumental error. At his request a summit meeting of sorts, without Salan, whom he had tried unsuccessfully to see in person (Salan refused to meet him), took place in the skyscraper offices of the Electricité et Gaz d'Algérie overlooking Algiers. Sar-

---

* According to Anne Loesch, Sarradet's plan was to carry out a raid at the next meeting of the OAS general staff, seize the leaders—Salan, Gardy, Godard, Susini, Perez, *et al.*—and hold them captive at a specially prepared hideout. Z Commandos would neutralize OAS sector chiefs in Algiers by raiding their arms caches and occupying print shops where clandestine tracts were prepared. This action was to be entrusted to Leroy, while Sarradet flew to Paris to negotiate the creation of a *pied noir* republic "on a pragmatic basis." Upon his return, the government radio, posters and tracts would acquaint the population with what was no less than a *coup d'état* within the OAS. A special commando would be held in reserve to deal with any possible riposte by Degueldre's Deltas.

radet, Leroy and René Villars, leader of the semi-autonomous France-Résurrection movement, attended, as did the increasingly powerful sector chiefs of the OAS—ex-captains Guy Branca and Pierre Montagnon, Philippe Le Pivain and Jacques Achard, who constituted among themselves the so-called *soviet des capitaines,* the group of young officers who laid down the law in entire *pied noir* neighborhoods.

Sarradet's purpose was not altogether clear, and his tactics by no means straightforward: he still hoped to wring some support for his ideas out of the OAS, whose cooperation could be invaluable; but he did not disclose his parallel overtures to the government, and he implied that if the Organization rejected his partition plan he was ready to drop it—which he was not.

The sector chiefs listened to his eloquent defense of the desirability of partition; unmoved, they volunteered simply to transmit his ideas to Salan. Anne Loesch thought it clear they felt that splinter groups should submit to discipline without discussion. The sector chiefs were deserters, but their outlook remained undeviatingly military.

Sarradet's risky, not to say foolhardy, move had aroused their suspicion without gaining their cooperation. From this point on, Sarradet went about armed and accompanied at all times. He now based his hopes exclusively on a favorable reply from Paris.

But in Paris, after hearing the proposals transmitted by Petitbon, Louis Joxe snapped: "We don't deal with *factieux*—with subversives." Some have charged that this reply slammed shut the door on a unique opportunity to destroy the OAS, that a more flexible reply might have averted the harrowing months that followed. But any possible inclination on the government's part to exploit Sarradet's proposals ran into the stone wall of de Gaulle's principles; he was not about to stoop to a deal with an outlaw movement, still less minuscule opposition within it, nor was he about to search for a blander solution to the *pieds noirs'* future; his feeling was that they must learn to live with the Moslems in peace or clear out.

Undeterred by this negative reaction, Sarradet and Leroy organized a series of further secret meetings at Bainem to persuade *pied noir* businessmen and professionals, hesitant elements within France-Résurrection and the Front Nationaliste of the rightness of their views. To these disparate groups, Sarradet stubbornly preached the advantages of settling for a coastal strip, not deep perhaps, but bigger than Israel—a *pied noir* republic where the Europeans would build a distinct ethnic and cultural nation, where the West would continue to have a toehold on the southern shore of the Mediterranean. In his enthusiasm, he prepared a draft declaration of independence and even the design of a national flag. Perhaps the idea in itself had merit—the merit of youthful idealism—but under the circumstances, given the mood prevailing within the Organization, it was suicidal.*

By early January, Sarradet and Leroy decided they were strong enough to force a showdown. They estimated that, with Villars, they controlled 70 percent of the real power of the OAS in men and arms; the Z Commandos would follow orders, and some Delta commandos were wavering, ready in a crisis to switch sides—or so, at least, believed Sarradet, who also thought leaders like Perez and Susini were unpopular with the rank and file and could easily be eliminated. In all this, Sarradet was the driving force; Leroy gave his assent, although with reservations; Villars had only a vague idea of what Sarradet was up to—he assented, but he was, in fact, so little in the picture that he was not even advised to carry a weapon when the others began to fear Salan's reprisals.

In the second week of January, Leroy handed Gardes, his nominal superior in the Organization, a set of four demands: scrap the dogma of *Algérie française;* accept partition; enter into contact with the government; and make room for two Front Nationaliste leaders on the OAS's general staff. A refusal, Leroy said, would lead to the formation of a breakaway "second OAS."

Extreme naïveté and courage seem to have possessed Sarradet and Leroy. From the Organization's point of view, the ultimatum implied the end of the OAS as such; and it came at a critical moment, when Salan was trying to weld the movement into a unified, disciplined whole. The gravity of the threat led to an emergency meeting in an apartment in the Télémly district, not far from Perez's headquarters. There are conflicting versions of what followed. It is certain that Susini viewed Leroy's apostasy without indulgence. Susini himself says that the OAS command as a whole ordered the traitors executed. A list was drawn up of twelve names, including Sarradet's, then it was trimmed down to only two—Leroy and Villars. The Organization could hardly afford a mass purge at this stage.

---

* Furthermore, there was no guarantee the FLN would ever have agreed to negotiate with the dissidents.

It is unclear why Sarradet's name was removed at the last moment. Susini has declared that the OAS set out to punish only the two recognized leaders of France-Résurrection and Front Nationaliste as responsible for the threatened schism; but this account is unconvincing, for the guiding spirit was Sarradet—if anyone merited the OAS's wrath, it was Sarradet. It is more likely that friends intervened to spare him. The meeting ended when Degueldre with macabre appositeness turned over the execution assignment to Philippe Le Pivain.

Susini at a later date described Le Pivain as "one of the two real revolutionaries" he had known in the OAS (Degueldre being the other). If, by "revolutionary," Susini meant cold-blooded fanaticism, then he was right. The son of a right-wing admiral, Le Pivain had deserted his post in the summer, joined the OAS under the code name "Cap," and assumed command of the suburban Maison Carrée sector about September. Underground, this blue-eyed dreamy Breton waged a pitiless war against the FLN, convinced that his cause was objectively justified. For all his "revolutionary" commitment, however, he was suspect of sharing the Front Nationaliste's ideas on partition; furthermore, he was a close friend of Leroy and his wife. In Degueldre's grim view, the surest way for Le Pivain to prove his purity of intentions was to kill his friend. Le Pivain accepted. Whether he registered hesitation is unknown; it is probable that he did.

On the evening of January 18, after receiving the murder order, he dined with the Leroys. He was a good guest, friendly and considerate. Leroy was well aware by this time of a brewing storm but displayed indifference to the possible danger; he had acted as he believed right, and that evening he was at ease. If there was one man he trusted fully within the OAS, it was Le Pivain, the godfather of one of his three children.

The next morning, Le Pivain summoned Villars to his headquarters. The chief of France-Résurrection suspected trouble and turned up with several bodyguards. As the group stepped into the sector office, Delta commandos turned submachine guns on them. All of Villars's men but one fled; the one courageous man in the lot ran up to Le Pivain, shouting that he did not understand, and was promptly disarmed. Le Pivain and several Deltas drove Villars to the neighboring town of Fort de l'Eau, escorted him to the deserted beach, and cut him down with automatic pistols behind a dune.

On the same morning, Leroy stepped out of his apartment into the arms of four men who displayed police cards and took him into custody. Leroy's wife witnessed the incident and saw the car drive off down the busy street. Panic-stricken, she alerted Sarradet. He was convinced that her husband had been kidnaped by *barbouzes*—and so, for that matter, was Leroy himself. Instead of driving to police headquarters, his captors led him to a villa and held him in the cellar. An inkling of the truth occurred to him later in the day when he recognized the guard who brought him food as a Delta. Leroy demanded to see Degueldre personally.

Degueldre came in the evening with Le Pivain. They drove Leroy to a secluded clearing in the forest of Bainem. With indomitable certitude Le Pivain expounded the reasons why his friend had been condemned for treason and must die. Leroy listened to this explanation, then said simply, *"J'ai joué, j'ai perdu."* He asked the two men to take care of his family, which they promised to do. Then Le Pivain shot him down.

Sarradet went wild with fury and frustration the next morning when he learned that Villars's bullet-riddled body had been found near Fort de l'Eau. There was no news of Leroy's fate. On crutches Sarradet reached the apartment of one of Susini's friends, Charles Bastianetto, and transmitted an ultimatum giving Susini twelve hours to hand back Leroy alive, on pain otherwise of seeing the entire movement torn apart by internal war. The reply arrived within two hours: Leroy was dead, executed, and Sarradet himself was summoned before a special OAS court.

Strangely enough, he heeded the summons. Leaving his bodyguard in a side street, he arrived by dark at an unfurnished villa where he was searched, then admitted into the presence of Susini and the sector chiefs. The atmosphere in the bare room was grim. Sarradet blustered a bit. He stated that he would not forget the murder of "two patriots," but was willing to set grievances aside temporarily to fight for a common cause. This won him a reprieve. After pledging allegiance to the Organization, Sarradet was reinstated but broken—given the thankless task of organizing the finances of the Maison Carrée sector *under Le Pivain.* (Susini's pitiless irony can be detected here.)

In fact, Sarradet had little choice; his followers were no match for Degueldre's Deltas. The Z Commandos were lying low in a cold sweat after hearing of the two executions. Few ventured to the morgue or the cemetery to pay respects to their former comrades in arms, Leroy and Villars, for fear of falling into an ambush.

The threat of internal opposition had been exorcised. The Z Commandos came under the sector chiefs' orders. There would be no further revolt within the OAS, but the double execution left a bad taste in many mouths.*

"What You Should Know About Plastiquages," read the lengthy newspaper article. It contained useful advice for Parisians not only about plastique but also about melinite, dynamite and TNT. It advised apartment dwellers to beware of shoeboxes and wrapped parcels deposited in a stairway; to remove doormats and put children to bed in rooms farthest from the landing; to place garbage cans as far away as possible from walls at night; to leave at least one window open at all times to dissipate the force of the blast; to keep an eye out for strangers seen carrying a package into a building, and to fall flat to the floor if one spotted a smoking, dark-colored fuse. . . .

Such was the atmosphere in the French capital in January.

Whether it was justified can be endlessly debated. It was true that, unlike Algiers, Paris had not lived closely with urban terrorism for five years, and each *plastiquage* and *attentat* tended to be amplified tenfold. De Gaulle, who never panicked, was known to be irritated by the panic some Parisians showed.

The dangers, however, were not entirely theoretical. A bomb blew up at the French Foreign Ministry, killing one employee and wounding twelve. Eighteen explosions rocked the city in less than four hours during the night of January 18; the OAS's intended victims, none of whom was killed, included two Gaullist parliamen-

---

* Le Pivain likewise met a violent death. On February 6, 1962, he was killed while trying to force a police roadblock in Algiers. The circumstances of his death—whether he was betrayed to the police by Sarradet's friends or by restive *pieds noirs* under his command—remain obscure. According to Susini, Degueldre appeared moved only twice during his career in the OAS—by the deaths of Leroy and Le Pivain.

tarians, a Leftist magazine editor, a judge, the habitués of a Moslem coffeehouse and several Frenchmen accused of aiding the FLN. It was a record to date; with unsuspected poetry the press dubbed the wave of attacks *la nuit bleue*. More sleepless nights were forecast. Just in time the police learned of plans to dynamite the Eiffel Tower's television installations, assassinate *gendarmerie* Colonel Jean Debrosse* and set off forty-eight explosions in a holocaust called Operation Budapest.

A situation was developing where the public, with apprehension or resignation or gratification, as the case happened to be, wondered: If the government no longer controlled the other side of the Mediterranean, could it maintain control in France itself? In many ways, the facts of the matter did not warrant this doubt, but the important and dangerous development was that the public thought they did. Average Frenchmen had little inkling of trouble within the OAS, but disorders in Algiers and daily *plastiquages* at home were realities.

A certain wavering—unavowed but ominous—began to be felt in the telltale civil service, where a few bureaucrats softly proclaimed their neutrality and others took prudent steps (undeclared donations to the OAS and offers of information) to safeguard themselves against a shift in the political weather. And while Morin worried about insurrection in Algiers, Interior Minister Frey, with less reason, feared a putsch in Paris itself. In early January five thousand CRS troops were brought into the capital to parry an eventual thrust; *gendarmerie* tanks and light-armored cars were held ready. Police, who now carried shoulder arms instead of the habitual side arms, searched hundreds of houses, stopped literally thousands of cars and checked the papers of still more Frenchmen on foot.† The police received orders to use their arms if attacked, if motorists tried to crash through checkpoints, and if roadblocks could not be defended otherwise. The government packed off suspect Rightists to a new internment camp at St. Martin de l'Ardoise in a barren, windswept area of Languedoc.

For most Parisians, life seemed to continue normally. But an

* The colonel who had arrested Gingembre and led anti-OAS operations in Algiers.

† The Police Prefecture said 9,826 cars were inspected and 29,950 persons were questioned during the single weekend of January 27–29. If nothing else, this indicated the degree of government nervousness. (Cited in *L'Aurore*, January 30, 1962)

undeniable tension overlay daily life, family quarrels over politics were painful and bitter, the Stock Exchange behaved erratically, reflecting the prevailing uneasiness, street brawls erupted between "anti-Fascist" and "anti-Communist" students. The far Left deliberately exploited the existing anxiety by calling on its militants to form "action groups."* France had split wrenchingly into two before, in the upheaval of 1789, at the time of the symbol-ridden Dreyfus affair, and during the national humiliation of 1940. An atmosphere of similar fratricidal hatred was seeping into the mainland from overseas, where Frenchmen were killing Frenchmen in a three-sided war in which the Moslems were often all but forgotten. A threat of civil war hung palpably like the smell of snow in the air.

In mid-January Lucien Bitterlin flew from Algiers to Nice, to visit Goulay, who was recuperating in a Riviera clinic, then on to Paris, to try to smooth out the serious disagreement that had arisen with Jacques Dauer. Jim Alcheik, the Tunisian judo expert, accompanied him. Upon arriving in Paris the two men learned that Debré had issued a personal order barring their return to Algiers.

It meant that the *barbouzes* at Rue Favre and Chemin Reynaud were left to their own devices, on the defensive in a hostile city, at the mercy of the active ill will of the *pieds noirs* and Degueldre's lethal Deltas. Far from easy in his mind about the *barbouzes'* security, Bitterlin endeavored to get Debré's order revoked—without success.

Then unexpectedly, on January 23, Alcheik received an entry visa for Algeria. He was enthusiastic over the prospect of seeing more action, and Bitterlin was relieved that the forty men left in the two villas would come under some sort of leadership.

* The PSU (Parti Socialiste Unifié) took the lead and created the semiclandestine Groupes d'Action et de Résistance, whose purpose was to fight violence with violence. Marc Heurgon, a party official, estimated the enrollment at 2,500; a police report in the author's possession cuts the figure down to 800. Various Communist municipalities in the Paris area recruited volunteers for "self-defense groups," at Orly, Gentilly, Châtillon-sous-Bagneux, Aubervilliers, etc. These groups patrolled the streets at night and were prepared to defend town halls against a putsch. However, none of these groups proved particularly effective, and the idea was soon abandoned. The French Communist party laid greater stress on organizing joint action with other Leftist parties including the Socialists.

Alcheik planned to start stepped-up printing of MPC posters and anti-OAS tracts. A 400-pound press had been purchased in Paris before Christmas and shipped to Algiers in his care under the cover name of Pierre de Lassus. It was waiting for him under consignment at the docks. It had been there unclaimed for the past two weeks.

On January 29, a few days after Alcheik's return, movers loaded the big crate aboard a truck and delivered it to Villa Andrea. The press arrived at an awkward moment. The *barbouzes* were holding three men captive in an improvised guardroom—a young radio technician named Alexandre Tislenkoff, the French-born son of a Tsarist officer; an ex-paratrooper; and a shop foreman. The three were suspected of operating a pirate radio transmitter. Tislenkoff admitted belonging to the OAS.

The only available account of what happened to Tislenkoff is Tislenkoff's; he published a book that contained signed corroborating statements accusing the *barbouzes* of torture. The book was banned in France. According to this account, he was kidnaped, led at gun-point into Villa Andrea, bound, slapped about and beaten by two Vietnamese and a stocky, dark-haired European. His captors wanted the names of other members of the network and the transmitter's location. One interrogator pressed a knife-point against his eye, and threatened to pop it out unless he talked. Tislenkoff gave some information. The interrogators remained unsatisfied. Two more prisoners were dragged into the guardroom, one with cigarette burns on the soles of his feet. Then a hooded man strapped Tislenkoff into an improvised electric chair and doused him with water preparatory to giving him an electric shock.

The arrival of the printing press interrupted whatever was about to happen. The movers unloaded the crate and carried it into the ground-floor living room. When he learned that the machine had arrived, Alcheik hastened from the guardroom, leaving one Vietnamese to watch over the prisoners.

A Moslem member of the team brought a hammer and a screwdriver, and jimmied loose the metal straps that circled the crate. Then he began to pry open the top. Inside was a 60-pound plastique charge—thirty times the amount used for intimidation raids, enough to demolish a military objective.

Just then the phone rang. The call was for Mario Lobianco, who was upstairs taking a nap. He was starting down the stairs, when an ear-splitting roar shook the house, smoke poured out of the shattered windows, a wall slowly crumbled, flames leaped up from the heap. The explosion was followed by a stricken stillness; a few seconds later there were faint cries.

One after another the three prisoners emerged, feet chained, dazed but alive, from the guardroom, the only room not destroyed by the blast. They stumbled out into the courtyard and found a shambles of rubble and mortar. Their Vietnamese guard had been killed at once, his skull crushed in. Alcheik's body had been torn to bits.

The orange trees were coated with plaster dust, and into the silence intruded the wail of an approaching ambulance. A few of Bitterlin's men were grouped together in the garden, panicky and dangerous. Under their machine guns Tislenkoff and the two other prisoners set to work, gathering up the bloody mess.

The extent of the disaster was almost unimaginable. A whole side of the three-story house had caved in like a sand castle under the tremendous detonation. A quick count showed twenty men missing, although in that gray, smoking heap it was impossible to tell exactly how many had perished, decapitated or pulverized. Lobianco did not struggle out of the house, nor Bui-The. One survivor said a corpse seemed deflated by the concussion. It was by far the deadliest setback the OAS had inflicted on the *barbouzes*.

From the blasted windows of two adjoining houses, *pieds noirs* taunted the group in the garden and were almost fired on point-blank by the enraged men. Police held back a crowd at the gate and were careful not to approach the survivors or try to disarm them. Tislenkoff murmured a prayer of thanks for the police's presence, which saved him, he thought, from being liquidated on the spot as an embarrassing witness. An MPC poster fluttered in shreds from an intact wall with its hopeful slogan: *Ni valise, ni cercueil. La coopération.* The acrid wartime smell of bombed-out building foundations and burning skin moved slowly across the neighborhood.

Salan called for more terrorism; he had no choice. Borne on by the OAS's impetus in a political void, he recommended the "spectacular kidnaping" of Gaullist families, for which he proclaimed his readiness to assume responsibility, even for the inevitable errors this order would entail. This was going very far. He defended this order as a "response" to Morin's security measures, which he termed a "provocation"—although this was patently absurd.

Marcel Ronda, the Algiers activist of pre-Barricade days, now saw a good deal of Salan and found him laboring under a burden of profound doubt. He gave no thought to giving up, but he was increasingly conscious of the difficult nature of this freakish, unavailing battle in a half-light. "The others will throw everything they have into this fight," Salan said one day. "They're very strong, but we are committed to the end."

17

The Meeting in the Snow

THE PLASTIQUEURS erred. Their intended victim was Culture Minister André Malraux, who occupied the upper two stories of the town house at 19 bis Avenue Victor Hugo, in fashionable Boulogne, outside Paris. But the men who arrived in the afternoon placed the puttylike strips of plastique on the ground-floor windowsill. A few seconds later the charge exploded, driving a shower of glass splinters into the face of four-and-a-half-year-old Delphine Renard, the daughter of the couple who owned the house. Malraux was not in the building at the time.

The little girl was immediately transported to Cochin Hospital, where doctors sewed one hundred stitches to keep her from being disfigured; but her right eye was lost, and for a time there was fear for the left eye too. French newspapers, even those normally pro-*Algérie française,* ran huge blow-ups of the victimized child and the blasted playroom that did nothing to endear the OAS to parents throughout the country. "France wants no more of this," editorialized one caption. Interior Minister Frey, in his sharpest attack yet on the OAS, denounced the "vile bunch of murderers, crooks and extortionists who are trying to dishonor our country."

The bombing was not the only one that day, February 8; ten rocked Paris in full daylight. It was too much. Trade-unions, Leftist student and youth organizations, liberal leagues and clubs, Communist party sections called a mass demonstration that very evening similar to earlier anti-OAS protest meetings and work stoppages in April and December 1961.* At this point, Frey committed a mistake. He upheld a government ban on all public gatherings "of a political nature," a measure that had been applied during the April putsch but was much harder to justify in the present context. The demonstrators decided to ignore the government warning.

They assembled in force, some ten thousand, at six o'clock in the vicinity of the Place de la Bastille, the rallying point for Paris working-class demonstrations. They stood in dense rows and chanted: "*O-A-S—As-sas-sins!*" As soon as riot police attempted to prod the front ranks back toward the Place de la République, fights broke out. The police lobbed tear-gas grenades and charged with poles to disperse the hostile crowd; the demonstrators had come equipped with spade handles, cobblestones, rocks and bolts, not to mention the detachable circular iron grills which the city of Paris plants around its plane and chestnut trees and the people of Paris rip up and wield to vicious effect whenever they clash with police. Fierce clubbing and jabbing erupted in spurts along Boulevard Beaumarchais and Boulevard Voltaire. In a sense, this was predictable; each side expected the other to react as it did. The desultory, mean-tempered skirmishing had lasted almost three hours when suddenly, at the intersection of Boulevard Voltaire and Rue de Charonne, the police charged.

Some demonstrators fled for safety down the stairway to the Métro station, where they ran up against iron gates shut and padlocked because of the street fighting. They could get no farther; meanwhile, in the confusion a growing number of demonstrators and onlookers stampeded down the stairs, crushing up against the others. The police then went berserk—there is no other word for it. They grabbed one or two men and flung them bodily over the railing, they threw marble-topped tables from café terraces down upon the heads of the trapped group below. There were screams and a mad, panicky scramble to escape. When it was all over, eight bodies, including those of several women, were recovered—a few dead of heart attack, others of suffocation. Among the police were

* On December 19, Communists, Socialists, Popular Republicans, the Parti Socialiste Unifié and the major trade-unions staged a fifteen-minute "symbolic strike." Up to that date, it represented the biggest joint endeavor by France's anti-OAS forces.

more than a hundred injured, and the same number among the demonstrators.

It was the bloodiest street riot since February 1934 when Popular Front supporters and pro-Fascist groups clashed before the Chamber of Deputies. Both sides drew back in stunned silence. Then there was a vast uproar on the Left: Was this the Gaullist government's way of defending the Republic against right-wing subversion?

Within hours, a worried Frey issued two communiqués blaming the outbreak of violence on the French Communist party, and accusing "organized bands of rioters" of fomenting trouble by taunting and attacking the police in the first place. The second charge may have been true; the first was misleading, for the Communists had been far from alone in persisting in the illegal demonstration.

A political writer for *Le Monde* noted: "The government's aim is to appear under no circumstances as an accomplice of the Communist party in the Army's eyes, for fear of seeing the Army swing over to the OAS. . . ."

Although Frey continued to maintain that his ban was the "surest way of maintaining order," the government in its eternal hesitation-waltz between two extremisms had badly overreacted. The mishandling of the Charonne incident brought about just the threat the government had sought to avert—the momentary vision of a new Popular Front.

On February 13 the working-class population of Paris turned out to escort the eight dead demonstrators to Père Lachaise Cemetery. This time, Frey wisely made no move to ban the gathering. Long before the winter day broke, a crowd began to form at the Place de la République. Driving rain, sleet and a chilling wind struck out at the mourners, whose wreaths sagged forlorn and drenched. The crowd grew so thick and fast, the cortege was two hours late getting underway. Onlookers watched in the downpour from rooftops and balconies. A trade-union orchestra played Chopin's "Marche Funèbre." In the forefront marched the rival leaders of the French Left— Pierre Mendès-France, François Mitterand, Maurice Thorez, Jacques Duclos, Benoît Fachon—for once united and thus potentially effective. The hearses advanced slowly through the heart of working-class Paris. No cries resounded, no slogans; a silence that rendered this gathering far more impressive politically and emotionally than the demonstration six days before. Estimates of the crowd's size ranged from several hundred thousand to more than a half million.

By general consensus it was the biggest street turnout Paris had seen since the Liberation. All who attended were vaguely aware of a turning point being reached that day. Not only the OAS, but the Gaullist regime was being judged; the government would have to move more firmly than ever against the OAS if it was to survive itself.

It has been estimated that ten determined men, drawn from the staffs of Debré, Frey and higher echelons of the police, fought and won the battle against the OAS in France. What they brought to the struggle were intelligence, political acumen, level-headedness and personal toughness. Several names became known almost at once to the underground—Constantin Melnik, Debré's chief adviser on police affairs; Jean Bozzi and Paul Parat, of the Sûreté; Daniel Doustin, then head of French domestic counterespionage. But the man who became most identified in the popular mind with antisubversive operations was Alexandre Sanguinetti, a well-read, politically ambitious, tough Corsican, a veteran of Free French amphibious landings on the island of Elba during World War II (in which he lost a leg), a member of the inner "Gaullist mafia."

A reader of Clausewitz and Trotsky, a student of revolutions and counterrevolutions, a man who knew the value of holding his tongue, and a flexible politician who had not always disbelieved in French Algeria, he emerged more and more frequently in the press during the winter of 1961 as "Monsieur Anti-OAS," a silly title which he did not covet, but which described, broadly if crudely, his functions.

From the outset Sanguinetti, like Tricot, dismissed the political and revolutionary aspect of the mainland OAS. Without a solid voting bloc, this presented no real danger. The Organization's troublemaking potential was something else again. Since the government to an uncommon extent reposed on one man, the OAS by assassinating de Gaulle could totally disrupt the French state. If it succeeded in killing de Gaulle, all its other blunders would be effaced and numerous wavering elements in the Army and police would rally to the side of the strongest. By the same token, the selective killing of the ten men who controlled the police apparatus in France could cripple the anti-OAS effort. There was a still grimmer contingency. If the OAS adapted and expanded FLN guerrilla tactics and blew up freight trains or main switches on railway lines, this—unlike the *plastiquages*—could do real harm and paralyze the nation; it might trigger a violent reaction by the Left, which the government, tied up in its anti-OAS campaign, could not control. The country would then slide surely toward civil war. Assassination and blind terrorism were the two OAS actions the government feared most. Some ministers and staff aides took to carrying guns, sent their children away and changed lodgings daily. They remember this period of their lives with considerable distaste.

To counter the double threat, Sanguinetti waged a day-to-day war. He has since said that he had no master plan, no deadline for crushing the OAS—he improvised; and this, as it turned out, afforded him greater flexibility.

Sanguinetti is not loquacious about his methods, but it is known that, in addition to using police tipsters, double agents and anti-OAS groups, he received information from thousands of private citizens loyal to the government. He enjoyed one signal advantage that did not exist in Algiers: the enormous police machinery as against the relatively small number of activists.* A newly created liaison bureau was functioning between the rival police services, and the gain in efficiency was immediately apparent. (Sergent's commandos found it especially difficult to guard against penetration by *several* police forces.) Determined to counter Leftist accusations of softness and block the rise of a new Popular Front, the government also carried out a belated but effective shake-up of police personnel. New inspectors turned up who had no emotional tie with the former battle against the FLN and were dedicated to fighting the OAS. Activist networks were the first to sense the abrupt change: the sometimes overt sympathy they had benefited from was swept away in a month's time, useful sources dried up. All this amounted to the "veritable mobilization of police" Debré had called for in January. And in addition accurate information was now arriving from Michel Hacq's Mission C in Algiers.

The real problem, in Sanguinetti's analysis, boiled down to a matter of identifying and tracking Organization members with no past political record. He suggested the police were wasting time

---

* The total *official* police force in France numbered 90,000 men, made up of the Paris Prefecture's 25,000 policemen and the Sûreté's 65,000 employees. Anti-Gaullists estimated there were 100,000 policemen of one sort or another on the payroll.

searching only in traditional Rightist milieus, notably among Army career officers, industrialists and aristocrats. An activist who volunteered for a terrorist mission might just as easily be found, he thought, in other classes threatened by social and technological upheaval in France—small shopkeepers, craftsmen, small landowners. When the police began to redirect their investigation among these groups, it paid off; throughout the provinces, each week a local OAS leader or two fell into the law's hands. To this day, Sanguinetti believes it was his chief contribution to the anti-OAS drive.

The OAS, at any rate, saw him as its chief enemy—a free-wheeling *chargé de mission*, responsible only to his stanch friend Frey, who acted outside channels, hired his own agents and could exercise heavy pressure on recalcitrant police officials by threats of transfer and spur others to greater effort through promises of bonuses. Yet it dared make no serious attempt to assassinate him.

This and the lack of attacks against other government leaders deepened Sanguinetti's contempt for his adversary. "There isn't a winner among them," he said.

The police—in particular, the Police Judiciare, whose basic function is to arrest lawbreakers, not stamp out political subversion—bore down on the problem with a capacity for methodical effort, an unsung talent for sustained examination of dull records, statistics and minutiae that was to prove extremely useful. IBM computers at Place Beauveau filed, cross-filed and memorized information about tens of thousands of cases. If a Frenchman had experienced any unpleasantness at the Liberation on charges of Pétainist sympathies; if he had ever belonged to a right-wing student organization; if he had relatives in Algeria; or if he had merely received a letter from an activist Army officer—any of these leads was enough to interest the police. The mails were minutely screened. Family and friends of suspected terrorists were put under heavy surveillance. And to be a Gaullist in good standing was no guarantee of immunity from investigation, for Frenchmen's political allegiances are notoriously fickle. The payroll for overtime at the Interior Ministry soared. By February the government claimed that activists already carried on police files were either in prison, in internment camps or in flight. This was a sweeping statement, and it happened to be more or less true; but it did not tell the whole story. To be sure, there were some significant arrests—Philippe Castille's in January, and the discovery that this former Indochina paratroop officer cornered at the Pam-Pam restaurant near the Opéra was the perpetrator of *la nuit bleue;* now in late February, Jean-Marie Vincent, the young Algiers law student who had organized the *plastiquage* that took Delphine Renard's eye. But editorialists noted that a group of dangerous, determined OAS leaders at intermediate level —Sergent for one, Canal for another—remained at liberty. To which the police replied that it was hampered by the perennial shortages of manpower and of means.

Toward the end of January, Sergent boasted that the Metropolitan OAS had built both a horizontal and a vertical infrastructure and enjoyed support at all levels of French society. In fact, this was precisely what it lacked; at the grass-roots level, in small towns and communes, the only infrastructure that existed was on paper.

In the eyes of millions of Frenchmen who regarded the war as virtually over, the OAS in France appeared as the principal troublemaker.[*] The tag of "OAS—Assassins!" zealously chanted by Gaullists and Leftists began to hurt. For all of Susini's efforts to the contrary, the OAS was labeled as neo-Nazi, exploiting *Algérie française* as a pretext to impose a Fascist regime upon an unwilling country. The Madrid exiles' diatribes, the William Levy affair, Sergent's inability to shake off extreme-Rightist support and unskillful propaganda had combined to create this impression.

There was lassitude in France with growing casualty lists and mounting costs of sixteen years of almost uninterrupted warfare since World War II, in Indochina, Morocco, Tunisia. The majority of Frenchmen were only grudgingly satisfied with de Gaulle's handling of the Algerian problem; but all the alternative solutions appeared still less desirable. The OAS could parade no positive accomplishments; it lacked a leader remotely comparable to de Gaulle in stature and prestige; Salan was unknown to many, dismissed by others as a politically capricious general. For practical purposes, Sergent found his activity limited to uprooted *pieds noirs* and restless Army reservists and veterans who had served in Indochina and

[*] "In France the FLN fought a war with the police but not the population. The OAS clumsily did the opposite." (Roland Gaucher, *Les Terroristes*)

Algeria; but these were precisely the groups the police kept under permanent surveillance.

By midwinter the situation was such that the OAS in Algeria directed Sergent to suspend *plastiquages,* which were doing more harm than good, and switch to terrorism against key government figures and the Communist party, with which it considered itself "at war." In short, Algiers urged upon Sergent the same plan of action Sanguinetti thought the OAS must carry out to be effective. But to add to Sergent's problems, there was not one but many OASes in France. Some local networks in the fastnesses of Brittany dreamed of a monarchist restoration, and in the southwest, of tax reform; in Lorraine and Champagne they were permeated by out-and-out nationalism.

To weld these groups together—and Sergent was in a hurry, since Canal's arrival upon the scene—an officer with authority was needed, a home version of Degueldre. Sergent, whose own authority was far from secure, found the necessary man—or thought he did—in a thirty-year-old deserter, Captain Jean-Marie Curutchet.

Readers of this book will find even the briefest account of Curutchet's past familiar—one more repetition of an unvarying pattern. The son of a retired naval officer, he had commanded a company of paratroopers in Algeria, had drawn thirty days' fortress arrest for his open sympathy with the April putsch, then had been transferred to France and inexplicably promoted to captain. On October 7, 1961, the Army carried him as absent without leave. He wrote a letter to his commanding officer to explain his reasons for joining the OAS: "A certain number of young officers do not believe in the inexorable process of predetermined facts," declared Curutchet. It is not difficult to puzzle out where he had found this notion—in Spengler, with his celebrated dictum that "in the last analysis it has always been a platoon of soldiers who saved civilization." Candidly, Curutchet added that he wanted to save the "patrimony" of French Algeria, which made sense, since he was married to a *pied noir* girl. He had black close-cropped hair, symmetrical features, and a wooden expression that led the Paris newspaper *Combat* to note mercilessly, "Every time he blinks, one is surprised." He denied that he was "a romantic revolutionary, a professional agitator, a crusader or leader of a gang"; nonetheless he combined a bit of all these callings. Georges Bidault thought of him as *"un jeune chien—charmant mais assez léger."*

Much of the terrorism that afflicted Paris at this point—the *plastiquages,* the machine-gunning of Communist party premises, the forays against Moslem cafés—was imputable to Curutchet. Sergent instructed OAS clandestine chieftains throughout France to take orders from him for all intelligence, sabotage and terrorist operations. With disconcerting ease he found ideological justification for the attacks. He described *plastiquages* as "politico-psychological operations"; the Communists were mortal enemies whom one struck down out of self-defense, the Moslem cafés were in reality "secret FLN courts." All this was not terrorism, he argued, but "a battle for public opinion," to open the population's eyes and turn it against the "FLN and its allies."

To a great extent his tactics misfired. Bombings had no noticeable restraining effect on the FLN; the Communist party did not leap to the challenge, as he had expected, and make the mistake of indulging in violent counteraction—after several OAS night raids, the party's only reaction was to post eight guards around the print shop of *L'Humanité* and Central Committee headquarters at Carrefour Châteaudun.*

Yet at about this time Curutchet issued violent new instructions for steadily increasing sabotage and terrorism, to begin within seventy-two hours of the signing of a cease-fire and to reach a climax a month later. This was Operation Paso Doble. The two-page order prescribed sabotage of high-tension lines and sluice gates, telephone lines and railroad tracks throughout France; setting fire to cars in parking lots and airplanes at various airfields; random armed attacks on pedestrians and motorists; and bombing of cafés, bars and theaters at curtain time. The terrorism was to be carried out by rural *maquis* and fifteen urban commandos, numbered 101 to 115, under the orders of an activist named Henri Armagnac.

Evidently, Curutchet had pored over the voluminous material describing FLN terror tactics and absorbed every detail. By no means all of Mission II agreed with his program; some activists saw the use of violence as a sure prelude to civil war, which they did not want. But Curutchet was seized by a feeling of urgency, for now it was an open secret that cease-fire negotiations between the French

---

* Curutchet finally gave up harassment of the Communist party. At his trial, he claimed the party refused to fight because of "sclerosis or political calculation," as though the latter, on his enemy's part, were outrageous. Curutchet claimed to feel some sympathy for the Communist rank and file.

government and the FLN would resume, soon and no doubt conclusively.

De Gaulle had clearly hinted at it in a speech that month.

The unlikely meeting place for new negotiations was a chalet the French Highway Department used for garaging snowplows and road-maintenance equipment. It stood close to—only about a mile from—the Swiss frontier, in the mountain hamlet of Les Rousses.

Louis Joxe headed the seven-man French team which arrived at the Chalet du Yeti on February 11. He was tired after a winter of diplomatic frustration; de Gaulle had assigned him two top-flight aides to help carry on negotiations, Public Works Minister Robert Buron, an advocate of decolonialization, and Prince Jean de Broglie, a Gaullist expert on Saharan affairs. Before the three men departed from Paris, de Gaulle gave them a final piece of advice: "Don't worry about details . . . don't get bogged down . . . do for the best."

The Algerians—they also numbered seven—arrived from Switzerland bundled up against the paralyzing midwinter cold, to which they were unaccustomed, via a circuitous route on ice-glazed roads. They had consented to the detour without protest. The possibility of an OAS commando raid was taken quite seriously by both sides.

For the moment, the unmarked cars burdened with skis and winter-sports gear, the delegates in parkas and hoods threw the OAS—and the press—off the track. Both sides settled down quickly to work.

The new meeting had been decided upon after sporadic contact throughout the winter in Switzerland and Italy, contact that had turned out far from encouraging. If Frenchmen and Algerians met now, it was through mutual necessity, because both were in a hurry; but neither side exhibited much optimism. These were official but not formal discussions. They sat down with the intention of talking and seeing what, if anything, could be done.

The stumbling blocks remained the same, as emotion-ridden, thorny and unpredictable in their consequences as they were the summer before: the Sahara's future status; the setting-up of a provisional executive and a *force locale* to maintain order during the interim period after the cease-fire; and above all, guarantees for the embattled Europeans.

With the French, this last point was essential. The government at this stage estimated that only one out of five *pieds noirs* would pack up and leave after independence; peaceful coexistence between Europeans and Moslems, though imperiled, still seemed possible, so it was deemed absolutely indispensable to secure guarantees. The FLN meanwhile balked at the proposed choice of Abderrahmane Farès, former president of the Algerian Assembly, as head of the provisional executive. In his countrymen's eyes, Farès, a dapper little Kabyle notary with a foot in both Paris and Algiers, passed for useful but superficial.

The February sun gave a blinding glare to the snowy fields. There were frequent breaks outdoors in the knifing cold, then the two delegations reassembled in the chalet's refectory in a stifling atmosphere of cigarette ash and overheated air. Over both teams hung a sharp awareness of time passing, yet disagreement persisted. After eight days' haggling, word reached them of an OAS air raid against an FLN camp at Oujda, in Morocco, the first time the Organization had struck openly outside Algeria.* The implication was plain: if no agreement were reached soon, the OAS might undo the two delegations' work, embroil the French Army in new hostilities and plunge Algeria into full-scale civil war.

Under this sort of pressure, they agreed on several things: on Farès' appointment, the need for written guarantees for the European minority, and the opening of formal cease-fire negotiations within a month at Évian. It was as much as could be realistically hoped for. At 2 A.M. on February 19, the exhausted Algerians drove back to Switzerland. The bone-weary French caught some sleep, then flew to Paris to report to de Gaulle.

He listened to Joxe's sober, hour-long report, then briskly congratulated the negotiators and told them that the agreement was a good and honorable one. "France," he said, "must be freed from a situation that has brought her only misfortune."† Then he called

---

* On February 18, an activist lieutenant and sergeant took off from La Senia airfield, outside Oran, aboard two T-6 training planes, headed across the nearby Moroccan border, strafed an FLN camp near Oujda, then flew back to a small airstrip at Saïda, in Algeria, and disappeared into a waiting car. In a pirate broadcast, Jouhaud congratulated the two deserters. The FLN claimed the attack killed five and wounded thirty guerrillas.

† Cited by Louis Terrenoire, *De Gaulle et l'Algérie*. Much of the material in this section derives from an interview with Jean de Broglie and from Robert Buron's firsthand account of the negotiations, *Carnets politiques de la guerre d'Algérie*. Buron published his account with what was judged undignified haste by the Élysée Palace, and his political career suffered in consequence.

upon each cabinet member individually to approve or disapprove the result—a procedure he had resorted to only twice before on the eve of major decisions: prior to his September 1959 speech and during the Barricades. The cabinet unsurprisingly gave its unanimous approval.

Buron, one of the three negotiators, saw de Gaulle at this moment as a man for whom Les Rousses represented a starting point, not a conclusion, a man who had not once lost sight of the Grand Design of his foreign policy.

Debré appeared wretched, patently torn between loyalty to de Gaulle and unhappiness with the outcome, which amounted to an FLN political victory.

Buron himself saw the week's negotiations as marking a moment when, perhaps for the first time in seven years, the two camps' aspirations coincided.

Algiers had a new prefect of police—a southern Frenchman picturesquely named Vitalis Cros, whose swart Mediterranean features could appear as native as any *pieds noir*'s. He had arrived from the Ardennes in November with personal orders from de Gaulle to shun all compromise with the OAS. Like Le Thiais in Oran six months earlier, Cros found a situation for which no amount of Paris briefings could possibly have prepared him.

His personal escort comprised eight CRS guards from France— four detached to protect his villa in Hydra, four who followed him around the city. Their leader was a Catalan; whenever he turned up personally at the start of the day, Cros knew that a particularly trying twenty-four hours lay ahead.

One morning, shortly after his arrival, as he set out with the Catalan on official business, Cros found his vehicle hemmed in at a busy intersection by a car in front and one on each flank. From the three vehicles, men silently pointed submachine guns out the windows at him. The Catalan jumped out and, brandishing his own machine gun, said: "Well?" The OAS cars drove on.

This, Cros learned, was minor byplay for Algiers; in succeeding weeks he escaped countless attempts at assassination by gun and Molotov cocktail.

By February he had formed a team on which he could count, but within the local police he still encountered passive resistance. To some extent he overcame this by issuing a blanket warning that he would literally kick in the behind anyone he came upon interfering with normal administrative service. Among his hand-picked staff there were other problems—too little sleep and too much drink; they were, in Cros's words, "leading a garrison life without being in the Army."

Under these conditions it became apparent that a holding operation was the best he could hope for until, at another level, the problem of Algiers' future was settled—by negotiation or destruction.

In an atmosphere of spreading decay, the *barbouzes* fought their last stand.

After evacuating the two villas on the heights of Algiers, the survivors and some new recruits were now concentrated at the Hotel Rajah, a shabby two-story building on Avenue Anatole France in La Redoubte district. The new headquarters did not go undetected for long. Guards around the hotel heard insistent sounds of digging at night and decided that Delta gunmen were burrowing a tunnel to blow the Rajah up. The guards could find no entrance to the tunnel, and from this time on, the twenty-five men in the hotel lived on their nerves, under a state of siege, barricaded behind shuttered windows, virtually out of contact with the surrounding neighborhood. For all the promises of extra hazard pay made in Paris, they had drawn only nominal advances and were running short of money; what remained shifted hands at nightly poker games under dimmed lights.

Then on February 14 a car drove up, a priest and two men alighted and approached the building. Suddenly they whipped out automatic pistols from their coats and began to fire point-blank at the ground-floor rooms. The *barbouze* guards inside killed the three men on the spot, as well as a Moslem child caught in the line of fire. This, at least, was one version that filtered back to Delta headquarters; according to another, guards had found several *pieds noirs* loitering suspiciously about the premises, collared them, discovered weapons in their pockets, lined them up against a wall and shot them. There were, at any rate, three Delta gunmen dead. Degueldre, with his obsessive itch for violence, responded automatically to the challenge. He decided to command personally an all-out attack to get rid of the *barbouzes* once and for all.

Five days later, in the late afternoon, two half-tracks rolled up within range of the Rajah. No one found this odd; Army vehicles were constantly on the move in Algiers' streets. As soon as the two armored cars came to a halt, the Deltas manning them opened bazooka fire, shattering windows and severely damaging the hotel façade. The *barbouzes* inside immediately returned fire. Covered by a heavy machine gun on the rooftop, several men burst out of the building and charged Degueldre's commando. As they reached the street a withering fire dropped them dead in their tracks. It was hopeless resistance. The others fled through the rear.

One group made it to a *gendarmerie* caserne at Maison Carrée, another arrived at Maillot Hospital, near Bab el Oued, with one wounded man.

Degueldre did not give up easily.

The next morning, a half-dozen Delta gunmen took up positions with little effort at concealment outside the hospital main gate. For the next hour they kept an eye on a beige Peugeot with Paris license plates in the courtyard. Civilians received orders to stay off the streets in the vicinity. Local police made no attempt to interfere. Shortly before noon, four men sat down in the car and drove off. As the Peugeot came through the gates, the Delta commando chief took careful aim and fired into the front tires. The car skidded out of control down Rue du Dey. As the three passengers clambered to get out, five gunmen standing in the roadway sprayed the vehicle evenly with their machine guns. Losing speed, the Peugeot crashed into a wall and exploded. Then the *pieds noirs* of Bab el Oued who had witnessed the attack from their windows surged into the street and added a barbaric note of their own. They rushed up and threw jerry-cans of gas onto the funeral pyre to make sure it flamed still higher. "Let them burn! Burn them!" cried several men. Then they danced, frenzied and mindless, around the roaring fire.

By the time a fire truck arrived and put out the blaze, it was far too late; four charred bodies were removed.

Only one potential victim survived the ambush—the wounded *barbouze* who had been escorted to Maillot Hospital for treatment. He lay on the floor of the ambulance that drove out of the courtyard in the Peugeot's wake. The Delta gunmen stationed along Boulevard de Champagne took no chances and fired a volley broadside at the ambulance too. The man inside watched bullets stitch a horizontal line just above his head, but he was not hit.

For practical purposes, the incident put an end to the *barbouzes*. A majority had been identified, pursued and liquidated; the OAS slapped up posters with their photographs and biographies, and a black X triumphantly scrawled across the faces of those who were dead. A remaining dozen sought refuge in the only relatively attack-proof enclave in Algeria, the Rocher Noir complex. Debré angrily ordered them flown back to France. So ended this strange, unproductive, poorly thought-out counterterrorist campaign. By now, the political situation was changing: the attack on the Hotel Rajah coincided with the successful negotiations at Les Rousses, which presaged a cease-fire; the Army showed less readiness to tip its weight on the OAS's side, an eventuality which only two months before had been a major government preoccupation. In the new context the *barbouzes* were no longer needed.

So the suspicion arose—and persists—that the *barbouzes* were dispatched to Algeria as bait, to draw enemy fire and be sacrificed. One survivor, a mild-spoken but glint-eyed French radio technician, charges flatly that the unprofessional bumbling, the lack of elementary security precautions and the recruiting of Vietnamese were not irresponsible, as it seemed, but deliberate; the unspoken assumption was that the *barbouzes* would fight the OAS but not return, for back in France they would be an embarrassment. This speculation cannot be ruled out. Certainly the explosion at Villa Andrea has never been fully explained. Why was a printing press sent from Paris when it could be procured in Algiers? Why was it stored on the docks where the OAS was sure to learn about its existence? Why was the crate allowed to remain temptingly in a warehouse for two weeks?

Perez, who fought the *barbouzes*, likewise concluded at a fairly early date that they were in Algiers on a suicidal mission. He says today: "The only thing they did not do was to put up a flag saying, '*Barbouzes*—Shoot Here.' They were clearly expendable. . . ." Perez himself thought it a waste of time to pursue and kill the decoys, but he claims that by the time he sought to call off the grimly efficient Degueldre, it was too late, the *barbouzes* had virtually been eliminated.

Whatever the real motivations, the price in lives was unarguably high. At the lowest estimates, nineteen died in the blast at El Biar;

twenty-four according to another count. The dismembered, uniden-
tifiable victims were buried without speeches or publicity in the
cemetery of the tranquil little community of Santeny, near Paris.
The survivors found the tag of *barbouzes* an ugly handicap in resuming and readapting to civilian life. Widows and relatives encountered difficulty claiming life-insurance benefits, for there was
trouble obtaining death certificates because of the impossibility of
identification of several corpses; moreover, in some cases *barbouzes*
had mutually listed one another as beneficiaries, and now were
dead.* The Gaullist government denied steadfastly that it had ever
employed a parallel police.

Lucien Bitterlin continues to wear a black tie in memory of the
companions who died at El Biar. He says: "What did we accomplish? It's a question that I still ask myself seven years later. Was it
worth twenty-four lives?" He has found no entirely satisfactory answer.

The shadow of another sort of violence lay across Algiers. The
two communities were physically splitting apart. Meeting in Morocco, the Algerian Provisional Government had proclaimed an all-
out offensive against the OAS, and at the prodding of FLN agents,
Moslems were beginning to regroup, moving out of mixed neighborhoods and clustering among themselves, at first with some
unwillingness, then accelerating the packing-up process as attacks increased. The Organization warned *pieds noirs* to fall back on the
heart of the city where they could be defended. Both groups knew
that the end was in sight.

Algiers was not Berlin, there was no Wall, exchanges subsisted;
but Europeans and Moslems eyed each other, in the words of a
former Algerian governor general, Edmond Naegelen, "as through a
latticework gate"; and what each saw on the other side was fear.

Nothing was tangible yet, but in the slum fastnesses of Belcourt
and Bab el Oued and Clos Salembier, the Casbah, Hussein Dey,
Hamma, down reeking courts, in fetid back alleys and grimy bi-
stros, up and down Algiers' steep ravined hills lurked two terrorisms,
neither triumphant, each observing the other intently. It was like a
pestilence that is in germ but has not yet broken out.

* It is the author's understanding that the insurance companies made resti-
tution at a later date without publicity.

18

The Deadly Streets

THE WIND rose and rattled the palm fronds around the Hotel Mayantigo every evening at dusk, the water slanted down from the horizon
—a reach of infinite gray on which a few late-returning fishing boats
dropped steadily landward in the clear failing light. In the inland
valleys, the cool abruptly extinguished the day's terrific burst of
equatorial heat.

Tropical exile for the Madrid activists was uneventful and devoid
of hardships, if one excepted boredom, which gnawed at them all.
Sitting on the smallest, westernmost of the Canaries, seven hundred
miles out in the Atlantic, they listened bitterly to radio reports of
the OAS's growing strength. It was galling to think that Salan,
Susini, Godard and the others, whom they had so casually accused
of betrayal, represented a force with which the Gaullist government
must now reckon. It was even more galling to realize that each day
spent on Santa Cruz reduced their own ambitions. They had badly
miscalculated; the dissident Directory formed on the eve of their
departure for exile had no effect and made them seem ridiculous.
Sensing this, Argoud had reversed his position, announced his unqualified support of Salan, then prodded the others into doing the
same. But the turnabout drew no acknowledgment from Algiers; it
came too late and was transparently too insincere. They were cut
off from the OAS.

So time passed—three wasted months, a dull winter of introspection in the islands. Each afternoon for exercise they went on an authorized walk in the company of their guards, eight placid, unathletic *guardias civiles*. Argoud, the hiker and climber, soon reached a tacit agreement with the soldiers: while he marched up and down volcanic hills and craters, they waited at a convenient roadside *posada* with the others. His solitary promenades lasted some two hours, after which he often went straight to his room without dinner. The compromise involved no risk, for where could he flee to in the interior? Santa Cruz de la Palma is a small, thinly inhabited island, and it has only one airport, which the police watch sedulously.

The four men did indeed have a common escape plan, but it had nothing to do with Argoud's expeditions. It centered about ex-Lieutenant Michel de la Bigne, the enterprising young activist officer who had flown to Algiers to participate in the putsch. He had subsequently deserted, made his way to Spanish Morocco concealed aboard a fishing boat under a bed of crushed ice, then reached Madrid. Here he joined forces with Lagaillarde and Argoud. In October he had avoided arrest and immediately contacted the other activists while they were detained at Canillejas. When they arrived in the Canaries, they received a message from him.

He was in Morocco making arrangements to charter the same fishing boat on which he had escaped a year before. The boat would sail for the Canaries, pick up the four activists at night while their guards slept, then sail due east for Mauritania, where they would land and make their way to the Algerian frontier.

Lagaillarde, in particular, was impatiently counting the days until the boat's arrival. Unknown to him, Argoud had readied his own escape plan—for just one man.

On February 25, the activists returned to the Mayantigo at sunset from their customary walk. As they crossed town, Argoud lagged behind the others. At an intersection he moved off unobserved down a side street. When the group entered the hotel, Argoud's wife, who was staying with him at the Mayantigo, said that he would not be coming down to dinner. In the hubbub the *guardias civiles* assumed that he had already gone up to his room.

Down the street Argoud found a raincoat concealed by prearrangement behind a hedge. He slipped it on and, still unremarked, struck off swiftly for the port. The evening ferry for Tenerife was leaving on schedule. He bought a ticket and went aboard. It is an overnight crossing to the biggest of the Canary Islands. Upon landing, he went directly to the Iberia Air Lines office; the fare for one passenger to West Germany via Madrid had been paid for by a young Frenchwoman.*

When the alarm was given that morning, *guardias civiles* combed the hills of Santa Cruz on the theory that Argoud was awaiting an opportunity to escape from the island, hiding in the steep pine woods where he had walked alone so frequently. It took local officials some time to grant that the colonel was not only off the island but out of the Canaries altogether, and perhaps even out of Spain. Then they did the only thing still feasible: they reinforced the guard about the other internees.

The Spanish government, which had shrugged off Salan's flight to Algiers a year before, expressed its "indignation and irritation." The press speculated that Argoud was on his way to the Spanish Sahara.

Lagaillarde was very, very angry; once again, as in Madrid, he had been left in the lurch.

One must add a sequel to this incident: Two days later, at dawn, a fishing boat dropped anchor around the point from the Mayantigo. De la Bigne was aboard. Taking advantage of the morning mist, he rowed to shore alone in a dinghy. He must contact Argoud and Lagaillarde, and take everybody aboard under cover of dark in ten hours' time; it meant several trips by dinghy, and he hoped that it would be a moonless night. Up to this point his plan had worked without a flaw. He started along the beach and had come halfway to the hotel when he saw a slight blond woman strolling on the shore. It was Pierre Lagaillarde's wife, Babette. She advised him of Argoud's disappearance, and warned him to clear out at once. The island swarmed with police; the other internees had no hope of evading surveillance. De la Bigne hurried back to the dinghy, and reached the boat, which sailed immediately. The next day it ran into heavy seas, and de la Bigne and the crew were almost shipwrecked off the African coast. Eventually the storm subsided, and they reached Dakar. There was nothing more de la Bigne could do for the internees on Santa Cruz de la Palma. Some time later he flew to Germany and rejoined Argoud.

* Presumably he also found waiting the identity papers he needed to clear passport control.

In February, both Debré and Frey received wrathful letters from Salan. In the first, Salan accused the Premier of betraying a cause, of attempting to suborn lower echelons in the OAS with offers of money, arms and ammunition. Grimly recalling Leroy and Villars's fate, Salan warned that he would be merciless in checkmating any further attempts at division. In the second letter, he blamed Frey for "a major share" of the civil-war atmosphere in Algiers through the commitment of *barbouzes.*

The correspondence aroused little emotion at the Hotel Matignon or the Place Beauveau. Constantin Melnik, Debré's aide who was accused by name of subornation, commented acidly, "He should have sent a killer, not a letter." There was, to be sure, something odd about an underground chieftain with an unquenchable need for communicating with his enemy instead of destroying him; it led to the remark that "he was more interested in correspondence with *Le Monde* than in commandos." As usual, this was a half-truth. The OAS had already ordered a great many killings, and more were in prospect.*

But after the dwindling of the January threat of insurrection, Salan was still charily biding his time. When Godard sought his approval to extend terrorism to the Sahara and blow up oil wells and pipelines near Hassi Messaoud and Ouargla with the complicity of pro-OAS oil-company personnel, Salan turned the scheme down and gave no explanation.

To render him justice, he was not wholly indolent; he had considered proclaiming an autonomous Republic of French Algeria before the inevitable cease-fire occurred, but on this score he encountered stiff resistance, notably from Susini and Godard, whose aims coincided although, as was to be expected, their reasons differed. A breakaway government implied the elaboration of a political platform and a doctrine, but Susini still mistrusted any doctrine other than his own. Godard feared that a publicly formulated Rightist program, while gaining supporters, might alienate many more potential allies. Together they managed to kill the idea.

The OAS's only official doctrine continued to be "Algeria a

---

* Beginning in January 1962, the OAS was responsible for about ten dead and thirty wounded a day. (Marie-Thérèse Lancelot, *Organisation Armée Secrète*)

French province." It was enunciated as a life-or-death article of faith; true believers must abide by it or be punished. It made no difference that the Organization lacked support in France, could not count on the Army and had not dared seize the coastal cities in January; the pirate radio continued to proclaim, "*Vive l'Algérie française!*"

Then news of Les Rousses reached Salan. He could delay a strategic decision no further.

Within a week he issued a new, six-page directive. "The irrevocable is about to happen . . ." begins Instruction No. 29, dated February 23. "I want us, wherever possible, to control the situation. I want to bring events about: in short, at the outset, I reject any idea of defense in favor of a generalized offensive . . ." As soon as a cease-fire is proclaimed, the directive adds, "I order the opening of systematic fire against CRS and *gendarmerie* units . . ."

This sounded like an entirely new and self-assured Salan; it was as though he were retorting to all the criticisms of passivity fellow officers and plotters had uttered throughout his two careers as general and terrorist. But he immediately weakened the effect of this declaration by cautioning against a putsch. Although time was running out, he was still not ready to gamble on a single throw of the dice; he wanted a three-stage offensive deployed in "space and time" to weary the Gaullist enemy and eventually overwhelm him. Regional commanders were to create insurrectional zones in the countryside; the OAS was to undertake systematic harassing of security forces in the cities; and in a final phase, "when the situation has developed to a sufficiently favorable point," armed civilian crowds, a "human wave" (*une marée humaine*) would be committed against the enfeebled and demoralized enemy.

To anyone who read it closely, this directive had a negative ring. For all Salan's talk of eschewing the defensive, H hour was pegged to the cease-fire, which meant granting de Gaulle the initiative once more. It seemed curious, moreover, that in a directive where he acknowledged that "we have only a few days left," Salan ordered action that relied so greatly on sufficient time and preparation.

Perez, for one, gloomily thought the directive came much too late in the day. In his view, the OAS was still hobbled by Salan's stubborn conviction that some units in the French Army would never accept a cease-fire.

Instruction No. 29, shot through with further contradictions, was unambiguous in one respect: by ordering his men to open fire against CRS and *gendarmerie* forces as soon as the end of hostilities was announced, Salan made a showdown with the Army in the coming days inevitable.

The imminence of a cease-fire and the OAS's increasing belligerence had drawn scores of foreign journalists to Algiers—many to the Aletti Hotel, the city's famed white bulbous landmark on the waterfront. The Aletti deserves some mention in any history of French Algeria's final days. Unlike its great rival, the Hotel St.-Georges, which rose in Moorish splendor among its own gardens above the city, the Aletti was located downtown near the Algerian Assembly and the shopping district, square in the midst of whatever was happening. It was several shades less grand than the St.-Georges, and its guests ran to traveling salesmen, small farmers, repertory actors and newsmen; in a sense, it symbolized Algiers' middle-class hustle.

Conditions here were radically changed these days; the gaming rooms closed at ten o'clock, the huge restaurant was half empty and wholly forlorn, only the bar prospered—a vortex of muddy rumors and counterrumors. The crowd of journalists at the bar was thick when two Europeans burst in on the night of March 3, seized two Italian correspondents, Giovanni Giovannini of Turin's *La Stampa* and Bruno Romani of Rome's *Il Messaggero*, and led them away at gun-point. Their crime was obvious enough: they had signed a number of stories hostile to the OAS. The kidnapers drove the Italians uphill to La Dolce Vita, a restaurant in the Télémly quarter notorious as an OAS haunt. Inside a backroom—as Giovannini later told it—an unidentified *pied noir* accused Italians in general of being the biggest liars in the press corps, confiscated his two captives' cameras and gave them twenty-four hours to fly out of Algiers. If not, he warned, they would get hurt. Until this time the OAS had wavered in its dealings with the press; it facilitated interviews for the few correspondents favorable to French Algeria, and it accused the others of being anti-French; it shied away from most journalists for security reasons and made no serious effort to justify its terrorism.

When the Italians returned to the Aletti an hour later, the hotel press corps was in an uproar, and highly excited at the prospect of a good story. Another Italian newsman, Corrado Pizzinelli, led a delegation that roused the government information officer, Philippe Mestre, and protested the lack of protection for correspondents reporting upon the camouflaged civil war. Mestre dismissed the abduction as a "barroom incident" and did nothing.

Nine of the ten Italian newsmen in Algiers thereupon packed up and flew out next morning. In Rome, they published hotly indignant reports of the French government's powerlessness. "Chaos reigns in Algeria. Never before has freedom of the press received such a blow!" wrote *Il Messaggero*, which was overstating it by a mile. The incident had its farcical side and was not repeated—other journalists continued to work in Algiers without being kidnaped*—but Mestre's handling of it came in for considerable criticism; it appeared to reflect not only official confusion but indifference to what was happening in Algiers.

Sunny days, forerunners of spring, drew crowds of soldiers, civilians and students to the sidewalk terraces on Rue Michelet and Rue d'Isly. Often, while lunch was being served, a shot rang out and somebody lurched to the ground. If gendarmes materialized, the murderer raced off through the midday traffic; otherwise he returned to his interrupted meal. If the victim was dead, a sheet of newspaper was placed over his face. If he was not, he lay on the sidewalk. Some passers-by detoured around him, very few would stop to assist him. An ambulance eventually arrived and he was removed. Firemen hosed off the bloodstains on the pavement. Then through unspoken convention, conversation resumed and drinks were served again on the sunny café terraces.

Algiers was now averaging between thirty and forty violent deaths a day, not to mention the wounded. Such statistics—the

---

* They did receive threats, however. John Casserly, an ABC correspondent, became aware through hints at the Rue Hoche studio that his broadcasts were causing some dissatisfaction. Finally, he was approached by two men in a bar across from the Hotel Aletti—a Frenchman and a Spaniard. Both carried arms. They gave Casserly forty-eight hours to leave Algiers. When he protested that his reporting had been impartial, they noted that his broadcasts were monitored by the OAS. As matters turned out, another correspondent was already on his way to Algiers to relieve Casserly.

Japanese journalists had another problem. They were mistaken for Vietnamese *barbouzes*. Out of self-preservation they took to wearing small Nipponese flags in their lapels.

"statistics of horror," as one Frenchman dubbed them—are not impressive when stated in the abstract. It is more relevant to note that one day, between 11:20 and 12:50, thirteen persons were shot dead within a radius of five hundred yards. The long French noon break provided a high number of deaths, for part-time Delta gunmen had discovered that they could fit lunch and murder into their schedules and return to work without haste.

The thirteen in question were not all killed at once, it was not a massacre, each was thoughtfully singled out and dispatched. The murderer did not know his victim, had no curiosity about him, and the death was unlikely to affect the outcome of French Algeria's agony. But Salan had ordered more terrorism, and Degueldre's Deltas dutifully complied. Moslem pedestrians became the chief targets, in general because they symbolized the FLN, the enemy, and in particular because they happened to fall athwart a gunman in the streets.

A *Paris-Match* reporter filed a harrowing description of one death:

> . . . On Avenue de la Bouzaréah, in Bab el Oued, a Moslem lay wounded, shot. An OAS gunman came up, took aim again and fired—but the gun jammed. Lying there, the Moslem, trembling uncontrollably, managed to clutch his jacket to his face. The gunman looked down, studied him and pulled the trigger—but the gun jammed a second time. Finally it went off.

Whether this new phase really reflected Salan's wishes, it is impossible to say, but few records exist and Salan himself has remained mute, except to claim full responsibility for the OAS's actions.

Murder in the streets no longer shocked, it was an hourly occurrence; the manner of dying sometimes differentiated victims, but the grisly process itself was mechanical. From balconies, Europeans watched the gunning-down of Arabs and commented on it as on a sporting match. When an Arab fell, young *pieds noirs* did not break off conversation with acquaintances.

Still, the psychological strain on the living was tremendous. Newcomers were struck by an oddity: Algiers' inhabitants, European and Moslem, avoided overtaking one another on the sidewalks; every few feet they turned to check whether they were being followed, and when in doubt they rapidly crossed the street. When they reached their destination safely, their faces were tight and blank.

That month the Organization forbade airlines and steamship companies to sell tickets to any *pieds noirs* seeking to leave Algiers without a properly signed and stamped OAS visa. The measure had a twofold purpose: to discourage departures and mainly to reinforce the OAS's position as the real power in the city.* A few days later, an airport bus was machine-gunned. Thus challenged, the government ordered both Air France and Air Algérie to fly customers out without OAS visas. Finally, under heavy pressure, both carriers did, but new take-off procedures at Maison Blanche airport were a sign of changing times. At the last moment, passengers with boarding passes were taken past a decoy plane wheeled into full view on the field to another plane, parked inconspicuously near a hangar. Here baggage was stacked around the craft. Each person was required to claim and carry aboard his own belongings, a not superfluous precaution against bombs. Passengers paid the fare upon safe arrival at Marseilles.

Most Europeans and Moslems, however, were not flying out of Algiers, but hanging on grimly, preoccupied by day-to-day concerns that bulked large in their lives.

Increasingly, the *pieds noirs* were thrust upon their own resources. Mail was no longer delivered since the OAS had killed five postmen—with fine indiscrimination, two Catholics, a Jew and two Moslems; only one newspaper, the *Journal d'Alger,* still appeared, and it carried lengthening columns of bankruptcy notices and real estate knocked down for quick sale. No one bothered with house repairs any more. Strikes broke out at any moment of the day—among trolley-car conductors, dockworkers, doctors, telephone operators. Shopkeepers rolled down their iron shutters directly it grew dark, long before the normal closing hour.

Yet—although not even the most obtuse could claim that condi-

---

* Local moving companies were also intimidated. One firm even balked at shipping the effects of a member of the United States consulate unless he produced an authorization from the OAS; a sub-sector chief of the Organization made it clear he was prepared to issue an "exit visa" in return for payment of a "fine." The consulate successfully ignored this attempt at extortion. But at about this time it burned some low-level classified material for fear of an OAS raid on the consulate grounds.

tions would ever be what they had been, that it was simply a matter of holding out and resisting change; in spite of the shadowy struggle for power that raged behind a "thin and cracked" façade of authority; and in spite of daily murder that each side knew about and watched with frozen-faced acceptance, even satisfaction—normality of sorts persisted. Stores ran bargains, cinemas and cafés remained open, downtown traffic had not noticeably thinned out, parties took place.

The Moslems went to work each morning, to support their families, even if it meant crossing a gunman's path—and human nature being what it is, after a few days' care they reverted to shortcuts through the European quarter, in preference to detours through safer neighborhoods. Or out of stubbornness and sheer curiosity they ventured into hazardous areas, to visit relatives, to shop, just to see what was happening, to stare. FLN agents gave up trying to stop these expeditions; you can coop people up for a few days, but not indefinitely.

The ambulances were overworked, and so were the funeral parlors and the morgue of Mustapha Hospital, where assassinated Europeans and Moslems briefly lay side by side in unfamiliar communion. Burials themselves became a problem: coffins were scarce, and so were undertakers' men; for security reasons, police prohibited funeral processions on foot, whether to the cemetery of St.-Eugène, whose fresh graves drew black-clad European widows, or to that of El Ketar, where women in shapeless white *haiks* lamented. "Algiers, Capital of Sorrows," Albert-Paul Lentin, the writer, called his native city.

This was the shifting anticipatory explosive atmosphere when formal cease-fire negotiations opened on March 7 in Évian.

The French and Algerians returned to Évian convinced that this time an agreement would be reached, although how long it would require was uncertain. This optimism stemmed from Les Rousses, where the two delegation leaders, Algerian Affairs Minister Louis Joxe and GPRA Foreign Minister Saad Dahlab, had taken each other's measure personally; where the atmosphere in the snow-ringed chalet had been, in one delegate's words—*"très dégagée"*; where the two camps had, after months of secret thrust and parry, shown a mutual willingness to make concessions.

The Algerians found Joxe well-briefed and intelligent; by and large, they had no complaints about the three chief negotiators sitting opposite them. The French regarded Dahlab as an able minister, with a broad, statesmanlike view of the problem, and the FLN team as one that apparently had more latitude to negotiate than those in the past—which was a relief.

In this encouraging atmosphere the conference began on March 7.

It was, therefore, all the more frustrating when the talks became mired in familiar treacherous areas of dispute. No voices were raised, but progress was nil. The strain bore home the truth of ex-premier Félix Gaillard's skeptical assessment: "It's hard to keep Algeria, harder to lose it and still harder to give it away." In Paris, Debré made no secret of his belief that it would be eternally impossible to wring a binding agreement out of the FLN; according to Robert Buron, he instructed the French delegation not to hesitate about breaking off contact if necessary.

Wednesday, March 14, has been cited as the day when nerves were strained to the utmost. Joxe was bone-tired and suffering from flu. Dahlab, Belkacem Krim and the others packed up their briefcases and took the helicopter back to their temporary Swiss residence at 6 P.M., two hours before the session's scheduled end. Once again, the vital negotiations were stalled.

Next morning three young men armed with automatic pistols drove up to the Domaine du Château Royal in El Biar, a social-service center founded by Jacques Soustelle in healthier days to promote Franco-Moslem cooperation. Inside, two school principals and four social-center inspectors of French and Algerian nationality discussed vocational-training plans for homeless Moslem children.

Brandishing their pistols the newcomers read out a list of seven names. One man was missing from the roll call. The commando led the six others outdoors after assuring them they would suffer no harm but would be obliged to record pro-*Algérie française* statements for an OAS pirate broadcast.

In the courtyard they lined the educators up before a wall and collected their identity papers. Then they opened fire, shooting first in the legs, then finishing the six men off where they lay on the ground.

The scene was witnessed by an old woman and a child in a nearby field. The young men had entered the social center at 11 A.M. By 11:15 it was all over.

The last to fall, killed by twelve bullets, was Mouloud Feraoun, a Kabyle writer awarded a literary prize, the 1953 Prix Populiste, for his novel *La Terre et le sang*. In the days of extremists he counseled moderation. Several days before his execution he wrote in his diary: *"La guerre d'Algérie se termine. Paix à ceux qui sont morts. Paix à ceux qui vont survivre. Cesse la terreur."*

That evening, a liberal European lawyer was assassinated in downtown Algiers. And as a line of Moslems waited in the dark before a bus stop at Hussein Dey, a car slowed down and a machine gun raked them, killing ten.

The question was: If more time were lost at Évian, would an agreement still have any practical meaning?

Every night Joxe was badgered about the day's accomplishments, or lack of them, by de Gaulle, who gave his negotiators the impression on the telephone that he was not convinced they were doing the very best they could. *"Où en êtes-vous de vos bergers?"* growled the unmistakable testy voice in Paris. The others watched Joxe. He was nervous and harassed, ill with flu, and they feared that he might follow Debré's advice and break off contact in a fit of anger. The talks had already dragged on more than a week.

The Algerians were preoccupied by three concerns: the reaction of Ben Bella and his four fellow inmates in France to whatever terms they obtained; Tunis's attitude; and the OAS's stated intent of rendering any agreement impractical.*

The breakthrough came all of a sudden after days of interminable hairsplitting. On Sunday, March 18, at five-thirty in the afternoon, the two sides signed a 76-page protocol putting an end to a war that

---

* Following the informal agreement reached at Les Rousses, the FLN's supreme instance, the Conseil National de la Révolution Algérienne, met from February 22 to 27 in Tripoli. At this next-to-last meeting before independence, the FLN gave itself—according to a French writer, Jacques Duchemin, closely acquainted with its deliberations—until November 1962 to be installed physically in Algiers: if not, it would mean de Gaulle's government was unable to subdue the OAS. If it came to the worst, the FLN let it be known, it had ready a substitute plan for separate negotiations with Salan. To some extent, this was bluff intended to wring negotiations out of the French at Évian—but not wholly.

had lasted seven years, four months and eighteen days and claimed tens of thousands of lives*—the second-longest war (after Indochina) France had fought in modern times. What began in the desolate Aurès mountains on All Saints Day, 1954, as a local nationalist uprising with a handful of men and five hundred rifles and was subsequently so woefully misunderstood by various French governments and the French Army was now, after great consumption of lives, matériel, money and good faith, at an end.

The protocol stipulated that military operations would cease the next day at noon. It called for a self-determination referendum to be held on Algerian soil between three and six months from that date; the language clearly implied the presumption that the country's nine-million Moslem majority would vote for an independent state and economic "association" with France. Guarantees for the *pieds noirs'* future—economic, social, juridical and cultural—were painstakingly spelled out over twelve pages. They would retain French citizenship but have the right to vote in Algeria and to be elected to office; the French language would be maintained in schools and public institutions; the hitch was that such guarantees would apply for only three years. In addition, there were six "Declarations" on military and technical cooperation and joint exploitation of the Sahara's natural resources. The central idea behind the agreement was to end hostilities and give Algerians an opportunity to vote in an atmosphere of relative order and stability. But as one French official noted, a cooling-off period would be needed for "passions to die down, rancor to subside, vengeance to be forgotten"—hence the three months' minimum delay before the referendum.

Now that it was over, both sides came round the table and for the first time shook hands.

Belkacem Krim felt relief. He was confident the cease-fire would be observed and the coming referendum would bring independence. As for the OAS, he voiced a minority belief within his group that not all *pieds noirs* belonged to it; after independence, some diehard elements would have to be expelled, that was all. This was a sanguine view.

* From 1954 to the end of 1961, *Le Monde* reported, the French Army suffered 12,000 dead and 25,000 wounded; the FLN, an estimated 141,000 killed. These figures, drawn from official sources, concerned military casualties only. There were thousands of civilian casualties.

The Algerians, however, already felt concern on another score. To the French, Saad Dahlab confided: "Now our troubles begin." And the French realized he was referring to the lengthening shadow of Ben Bella.

Willful and relatively young at forty-five, sprung from the lower middle class, a symbol of the new Algerian generation coming to the fore, Ben Bella might easily sweep aside the older, more conservative nationalist leaders, like Ferhat Abbas and Belkacem Krim, who wanted a limited and moderate social revolution along the lines of Habib Bourguiba's regime in Tunisia. During five years' imprisonment, Ben Bella had foresightedly cultivated an image as an Arab man of action, a new North African Nasser unsullied by political haggling with the French; still detained by the Fifth Republic, he had given his verbal consent through Moroccan emissaries to the Évian agreement, but significantly he had not signed it. He was now free to criticize and repudiate the terms. The FLN delegation had asked for his release from internment with extreme reluctance—as one French diplomat put it, *du bout des lèvres.*

The French themselves signed the protocol because they judged it necessary, but without enthusiasm. They were tired and morose. They had obtained guarantees for the *pieds noirs,* but the feeling was that the only worthwhile guarantees would be those buttressed by French economic aid, to be granted on a strict *quid pro quo* basis. Privately, the French delegates expressed doubt whether more than half the Europeans would remain in Algiers; it seemed unlikely that they could be happy in a country where they had lived as masters. One delegate expected to see politically compromised *pieds noirs* leave first, then those so attuned to colonialism that they could not stomach new ways, then ultimately those with enough means to wait for a good price before selling. But there was the same optimism as Krim's about the OAS: the cease-fire, the French reasoned, would demonstrate the uselessness of further resistance (although some feared that more terrorism might simply cross the Mediterranean to the mainland). The two sides shared the consolation that, without Évian, bloodshed could have continued indefinitely in the Algerian countryside.

Elsewhere, the agreement brought sharply differing reactions. In Tunis, Ben Khedda, president of the Algerian Provisional Government, claimed that with the cease-fire the Algerian revolution had triumphed and attained the aims for which it was fought. But he omitted to say that like all revolutions it contained the seeds of internal strife.

What did de Gaulle think? The answer, of course, is central to this story, but in view of his pragmatism and his moral solitude, only a guess can be hazarded. Some French writers have described the "lugubrious atmosphere" at the Élysée Palace when he met with Debré and the returning negotiators. If one grants that for a man of his generation and background and proud nationalist instinct the end of French rule in Algeria—that is, to all intents the knell of the French colonial empire—cannot have been altogether gratifying, this is as far as one can go in this vein. He strongly mistrusted the lure of colonies; he thought they swallowed up the energy and budget of a nation, and he shared with Pétain a lingering distrust of overemphasis on the Army's task of defending empire at the sacrifice of continental (that is, European) strategy. As he saw it, he had inherited a booby-trapped problem from the Fourth Republic, which prevented carrying out the Grand Design of his foreign policy. NATO, an Opening to the East, relations with the underdeveloped African countries, strategic overhaul of the French Army—all had waited until Algeria was out of the way.

At a cabinet meeting the next day, March 19, he thanked the three main negotiators, observed that his aim had been a cease-fire and a way both parties could take out of the quagmire. Realistically, he foresaw that the guarantees might prove worthless, but— "We could not prevent her from being born," he said of Algeria, "and now we must give her a chance."[*] His long-time friend and admirer, François Mauriac, was moved to exclaim at the "incredible force of this old man whose downfall everybody is hoping and waiting for—and preparing." True to character, de Gaulle himself briskly told one negotiator, Jean de Broglie: "Now we're out of that hornet's nest."

Michel Debré remained silent and loyal, struggling with the technical problems rising from a solution he had bitterly opposed.

In France, opinion split sharply. In some families there was relief and joy at sons returning from war; in others, misgivings and stupefaction at the loss of the huge chunk of territory. In the National Assembly, cries and countercries of "Treason!" and "OAS—Assassins!" resounded. Maurice Faure, president of the Radicals, declared soberly: "I have learned the news of the cease-fire with satisfaction

---

[*] Cited by Louis Terrenoire in *De Gaulle et l'Algérie*.

but without joy"—a summing-up which spoke for many. The satirical weekly *Le Canard Enchaîné*, much to its readers' surprise, published a front-page editorial with unprecedented praise for de Gaulle. But church bells rang out in only one small village on the Channel coast; elsewhere, it was indeed a cease-fire "without bugles."

The Army swallowed the news without protest; most officers were cowed, conscripts thought of it essentially in terms of quick demobilization. Some observers went so far as to say the cease-fire prevented the by-then neurotic Army from disintegrating completely. At La Reghaia, General Charles Ailleret issued a new order of the day to his troops: "The cease-fire puts an end to more than seven years of combat during which our Army had the mission of opposing an often overexcited but always courageous enemy. . . . Military conditions were assured that were necessary for the solution of a very serious political problem. The Army's mission is thus accomplished . . . but its role here is not finished. It must, by its presence, and if necessary by its action, contribute to prevent disorder from prevailing, no matter who should try to unleash it again."

Gaullists hailed this brief order of the day as a masterpiece of tact, which danced lightly on the passions of the past seven years and carefully stressed the predominance of the political over the military outcome.

The Right was inconsolably bitter. "It isn't an army that has been beaten, but it is our nation—for it isn't our army that has yielded but our resistance and our energy," wrote one polemicist. Algeria's former Governor General Edmond Naegelen was particularly caustic: "Ailleret's order of the day deserves to go down in posterity. He professes a new concept of strategy and the consequences of battle. In curt, concise military language: 'We have won, hence let's beat it.' And to the enemy: 'You're licked, hence we're allowing you to move in.' Here is a doctrine well suited to encourage young Frenchmen in future to let themselves be killed in defense of a position. . . ." The cease-fire, Naegelen pointed out, had been signed alone with the FLN, "without and against" the *pieds noirs*. In Algeria he foresaw a "violent movement of despair and anger."

In Algiers, the sky had been overcast and rainy all day. First news of the cease-fire reached the city late that Sunday evening.

Vitalis Cros the police prefect learned of it through a code word, *Iris*, flashed over the official communications network. Within an hour he summoned local FLN leaders to his office at Palais Carnot and obtained their agreement to halt further terrorist attacks. Cros says he wanted to call in OAS chiefs, but he could not, because they commanded no official status; the Évian agreement, theoretically at least, did not concern them.

Somewhere in the city, hidden in an apartment, Salan heard the radio flash. He reacted somberly. Whatever Moslem support the OAS had enjoyed was now automatically ended; with independence a tangible prospect, it could scarcely be otherwise. De Gaulle would withdraw still more troops from the countryside and concentrate them in an iron ring around Algiers. Salan immediately arranged to speak on the pirate radio. In his innermost self he had never believed this day possible: "You do not have the right to do this," he declared. But the hard fact subsisted: the Organization had failed to block the cease-fire. Three precarious months were left, until summer, to prevent the referendum from being held—through total destruction, if necessary.

The cease-fire did not ignite the explosion of popular fury Naegelen had prophesied. The *pieds noirs* were sure Salan had a master plan to save them. They stayed indoors, glum but on the alert; shutters everywhere were drawn, but behind them the faint, obstinate thump of *"Algérie"* on kitchenware brought the immediate answering beat next door of *"française!"* It was pitch dark outdoors: Électricité d'Algérie employees had cut the power. There was not a taxi or a car abroad.

After the nine-o'clock curfew, a security patrol moved cautiously up the street under the weakly lighted arcades of Rue Bab el Azoun, past blasted-out stores and incinerated cars. Rifles ready, the soldiers crossed the street, expecting a grenade, a Molotov cocktail, a machine-gun burst. There, somewhere in the dark, lay the OAS. It rejected the cease-fire, it had just been ordered by Salan on the pirate radio to start immediate harassing operations. The patrol reached the corner. Its footfalls echoed and died down the silent, dangerous street.

PART FOUR

Just as an individual, subjected to certain inner pressures beyond his endurance, will suddenly go mad and destroy himself or those around him, so too, apparently, can a segment of society take leave of its senses and deliver itself to the forces of destruction.

—STANLEY LOOMIS,
Paris in the Terror

19

The Showdown

AFTERNOONS THE Place du Gouvernement was always thronged. The steep teeming alleyways of the Casbah flowed downhill here, past what was the great stone bulk of Saint Philip's Cathedral, the old Ketchaoua mosque, and emptied out into the leafy square, which in spite of its name housed few administrative services in those days but spawned a rich variety of outdoor trade and barter. Trays of lemonade and sweetcakes, lamb roasting on a spit, mounds of grilled fish and loops of the inevitable *merguez** sweated under clouds of bluebottle flies. Shoelaces, work pants, combs and henna were on sale. Merchants and women haggled in shrill pleasure, old men in bronze jelabs sat under fig trees near the rusted equestrian statue of the Duc d'Orléans watching the activity in the port. Here buses left for the suburbs. Here Moslems came at prayertime to the two mosques on Boulevard Anatole France facing the scummy waters of the tidal basin.

That afternoon—March 21—still more Moslems than usual—certainly several hundred—loitered or sipped mint tea or did business in the neighborhood, reassurred by a lull in terrorism following the cease-fire. Few *pieds noirs,* however, approached the broad square; they had received a tip to stay at some distance.

At 4:15 P.M., on a nearby rooftop in Bab el Oued, a deserter lieu-

* Mutton sausage with red peppers: an Algerian delicacy.

333

tenant stood beside the Algiers OAS's only mortar, carefully checked range and trajectory, then gave orders to two Delta gunmen to fire. One right after another, four 60-mm. shells rose, arched high through the pale afternoon sky, and exploded with perfect deadliness in the center of the Place du Gouvernement.

The impact was terrible. A flash, followed by another, then debris, smoke, cries, moans—the square drew itself into a whirring cylinder of confluent damage, winds and heat, then flew apart into separate components of distress. Three men lay dead. An old woman supported by several boys collapsed with slow deliberation against a blood-smeared wall. Scores of wounded sprawled on the pavement. A newsstand crackled into flame. A car lay overturned, leaking oil, and burst into fire.

There was incipient panic, when it seemed the bombardment might resume; then a spontaneous surge to help victims. A Moslem street crowd ignites quickly to anger. It began to form threateningly about a Moslem noncom, probably because he was the first scapegoat visible in French Army uniform—anything European appeared under the circumstances inimical. Bystanders shouted. The noncom backed off, fumbling at the safety catch on his gun. A French major hurriedly pushed his way through the crowd, strode up to the sergeant and smacked him hard across the face. This helped; perceptibly the crowd's nervousness eased off. A gendarme hustled the sergeant out of reach before the uncertain mob changed its mind. For the first time in Algiers' history, French officers and FLN neighborhood leaders cooperated in restoring a semblance of order to the blasted square.

In the adjoining Casbah FLN agents kicked and prodded Moslems back indoors. "Don't fall for their game . . . keep calm . . ." the word sped up and down the whitewashed identical passageways. "*Dor lou dia koum!*" [Back inside!]," someone roared. A zouave patrol caught inside the Casbah when the mortar attack occurred was allowed to continue unlynched on its way.

Once again, a miracle had prevented the worst—a full-fledged racial riot—from taking place.

The Moslems did not flail out in retaliation, for a number of reasons. Five years earlier, French paratroopers had thoroughly dismantled the FLN's local underground network, the *Zone autonome d'Alger;* in the interval no serious attempt had been made to reconstitute it. Ben Khedda and other nationalist leaders abroad were aware that the French Army was extremely touchy on this point and was not likely to suffer the zone's reestablishment until a formal cease-fire. Thus, in Algiers itself, no effective organization existed to strike back at the OAS.

Moreover, the FLN legalistically persisted in dismissing the OAS as an internal French problem. According to this view, until the signing of the Évian accords the French Army was responsible for maintaining order in Algeria; thereafter the task fell to the newly constituted *force locale*—although it was manifestly incapable of doing so.

Among the Moslems who lived in Algiers and Oran in daily fear of attack, the same dispassionate attitude scarcely prevailed. Moslem teen-agers strained a bit more each day at the leash for a chance to square accounts with *pied noir* youths. At this juncture, anonymous neighborhood FLN *responsables*—men who were known only to a few families, but carried weight as the movement's representatives —played a significant part in upholding morale and imposing discipline on the population. They preached patience in the teeth of unbearable provocation. They argued that the battle was half won; difficult days lay ahead, but it needed only a few more months to independence. Somehow they were listened to.

The average Arab city dweller exhibited uncommon political sophistication during this ordeal. The terrorists were bent on terrorizing to a degree where the Moslems would storm mindlessly into the streets for revenge, run up against the French Army, and precipitate riots that could jeopardize the cease-fire. At some point, knowledge of the enemy's tactics was impressed upon the inhabitants of the Casbah and Belcourt and El Kettar. They thereupon chose a course of tenacity, silence and endurance.

Inbred Arab fatalism perhaps rendered the choice easier. The worse the OAS attacks became (reasoned some) the more cause there was for hope, since obviously the enemy was being driven to extremities. Poetically one Moslem noted of this unpoetical period: "The wind in the sails drives the boat."

Since March 19 a heavy burden lay on the OAS of trying to undo what was done. The Évian agreement had cut the Organization off from the homeland, where a poll showed public opinion running strongly in favor of de Gaulle.* In Algeria, the OAS had failed as yet to mount a single major coordinated offensive against either of its two enemies, the FLN and the French Army. But strikes, sabotage and local uncoordinated actions were obviously no longer enough to counter the march toward independence.

It is interesting to note that an official at the United States Consulate General at this point considered the OAS "one of the most efficient terrorist organizations in modern history." Even allowing for its internal weaknesses, the Organization numbered almost two hundred well-armed gunmen and several thousand militants.† With this weapon Salan could reasonably hope to fight a vicious delaying action. The *barbouzes* were beaten, the Deltas carried out bank holdups at will, Morin and his staff at Rocher Noir were isolated; their authority, it was said, ended at the barbed-wire fence around the complex; in Oran there was growing anarchy. The now-legal FLN did not weigh in the balance in the cities, where it was disorganized and on the defensive. In Algiers itself, there existed no force to oppose Salan—except, perhaps, the French Army.

On March 20, twenty-four hours after the cease-fire, Jacques Achard, OAS chief of the Orléans-Marine sector including Algiers' waterfront, issued an unprecedented ultimatum to the French Army and security forces in Algiers. He gave them until zero hour, Thursday, March 22, to withdraw "from the neighborhood delimited by Caserne Pélissier, Caserne d'Orléans, St.-Eugène and Climat de France." Beyond this date, the warning said, French troops intercepted in the streets would be considered a foreign and hostile occupation force. For practical purposes, the area described corresponded to Bab el Oued.

For the past year, Achard, a violent, impulsive, hard-drinking ex-

---

* To the question, "Do you approve of the cease-fire?" 87 percent of those queried replied Yes, 3 percent No, and the remainder had no opinion. The poll included a further question, "Do you think the OAS has lost?" Forty percent replied Yes, 20 percent No, and the rest did not know. (*Le Monde*, March 22, 1962)

† The Délégation Générale in March estimated the OAS's total strength at between 100–150 killers, 1,500–2,000 shock commandos (including Z Commandos), 3,000–4,000 militants. Another estimate set the number of militants at 5,000. The last figure seems high. Susini contends that the OAS never amounted to more "than 300 or 400 individuals"; but this seems overmodest.

colonial administrator, had counseled transforming Bab el Oued into a military bastion—with the intention, according to his detractors, of ruling over it singlehanded. Encouraged by Salan's Instruction No. 29, he was spoiling for a fight. He was not alone; Perez and Roland Vaudrey, Godard's former aide in the Algiers Sûreté, also felt the time right for a showdown.* The FLN operated with impunity in Moslem quarters; the OAS, they reasoned, should have the same right in a European quarter.

Bab el Oued seemed the logical choice—at least psychologically— for a showdown. The OAS *was* the law there. Neighborhood toughs bragged: "To drive us out, they'll have to destroy Bab el Oued house by house." Always extremist in its attitude, the hotbed of Algiers activism was an enclave of brooding rebelliousness. The once good-tempered rhythm of life in its turbulent streets was sullen; the curfew, the slump in business, the cease-fire, the FLN, de Gaulle—the *petits blancs* lumped all these together under the same heading of stark injustice: *la sckoumoun,* "bad luck" in their argot. More insecure than ever, rubbed raw by a year's unbroken string of frustrations and defeats, they were ready to lash out at the highly visible enemy they held responsible for their misfortunes—the gendarmes and the Army. To cite Albert-Paul Lentin once more, "If there is one city whose inhabitants never know when to stop before going too far, it's Algiers."

Achard meant his ultimatum as a test of the Army's will to fight back. He instructed the *pieds noirs* in his fief to defy house searches by going out into the streets; to circumvent roadblocks by alighting from cars and continuing on foot, and to attack roving patrols with grenades. He promised the OAS high command there would be a minimum of bloodshed. The Army had, to be sure, shown hesita-

---

* Vaudrey's role as a Paris plotter and his arrest during the April putsch are recounted in Chapters 3 and 5. In September 1961 a military court sentenced him to ten years' imprisonment. On September 25 he was taken under guard to Beghin Hospital in St.-Mandé, outside Paris. Vaudrey slipped out through a side door and found a car waiting at the curb, as prearranged. Godard had set up his former deputy's escape. Vaudrey arrived illegally in Algeria the following month, joined the OAS under the code name *Scipion Hannibal,* and assumed command of the sector chiefs. His headquarters was a two-story apartment fitted with false partitions and closets on Boulevard du Télémly, where he remained for days at a stretch without coming outdoors. The colonel, once hailed as a "resolute and magnificent officer," was described at this stage as "hating de Gaulle more than he wants to save French Algeria." (Robert Buchard, *Organisation Armée Secrète*)

tion at siding with the OAS, but this reluctance was not synonymous with willingness to crack down on the Organization. To refrain from firing on Frenchmen, the Army would give the quarter a wide berth; the detested gendarmes might penetrate into its streets; but if they were mauled by OAS commandos, they would think twice about venturing into the neighborhood again. All of this was predicated on two assumptions: that the population would not hesitate to open fire on a "foreign oppressor," while conversely the Army would recoil at firing on Frenchmen. It bore out the dictum that it is a prime French vice to stake all on brilliant theories proceeding from questionable hypotheses.

Achard was persuaded the conscripts were not prepared to die in anti-OAS warfare, that the Army would never dare to risk committing Legionnaires or paratroopers against *pieds noirs,* and the gendarmes would prove less effective in crushing an insurrection than at riot-breaking. He saw the stake as a major one: if the OAS succeeded in establishing permanent daylight control over Bab el Oued, its power would subsequently spread to other European districts. Willfully or not, he had misinterpreted Salan's directive, which stressed avoidance of a pitched localized battle. And it apparently did not occur to Achard that matters might get out of hand to a point where the Army would have no choice but to riposte.

Militarily, his plan made no sense. Bab el Oued was dominated by heights, from which the Army could easily pour down annihilating fire in the event of prolonged resistance. And the district adjoined the Casbah, whose Moslem mobs could conceivably swarm out to attack the Europeans. General Bernard Cherasse, the *gendarmerie* commander, considered Bab "indefensible."

Not everyone in the OAS favored the operation. Degueldre refused to commit his Deltas; he undertook merely to carry out diversionary tactics on the eve of Achard's planned showdown. The reasons remain unclear. Susini viewed Bab el Oued's secession—this was what it amounted to—as a desperate last resort; but he did nothing to check Achard.

Salan's share of responsibility for what ensued is hard to assess. He states vaguely today that he followed the operation stage by stage from a lodging near Bab el Oued; it reminded him of the Spanish Civil War. His Instruction No. 29 did indeed call for immediate systematic harassment of the enemy. Yet Achard's ultimatum went directly counter to his strongly expressed warning against being lured into battle against a superior force in a circumscribed area. Moreover, if a showdown was approaching, it called for coordinated OAS action throughout the city; but next to no such action took place. It is inconceivable that the former commander in chief in Indochina and Algeria overlooked the need for this. It is much more likely that he did not exercise the control over the Organization he claims to have exercised. Other OAS leaders interviewed by the writer maintain that Achard issued the ultimatum on his own authority; then, once it was done, the Organization could do little, in spite of misgivings, but back it up; Salan once more, as in the William Levy affair and with Sergent, covered up for impetuous underlings.

The ultimatum awakened little apprehension at first in Algiers Army Corps headquarters, where it was seen as part of Susini's relentless psychological-warfare campaign. Nonetheless, two days before its expiration, heavier numbers than usual of security forces appeared around Bab el Oued. After the nine-o'clock curfew, tanks and scout cars rumbled down the winding streets. For all this, troops under General Ferdinand Capodanno, the local commander, did not want a showdown with the OAS, least of all in Bab el Oued, where the activists were considered particularly mobile and tough.

In the same period, local *pied noir* garage owners built up a stock of oil drums and nails; and OAS commandos from other districts slipped during the night into the *petits blancs'* bastion. The showdown Achard wanted and Salan had cautioned against was approaching. Achard, Perez and Vaudrey awaited it with confidence.

A red signal rocket streaked into the moonless sky. Immediately a bomb blew up at the Police Prefecture and a *gendarmerie* barracks near the Délégation Générale came under bazooka attack. This was Degueldre's contribution to the forthcoming battle. Throughout the night of March 22—hours after the expiration of Achard's ultimatum—there was intermittent gunfire. Nervous gendarmes just flown in from France waited at the Tunnel des Facultés to be committed against an unseen enemy. When a pistol shot cracked nearby, they opened indiscriminate enfilade fire with heavy machine guns down an empty street.

During the predawn hours the city quieted down, but it was an oppressive, watchful quiet. Volunteers crept out and spread oil and nails on the street surface before Caserne Pélissier, Army Corps headquarters.

Just before 8 A.M., an OAS commando intercepted a foot patrol advancing through the still-deserted streets near the Caserne, and disarmed it. The soldiers offered no resistance, save for one draftee, who was clubbed to the ground.

Throughout the quarter other commandos armed with bazookas and grenade launchers began taking up positions. For the moment, the OAS securely controlled Bab el Oued.

Two hours later, the first serious trouble occurred. A convoy of two Army Signal Corps trucks was stopped outside the Bastos cigarette factory on Rue Christophe Colombe. Twelve youngsters carrying submachine guns surrounded the vehicles and ordered the conscripts inside to hand over their weapons. A Moslem soldier in the second truck blindly grabbed his rifle. At once the commando opened fire, killing the lieutenant in charge and two enlisted men. The windshield shivered in front of the stricken driver. The firing continued. Several other soldiers slumped against one another. Two fell off the truck, wounded. As soon as the fusillade was over, the teen-agers snatched the dead soldiers' weapons, and fled; they knew the attack spelled trouble of a sort Achard had not foreseen.

Word of the murderous ambush spread rapidly through the Army. Most units stationed in Algiers were made up of conscripts gratified by the end of the war and eager to return home. They felt little sympathy for the *pieds noirs,* and none at all for the Organization. Some saw bloodstains on the ambushed truck as it was being towed away; others heard the wail of the Medical Corps ambulance evacuating the wounded—draftees like themselves.

Shortly afterward, CRS troops and *gendarmes mobiles* began to surround buildings on Rue Mizon, near the scene of the attack. Except for sporadic shouts, Bab el Oued lay still—too still; word of the deaths had circulated among the population too, and the entire neighborhood wore an air of expectancy. Families watched armored scout cars approaching down the narrow streets. Some vehicles were equipped with makeshift brooms and brushes attached to front bumpers to sweep away the oil and nails. Earlier in the morning, a woman's car had skidded on an oil slick and crashed into a wall. She emerged with a broken arm.

Suddenly the gendarmes came under fire from a café in a tiny square. The windows shattered as they poured fire back. Several Molotov cocktails exploded in the street.

An infantry patrol simultaneously came under attack at another entrance to Bab el Oued. The ensuing skirmish left two soldiers dead.

The prenoon fighting was still limited to isolated incidents; but where the Army had not yet penetrated, armed civilian commandos moved swiftly through the streets and assembled at corners and beside rooftop chimneys.

Then the antagonists called a tacit truce for lunch—they were, after all, Frenchmen. Outdoors it was hot for March, and there was no movement. *Pied noir* men observed the gendarmes; they were obviously waiting for further orders, either to withdraw or move out and occupy the entire quarter. At two-fifteen they were still there, concentrated at several checkpoints. A platoon of zouaves began to string up a barbed-wire entanglement across the street. Without warning it came under fire. An OAS commando raced up and ripped down the wire coils. Then the entire squalid overcrowded neighborhood of 50,000 seemed to explode simultaneously into rebellion. Everywhere there was heavy sustained fire. Onlookers fled from their balconies.

Tanks rumbled down Bab el Oued's main shopping street, Avenue de la Bouzaréah, their turret guns firing at anything that moved. As an ambulance sped up the avenue, it was hit and crippled by a bazooka shell. *Gendarmerie* helicopters hovered low over the fighting. Rooftop snipers were holding up the advance of a column of military vehicles. A helicopter dropped grenades on one roof, then whirred away as it came under rifle fire. This had never been seen before—an entire European quarter of Algiers clashing with the Army.

At the Place des Trois Horloges, where he had briefly established his headquarters, Achard was on his own. No other OAS leaders were in Bab el Oued. The European population was abetting the OAS, but not actively taking part in the battle; men and women hurled bottles and flowerpots at the troops, but it was far from being the generalized, Budapest-style uprising Degueldre had dreamed of. The Army was moving in to surround the neighborhood, and the OAS was fighting to break out of the potential trap.

Ailleret had driven at breakneck speed from La Reghaia to Army Corps headquarters at Caserne Pélissier to direct operations personally. From reports reaching him he found it difficult to decide what size or sort of force faced the Army; commandos formed and melted every few minutes. By midafternoon he judged that Bab el Oued was in a state of open, armed insurrection. He remained in constant telephone contact with Debré, and from Paris came two peremptory orders: Ailleret was to prevent at all cost a head-on collision between Europeans and Moslems, and he must smash any attempt to set up a redoubt in Bab el Oued that could fester and cause trouble for days, as Joseph Ortiz's bastion had done during Barricades Week. The fleet cruising along the coast was put at the commander in chief's disposal. Ailleret thereupon ordered four more squadrons of *gendarmerie* armor sent in to control the area.

Scout cars progressing slowly toward the center of Bab el Oued past Boulevard Guillemin amid clouds of smoke and dust were now firing point-blank every five seconds on buildings from which commandos tossed grenades into the street. Several gendarmes fell to the sidewalk. A young lieutenant pale with emotion shouted at a reporter: "Do you still think we're for the OAS?"

There was a brief lull, then scattered sniping fire resumed; presently it grew into concentrated, automatic-weapons fire from a row of apartment houses. Young girls who were shopping took shelter under an arcade to escape the lethal cross-fire.

The OAS was falling back building by building, but continued to show fight. A call arrived from one zouave platoon for relief. Finally losing patience, Ailleret decided it would be faster to get the thing over with by committing aviation. He called up General Michel Fourquet, commander of the 5th Air Force Tactical Wing.

By four-thirty, guessing that the Army was about to invest the Place des Trois Horloges, Achard gave orders to all but a small rear guard to break off contact.

At five, the first wave of four T-6 training planes coming in from Boufarik Air Base swept over the quarter, making warning passes and firing into the sea. A burst of Bren-gun fire replied from a rooftop. Immediately the second wave arrived: this time the T-6s dived and strafed the clearly visible figures on the flat, open roofs of Algiers; and for good measure the planes launched four rockets.

That did it. Protected by covering fire, Achard and his commandos slipped away and reached the Pont des Deux-Moulins leading to the adjoining neighborhood of St.-Eugène. They retreated over the unguarded bridge, then blew it up and disappeared among the *pied noir* population.

An hour later, the battle was over. Tanks rumbled into the center of Bab el Oued and lined up, their guns trained on balconies and public squares. Some sporadic fire continued until evening, and tracer bullets illumined the dusky sky, but organized resistance was at an end.

The Army counted up fifteen dead and seventy wounded among its own. The number of civilian casualties was surely high, although impossible to ascertain exactly; OAS volunteers were being treated and hidden in *pied noir* homes; hospitals in Algiers reported no record of admittance of any wounded civilians. Several estimates ran to twenty dead and eighty hurt.

As was to be foreseen, official countermeasures when they came in the wake of the OAS's rout were harsh and spared few in guilty Bab el Oued. That evening, thousands of CRS troops and gendarmes threw a security cordon around the entire quarter, sealing it off from the rest of Algiers. Until 4 A.M. no ambulances were authorized to enter or leave, and it was only following the Red Cross and local clergy's intercession that the ban was relaxed. White-smocked interns arrived to give blood transfusions and vaccinations. Then gendarme search parties swept through the Europeans' apartments.

Photographs and eyewitness accounts leave no doubt that the infuriated gendarmes' handling of the population was brutal. They staved in doors, smashed TV sets and chinaware, confiscated transistors, overthrew bedroom furniture, forced women to disrobe, arrested five hundred suspects and hauled all male teen-agers off in trucks to internment camps. Some troops made a point of driving the youngsters at reduced speed through Moslem neighborhoods; onlookers in the street jeered and stoned the *pieds noirs*, but made no attempt to seize them, as had perhaps been hoped.

Next day it rained—a sopping, mournful downpour. Soldiers shut off Bab el Oued's streets with iron palings and sawhorses, half-tracks blocked intersections. Sound trucks called on the population to get hold of itself; "Yesterday's events prove the forces of order will go the limit to do their duty," a Police Prefecture communiqué said with terse truthfulness. Yet at first passive resistance showed no sign of letting up—women were not stopped and searched in the street, and they used this advantage to pass arms and Molotov cocktails back and forth, from neighbor to neighbor, to foil house searches. Wounded OAS commandos slipped through the cordon into other parts of the city disguised as ambulance drivers and stretcher-bearers.

The quarantine lasted almost a week. It has been contended that the government's intention was not to capture Achard's dispersed commandos so much as to put the fear of God into the neighborhood and damp its taste for activism. If so, it succeeded. Housewives were allowed one hour a day to go out and do their shopping. Telephone contact with the rest of Algiers was cut off. Families got no information where fathers, brothers, sons had been taken, or for that matter whether they were alive. Forgetting their own part in the disastrous showdown, the *pieds noirs* wallowed in self-pity. Alarmist rumors spread that the Army planned to disrupt Bab el Oued's food supply. This was nonsense, but the Prefecture felt compelled to issue a further communiqué denying inhumane treatment of the blockaded quarter.

On Friday, March 30, the six-day siege and curfew was lifted. During the following weekend relatives, friends and the merely curious attired in their Sunday best poured into Bab el Oued for a look at the battle area and found enough to satisfy their taste for the spectacular: burst water mains; tree trunks sawed in two by machine-gun fire; burned cars flattened by tanks; doors riddled with bullet holes. Demoralization among the inhabitants ran high. Many families had been utterly unprepared for the pitched street battle and thus had taken no precautions to shelter women and children. Some had been struck by flying glass and stray bullets. They had not expected the French Army to fire on their menfolk. One little girl was dead of a bullet wound; the people of Bab el Oued bitterly referred to her as *"our* Delphine Renard."[*] They took note that Salan, Susini, Gardes and others had not, contrary to rumor, fought with Achard's commandos but had remained safely out of the neighborhood. Psychologically and militarily, Bab el Oued was knocked out, its capacity for revolt exhausted.

For the OAS, the insurrection proved to be a greater defeat than either side realized at the time. Ailleret thought then that it represented a transition from the first to the second phase of Salan's

[*] The child blinded in the unsuccessful attack against André Malraux's apartment in Paris.

strategic plan and kept troops in reserve to deal with a new outbreak. In fact, no more full-scale battles took place between the
Army and the OAS in Algiers; the Organization had, with this
single, short-lived, dispiriting rising, reached the high-water mark
of its military effort. The long-sought showdown demonstrated two
facts conclusively: the French Army would not hesitate to fire on
pieds noirs; and the Europeans' much-touted determination to oppose independence to the death could collapse with significant
swiftness. Thus, two myths, in which OAS leaders like Achard and
Vaudrey themselves believed, died simultaneously.

As soon as the full scope of the defeat became apparent, criticism
raged among Rightist supporters of the OAS in France. The operation was deplored, not because Frenchmen's blood had been shed,
but shed without profit to the Organization. Perez retorted that the
Army had seized at least 600 pistols and 600 rifles in *pied noir*
homes, *none of which had been fired*—which proved, according to
him (and the facts bore him out), that Bab el Oued's verbal defiance
and bluster were sharper than its will to fight and take punishment.
Thus, mutual recriminations flew for what went wrong.

Susini called the outcome a catastrophe.

There was little doubt in the *Oranais'* mind about the identity of
the broad-shouldered, military-looking man who strolled each
evening along the seafront past the huge electric sign that proclaimed *"Ici la France."* It was Jouhaud, "Compagnon" in the underground, taking few pains to conceal his presence. He could
derive solid satisfaction from the formidable power the Organization wielded in Oran.

OAS commandos moved openly about town in jeeps and trucks,
entered restaurants to check soldiers' papers, and mounted checkpoints of their own near *gendarmerie* barracks.

A group of youngsters raced down Rue d'Alsace-Lorraine at dawn
shouting, *"Édition spéciale! OAS!"* and hawked 20,000 copies of a
pirate edition of *L'Écho d'Oran,* the city's most widely read newspaper. The newssheet, prepared with the complicity of local type-
setters, carried the text of a Jouhaud speech, his picture and OAS
slogans.

Without opposition, another commando of fifteen men entered the
Banque d'Algérie on Boulevard Gallieni ten minutes after closing

time on March 22, swept through the ground-floor and upper-story safes and made off with $4,700,000 in French and Algerian banknotes. The *pied noir* population—presumably including depositors—applauded this exploit, and took pride in its setting a world's record for a bank holdup. The OAS could scarcely ask for more cooperation.*

Oran had reacted with less despondency than Algiers to the cease-fire. When the news broke in the evening, crowds of Europeans poured into the Place des Victoires disregarding the curfew, crying and shouting *"Salan au pouvoir!" "De Gaulle au poteau!"* singing the "Marseillaise" and firing guns off in the general direction of the Moslem quarters. It was only after several days, following a spell of steady rain, that the *Oranais* subsided into what had become their normal state of sullen apprehension. They refused to read leaflet condensations of the Évian agreement; it was inapplicable, they said.

As in Algiers, each community drew into itself. In the European quarter, huge painted black feet blossomed on shop fronts, above posters cautioning: *"Taisez-vous, une parole de trop, un patriote de moins."* Barbed wire strung up by the Army cut into two a neighborhood of mixed population, Les Planteurs, to prevent the inhabitants from springing at each other's throats. The Jewish quarter behind the Hôtel de Ville lived on a virtual war footing, its young organized into self-defense groups who received summary training in the use of small arms and fought alongside OAS commandos; Jouhaud praised their aggressive spirit.† Ville Nouvelle,

* The commando arrived at the bank with empty sacks, but cooperation proved so extensive among employees that they "lent" more sacks to the OAS to haul away all the booty.

† The overriding concern of Algeria's 135,000 Jews was to retain French citizenship. There were behind-the-scenes negotiations with Algerian Affairs Minister Joxe to ensure this. Most Jews feared that after independence an Arab state might hold them as hostages in the event of a new Arab-Israel war. As it turned out, upon independence more than ninety percent emigrated—most to France, and about 13,000 to Israel.

Within the Jewish community, a whole range of opinion existed from extreme-Left to Right. Many community leaders condemned "all excesses." However, the threatened loss of businesses and various privileges led to considerable sympathy for the OAS. No leading members of the Jewish community joined it, but it attracted hotheads including some Jews who belonged to Irgun Zvai Leumi, the Israeli underground military organization. They were recruited by the OAS as specialists in clandestine warfare. The best-known was Jean Ghanassia, a teacher who had fought in Palestine.

In Oran, as the situation degenerated in 1961, self-defense groups, Haga-

Oran's Casbah, was in FLN hands: volunteer police composed of young men sporting green-and-white armbands systematically searched all strangers, European and Moslem alike, who entered the neighborhood; fear of extermination by the OAS was very real.

Many afternoons, in the heart of town, three-way gunfire erupted between activists, Moslems and gendarmes; and the pedestrians who scurried for cover had no idea who was firing, or why.

The new Army commander recently arrived from Perpignan, General Joseph Katz, a burly up-from-the-ranks officer reputed for his loyalty to the Republic—whether Fourth or Fifth—had hesitated at accepting the assignment and drew partial consolation from the remark of his friend, novelist Serge Groussard, who observed with more eighteenth-century wit than twentieth-century realism: "One should never miss the chance to be in a revolution." Katz installed himself in the sandbagged Police Prefecture, placed his cot on the floor to be out of the line of fire of OAS snipers and, since he could not sleep at night for the recurrent boom of plastique, read the memoirs of Saint-Simon. He called in the *pied-noir* officers under his command, and outlined three courses of action open to them. "You may carry out government orders; this will be difficult for all of us, but it may become impossible for you. You may ask for a transfer; and I'll see that you get it without prejudice to your careers. Or join the OAS. I hope you choose the first; but once your minds are made up, I don't want any wavering." Almost all stayed at their posts. But, as Katz admitted, those who believed in the Organization had already deserted.

As March began, Katz worried about the prospect of full-scale civil war in Oran's streets, and he scaled down the civilian casualty lists he sent to Rocher Noir for fear of the demoralizing effect the true figures would produce.

For the Oran OAS enjoyed at least one superiority over Algiers: it was better armed. Thanks to the nearby presence of the Foreign

---

nah Magen (Shield of Defense), were established clandestinely among young Jews. They received training in small-arms use and guerrilla tactics, and fought alongside the OAS *collines* (as the sectors were known in Oran), although their action was not always coordinated with the *pieds noirs'*. Official Israeli delegations in Algeria to organize emigration of Jews from the coastal cities were not averse to aiding these self-defense groups. The Israeli government, however, never confirmed any connection with them. At least one political party in Israel, the Mapei, considered the *pied noir* cause doomed, and privately urged the departure of Jews as early as 1960.

Legion depot at Sidi bel Abbès, its arsenal included several stolen 80-mm. mortars, and beginning at this time it laid down a mortar barrage almost daily on Ville Nouvelle. Inevitably, bloody reprisals followed. An atrocious incident occurred on March 1, when a Moslem mob in broad daylight broke into the home of a *pied noir* stadium watchman at Mers el Kebir while he was absent, attacked his thirty-year-old wife with hatchets and iron bars, mutilated and killed her, then seized the couple's two children—five and four years old—and smashed their skulls against the wall. The reaction was fast and predictable. Black-jacketed European youths surged into the streets and set fire to Moslem shops; four Moslems were killed "while attempting to evade arrest." Several days later, a convoy of cars and jeeps drove up to Oran's old-fashioned Prison Civile in the evening. Thirty men in paratroopers' leopard-dress and forage caps emerged with automatic pistols, seized and disarmed the guards, then drove two cars loaded with butane-gas containers and jerry-cans of gasoline up to the prison wall. From a safe distance, the men opened fire on the cars. The deflagration blew an enormous gaping hole in the wall, tore two Moslem inmates to pieces, and set a raging fire, which threatened to burn alive more than 150 other prisoners. A panic ensued inside the building. Firemen called to the scene used blowtorches to reach some cells and evacuate the occupants, but it required hours to bring the fire under control. That not more than two prisoners died appeared to many impartial witnesses as providential. The OAS justified this raid by noting that the prison housed FLN terrorists under sentence of death.

Terrorism moved from one community to another, apparently uncontrollable. A parish priest sizing up the situation in March wrote in his diary: "We are more and more in the hands of God." The man nominally responsible for the chaos in Oran was Jouhaud.

Military Security had for some time identified Le Panoramique, the fifteen-story modernistic building on Boulevard du Front de Mer, a skyscraper by North African standards, as an OAS hangout, but no one knew whether it harbored rank-and-file militants or bigger game. Then on March 26 a break occurred, in Paris. A senior officer suspected of OAS sympathies admitted under interrogation having met Jouhaud in a "particularly high building on Oran's Front de

Mer." Only one edifice corresponded to this—Le Panoramique. The tip was relayed to Katz.

He took special precautions. The next day he issued sealed orders and mobilized ten squadrons of *gendarmes mobiles* and several infantry battalions—all told, some 2,500 soldiers. Exactly at 1 P.M. he sent some of his forces into the city to search for a pirate transmitter. Katz says this operation was genuine, but it can be assumed one purpose was to prevent the OAS from realizing what was up.

The OAS pirate radio immediately interrupted regular broadcasting with a terse code message: *"Les fleurs vont être arrosées,"* * which meant that security forces were hunting down the transmitter's site. This, presumably, was just what Katz hoped for.

Armed civilians and deserters, some in paratroop uniform, some with black OAS armbands, surged into the streets of downtown Oran to hamper the seek-and-destroy mission. They punctured the tires of buses, overturned them and set them afire. There was a hail of gunfire from OAS commandos manning rooftops. In a matter of moments, a battle was raging between the OAS and security forces. The heaviest fighting centered about the cathedral. Sniper fire seemed to be coming from one of the spires. *Gardes mobiles* turned a heavy machine gun on the edifice but could not advance. For the next two hours, the OAS controlled streets around the cathedral. It was a small-scale replica of the rising at Bab el Oued, and it drew attention from the finetooth-comb search Katz's other forces were carrying on of all buildings along the seafront.

Jouhaud meanwhile was holding a strategy meeting with several aides in Le Panoramique, oblivious of the approaching danger. One must say a few words about his ideas and morale at this stage. He thought violence in Oran inevitable, "as inevitable as when the Sinn Fein fought the British, and the Irgun fought the British"— yet after the cease-fire he had few illusions. Far more sincere in his motivations than Salan or Challe, fighting out of an uncomplicated desire to preserve the soil from which he sprang, he thought uncomfortably that the momentum toward independence was too powerful to brake—sooner or later, in the progression of ambush and counterambush, something must crack. Until now he had led a charmed life through Army complicity; but in the wake of Bab el Oued, Army officers were less ready to shield an OAS leader.

In their methodical search *gardes mobiles* had reached the eighth

* Literally, "The flowers are going to be watered."

floor of the high-rise building. They entered an apartment occupied by four persons—a young, well-dressed brunette and three men. When the search party arrived, the four were nibbling biscuits and discussing the gun battle in town. Of the three men, one was thick-set and middle-aged, wore a bushy mustache and goatee, and had identity papers describing him as a school superintendent named Gerber. Another was an *Oranais* doctor, Edmond Sabatier. Their papers were in order, but the *gardes mobiles* found next to the girl's handbag a roll of one million old francs for which she could furnish no convincing explanation.

The group of four was driven with twenty other suspects to *gendarmerie* headquarters for further questioning.

It was only a short time before word spread through the OAS that security forces had made an important capture at the Front de Mer, although no one knew who was involved. The street battle resumed. One OAS commando detaching itself from the main group reached the *gendarmerie* caserne and tried unsuccessfully to storm it, killing one officer and wounding eighteen men.

Inside the sprawling building, a team of police and Military Security officers conducted the interrogation. Sabatier seemed to be a genuine doctor, and Gerber aroused no suspicion. After a half-hour the two men expected to be released. Katz was puzzled by the inaccurate tip relayed from Paris. One by one, the other suspects were freed or booked on minor charges.

Then Gerber was taken into another office and questioned by two inspectors from Paris. They compared him with photos of Jouhaud in middle-age taken from various angles. One inspector took Gerber's photo and drew a white chalk mark across the mustache. Some resemblance undeniably existed between the two men. Gerber floundered as a barrage of questions was fired at him about Oran's school system. He had trouble distinguishing the rector of the university from the vice-rector.

The ordeal lasted more than six hours. Gerber vigorously denied any connection with the OAS.

Finally, past eleven o'clock at night, one inspector said, "I think it's no longer necessary to keep this up. Do you know what I'm talking about?" In a hardly audible voice, Gerber admitted that he was Jouhaud and signed a statement. After being searched for poison, he asked for a blanket to ward off the night chill. Sabatier simultaneously confessed to being Major Julien Camelin, "Compagnon's" deputy.* The third man was an OAS liaison agent. The girl had acted as Jouhaud's secretary.

They were put into a truck under heavy guard and driven to La Senia airport. It has been said that Jouhaud was draped in a burnoose, to create the impression among the few *pieds noirs* about in Oran's curfew-silenced streets that the Army had captured an FLN guerrilla chief. Jouhaud denies this. At four in the morning, a Nord 2501 with the four prisoners aboard took off for Paris.

In Algiers, when he heard the news of Jouhaud's arrest on a Europe Number One radio flash, Salan murmured: "De Gaulle will shoot him . . . unless he captures me first."

During the battle of Bab el Oued, de Gaulle had dispatched a curt, three-sentence missive to Debré:

"Immediate action must be taken to smash the criminal action of terrorist bands in Algiers and Oran. I have entire confidence in the government, the High Commissioner, the commander in chief and forces under his order. Please tell them this. Very cordially, Charles de Gaulle."

His concern was far from feigned; the insurrection threatened to undo the entire settlement he had so laboriously achieved. But later, following the rout of Achard's commandos, de Gaulle reverted to his earlier estimate of the situation. Visibly the Europeans as a whole were not ready to stage a mass uprising: the middle-class instinct for security had triumphed over the desperation of the *petits blancs*. Algeria was not Israel; further urban guerrilla warfare lay ahead, in Algiers and Oran, but there would be no apocalyptic struggle to the last man.

So, within the formal privacy of the Élysée Palace, de Gaulle turned his attention more and more to the forthcoming April 8 referendum that would enable French voters to approve or reject the Évian agreement and, if they approved, give him legal power to apply it.

Outside, a wet, shivering Paris presented a curious, uncommonly

* A promising Foreign Legion officer, Camelin had sided with the putschists in April 1961. He subsequently drew a three-year *suspended* sentence, retired from the Army and lived in Paris until October 1961, when he returned to Algeria and joined the OAS. Another of Jouhaud's aides, Navy Lieutenant Pierre Guillaume, was arrested near Oran at the same time. He too had drawn a four-year *suspended* sentence for his role in the putsch.

grim aspect as winter ended. Tourists arriving in the capital found the Eiffel Tower draped in barbed wire and antigrenade nets; the Arch of Triumph, closed to sightseers until further notice, was in use as a command post to coordinate security measures; antiaircraft guns bristled on the roof of the Ministère de la Marine at the Place de la Concorde.* Police and gendarmes patrolled the streets and checked cars. Scores of arrests were made. Parisians considered all this with mingled irritation and fascination; it was like an early American gangster film brought up to date against a French backdrop.

A police report referred to this period as the moment when the OAS in France "seemed to reach or at least could reach its most dangerous point." The bombings grew much deadlier. In the early hours of March 9, a van blew up as the left-wing Mouvement de la Paix prepared to hold a national congress in suburban Issy les Moulineaux. The sixty-pound charge exploded with such force that a bus was overturned, two patrolmen and a janitor were killed, and the blast was heard throughout the west of Paris. Perhaps impressed by the resultant public outcry, the OAS denied responsibility for the attack and blamed *agents provocateurs.*†

Unknown to the general public, the tug of war between Mission II and Mission III continued. Some time in early March, Canal—*le Monocle*—arrived at a bar in the highly respectable Sixteenth Arrondissement expecting to meet his fractious rival, Sergent, face to face. Instead he found himself surrounded by Mission II gunmen, all armed, who gave him a choice of recognizing Sergent's authority throughout France or being liquidated on the spot. Canal, with

---

* As a security measure, the Interior Ministry had forbidden all non-scheduled commercial flights and private planes from taking off or landing at French airports or flying over French territory.

† But former OAS members whom the writer interviewed in Spain claim they were responsible for the *attentat*. Their harrowing idea was to kill a good number of delegates to the peace congress. This in turn would have led to nationwide protest strikes, embittering the situation, and solemn funeral rites. The OAS counted upon a major turnout of Communist and other Leftist leaders in the forefront of mourners. One commando had arranged to occupy a vacant apartment overlooking the probable route of the funeral march, and set up a Sten gun with which it planned to mow down its enemies. The result, it was hoped, would be a state of civil war. As it was, the charge exploded three quarters of an hour before the delegates arrived. To the OAS's dismay, the three victims were not considered worth a mass funeral procession. This version of what might have happened is uncorroborated. Paris police say there has been no determination of who is to blame for the Issy les Moulineaux attack.

great courage, stood his ground. He was held prisoner all night, then finally set free. The incident settled nothing. Each activist leader continued to wage his own terrorist campaign, but neither could mount the spectacular assassination needed—in the police's opinion—to reverse the situation in France; and time was running out. Whoever won the tug of war for the Metropolitan OAS's leadership, it would make no difference to the decisive outcome in Algiers.

As soon as he heard of the scheduled demonstration and march, Algiers Police Prefect Vitalis Cros forbade both, terming them a "call to insurrection." At his headquarters on Boulevard Carnot, he told his staff: "In France, demonstrations are forbidden; they will be forbidden here."

This was on March 25. Bab el Oued was still quarantined. Cros had just learned of a tract urging Algiers' *pieds noirs* to attend a meeting at the War Monument and take part in a protest march upon the blockaded "ghetto." The ostensible reason for this new action was to demonstrate solidarity with the embattled residents of the downcast neighborhood. The real reason appears to have been to try to recoup some political advantage from a military blunder; portraying the residents of Bab el Oued as martyrs might curb demoralization and loss of faith in the OAS. The authors of the tract were the two men chiefly responsible for the calamitous showdown with the Army: Jacques Achard and ex-Colonel Roland Vaudrey.

Susini this time warned Vaudrey that a street demonstration, if organized at all, must be "static"—that is, immobile—to minimize the risk of violence. This sudden interest in law and order must have seemed surprising on Susini's part, but it reflected common sense; in each succeeding clash with *pieds noirs*, he noted, security forces had displayed growing bellicosity. Bab el Oued was a stark case in point.

The tracts were already distributed, however, and Vaudrey disregarded both the police ban and Susini's advice. Once again, the Organization did little about internal disobedience.

On the afternoon of March 26, shortly after one o'clock, the first contingent of youthful demonstrators assembled on Rue Michelet. The weather was sunny. Vitalis Cros and the Army had taken precautions: motor traffic was banned in the center of Algiers, roadblocks were set up, and every one hundred yards along the main access routes to Bab el Oued, colonial infantry regiments manned checkpoints.

At about this moment, Jean Ferrandi, Salan's aide, set out to remonstrate with the general about Vaudrey's increasing tendency to act on his own.

Debouching from sidestreets, more *pieds noirs* began to move down winding Rue Michelet, first one hundred, then five hundred, soon more than two thousand. They were in a festive mood; they sang the "Marseillaise"; some were accompanied by children and dogs; they considered a march in their own part of the city a traditional and inalienable right. Pressure from late-comers at the rear pushed the front rows forward, and like a broad stream they flowed about one checkpoint, then another, submerging the soldiers—"submerging" was the word employed by eyewitnesses, but these colonial-infantry units were sympathetic to the *pieds noirs'* cause and allowed them to get past without challenge. In a matter of moments, borne by its own impetus, the flag-waving crowd found itself in downtown Rue d'Isly, face to face with a detachment of a dozen Moslem *tirailleurs* under command of a young French lieutenant. This was a different matter.

The Rue d'Isly was a busy, commercial street that ran straight and nondescript from the general post office past real-estate offices, travel agencies, boutiques and snack bars to the poorer quarters near the Place du Gouvernement. The Rue d'Isly and similar streets made French Algiers tick and gave the *pieds noirs* the illusion they were living in a city as undeniably French as Marseilles or Toulon.

The lieutenant shouted in a strangled voice that could hardly be heard above the uproar that he had orders to fire if necessary.

As the front ranks hesitated, others in the rear began to pile up and push. By this time the crowd numbered more than three thousand. Some darted down Boulevard Laferrière and emerged on the far side of the checkpoint. They raced toward Bab el Oued along Rue d'Isly, then pulled up short several hundred yards farther on at Square Bresson. Confronting them was a solid phalanx of black-uniformed CRS troops, helmeted, armed and motionless.

Women cried *"Algérie française!"* A helicopter whirred overhead and dropped several grenades, a cloud of whitish tear gas enveloped the marchers, who doubled back in confusion toward the post office, where the detachment of Moslem soldiers stood.

These *tirailleurs* were exhausted and tense, they were just back from field operations, they had no training in riot-control techniques. As the crowd on both sides eddied about them, they were patently terrorized and uncertain how to handle the situation. A *pied noir* woman rushed up and hugged one soldier, who struggled clumsily to disengage himself. Another *tirailleur* held a Bren gun ready only ten feet from some demonstrators. He was, eyewitnesses said, shaking like a leaf.

"You're not going to fire on us!" someone in the crowd shouted —whether in challenge or query, it was difficult to say.

At this moment, in an office building on an adjoining street, Ferrandi said to Salan angrily: "You can't allow this. Vaudrey has to be disciplined."

A cluster of flat, dry reports broke the silence on Rue d'Isly. There had been no order, no warning shots in the air. The Moslem soldiers began firing their automatic weapons point-blank in a panic, emptying whole clips. The crowd stampeded, running and separating helter-skelter in all directions. Some threw themselves flat on the street to get out of the line of fire, others crouched in doorways or behind kiosks and cars. An elderly man trembled, hit in the back.

The firing suddenly became heavier. A woman ran forward to reach the inert figure of a man outstretched on the cobblestones. A *tirailleur* raced up to a pharmacy, hesitated, swung his rifle butt at the plate-glass window, shattering it, then spotted a group of civilians cowering in a doorway waving handkerchiefs and rushed up with his rifle ready, only to be ordered away by an officer standing just out of sight indoors. Before a bank, two other soldiers, their faces pale and drawn under their olive color, were squeezing off burst after burst from the hip, mechanically, obsessively, viciously, at what moved and what did not. "Stop shooting!" cried someone. "We're not armed." Immediately the two soldiers spun around and fired in the direction of the voice.

The firing suddenly ceased, then resumed again. A woman writhing in pain stumbled toward a maternity shop and sat down on the sidewalk while bullets hissed and ricocheted off the curb, then got up with an effort and managed to reach the door, which immediately opened for her. Down the street another woman screamed hysterically, hit in the face. In the sporadic intervals of calm, stretcher-bearers raced out into Rue d'Isly, ducking and weaving.

The original fusillade had lasted perhaps eight minutes—which is very long if one is under fire. As it died out, jeeps tore into the area, to begin evacuating the wounded. The detachment of Moslem *tirailleurs* was gone, replaced by a unit of French draftees, who looked aghast at the carnage.

Another woman came out into the street and began to turn over bodies, looking for her husband. A profusion of handbags, eyeglasses and shoes littered the pavement where people had fallen or thrown themselves to the ground to save their lives. Some demonstrators tottered away toward Rue Michelet, where they had started out two hours before. A priest retrieved a fallen tricolor flag and furiously dipped it in an uncongealed bloodstain on the pavement. Jean-Pierre Farkas, a reporter for Radio Luxembourg, returned to his hotel room and vomited; an Army veteran, he says: "I had never seen so much blood in my life."

Intermittent shooting persisted until the evening.

The next morning, groups of embittered Europeans re-formed on Rue d'Isly, examining the bullet holes in shop fronts and passionately reviewing in detail, for the hundredth time, the events of the day before. When a Moslem patrol passed, they cursed and spat at it. The battle of Bab el Oued and Jouhaud's arrest were forgotten, outstripped by this larger disaster, which had seen the French Army fire not on *petits blancs* in a state of insurrection but on unarmed Europeans of all classes and neighborhoods.

Casualty figures varied considerably: the Army reported thirty-six dead and eighty wounded among the demonstrators; European sources in Algiers set the figure at eighty dead and two hundred wounded. Who fired first? The Army quickly disclaimed responsibility for the bloody afternoon and said the fusillade had been touched off by unknown, unidentified snipers firing from rooftops on surprised troops below, who then returned fire in self-defense. This implied that OAS commandos had exploited the tense atmosphere in Algiers and provoked the slaughter to create an irreparable breach between the two sides. French journalists did indeed find empty shells on roofs overlooking Rue d'Isly, but non-French journalists who witnessed the confused sequence of events said they heard no opening fire from rooftops.

Seven years later, the fusillade on Rue d'Isly remains one of the most controversial episodes in the last days of French Algeria. The extreme Right in France published a White Book with dozens of eyewitness accounts that unanimously set the blame on the nervous Moslem *tirailleurs:* this version hinted at a deliberate plot between the Gaullist regime and the FLN to massacre the *pieds noirs.* Such accusations were never proved, and the French government banned the book. Senior French officers have acknowledged privately that the Army was at grave fault in assigning Moslem troops with no crowd-handling experience to stem a hostile European demonstration. In view of the unbearable atmosphere in Algiers, a clash was inevitable as soon as the *pieds noirs* met the Army head on; some officers had expected it long before. But beyond this blunder loomed the much larger question of Vaudrey's responsibility in organizing the prohibited march. Subsequently he was relieved of his command within the OAS and left for the countryside.

Only a week had elapsed since the signing of the cease-fire, and the standoff in Algiers appeared as grim as ever. A journalist arriving from France found the Europeans "at the extreme limit of exasperation," and he wrote: "It is a situation that can go either way." He meant that it could lead to still bloodier incidents or the *pieds noirs'* departure from Algeria.

As it turned out, the Rue d'Isly affair would lead to both.

20

The Fortunes and
Misfortunes of War

AT NINE o'clock on the evening of March 27, a special train comprising one locomotive and six freight cars rolled out of Algiers' Hussein Dey station bound for Orléansville, one hundred twenty miles to the west.

The stationmaster had received waybills made out for a shipment of agricultural machinery, and the train was cleared without difficulty. Beside the engineer stood a chunky, thirty-six-year-old *pied noir*, who watched the hillside lights of Algiers dwindle, then disappear altogether. His face registered no emotion. The man was ex-Captain Guy Branca, OAS sector chief for downtown Algiers.

During the night, the train made several unscheduled stops, taking aboard small groups of armed men.

The next morning, several miles past the market town of Affreville, the train stopped in a narrow cut, and Branca and the men got out. The countryside roundabout consisted of melancholy plains; beyond rose the somber skyline of the Ouarsenis mountains. As the sun came up, the men hid in a ravine. Later in the morning trucks arrived and drove them to a number of abandoned farmhouses in the region. At one such farm, Branca settled down to await his superior in the OAS, Colonel Jean Gardes.

Without knowing it, the group had been spotted by Arab shepherds.

There was a breath of early-flowering spring in the countryside. On the prosperous Mitidja plain, vineyards and lemon groves and wheatfields ripened in the sun, rivulets swelled; far southward, in the untracked Hauts Plateaux, a cold sun shone down on newly fledged coveys of quail and immense fields of rising alfa grass.

Here the war had ended; the Armée de Libération Nationale moved into the douars to replace the French Army; rudimentary coexistence, which had never fully broken down during seven years of guerrilla raids, resumed between European tenant farmers and Moslem field hands, who sowed crops together. The Moslems urged the Europeans to remain after independence. Outside the cities, in truck-gardening centers scrupulously patterned after French models and in isolated settlements, the OAS was nothing but a vague and distant threat: the *pieds noirs*, realistically, had refused to rally to the Organization in the Aurès, the Hauts Plateaux, the Sud-Constantinois, where Arabs and Kabyles outnumbered them. A Moslem village chieftain was quoted as saying in Kabylia: "The activists know that if they raise a finger here, we'll flatten them out with our hand."

Yet the OAS now chose the countryside, paradoxically, to stage a supreme effort. The target area was the Massif de l'Ouarsenis, a rugged, sparsely inhabited but strategically important mountain region situated halfway between Algiers and Oran. This was not the Sahara, whose oceanic wastes began more than a hundred miles to the south, but it was wild, sterile, eroded country broken up into cedar-cloaked heights, treeless ridges and inhospitable plains dotted with a few gray clusters of stone and mud huts that survived winter and waterlessness, icy winds and endemic poverty, but just barely.

If the OAS managed to seize control of this area, it could drive a wedge between the two coastal cities and separate both from the hinterland. Salan's Instruction No. 29 had called for the implantation of *maquisards* and creation of insurrectional zones. The OAS deemed its greatest chance of success lay in the Ouarsenis. A sizable force was to capture key military outposts in the region by surprise, rally anti-FLN elements among the Moslem population, and consolidate its hold with the help of the local pro-French potentate, the *bachaga* Boualem. The rocky slopes of the Ouarsenis are difficult of access and easy to defend. The area would become a sanctuary to which OAS commandos could repair after fighting in the cities. The operation itself would force Ailleret to transfer troops to the countryside and relieve pressure on the cities; and the regular French Army could not be asked to attack Moslems who proclaimed their readiness to die to remain French. At the same time, nearby Foreign Legion units opposed to the cease-fire would fall upon unprepared ALN troops and wipe them out, thus wrecking any hope of a permanent peace between the FLN and the French government.

The preliminary planning for this operation antedated Bab el Oued by a month; but lack of agreement and Salan's unwillingness to budge before the cease-fire had delayed its implementation. The showdown in Algiers now made it imperative to act with the greatest speed: the Organization had to break out of the cities, where it was being slowly throttled.

At first, Jouhaud had been designated to command the *maquis* personally. With his capture, the officer entrusted with operational planning, Colonel Jean Gardes, gradually assumed over-all responsibility for the Ouarsenis expedition. An unemotional, thin-lipped product of St.-Cyr, Gardes had served under Salan in Indo-china, then headed the Deuxième Bureau in Rabat in 1955–56, when Morocco gained its independence from France. In the Far East Gardes acquired a reputation as a zealous and useful, if not overly bright, information officer. In intelligence work in Morocco, he struck few sparks; duty that requires intuition, silence and, above all, realism was apparently not his forte. Applying the classic colonial principle of divide and conquer, he dabbled in subversion and promoted an abortive revolt by the governor of Tafilalet, the *caid* Addi ou Bihi, against the Sultan's central authority when the Royal Moroccan Army was being formed with the help of some French officers. Gardes was already notorious for tearing up every copy of *Le Monde* he could lay his hands on because of its liberal views on decolonialization.

In 1958, he succeeded Colonel Charles Lacheroy as head of the increasingly influential Cinquième Bureau—the psychological warfare office—in Algiers. At this task he fared somewhat better; expounding the case for *Algérie française* to newsmen, he was effortlessly eloquent. Nonetheless, his aptitude for political analysis proved abysmal. He hailed de Gaulle's return to power in May 1958 as a psychological-warfare victory, when in fact it had resulted—as practically all informed Frenchmen knew—from widespread impatience in France with the Fourth Republic's recurring lackluster crises, the various Gaullist networks' determination to put their hero back in the saddle legally or illegally to save the country, and the same Gaullists' brilliant takeover of a parallel, activist antigovernment and pro-Army plot in Algiers.

As time passed, Gardes ran the Cinquième Bureau more and more according to his own ideas, sublimely heedless of the shift in official policy from integration to self-determination. Gardes's way, it turned out, consisted of interpreting de Gaulle's choice of three solutions to the Algerian problem—integration, association and independence—as a veiled summons to impose all-out Franco-Moslem integration upon the territory. So once again he was out of step, at least with the official line. Fellow officers recall that he was altogether incapable of listening to the other side; if someone suggested a more moderate and flexible approach to Algeria's future status, Gardes turned white from the effort of restraining himself.

His Algiers office became a "permanent meeting place of the *crème de la crème* of activists." He met interminably with fellow conspirators in the Army, leading civilian agitators like Ortiz, Lagaillarde and Susini, and pro-French Moslems. He saw no other Arabs. Somehow he acquired a reputation as a specialist in Moslem affairs. Nothing could have been more misleading.

During Barricades Week, he unabashedly appeared beside Joseph Ortiz on the latter's balcony (Gardes's presence appeared to represent Army endorsement of the insurrection) and predicted that French home opinion favored the insurgents—again, a misreading of prevailing currents. This error resulted in his being the only officer prosecuted at the Barricades Trial. In court he stood up in a crisp new uniform with his medals, stressed his sense of mission, and made a favorable impression as a dedicated, forthright officer, which, in reality, he was. Acquitted, he emerged from the dock unrepentant and proceeded to plot anew against the government with undiminished enthusiasm. Thus, almost automatically he found himself embroiled in the Generals' Putsch and the OAS.

His underground code name, "Fleur," later transformed into the contemptuous "Fleurette des maquis," gives a good idea of the

Organization's feelings about him. He was regarded as honest, altruistic, disingenuous, something of a fool and more than a bit of a nuisance. When Susini bemoaned the OAS's lack of arms, Gardes *tut-tutted* that *pied noir* housewives could fling flowerpots at gendarmes' heads to show disapproval. This sort of homily obviously did not sit well with the group of hard-pressed men who ran the Organization. Godard thought of him as a "Boy Scout."

For the past month Gardes had painstakingly prepared the Ouarsenis rising. Here, finally, he had an opportunity to put his theories about Moslem integration to work. Not even the Bab el Oued fiasco curbed his optimism; what had failed in the city, he maintained, would succeed in the country, with Moslem support.

Gardes's entire plan was predicated on two major assumptions: the wholehearted commitment of the *bachaga* Boualem and the rallying of certain Army units.

Said Boualem, *bachaga* of the Beni-Boudouane tribe, could conceivably raise a private force of some three to four thousand *harkis* (armed Moslem auxiliaries) to harass the FLN, with which he was locked in deadly conflict. Boualem was fifty-six years old; he was gaunt and melancholy and rich, with hooded black eyes, the sorrowful face of a spaniel, and a thin nose. Clad in a white chiffon turban, a *gandurah* that sparkled with a triple row of French decorations, and spotless boots, this Arab chieftain—who also served as vice-president of the National Assembly and right-wing deputy from Orléansville—cut a figure dear to any colonialist's heart. Well educated and shrewd enough where his own interests were concerned, he ruled unopposed over 60,000 acres of the Ouarsenis from a big stone house at Lamartine, near Orléansville. Here he bred Arab horses and raised livestock. He opposed self-determination. The FLN had killed his brother-in-law and one of his sons in ambushes. While carefully noting that he "neither approved nor disapproved of the OAS," the *bachaga* had promised Gardes to commit his followers if a rising took place.

As for the French Army, officers and men of several disaffected regiments in western Algeria—the 28th Dragoons, the 8th Spahis, the 5th Tirailleurs stationed at Sidi-Ferruch, and the famed 1st Foreign Legion Infantry at Sidi bel Abbès—were to take to the *maquis*, neutralize whatever conscript units attempted to oppose them, and "organize" the Moslem population—that is, forcibly wean it away from any hankering for independence. Here, too, officers had made oral promises. Gardes did not expect all these regiments to defect; it was sufficient for the purposes of his scheme for one or two to do so. The important thing was for an entire unit to take the irrevocable step of breaking discipline; join the *marquisards* and attack an ALN *katiba—"créer l'irréparable,"* as the OAS was fond of saying. Other, undecided regiments would then surely follow this example.

As the spearhead of this *maquis*, Gardes counted on two thousand OAS civilian volunteers from Algiers and Oran.

Salan expressed doubt about the amount of Moslem support the rising in the Ouarsenis could muster. He also remained skeptical about the *bachaga*'s reliability. Godard strongly objected to stripping Algiers of sector chiefs to undertake a gamble in the countryside, and he dismissed the operation as an outlet for Gardes's love of the outdoors. Some unflatteringly called it *Opération Djebel Pelé* (which, loosely translated, means "Operation Scrub Brush"). Oddly, in view of his consistent disinterest in the hinterland and sharp distrust of the Army, Susini favored the plan—"I saw it as one chance out of a thousand," he has since said, ". . . therefore, I thought, let's try it." The Foreign Legion's proximity in the area struck him as an asset, although it was offset by the fact that most of the European settlers in this region, as elsewhere in the countryside, were obliged to get along as best they could with the FLN and manifested no support for the OAS, which knew that it could not count on them in an emergency.

In mid-March, two weeks before the launching of the operation, and before either the battle of Bab el Oued or Jouhaud's arrest had occurred, Gardes arrived at a clandestine command post set up in a farm near Affreville.

His purpose was to arrange for the arrival of a vanguard of one hundred European *maquisards*. Considerable food stores—canned goods, cooking oil, wine and flour—were distributed in various caches in the lonely countryside. Simultaneously, Gardes dispatched Perez and Degueldre to the *bachaga* Boualem to coordinate final plans for commitment of the *harkis*. Perez says—and other sources corroborate him—that a considerable sum, in easily negotiable gold coins, was turned over to the *bachaga* as the price for his collaboration.* Gardes also arranged to use pro-OAS European railway workers to move his men under the authorities' noses from Algiers to the Ouarsenis. This, the most imaginative aspect of his entire scheme, almost foundered when the railway union, in indignation over Bab el Oued's quarantine, unexpectedly called a protest strike. Gardes was obliged to step in, take *pied noir* union leaders into his confidence, and advise them that in view of the planned rising the strike would do more harm than good. It was called off. But as it turned out, of the two thousand volunteers Gardes counted on, only about a hundred assembled on the evening of March 27 at rendezvous points along the railroad track. The others arrived too early, drew suspicion upon themselves and dispersed—or too late, and missed the train.

The following morning Gardes drove out of Algiers. Dressed in civilian clothes and equipped with false papers, he was waved through *gendarmerie* roadblocks and reached the Affreville command post, where he held a final tactical meeting with his staff during the day and made some last-minute changes.† Branca was dispatched to Sidi bel Abbès to urge Foreign Legion fellow officers, who reportedly needed only minimal encouragement, to join the rising. His operational command was assigned to another paratroop deserter officer, Captain Pierre Montagnon. Then, past midnight,

---

* Georges Chaffard, in *Carnets secrets de la décolonisation*, sets the sum at $80,000.

† Gardes's staff included two other deserter officers, Lieutenants Pierre Delhomme and Roger Bernard. In the OAS, Delhomme, a career soldier with a brilliant wartime record in Indochina, served as one of Degueldre's deputies, and headed Delta 30. His near-arrest in a police trap at El Biar has been described in Chapter 13. Months before, Bernard had abandoned his platoon in the woods of northern France for the life of an OAS guerrilla. An avowed activist, he was inexplicably in charge of speeded-up training of officer candidates in the 143rd Infantry Regiment stationed near Lille. On December 13, 1961, he marched his men to an isolated fort, then sent them off through the frozen woods to breakfast, and deserted in a waiting car with all their weapons including a new-model, ultramodern submachine gun—a theft that gave the French Army a few bad moments. Senior officers favorable to the activist cause expressed outrage at this blow "to military honor." Their reasoning is hard to follow; it was apparently admissible for generals (Challe, Jouhaud, etc.) to revolt, but dangerous for a junior officer to take matters into his own hands.

Gardes left for an ultimate check-up of preparations with Said Boualem. Gardes was in for a surprise.

That morning the *bachaga,* on whom most of the operation's chances of success hinged, had driven to Orléansville to chat with General Pierre Boulanger, the zone commander in chief of French forces in the western Algerois. The *bachaga* assumed that Boulanger was going to participate in the rising. There is no record of what the two men said to each other, but apparently the general said flatly he had no intention of doing so. The *bachaga* then returned to his country house at Lamartine in a pensive mood. When Gardes arrived several hours before dawn, his host declared that the area was not safe and urbanely hustled him out.

That Gardes put up for a second with this shabby treatment reflects the OAS's real powerlessness as well as Gardes's own fantastic naïveté. He must have been under no illusion that the *harkis* he vitally counted on would still be committed. Meanwhile (but he probably did not know this) not a single disaffected regiment in western Algeria had risen; instead, an extraordinary number of officers had reported on sick-call that day at Algiers' Maillot Hospital. Once again, as during the putsch, some career-conscious cadres had second thoughts about defying de Gaulle; others were ready to march only if Boualem made the first move and proved there was Moslem support for the OAS cause in the Ouarsenis. But the *bachaga* suddenly had cold feet. It was, of course, much too late several hours before the attack to draw up an alternative operational plan. Gardes presumably still had time to scratch the undertaking. Instead, with less than five percent of his estimated force, he went ahead with his original plan.

Before 6 A.M., a convoy of trucks, with Montagnon's men divided into three combat groups, headed south along narrow military roads, kicking up smothering clouds of pebbles and dust, into the huge, cut-up boulder- and ravine-strewn area. There was only a faint silver flush in the sky. Arab shepherds and goatherds watched the convoy pass in silence. One truck contained a radio transmitter powerful enough to beam a signal throughout the Ouarsenis: Gardes confidently expected to use it to broadcast a message to all Moslems in the "liberated" zone.

Enjoying complete surprise, Montagnon's men took Hill 505, the first of three French Army outposts, in the early hours of the morning without a fight. One truck with fifty Europeans in stolen uniforms and *harkis* in brown jelabs drove up to the gate; Montagnon pretended to be returning from a field operation, and the sentry let the group past without difficulty. The raiders broke into a young lieutenant's quarters, seized him and confiscated the garrison's arms. Then they forced the lieutenant at gun-point into a jeep and roared off toward the second outpost, Dra Messaoud. Here they got past the sentry with just as little trouble. They repeated the trick at Moulay Abdel Kader.

By 8 A.M. the three outposts were in the OAS's hands. Zone officers in Orléansville knew that something was up, but the Army had not expected an outright OAS attack and had taken no precautions. It seemed for a moment as if the Ouarsenis venture might still succeed.

Gardes set up temporary headquarters at Moulay Abdel Kader, ordered the confiscated arms distributed to Moslem villagers, and assembled the three weaponless garrisons. He then delivered an extraordinary harangue, claiming that Boulanger supported the rising. Unimpressed, captured officers and men, with the exception of one *pied noir* soldier, refused to switch sides.

Gardes had no sooner finished his exhortation than the *bachaga* drove up. The ensuing confrontation must have been painful. Boualem had arrived primarily to gather a firsthand idea of what was going on in his fief, and in spite of the OAS's initial surprise victory, what he found confirmed his earlier, unfavorable impression. Foreseeing no opposition, Gardes had failed to cut or mine the roads leading to the three outposts and had no tactical reserve whatever. The *bachaga* flatly declined this time to play any role in the rising. Gardes's lieutenants threatened at first to hold him, then allowed him to depart; but his eldest son remained, a willing hostage, with the insurgents. Before leaving, the *bachaga* bitterly railed at his son and Gardes.

By this time, Zone Headquarters was concerned by the three outposts' radio silence. Upon reaching town, Boualem promptly proclaimed his loyalty to the Fifth Republic and alerted Boulanger. The Army swung into action with grim efficiency. If it had sometimes experienced frustration in hit-and-run urban battles with the OAS, the prospect of a fight in open country where it enjoyed overwhelming tactical and technical superiority was another matter. Boulanger rapidly gave orders for a huge combined land-and-air offensive to dislodge the raiders from the three mountain outposts. The *bachaga* meanwhile sent messengers to *harkis* throughout the Ouarsenis who had joined Gardes's ranks to desert at once.

Toward the end of morning, Air Force reconnaissance planes appeared in the cloudless sky, circled several times over the captured outposts, and left. Montagnon's men felt some uneasiness; the barren peaks were vulnerable to air attack. Moreover, they disliked Montagnon; for one thing, he had insisted, in the midst of the operation, on formal inspection of their kits and other parade-ground nonsense; for another, he had brought his *pied noir* mistress, attired in Foreign Legion uniform, into the combat area.

At Moulay Abdel Kader, Gardes remained optimistic. The Air Force would never dare attack French officers, he said. Montagnon drew up plans to seize a fourth outpost.

An hour later, as they sat down to lunch, T-28 attack planes streaked in low, making for Hill 505. Gardes is said to have exclaimed stupidly: "I never would have thought it!"

At Hill 505, bullets smashed into the outpost's baked-earth walls. Panic broke out among the occupiers, and they made a fatal mistake. Abandoning trucks, radio transmitter and hostage officers, they began to stream down from the heights onto the arid plain. This was on March 29.

The next few days' events can best be summed up as seen from the Affreville command post. The OAS rural zone chief, a young *pied noir*, had requested radio liaison with the commandos in the Ouarsenis. For all practical purposes, however, when Gardes's column disappeared into the stony fastness, contact with it was lost. For the next two days, the command post hoped liaison could be reestablished, in spite of a growing impression that all was not well.

On the fourth day, a few survivors began to straggle back, parched, exhausted and forlorn. The retreat had swiftly turned into a rout. Hill 505 was smashed and destroyed from the air by rocket fire. Helicopter-borne troops swiftly reoccupied Dra Messaoud and Moulay Abdel Kader. Moslem villagers surrendered the confiscated arms. The *bachaga's harkis* streamed back into Orléansville. Boualem comfortably called a press conference, gave journalists whisky and announced: "I did not want my *harkis* to spill French blood." The French press dutifully reported his loyalty to the tricolor flag, but he himself had the candor to add: "If the rising had succeeded, I would have joined it."

Montagnon's men fled northward, leaderless, waterless, guiding themselves by compass toward inhabited areas; but an armored column and motorized troops sent into the mountains waited at waterholes and passes to pounce on them. Some stragglers stumbled upon a douar, where hostile Moslem youngsters shouted FLN slogans and stoned them. Shepherds had already alerted the *gendarmerie*, which arrived just in time to save Gardes's two lieutenants, Delhomme and Bernard, from being lynched. The two men were haggard and coated with dust and could hardly stand. They meekly submitted to capture. Montagnon and the *bachaga's* son were arrested. If ever revolutionaries were like fish out of water, it was these city-bred commandos with no knowledge of *maquis* warfare. There was no evacuation plan, no rear zone upon which to fall back. Even friendly *pied noir* farmers were reluctant to shelter the fugitives as they withdrew in disorder.

At Affreville, there was worse news. Branca was back empty-handed from his expedition to Sidi bel Abbès, where not a single officer had agreed to participate in what the Foreign Legion considered a foredoomed venture. Humiliatingly, the commanding officer at Legion headquarters, Colonel Albéric Vaillant, had refused so much as to see Branca, a former fellow officer.

On the fifth day, Gardes managed to reach Affreville. Lean and spruce, he exhibited his customary unruffled air. "What do I do now?" he asked. On the part of an officer who had led one hundred men into a rock-bound wilderness, made no provision for a rear zone, utterly misread the Moslem inhabitants' feelings and retreated without glory, the remark seemed insufficient. He was driven back to a hiding place in Algiers.

The ill-fated Ouarsenis enterprise dragged on for another week. After Gardes's departure, a major named Bazin, a deserter from the 5th Tirailleur Regiment, arrived at Affreville with a commando of twenty-two men and a mule train. News travels slowly in the countryside, and there is reason to believe he was unaware of the *bachaga's* defection and the real scope of the disaster. Bazin's purpose remains obscure; presumably he meant to bring Gardes reinforcements. The group set out along a mountain path through the Ouarsenis on April 9. Near the town of Duperré they spotted an approaching FLN motor convoy, and instead of taking cover, then proceeding unmolested toward their destination, they engaged the guerrillas in battle, killed some and routed the others. But in this action their own mules were scattered, and precious time, a full afternoon, was wasted rounding them up. Meanwhile, Moslem villagers—the same villagers whom Gardes had expected to muster in defense of French Algeria—alerted a Wilaya IV *katiba* lying up in the nearby mountains.

The next day Bazin's commando resumed its trek. At 8 A.M. they reached a narrow defile, near Djebel Doui, whose crests had been occupied during the night by the *katiba*. As the mule train filed through the wadi, the *katiba* opened a murderous cross fire. The trapped men dodged for cover in the pass below and fought back. The battle raged throughout the morning—a local, vicious skirmish that marked the only time in French Algeria's final year when organized OAS and FLN bands clashed directly in the field. As was to be expected, each side attacked with pent-up ferocity. Both Europeans and Moslems suffered heavy casualties in proportion to their size. As the hot, dusty forenoon wore on, a squadron of *gendarmes mobiles* rumbled to the scene, but found only dead and dying; the *katiba* had melted back into the surrounding hills. Bazin had been wounded in the ambush and was left by his men to bleed to death. Five other Europeans and as many *fellaga* lay dead.

With this action, the Ouarsenis venture came to an end. The OAS tried to put a brave face on the campaign and termed it a "success," claiming that Army outposts had fallen without resistance; but this was only half—and not the important half—of the story. Survivors of Montagnon's and Bazin's commandos reached Algiers concealed in moving vans that belonged to *pied noir* farmers who were beginning to evacuate the countryside. The food dumps remained. Some are intact to this day; several have been discovered by Arab peasants, the surprised recipients—as one European bitterly puts it —of "OAS economic aid to independent Algeria."

The consequences were considerable. There were no more OAS expeditions outside Algiers and Oran; OAS cadres, never numerically strong, were seriously reduced in the rout—all together eighty-seven men and eight officers were taken prisoner. The gravest consequence of all, however, affected a man who had had virtually nothing to do with the operation and probably disapproved of it— Degueldre.

He turned smartly into the building at Pont du Télémly. The chief of Deltas wore civilian jacket and trousers and a brown felt hat; his short-cropped brown hair was dyed oat-colored. Papers in his billfold identified him as a grade-school superintendent named Esposito; on this score he had no worries; the counterfeit documents had already got him out of several tight fixes.

Moreover, although he slept in a different apartment each night, Degueldre made no serious effort to pass unperceived in Algiers. Those who wanted to managed with application to locate him—in his nearby penthouse headquarters, flanked by submachine-gun-toting bodyguards and Nicole Gardy, the general's tomboyish daughter. Here he held court for young deserter officers, journalists and admiring teen-agers from Bab el Oued. Local police prudently made no attempt to interfere.

Degueldre was locked in bleak introspection. The Deltas were killing more than ever, but Algeria was marching toward independence. The *pieds noirs* themselves leaked less information to the OAS, as they reevaluated its chances of winning. Furthermore, while he had foully criticized Salan for letting slip opportunity after opportunity, it was clear that his own determination to track down and slay every single *barbouze* had resulted in a waste of two precious months during which French negotiators and the FLN had signed the cease-fire. If it came to the worst and the OAS ordered evacuation, Degueldre thought dourly, he could and would leave Algiers a mass of ruins.

He was sourly aware of being considered a born killer, useful exclusively for eliminating the OAS's legion of enemies. This left him unaffected; but he was piqued at not being consulted within the Organization. Constant complaints to Godard had brought no change: for days in a row, he received no specific instructions. So, restless and frustrated but efficient, self-destructive and lucidly aware of what was happening, he continued to type up orders to kill.

Perez had summoned him to hear a report on the Ouarsenis debacle. Degueldre entered the upstairs apartment, which belonged to two *pied noir* girls, who made it available for impromptu meetings of the OAS leadership. Inside, Degueldre found six men present: Perez, Branca, Jacques Achard, Captain Raymond Mura, a paratroop deserter, and two other members of the Organization. They listened to Branca's report impassively. Perez, who has described the meeting, says they were not downhearted; above all, they were sustained by a curious belief in their own invulnerability among the mobilized, beleaguered *pied noir* population. But as the meeting proceeded, gendarmes surrounded the building.

The French police are extremely reluctant to discuss details of the capture of major OAS leaders, which resulted almost invariably from denunciations by double agents and informers. This had befallen Jouhaud, it happened now, and it would befall others later. It is established, however, that earlier that day the Sûreté had picked up in the streets of Algiers a German Legionnaire deserter. He had taken part in the Ouarsenis operation, wandered back disconsolate to Algiers, drifted penniless for a few days, come into contact with Perez and learned of a top-level OAS meeting at Télémly. Under interrogation, the German talked. Whatever loyalty he felt to the Organization had worn thin in the Ouarsenis.

Things went very fast. Halfway through the meeting, Achard and two other men left. Then, from a window, Perez spotted patrol wagons in the street and policemen on rooftops.

The four men present were prepared for such an emergency. With the exception of Degueldre, they hastily removed all papers and tidied up the room, turned off lights and drew open curtains, then moved to the bedroom and unlocked a white plywood partition at the rear of a roomy clothes closet that admitted them into a dark cubicle beyond. Then the partition swung back into place and clicked shut. It was an absurdly old-fashioned escape device.

Degueldre had confidence in his identity papers. He trusted his fantastic *baraka*, or luck; with the assistance of the *pied noir* population, for whom he had killed so generously and so pitilessly, he would somehow get through this strait, as he had before. It is futile to try to imagine just what crossed his mind. He felt no fear. He wondered about the person who had betrayed them, and he made a mental note to order his death once he had established the culprit's identity. He strode out on the landing and met several gendarmes, who eyed him curiously but allowed him to continue down the stairs. They were obviously unsure whom they were looking for. He was just leaving the building when a second patrol in the street hailed him.

Perez, Branca and Mura heard approaching footfalls. The gendarmes rapped at the door, shook it, then entered the apartment with a passkey and began to search it room by room. The gendarmes came up to the partition, said something inaudible—someone laughed —and after a moment's hesitation turned away and proceeded down the hall.

In the street the gendarme patrol surrounded "Esposito," searched him and relieved him of his gun. He was almost immediately identified. He put up no resistance. His thick lips cracked into a smile, a brief, wintry satisfied smile as though he were anticipating what would befall him.

At the Caserne des Tagarins, gendarmes toasted Degueldre's arrest with champagne; they were very relieved. The captain in charge approached the long, grim sun-baked figure and offered to wager a case of champagne that French Algeria would no longer exist within a few months.

"I won't be here in a few months to drink it," Degueldre replied simply.

A bloody legend came to an end in this way. Degueldre's career in the OAS had lasted a year. During this period, with a hunter's, a gunsmith's professional conscientiousness and pride, he had forged, handled and perfected a weapon—his Delta commandos. He had suffered no qualms about employing the weapon. As the Deltas executed their *danse macabre* about Algiers' slum quarters, there was no doubt in his mind that sooner or later he would have to pay for his action.

For the next two hours, Perez and the others waited in the hot, uncomfortable cubicle. Finally they exited and slipped away, with no idea that Degueldre was under arrest.

When they learned the news that night, Perez ordered Branca to take over immediate command of the leaderless Deltas. Branca declined. He was not interested, he said, in Degueldre's legacy of hit-and-run street-corner executions.

There is, of course, something glaringly incomplete about this version of Degueldre's downfall. Why, for example, did the gendarmes, after they identified him, fail to search the building thoroughly a second time for other OAS leaders? The truth is, Degueldre was betrayed, but whether by the German deserter alone remains unsure. He was by this time an embarrassment to many in the OAS with his fatalistic determination to stick it out to the bitter end.

Hardly a *pied noir* in Bab el Oued had not at some time brought

Degueldre an urgent message or helped spirit him past a road-block. They spoke of him with awe; even Jouhaud, in Oran, considered him "invulnerable." This reflected the OAS's dreadful gullibility in its own myths, for in fact there had hovered about Degueldre from the start—with his predatory instinct, his desolate and stony commitment to a historic oath, his terrible withdrawal from reality—an air of the gallows. If ever there was, in de Gaulle's blunt phrase, a "lost soldier," it was he.

The government went ahead with the task of preparing Algeria for independence, which still hinged, theoretically, on the outcome of referendums on both shores of the Mediterranean.

"The contrast was striking," wrote one Frenchwoman, summing up the period, "between the OAS's disorganized violence and the orderliness with which prereferendum institutions were set up."*

Six days after the cease-fire, Christian Fouchet, the new High Commissioner appointed to represent French interests during the interim period, had arrived at Rocher Noir. Fouchet was fifty, a tall, serious Parisian whose career to date had embraced diplomacy and politics. His knowledge of Algerian affairs was far from comprehensive (in fact, this marked his first assignment in Algeria, though not in North Africa), but his loyalty to de Gaulle went unquestioned; and at this stage, the latter undoubtedly counted for as much as the former.

Rocher Noir offered a study in stunning contrasts. It rose on a hot, treeless stretch of sand that sloped down to the open sea, twenty-five miles outside Algiers. The sprawling whitewashed compound was jerry-built. The cement walks had not yet hardened. Soldiers lived under tents. The site's main advantage lay in its physical remoteness from the murderous climate of Algiers. Those on Fouchet's staff who set to work at Rocher Noir thought of it, with gratitude, as "an oasis of tranquillity"—although at any moment they expected to be blown sky-high by the OAS.

Fouchet's arrival symbolized, at least in the government's eyes, a new determination to stamp out the OAS and keep the situation under control until the Algerians themselves assumed responsibility for order. His predecessor, Jean Morin, had done a fairly creditable

* Marie-Thérèse Lancelot, *Organisation Armée Secrète*.

job under particularly difficult circumstances; but from first to last, he had been saddled with *pied noir* civil servants who supported the Organization. Under Fouchet there was a palpable change of mood.

Addressing himself directly to the *pieds noirs* on television, Fouchet urged them to face facts and eschew "madmen and criminals" who were dragging them down to destruction. This possessed shock value; no other French government representative had done exactly this in exactly the same way before. The Europeans responded with a stir of interest, especially when this outlander, this *pathos* injected an unexpected note of sentimentality into his appeal. For this had been lacking all along; emotion was eternally on the *pieds noirs'* side, the icy wisdom of rationality on the government's. But Fouchet's speech came too late. The *pieds noirs*—the impoverished, the ignorant and the young in particular—were committed to the OAS to the hilt. They were voluntarily cut off from any meaningful exchange with the Moslems, France, the outside world, all of whom they blamed for their misfortune. Presumably, employed before, Fouchet's approach might have worked a change; as it was, it changed nothing, and his subsequent appeals were even less successful as the novelty wore off.

In early April, the twelve members of the newly created provisional executive—Abderrahmane Farès, its president, three Europeans, five FLN representatives, and three nationalist but non-FLN Moslems—also arrived at Rocher Noir. They were assigned villas, met with Fouchet, and the next morning, April 7 (the day of Degueldre's arrest), in a still uncompleted office amid bulldozers and cranes, they held their first official session. Algeria's difficult transition from French rule to independence began.

The next day in France voters overwhelmingly approved the Évian agreement.

The single question put to them in the country's first referendum since January 1961—that is, since the putsch and subsequent ceasefire talks—was deliberately murky: "Do you approve of the bill submitted to the French people by the President of the Republic concerning agreements to be established and measures to be taken in regard to Algeria on the basis of the government's declaration of March 19, 1962?" Voters, in short, were not asked outright whether they wanted Algeria to remain French or become independent; they were asked to write out a blank check for *all* measures de Gaulle might choose to adopt to settle Algeria's future status. Nonetheless, with the exception of the extreme Right, all parties, including even the Communists, somewhat to de Gaulle's discomfort, recommended a Yes vote. When the ballots were counted up, seventeen and a half million Frenchmen had voted Yes, fewer than two million No. The OAS's excesses during the past six months had certainly contributed to this result; among a population weary of terrorism, there was impatience to get the Algerian problem liquidated once and for all. However, more than six million eligible voters abstained, registering disapproval with de Gaulle's way of conducting the affair, more perhaps than with his aims.

Legitimate grounds for criticism existed on this score. The principle of a referendum itself reposed on shaky ground.* With even lordlier arbitrariness, de Gaulle had confined the referendum to Metropolitan France, which denied the *pieds noirs* and, by the same token, the Moslems, though both had voting rights and ruled the streets in Algeria, any voice in a matter that primarily concerned them. The least one can say is, this was a breathtaking piece of political willfulness.

Algiers reacted to the referendum with sullen, predictable resentment; the murders continued. In Oran, April 8 was a milestone. Nonparticipation in the referendum shattered the Europeans' last illusion. Women cried openly in the street. The OAS pirate radio vowed that Oran would become a "new Stalingrad."

---

* The authoritative *Année Politique*, which had no particular ax to grind, commented: "It would seem that this referendum, once again, did not wholly respect the text of the Constitution and exceeded Article 11 on which it was based. According to Article 11, only agreements with the French Community and international treaties can be the object of a referendum." Since Algeria still constituted part of France, it did not lie within the scope of Article 11. Moreover, in going straight to the nation, de Gaulle not only bypassed the National Assembly, but presented it with a *fait accompli*. The deputies held a debate on the government's cease-fire announcement from March 20 to 21. But on the very morning the debate opened, Jacques Chaban-Delmas, president of the National Assembly, received a letter from de Gaulle informing him that the referendum text would be published in the *Journal Officiel* next day. In other words, de Gaulle did not wait for the outcome of the debate to do as he pleased.

The debate took place and was marked by frequent interruptions and insults exchanged between the Communists and extreme Right. The latter, discredited by their earlier support of the OAS, were far too weak to stop events from unfolding as de Gaulle wished. They could give vent to their unhappiness, and warn of independence's consequences, but that was all.

At the same time, the *Oranais'* interest focused on the fate of a native son.

Jouhaud's trial did not take very long. It set no precedents and produced no surprises; the proceedings were cut and dried, the defense mediocre and the verdict foreseeable.

He stood on April 11 before the Haut Tribunal Militaire, the same court that had judged Challe and Zeller. He was a thick-waisted, bluff, ruddy undistinguished middle-aged man in a double-breasted blue suit; he was clean-shaven now; his only particularity in the arid Paris courtroom was his sunny accent. This linked him, in a way the Parisian judges and spectators imperfectly appreciated, with the fertile *pied noir* earth and made his otherwise inexplicable terrorist activities partly understandable. "I have only one regret," he said heavily, and he meant every word of it, "not to be able to die on Algerian soil." His defense strategy was to placate: "What is the OAS?" he asked rhetorically. "It's the entire European population and many more Moslems than one thinks . . . the OAS has played a moderating role, more than one thinks." For anyone in the courtroom who listened to radio reports of the swelling list of murders and mortar attacks on defenseless Moslem homes, this was hard to swallow.

The most unusual defense witness proved to be Albert Camus' widow, a misty, diminutive blonde, who made an eloquent plea that resumed the *pieds noirs'* dilemma. "I feel divided," she told the judges, "half French and half Algerian, and, in truth, dispossessed in both countries which I no longer recognize, since I never imagined them separated."

The judges, however, were not about to be drawn onto these treacherous quicksands. They were sitting in judgment on a general who had plotted, led the putsch, and sanctioned terror in Oran. He stood before them already condemned to death *in absentia,**
and must answer for specific acts, not a metaphysical puzzle—these were the misfortunes of war. It took them only two hours and ten minutes to find the accused guilty on all counts and sentence him to death.

There was total silence in the courtroom. Then Robert Cerdain,

* According to French law, a person convicted *in absentia* must, upon arrest, be retried.

the blind president of the Oran War Veterans' Association, who had testified as a defense witness, cried out: *"L'OAS vaincra!"* Jouhaud's wife hushed him.

The cabinet met at the Élysée Palace. The ministers took note of Jouhaud's fate, but they were more concerned with a drama in their own midst.

Containing his emotion with some effort, Premier Michel Debré read out his letter of resignation. He had sought a solution that would conserve French rule in Algeria at least for a few more years and permit negotiating with nationalist groups other than the FLN. With rare irony, de Gaulle had used him to carry out a policy that achieved the opposite. This paid a further dividend: as long as Debré remained in office, the OAS and its backers in France mistakenly thought, nothing could go wholly wrong in Algeria.

Now, without even the balm of parliamentary elections to take the sting out of a new premier's appointment, Debré was discarded, his current usefulness at an end.

The unsentimental occasion lasted twelve minutes. De Gaulle had already sent Debré one of his famed letters: "I think—and you yourself think, my dear premier—that it is in the public interest for you to retire, in order to prepare yourself, when the time comes and circumstances are different, for a new phase of your activity." Mellifluously, this promised nothing. Clearly, in de Gaulle's mind, the Algerian problem and the human crises and dilemmas it involved, were over. But there was still some unfinished business.

21

The Shadow of the General

THE NEW white building at the corner of Rue Desfontaines and Rue Daguerre—not far from where Degueldre had been arrested —was middle-class and sedate. The occupant of the fifth-floor apartment was equally sedate—a mustached, large-faced man of deliberate, stolid gesture, who dressed with a trace of aggressive vulgarity in pointed shoes, gaudy-patterned ties and suits that made him seem even broader in the waist than he was.

Salan had been in the same apartment for four months now. He was perhaps as safe here, in the midst of patrols and passers-by, near a villa Ailleret's staff officers used when they came to Algiers, as anywhere in the city. There is much to be said for hiding as close to the enemy as possible.

His life these chaotic days followed the same set pattern as in Spain. Habitually he arose late; then, while he bathed and shaved, Ferrandi, who still performed the functions of aide-de-camp and secretary, prepared OAS directives for his signature. It has been suggested that sometimes he signed these papers without reading them first, but this is unlikely. He remained hidden indoors throughout the day. It was only at twilight that he emerged to buy *Le Monde* and, through lifelong custom, stroll up the streets as they awakened to life after the siesta. He met with emissaries from the Organization —Godard, Perez, student leaders. He saw his wife and daughter.

But, in a fundamental sense, Salan was out of touch. Anne Loesch described him as being at this point "more isolated than the Dalai Lama." Salan has confirmed this—"I was very much alone. . . . I had several worthwhile people around me, but not very many." He spent considerable time reading and listening to the government radio, "which informed us," he now says wryly, "of our mistakes and our successes."

He had become, unwittingly, a symbol of omniscience and omnipotence, remote, vague, impersonal, somewhat like a monumental, shadow-veiled Buddha. Most *pieds noirs* had no personal contact with him, never saw him, and perhaps this was as well: some thought Salan retained the Europeans' confidence only by being a myth. His mysterious presence somewhere and everywhere in Algiers, his name leaping out from walls, his disembodied gruff, meridional voice on the pirate radio gave them irrational comfort. He still had a secret master plan, they insisted—much as Nazi diehards clung to a belief in Hitler's guile—which he would reveal at the proper moment to outwit de Gaulle and reverse the situation.

In fact, by mid-April, the OAS leadership saw the situation on the ground as virtually hopeless. Godard warned that things could not continue in the same way after the Ouarsenis debacle. But what he proposed, except to hold out in Algiers, was less clear. Susini spoke openly, for the first time, of negotiating a settlement with the enemy—by which he meant the FLN; but Susini's influence was on the wane. Salan ignored him and told Godard coldly that his duty was to continue as before.

But in truth Salan himself no longer believed that the OAS as such could achieve any of its goals; it had a bleak record of failure, in the cities and the countryside, in Algeria and France; and it is surely true that no organization could have weathered the series of disasters that had accumulated since March, without profound reforms.

Some time in late March or early April, Salan reverted to his original position: the only way to check de Gaulle was not through violence but through a broad spectrum of "respectable" opposition.

On April 1 a terse, three-line communiqué appeared in Algiers, designating Georges Bidault as the chief of a new National Council of Resistance in the event of Salan's own arrest. The OAS, as such, was finished.

It was a strange choice. Bidault—first a modest provincial teacher of history, then prestigious leader of the internal wartime Conseil National de la Résistance, premier and foreign minister—was by this time an embittered man in his early sixties, resentful of his exclusion from the mainstream of French political life under the Fifth Republic, starved for recognition and power that were not forthcoming. In the spring of 1962 he still represented the Loire department in the National Assembly, as he had been doing since 1945; but his political fortunes had shrunk.

His falling-out with de Gaulle went back to the Liberation: as the number-one Résistant in occupied France, Bidault had only grudgingly accepted orders from Algiers and London, then found himself progressively shunted aside and humiliated. Later, as the Fourth Republic declined, his hopes of being recalled to power with other conservative leaders were dashed, once again by de Gaulle.

A small, courageous man with a gift for corrosive prose, Bidault moved further and further to the Right, driven by an extreme nationalist outlook and wounded vanity. Like Jacques Soustelle, he rallied to the *pieds noirs'* cause. A people threatened with extermination has a sacred right to defend its interests in defiance of established authority, he wrote. While Soustelle railed against "white-shirted Fascism" (Gaullism), Bidault inveighed bitterly against the government's Algerian policy ("this renunciation of more than a century of history, of millions of compatriots of all creeds, of immense resources and on top of it all, of honor"), the Évian agreement ("this monument to follies and betrayal, of which France is the victim"), and the situation in France ("a conjuncture of cowardice, conformism, defeatism and communism").* He was under round-the-clock police surveillance as a parliamentary champion of the OAS; he went characteristically to extremes by declaring that Salan's decision to assume the movement's leadership involved far more dangers, difficulties and discomforts than de Gaulle's flight to London in June 1940!

Bidault's attitude of supreme hostility to de Gaulle struck some as basically psychological. "A study in political pathology," one

* The quotations are taken from Georges Bidault's *D'Une Résistance à l'autre.*

observer put it. From this point on, his path to self-imposed exile was unswerving. As one senior analyst of the United States Department of State has remarked, "The passage from legality to illegality becomes almost academic. When one is committed to a course, the dividing line gradually ceases to exist."

At the end of March, Bidault left his house in St.-Cloud, outside Paris, ostensibly to attend a colleague's funeral in central France; he vanished, then surfaced in Switzerland as an avowed foe of the regime.

Shortly afterward, a letter violently denouncing de Gaulle and the "illegal" April 8 referendum, in the name of the new National Council of Resistance over Bidault's signature, reached Paris editors. His exact whereabouts were unknown.*

To the reorganized movement Bidault brought little. He had no political power base in France, and Salan, it appears, had named him as a replacement reluctantly; there was no excessive admiration between the two men.

Why had Salan designated him? Because he was available, and few other known Rightist personalities were; because Salan had to take some action as the OAS foundered; above all, because of Bidault's Resistance record, which the Organization intended to exploit, hoping that it would strike a responsive, nostalgic chord among some. Most Frenchmen, however, found no common measure between Hitler's oppression and the Fifth Republic's relatively benevolent authoritarianism.

The designation aroused jeers in Paris. The cruelest reaction of all came from de Gaulle himself, who upon learning that Bidault had fled into the activists' ranks, rasped: "At last, some good news!"

Though there was little reason for him to remain in Algeria and the danger of capture grew daily, Salan resisted suggestions that he flee to Portugal, one of the few countries that might offer him sanctuary. His departure, he claimed, would prove the last, unbearable blow for the *pieds noirs:* "I was determined to stay to the end,

---

* Salan's April 1 communiqué designated Bidault as "chief of the OAS." But Bidault claimed to be connected only with the reincarnated National Council of Resistance; he said that he never acted as head of the OAS, and heard of Salan's designation for the first time while reading the Paris weekly *L'Express.* Beginning in April, tracts were often issued under the double letterhead CNR-OAS; Bidault said this was contrary to his wishes and instructions.

just as at the beginning, at the time of the putsch, I was bound to go to Algiers."

There was still one thing he could do to upset the balance of forces on the ground: gain a tactical alliance with the FLN's enemy, the rival nationalist group headed by Messali Hadj. The advantages were obvious: the Messalists could still penetrate into the Casbah (which no European could do) to track down FLN agents and carry on anti-FLN propaganda. Salan knew that a long-term alliance and a common political doctrine were out of the question— the OAS wanted French rule, the Messalists wanted independence on their terms; the only cement between the two groups was their deadly fear of the FLN. What Salan hoped for was simply a local, temporary, opportunistic arrangement, which both sides would feel free to scrap later; in return for the Messalists' aid, he promised that they would play a leading role in determining Algeria's future.* But obtaining even this limited cooperation was proving difficult. The OAS murdered Moslems every day, and boasted of the death rate; this bloody policy could hardly attract even the stanchest anti-FLN Moslems, and to date Messali Hadj had refused all contact with the "fascist Organization." As a last resort, Salan had addressed a letter to a splinter group among the Messalists, the FAAD (Front Algérien d'Action Démocratique). It was, tactically, his last card.

On Good Friday, April 20, Salan came down from his fifth-floor apartment to the ground-floor office he used for OAS business. He had an appointment at noon with a Frenchman, passed on by Jacques Achard, who was in touch with the dissident Messalists. Salan had refused to nibble at several similar contacts, suspecting a baited trap; but there was no reason to distrust this Frenchman, who had furnished the Organization in Paris with false identity papers and been held in Santé Prison for activist opinions. Salan was looking forward to the meeting. Ferrandi joined him. The man they were waiting for was called Lavansseau.

Lavansseau came up the street alone to the address he had been given. He was a youngish man who had worked with the Moslem

---

* Gardes, upon his return from Affreville, concentrated on this task. But when Messalists in one rural area showed some interest and demanded four hundred rifles, the OAS was in no position to meet the request.

civilian population in the hinterland as a native-affairs officer. He had obtained Salan's address only at the last moment and had been unable to communicate it to the people for whom he was working. But he knew that they were following him.

The neighborhood was quiet; Algiers lay drenched under pelting showers as the Easter weekend began. Few pedestrians were outdoors.

A black Peugeot 403 drove up Boulevard Saint-Saëns, turned right into Rue Desfontaines, overtook Lavansseau, and several hundred feet farther ahead slowed down.

OAS bodyguards in parked cars at the corner watched what was going on without alarm. They assumed the pedestrian was a visitor for Salan, and the men inside the Peugeot, a discreet Delta escort. Two government helicopters were aloft in the stormy sky, but they whirred far off. The bodyguards did not know that three squadrons of *gardes mobiles*—more than 250 men—surrounded the neighborhood. As the gendarmes moved up into position, their arrival touched off hostile *pied noir* comment in nearby streets but drew little real attention. The sealing-off of certain, suspect areas was a commonplace occurrence these days.

Through the rear-view mirror, the Peugeot 403 driver saw Lavansseau, whom he had been following for the past two days, turn into the corner building.

The driver reached for his radio-telephone, spoke to the Caserne des Tagarins and relayed an order to bar all traffic into and out of the neighborhood. The men seated beside him were Sûreté inspectors. The driver was the *gendarmerie* captain who had arrested Degueldre.

He braked the Peugeot at the curb, and they got out.

At this moment, Lavansseau knocked at the door of a ground-floor apartment in the building at 25 Rue Desfontaines and was admitted. Two men were in the room—Ferrandi and Salan. Introductions were perfunctory. Lavansseau turned over documents he had brought from Paris about the Messalists to Salan, who read them and nodded; they corresponded to information he already had. "We'll have lunch upstairs," said Salan. His wife and daughter were in the fifth-floor apartment, waiting. "There's no need to stay here."

Lavansseau hesitated and asked to go to the toilet. There was a knock at the door and noises in the corridor. Ferrandi looked through the judas and saw men on the landing. "We've had it!" he exclaimed. He thought of escaping through a back door, but before he could reach it Lavansseau flung the front door open and cried, "There he is." Ferrandi tried to slam the door shut, but a police inspector had already thrust his foot inside. Salan looked stunned.

He was led away before the bodyguards outside could react or, in fact, had realized what was happening. Police looked for a hollow tooth and a cyanide capsule in Salan's mouth, but found none. In his wallet were visiting cards with the name Louis Carrière, Paris businessman; he carried no weapon.

One inspector turned to the other prisoner and said as a matter of fact: "You're Ferrandi." Ferrandi nodded. In his pocket were auto-insurance and car-registration papers in the name of Jean Fournier, advertising agency employee; and additionally—it was a nice touch —a membership card in the pro-government Association pour le Soutien du Général de Gaulle. As they came out into the rain, a policeman draped a coat over Salan's shoulders.

Technically, it was a perfect operation—armored scout cars moved up into place; helicopters flew over the building; motor traffic was halted on Boulevard Saint-Saëns. The bodyguards did not make a move.

As the police car sped through the city, Salan sat speechless between two Sûreté inspectors; through the streaming window he saw *pieds noirs* unaware of his arrest jostling under the downpour into Algiers' churches. The three-hour observation of the Passion was about to begin.

At the Caserne des Tagarins, while Ferrandi replied to questions about his identity, Salan remained mute, teeth clenched. Once or twice he broke the silence, to deny angrily that he was Salan. A gendarme brought him a sandwich and a glass of red wine, which he drank. He was addressed as *mon général*. The fable that he was Louis Carrière gradually crumbled. He had fallen neatly into a trap, and that was that.

Finally, his will power cracked and he admitted who he was. "I saw too many people for idiotic reasons . . . people I didn't know," he lamented bitterly. "It had to happen. Now or later. What difference does it make? Everything was collapsing around us." Refusing for once to defend his subordinates, he added something especially acrimonious about "insane associates."

Gaullists put out descriptions of a drugged, broken figure craving heroin, but there is no evidence that at the time of his arrest Salan was doped. What is sure is that he was in a state of shock, emerging into the light after the mole's existence he had led ever since that windy night, a year before, when he and Jouhaud had fled from the Délégation Générale.

Hair dyed an unreal black, still sporting his profuse mustache, clad in a baggy business suit, he stood glaring under the flash bulbs into the police camera's lens. It is an astounding Rogue's Gallery photograph; behind this absurd and exaggerated getup somewhere lurks Salan, but it is hard to discover just *where,* as he stands there, stiff-necked, ceremonious and embarrassed, for all the world like a newly rich, middle-aged Italian country bridegroom before the wedding.

Within the hour he was transferred, handcuffed and flanked by gendarmes, to La Reghaia air base. Ailleret, whose death the OAS had plotted numberless times, ran into him in the waiting room on the field.

"Do you know who I am?" Ailleret barked. "Do you recognize me?" He was beside himself at the sight of a fellow general who gave orders to kidnap, bomb and murder.

Perhaps taking advantage of the situation, at any rate vehement in his outrage, Ailleret said what he thought of the OAS, and predicted that the man before him would pay for his crimes. Salan turned pale but preserved a grim silence under the tongue-lashing.

They were poles apart. One general embodied loyalty to de Gaulle through thick and thin, the other—it was hard to say what he stood for; his career had flourished, so to speak, amid enigmas, by twists and turns. Ailleret represented a trimmed-down new Army struggling into being, of technicians whose main problems resembled industrialists'; Salan sprang from the old-fashioned *armée coloniale,* with its simple trust in overlordship of native races, pageant and one-sentence patriotic concepts. Between the two men there could be no meaningful exchange. It was a cruel moment—for Salan.

Then, with Ferrandi, he was hustled aboard the DC-3 waiting to fly him to justice in Paris.

At first, it was only a rumor about an "important break." An hour later, Algiers learned something of the truth through a laconic communiqué from the Délégation Générale, which implied that Salan had been flushed out during a routine search for a pirate transmitter, like Jouhaud. No mention was made of how he had really been caught, nor of the painstaking month-long undercover work in France that had led to infiltration of the OAS's highest echelon, nor of thirteen previous unsuccessful attempts; the government was not anxious to expose Lavansseau, its double agent, to Delta retaliation.

Pied noir Algiers at first refused to believe the news; but shops began to close one after another along Rue Michelet and Rue d'Isly. Several hours later, the pirate radio confirmed Salan's capture and endeavored to reassure its stunned audience—"Salan remains the soul and spirit of the French Resistance. The fight continues." But would it? Salan, the *pieds noirs* bitterly noted, had been captured—like Jouhaud, like Degueldre—without a fight.

A heavy rain continued to fall on the city.

That afternoon Broizat waited with growing impatience in an Algiers apartment for two underground contacts. Bald and pallid, easily recognizable, the former seminarian went about in accentuated disguise somewhat like Salan's.

When no one turned up, he went home mystified. Later he learned that members of the network had got wind of the arrest of a stout, dark-haired man, assumed that it was Broizat and stayed away from the meeting for fear of walking into a police trap.

Godard learned the news from Madeleine Larroumet, activist daughter of Amedée Froger, Algiers' former mayor. Later that afternoon she too was arrested, and Godard spent a wretched night in his hideout expecting the police to rap at his door at any moment. But they did not.

Salan left behind an uncertain legacy. For months Algiers had trembled or rejoiced in his shadow magnified to superhuman proportions; but on Good Friday, "Soleil" suddenly cast no shadow— he was disclosed to be one more incautious activist in the toils of a clever and rather foxy government. The myth of the OAS leadership's invulnerability was dead once and for all.

Curzio Malaparte, writing of the Roman statesman Catiline, describes him as "a perpetually indecisive revolutionary as to the hour, the place and the means, incapable of going down into the streets at the right moment, a Communard hesitating between the barricades and conspiracy . . . a victim of the intrigues of a celebrated lawyer and the snares of the police."

No better description of Salan could be conceived.

Ailleret watched the plane contract into the sky, then turned and walked back to his office to telephone Fouchet at Rocher Noir.

22

The Pestilence

IT WAS a lost cause. Each day brought fresh confirmation of this. The number of murders climbed inexorably upward; but so did the number of arrests. *Pieds noirs* for the first time publicly criticized the OAS and spoke of packing up in spite of the Organization's ban on departures. The final issue of *Appel de France* forecast defiantly that the provisional executive would soon consist of the "permanently executed"; but between the newssheet's lines ran a sense of the approaching end.

The Organization was now, militarily, besieged. The hinterland belonged to the *wilayas* and the Armée de Libération Nationale, and first elements of the 40,000-man *force locale* were beginning to enter the cities. The OAS, "unlike the Israelis, the Viet Minh, the FLN," wrote Roland Gaucher, "could hope for no outside pressure or offer of material aid; no army was pressing on the city to bring relief, as it had to the Fifth Column of Fascist sympathizers within Madrid."*

A secret appeal by Perez for twenty European teachers, twenty lawyers, twenty doctors and all reserve officers to join the OAS at once, to replace the cadres lost in the Ouarsenis debacle, drew not a single favorable response from those solicited.

Under these circumstances, one wonders why the remaining

* *Les Terroristes.*

388

leaders continued. One suspects they were as cut off from the outside world and all sense of objectivity as the bewildered *pieds noirs*.

But just as the SS fought a meaningless rear-guard battle in the streets of Prague more than a week after Hitler's suicide, so the OAS carried on with Salan in jail.

On April 21, Paul Gardy, the retired Foreign Legion general, announced from Oran that he was assuming military command of the Organization. The next day, he signed a directive setting forth the OAS's grand, new objective: the only valid strategy now was to maintain a death grip on the urban centers, and *inch' Allah!* ("by the grace of Allah") force de Gaulle to postpone the July 1 self-determination referendum.

Delaying the inevitable—the OAS's goal was reduced to this, with all that implied in the way of confusion and excesses.

Police Prefect Vitalis Cros found the boulevard down which they drove oddly empty at that usually busy hour of the early morning. Housewives, pushcart vendors, street porters and schoolchildren had vanished. The avenue gleamed in a faint, steely light. Soon, as they approached an intersection and the chauffeur slowed the official car down, Cros saw the reason for the ominous quiet: four bodies were sprawled at regular intervals on the pavement, and from the puddles of uncongealed blood it was apparent that the murders had just been committed. He looked more closely and realized that the victims were, without exception, Moslem men.

Cros was being driven to work at his waterfront headquarters at Palais Carnot. Fifty yards ahead, he spotted a fifth Moslem hastening to get away from a determined-looking European boy, who was moving in the shadow of a row of warehouses, stalking him. Suddenly the boy drew out a pistol, broke into a trot, caught up with his quarry and aimed the gun at his neck. There was a flash and the Moslem fell awkwardly to one side. "Just one shot, like a rabbit," thought Cros, dumbfounded.

He sprang out of the car and raced up the street. The murderer looked round, surprised, and vanished down an alley. Cros hurried back to the motionless Moslem. While the chauffeur parked the car, Cros crossed the intersection, entered a café and asked for a telephone slug to call an ambulance.

"*Un melon de moins,*" grunted the *pied noir* owner. "One Arab less," he repeated; then added, indicating the telephone on the counter: "It doesn't work." Cros stared at him, picked the receiver up and heard the dial tone. He began to dial the number of police headquarters when, instinctively looking up, he saw in the mirror behind the counter a group of three men—*pieds noirs* by their looks, heavy-set and blank-faced—seated at a table near the door. They watched him wordlessly. Into the silence, one man, the biggest, said distinctly, "I don't think anybody should call an ambulance."

The owner came up to the telephone and murmured, "No trouble here." Cros felt cold sweat down his neck. Where they sat, the three men blocked the exit. He guessed, sensed, knew for sure that they belonged to an OAS Delta commando, and to make the call he had to turn his back on them. He carefully replaced the receiver in its cradle. No one broke the silence as he left the café.

Once outdoors, he heard guffaws, and it struck him with full force how untenable it was for him, the police prefect of Algiers, to be afraid.

By this time, his chauffeur-escort had run up to join him. Together they reentered the café, hands on their guns. The owner scowled. The men at the table set down their coffee cups. Ignoring them, Cros informed the owner that he was going to use the telephone, clap him in prison on charges of obstructing a police officer in the execution of his duty, and revoke the café's permit for three months.

During the call, the chauffeur kept the men covered.

Cros eventually made good on all three pledges. He is a steady-nerved man, but he has described this experience as his worst during those amazing days when it was difficult to succor the dead.

Godard and Susini saw each other seldom now. Salan's arrest had snapped the thin bond between them. They conducted their business as often as possible through underlings and intermediaries, at ever-changing rendezvous.

Susini inhabited a luxurious cliffside, glass-roofed villa near Clos Salembier, overlooking the Bay of Algiers. The marble house boasted several dependencies, was smothered in bougainvillea, and belonged to Fernand Pouillon, a controversial French architect. Susini had hid here at intervals during the preceding summer and fall, then left brusquely when gendarmes took up quarters nearby; following their departure, he moved back in with relish. He reveled in the house's

Oriental refinements, which he described as "exquisite as a poem by Hafiz."*

Psychologically, Salan's arrest—and Degueldre's even more so—had rendered Susini warier than ever, but it had also freed him of significant constraints. The eventuality of negotiating, of finding a political, rather than a purely military, way out of the OAS's impasse crept into his conversation with increasing frequency; he no longer feared a rebuke from Salan, or Degueldre's possibly deadly reaction. From the Villa des Arcades, he frequently drove down into the city to attend strategy meetings and press his views, flanked by two enormous bodyguards—the Saint-Just (some said the Robespierre) of the Algerian counterrevolution. If his confidence in revolutionary mass action was perhaps worn a bit threadbare, he was more voluble than ever. However French Algeria met its end—through negotiations or destruction—Susini planned to play a leading role in the outcome, without suffering Godard's interference.

The colonel lived in a hideout on Avenue Pasteur, in Algiers' very center. He had lost none of his truculence or professional wariness, and he continued to sidestep one police trap after another; but he exercised no command over operations, made no further decisions. A notable change had come over him. Unlike Susini, he showed little ambition to replace Salan; shrewd, withdrawn and bitter, Godard haunted the city he had sworn to defend and concentrated on gathering arcane information that could no longer be of the slightest possible use against an enemy who grew stronger every day. His sole advice was to fight on. An incontestably gallant yet perverse vision deformed his actions during this final phase. It marked the ultimate frustration of intelligence work carried on for its own sake in a void.

Both men, presumptive heirs to Salan's shaky throne, enjoyed seemingly unlimited immunity to arrest, since no *pied noir* was likely to inform on them; yet following the capture of Degueldre and Salan, neither felt safe any longer.

The period that follows is exceptionally confused. Significantly, within the Organization, Salan's disappearance went unmourned. Some *pieds noirs* worried that he might die "accidentally" while awaiting trial in Paris' Santé Prison (which revealed their basic

* Persian lyric poet who lived in the fourteenth century. Architect Pouillon was serving a jail term in 1962, in connection with a building scandal, and had no idea his showplace was occupied by Susini.

incomprehension of the Gaullist government's insistence upon outward observance of legality); but his former henchmen wrote him
off, with remarkable callousness, as a casualty of underground war.

Yet there was no new leader to draw on, whose word would automatically command obedience. Outside Oran, Gardy's authority
provoked only mirth. Chaos prevailed among the freebooting Delta
commandos. They had, theoretically, a new chief; he was Paulo
Nocetti, a well-meaning *pied noir* X-ray technician. There is no
need to dwell on his role within the OAS. In the month he lasted,
he exhibited none of Degueldre's murderous drive or his ruthless
ability to crack the whip over Legionnaire deserters. Nocetti got
the unenviable assignment, it seemed, primarily because Susini had
backed him. But Delta gunmen did as they pleased, and accepted
orders according to whim. In Susini's sardonic phrase, it was *le
règne des barons,* an era of warring lieutenants.*

In this disintegrating atmosphere, any man who retained direct
control over a cache of small arms and funds and the personal
loyalty of a few Delta commandos could lay claim to influencing
Algiers' fate. This proved to be Perez's case.

After Degueldre's downfall, the doctor had precipitously cleared
out of his headquarters on Boulevard du Télémly, expecting to
suffer imminent arrest. He dared not return to Bab el Oued, where
former neighbors and patients, including Moslems, were sure to
recognize him, so he moved to the La Redoute district and found
pieds noirs, motivated by admiration or fear—it is impossible to say
which—ready to shelter him. On Easter Sunday, two days after
Salan's arrest, he met Susini in an apartment on Boulevard Saint-
Saëns and advised him somberly: "If the current rate of arrests
keeps up, we have ten days left."

There was as little esteem between these two as between Susini
and Godard. Susini jeered behind the doctor's back that he was "likely
to put someone's eye out with his clyster," and Perez sneered at the
skinny blond teacher of violence (*le blondinet maigrichon*). Nonetheless, a shared instinct for survival drove them to reach agreement on a
few indispensable practical matters.

---

* Jesus Ginest, an Algiers taxi driver and local Delta chieftain, blossomed
forth as a celebrity, if only because he spouted nonsense with great gusto. The
Arabs might shortly invade Bab el Oued; so, for that matter, might the Rus-
sians, the Chinese and the Americans, proclaimed this desperado; the *petits
blancs* would throw them all back into the sea. Journalists made pilgrimages
to the Bar des Consulats, in the heart of Bab el Oued, to hear him declaim.

Orders went out through liaison agents to all remaining *maquisards* to fall back on the city. The six urban OAS sectors were consolidated into one (on paper, since they had never really materialized). Gardes's ineffectual Organization of the Masses was abolished —a tacit recognition that it was too late in the day to create a revolutionary infrastructure among the European population.

To Perez, this new strategy made sense. It was now a matter of fighting with limited means within a reduced perimeter. The doctor from Bab el Oued saw Algiers as a second Warsaw—supreme example, in his view, of a city resisting with its back to the wall. But he sourly acknowledged that, unlike the wartime Poles, the *pieds noirs* were not ready to die to defend a birthright, a homeland, a cause. To spur them to a state of permanent revolt, and have a lever ready for future bargaining with the enemy, the OAS would intensify citywide terrorism and destruction. The chief of O.R.O. favored both.

While it is difficult and probably unnecessary to give a complete idea of the stresses and strains that divided the OAS at various levels in this period, it is relatively easy to paint the decaying atmosphere in Algiers. It was made up of moments of spectacular violence followed by stretches of torpid, sullen resignation. There was no concerted plan of violence; the killing was as sporadic as the dust storms that flew up from the south. And perhaps, for the inhabitants, this was the most demoralizing realization of all—that no one was in charge, that the plague would have to work itself out uncontrolled and unchecked to the bitter end before a return to normalcy for the survivors could be achieved.

"Algiers is dying of a slow hemorrhage of murder, robbery and lawlessness," wrote British author Maurice Edelman, who knew the city well.

French Algeria's long journey into oblivion now entered its darkest phase. It was an extraordinary period. When people now speak of the OAS, this is the period they generally have in mind.

The OAS's rage reached a paroxysm. From 73 assassinations in the last week of April, the figure soared in the following week to 203. During this first week of May, it was said that people lost track of murders in the street, the rate was so fast and furious. Milkmen, fruit vendors, fishmongers, day laborers, gas-station attendants fell where they worked or on their way to work. Moslems—the despised *sidis, bicots, bougnouls*—were "knocked over like bowling pins."

"It was horrible," said Perez, "as an artillery barrage is horrible."

Hocine Djibran, a young Kabyle who had to flee Algiers to save his life and was pursued afterward in the streets of Paris for weeks, summed it up: "I think that until May 1958 the *pieds noirs* believed they could coexist with us and make integration work. When they started to kill Arabs indiscriminately, the *petits blancs* were intoxicated . . . they no longer thought straight."

Street directions were bizarre. Newcomers to Algiers were told: "Turn to the right, where they killed the baker"; or "The house you're looking for is on Rue Charras—you'll see a body outside the door." The churches were no refuge. A priest saw twenty Moslems killed, but could do nothing as the gang pursued the lone survivor into the rectory and slew him too.

A journalist, appalled, witnessed the following scene:

When a young Arab came out of a jewelry store with his fiancee, a small boy no more than thirteen came up and deliberately aimed a gun at him "as one aims a toy," pulled the trigger, killed him and then placed a newspaper folded into a cone which he had brought for the purpose over the dead man's face. A passing *pied noir* girl glanced at the body and said to her escort: "Do you think he's really dead?"

At first, many Europeans justified the murders. The Deltas, they said, killed only known FLN terrorists. Then they fell into the habit of disregarding the blood spilled at their feet, and proceeded pale and sleepwalkerlike on their errands.

But as time went by and the corpses multiplied, the *pieds noirs'* reaction changed to distaste, and finally, nausea and horror. A woman in the street sobbed, with a good deal of pertinence, "We may be next."

If the truth were told, the *pieds noirs* were fed up—as were the Moslems—with war and terrorism and revenge; the tragedy was that they could not communicate with each other except through murder.

The streets of Algiers—literally, in William Hanley's phrase, the "killing ground"—became a theater of operations for roving gangs of young, pitiless thugs who scoured one neighborhood after another for Moslem victims among a population frozen with fear. These gangs were modern counterparts of the mobs of ruffians who emerged from the Paris slums under the Terror. This was, in fact, a new Terror, and it lasted approximately a month. The atmosphere was steeped in racial malevolence, decay and nihilism, and its slogan could well have been the Spanish Civil War cry, *"Viva la muerte!* [Long live death]."

Murder was, so to speak, taken over by the young. The remaining OAS leadership lost all control over these teen-agers. Fourteen-year-olds lynched a Moslem with piano cord. Swaggering toughs in filthy blue jeans and armed to the teeth took over the cafés and held mock courts to decide whom they would assassinate. Some parents were proud and egged them on. Some *pied noir* girls slept eagerly with boys fresh from a murder. It was a bit as though Dead End kids had been given patriotic license to shoot down anyone whose looks they disapproved of.

Albert Camus had foreseen something of the sort—although in writing *The Plague* he had had the German occupation in mind. He warned in the celebrated coda of his novel that the pestilence of old could return to his native city of Oran; that the "plague would one day, for mankind's enlightenment and misfortune, rouse up its rats again and send them forth to die in a happy city."

Seemingly, for the moment, no one could do anything about it.

De facto segregation—"apartheid," as Susini virtuously called it —was now all but complete in Algiers. Moslems living at the Champ de Manoeuvre housing project, which bordered the European quarter, moved precipitously out. Europeans dwelling too close to Belcourt went into the center of town. This was what the OAS wanted, to inflame racial animosity still further. *Pied noir* employers received orders to fire Moslem help "discreetly"; when the orders went disregarded, as happened, the OAS took measures of its own to enforce it, which assumed the simple form of murder.

Some Moslem families living in predominantly European El Biar had a feeling of being "lost in the desert." Told not to show their faces on the street, they remained indoors, listened to the radio and subsisted for several weeks on a diet of macaroni and semolina flour, a staple in Arab households. At any moment they expected OAS killers to break in and exterminate them. At last, under gendarmes' escort, they piled their belongings together into a moving van and joined relatives in crowded Belcourt. But here no one could do anything about the daily mortar attacks.

Then on May 10, seven Moslem women, all servants, mistakenly assuming that the street attacks would be limited to men, were shot in the back of the head as they plodded to European homes where they had been employed for years.

"Terrorism is an arm of the weak," said Perez, "and we were weak."

Why? Why were old women executed? What did the OAS's leaders possibly hope to accomplish by this barbarity?

In late April, reports had reached Susini and Perez of active collaboration between French Military Security officers and the FLN in identifying and apprehending OAS members. The reports were partly true. Moslems of all political persuasion, sensing victory, were flocking to the standard of the FLN, which ordered them to report anything abnormal where they lived and worked. In a number of cases, individual Arabs gave information about suspect Europeans to FLN political commissars, who transmitted it to Military Security, which turned it over to the gendarmes for action. The danger of joint anti-OAS action by the two sides had always existed; but, for obvious reasons, as long as the war lasted, it could not be put into effect. With the cease-fire the situation was changed, and on May 2 Algérie Presse Service, the nationalists' news outlet, hinted broadly at the new policy when it rapped OAS fascism as the "common enemy" of the FLN and the French Army.

In the OAS leaders' eyes, this turn of events threatened their very existence.

"There were Moslems everywhere in Algiers, and our own security was lax. We had the impression," Perez said, "that with spies surrounding us, we would no longer be able to function."

It thus became essential to discourage *all* Moslems, including charwomen, from venturing into the European quarters. Penning the Arabs in the Casbah and Belcourt would, furthermore, create acute problems of hygiene and nourishment and show up the FLN's inability to cope with these problems.

There is a curiously unconvincing ring to these explanations, as though they served as a mask for simple racial bigotry, yet in separate interviews with this writer, Susini and Perez ticked up identical reasons for their action. They insisted that it did not spring from panic or confusion but represented a policy coldly adopted to meet a given situation.

They had no illusions about the effect it would have; but, when reproached for the excessive bloodshed, Susini said, "We didn't go into this to play games. The only justification for our action is to win." Perez thought of the murders as a survival operation. So the orders were given to the Deltas.* And later, when the two men developed second thoughts about the policy's usefulness, they discovered how much easier it is to set killers loose than recall them.

First a local problem, then a national one, the OAS drew shocked international attention. World opinion was exercised over the attacks. In France, a few extreme Rightists still defended the Organization's methods; they recalled that during the Battle of Algiers FLN terrorists had sometimes disguised themselves as *fatmas* (charwomen and house servants); thus, the OAS attacks on women were perhaps not on women at all, but on bona fide guerrillas. But, by this time, few responsible politicians, even on the Right, were prepared to support this point of view. United Nations Secretary General U Thant denounced the OAS's "bestial and inhuman crimes." The United States State Department condemned the indiscriminate murders as "without excuse, without justification . . . which can only lead to a dark future for Algeria." In view of the State Department's usual pussyfooting and the fact that Algeria was still legally an internal French responsibility, this constituted strong language and presumably reflected genuine indignation.

* Perez claims that Salan was informed before his arrest of the plans for blind murder and made no attempt to stop them. Perez's fears about Army-FLN collaboration were exaggerated: French Army officers have since minimized the usefulness of the information the FLN furnished.

Conditions were no better in Oran. The hot, fretful city was washed by rains. On Easter Sunday, two days after Salan's arrest, *pieds noirs* leaving church at the wet, windy Place des Victoires came upon the body of a forty-year-old European clad in pajamas, a bullet hole in his forehead, exhibited from a lamppost with a sign around his neck bearing the single word *"barbouze."*

A handbill nailed to a tree trunk proclaimed: "Salan has been arrested, but there remain Gardy, Gardes, Godard, Broizat—and you!" To the irreverent, this did not appear to amount to much, except for the "you." But after a brief interlude, the *Oranais'* morale revived; Gardy was in their midst, and the Organization's power left no doubt in any minds.

The same daily pattern of bank holdups, explosions and mortar barrages continued. Army troops these days ventured forth into the center of the city only in force. Gun fights broke out for no reason. Mail and telephone service had virtually ceased; even the undertakers struck, for lack of security at the cemeteries; schools were closed and occupied by *gendarmerie* squadrons. A mob attacked a group of Paris photographers after the OAS decided that news photos could help identify terrorists. And on the Organization's orders, the *Oranais* removed street signs and nameplates from letterboxes to make patrols and house searches more difficult. In the evening, street lights flickered on, went out, came on again and went out for good as electricity-company employees showed their support for the movement. In the dark, neighbors sniped at one another from balconies and attacked one another with knives in the street.

The Church in Oran sought unconvincingly to remain above the fray. On many a Sunday, a priest from his pulpit praised the OAS by name; many hid OAS arms and militants, and were continuously in trouble with the authorities. Some worried about encroaching Islam and restrictions on freedom of worship under a future, Moslem-dominated government. It was a short step from this to the concept of a crusade. One priest noted: "For Mediterraneans of Spanish blood, faith and violence are not incompatible."*

---

* In contrast with the Church's position in Oran, Monseigneur Duval, Archbishop of Algiers, continued steadfastly to preach equal rights for the two racial communities and exhort his flock to Christian charity—a stand that required, as the situation worsened, an ever-increasing sum of courage.

The members of Catholic Action and Catholic welfare organizations in Oran dispatched an open letter to France, which described the "violent reaction of the community" as legitimate self-defense, claimed that "decent *pieds noirs* at the risk of their lives protected Moslems," and made the astonishing assertion that the OAS was "trying to reestablish order where the state wished disorder." Such was the *Oranais'* unyielding and wholly committed attitude six weeks before independence.

Fantastic rumors flew through the streets. Jouhaud and Salan were really at liberty; the news of their arrest was government propaganda. The Moslems were about to descend en masse from Ville Nouvelle upon the European quarters; or, conversely, all Arabs were preparing to join the OAS. The Organization had a submarine waiting to embark its leaders to safety. With limitless credulity, "barricaded behind walls of absurdity," as one visitor described them, the *pieds noirs* listened to these stories, which alternately elated and depressed them.

There was at least one minor reason for their near-hysterical state. Katz, the local Army commander, still feared outright civil war in the streets, and—adopting Marshal Lyautey's famous advice to show force so as not to use it (*"Il faut montrer la force pour ne pas s'en servir"*)—he deliberately set out to rattle the *pieds noirs'* nerves and keep them off balance.

"I did things without reason to catch them off guard. . . . I'd set up checkpoints where no traffic passed, I sealed off a neighborhood, then did it again the next day," Katz later said. "The OAS never knew what I would do."

As of April 23 (Easter Monday) his troops received orders to fire without warning at persons loitering on balconies. If this did not work, he threatened to evacuate entire families summarily from apartment buildings that harbored OAS snipers, and bring in the Air Force to drive OAS commandos from the center of town. Feeling that the "rooftops commanded the situation," he placed gendarmes and CRS troops twenty-four hours a day on the roofs of the city's seven highest office buildings. He forbade motor and some pedestrian traffic in downtown Oran.

Up to a point, these tactics worked. Full-scale civil war did not erupt, and Katz discovered that what was true in Bab el Oued was equally true in Oran: practically no *pied noir* wanted to lose his life in defense of French Algeria.

But Katz himself became the OAS's principal enemy—a combined bogeyman and scapegoat. The Organization accused him of behaving "against the OAS the way Massu had behaved against the FLN in the Battle of Algiers." The *pieds noirs* vehemently accused him of issuing orders to his troops to spray the façades and balconies of apartment houses with machine-gun fire, and of releasing European suspects in Ville Nouvelle, where they were sure to be torn to shreds by the Moslems. The first charge appears to have been true; the second false. To boost their morale, the *Oranais* persuaded themselves that Katz had been kidnaped by the OAS, that serious disagreement existed between the Army and the *gendarmerie* on anti-OAS operations. To exploit this alleged split and wean away the Army from the gendarmes, the *Oranais* took the curious step one Sunday of organizing a street dance at Place Hoche, where armored vehicles blocked all civilian motor traffic. On OAS orders, local girls invited the alien, despised soldiers from France to dance, while older spectators offered them cigarettes and coffee. The hot, weary, thirsty soldiers certainly considered "Operation Charm" a success; but it was never repeated, for the tense *pieds noirs* could not put their hearts into it.

Katz was more concerned by the Foreign Legion's proximity at Sidi bel Abbès, only thirty miles away, and its "childish side." If one or several crack Legion regiments defected and marched upon Oran, he did not see how he could order his conscripts and gendarmes to stop them. If the Legion marched, Oran would be invested, then the outlying countryside.

The government knew that the OAS—in particular, Gardy and Micheletti, his civilian deputy—were thinking of creating an autonomous region, a territorial platform comprising Oran, Sidi bel Abbès, Aïn Témouchent, Mascara, Relizane and farm centers in the interior, from which to wage desperate, last-ditch resistance against the FLN. According to Gardy's plan, the enclave would stress its attachment to French ideals, welcome anti-FLN Moslems, and proclaim its temporary separation from France until de Gaulle's overthrow. From a long-range point of view, the government had little to fear, for such a redoubt implied the expulsion of tens of thousands of pro-FLN Moslems and a consequent manpower shortage, which would make it economically unviable. The region's water supply alone would be vulnerable to guerrilla attacks. But if, in the short term, Oran rose and the Foreign Legion sought to defend the rebellious zone, the *wilayas* and the Armée de Libération Nationale camped in neighboring Morocco would probably intervene; and this would surely lead to skirmishes and the wreckage of the cease-fire.

The government was determined not to allow any of this to happen. It could not permit the establishment of a breakaway region. For once, the orders it issued were unequivocal. If Gardy attempted to create an Oran redoubt, Katz and the 20,000 men under his command were to put it down. There was every reason to believe that he was tough enough a general to do the job.

As dawn splashed over Algiers on this May morning—May 2— more than a thousand Moslem longshoremen milled outside the hiring hall at the docks, waiting to be called. A truck loaded to capacity with scrap iron stood parked before the hiring hall. At 6:10 A.M. it blew up.

The first blinding flash literally cut a swath through the crowds of waiting men. The booby-trapped vehicle collapsed on its wheels, pulverized. The hall was a twisted, singed shambles. A giant coil of black smoke unwound skyward.

The howling mob fled down Quai de Calvi for safety. Some were mowed down by OAS commandos who opened fire through the smoke from nearby buildings that overlooked the docks. The Moslems fell upon the first European in their path—an oil engineer— and cut his throat.

When the dead were finally counted up, there were sixty-two. When police arrived, the survivors angrily insisted on cleaning up the mess without the aid of Europeans—and did so. The longshoremen had been preparing to unload food supplies for the *pied-noir* population.

Later in the day, mortar shells rained down on two Moslem quarters, Belcourt and Climat de France, killing thirty more.

That evening the Europeans retired early, but as the warm, orange-scented night fell, their uneasiness grew. They could almost feel the mounting terrible anger in the Casbah's white recesses.

That week, de Gaulle phoned Fouchet at Rocher Noir and coldly informed him that the OAS must be smashed by all means. But the French government had ceased being an effective force in Algiers.

Major Si Azzedine, former deputy chief of Wilaya IV, returned to Algiers in April. He turned up, less than a month after the cease-fire, entrusted with a key mission—the reconstitution of the underground ZAA, the Zone Autonome d'Alger.

As has been noted, the original Zone had been smashed and dismantled by French paratroopers in 1957.* Since that time, Algiers —from the FLN's point of view—was divided into two sectors composed of nationalist elements in contact with Wilaya III and Wilaya IV in the neighboring countryside. Between the two *wilayas* there existed intermittent rivalry for control of the city's Moslem population.

In Si Azzedine's present assignment, political considerations outweighed tactical needs. Mindful of the growing shadow cast by Ben Bella since his release from internment and his arrival in Morocco, the Algerian Provisional Government's leaders in Tunis were anxious to reactivate the Zone before independence as a solid anti-Ben Bella nucleus. It goes without saying that they acknowledged nothing of the sort. They declared that the Zone Autonome would serve as a base to organize and coordinate anti-OAS action in Algiers; and it was true that since the cease-fire the FLN no longer considered the OAS as a useful political scapegoat but a clear and present evil that must be crushed. Nonetheless, this purpose was secondary.

The slight, dark-haired major had volunteered for the assignment. He already knew the inside structure of Wilaya IV, and he was acceptable to Wilaya III; he possessed physical courage, and there were few other qualified candidates.† After some reflection, Tunis agreed to send him.

* See Chapter 19.

† On November 17, 1958, French paratroopers in a bloody skirmish with FLN guerrillas wounded and took prisoner Si Azzedine, then deputy chief of Wilaya IV in the region around Algiers. The capture occurred at a period of the war, six months after de Gaulle's return to power, when there was considerable wavering in the *wilayas* about prosecuting guerrilla operations.

General Jacques Massu thereupon decided to win over Azzedine and put him in the hands of Captain Bernard Marion, of the Deuxième Bureau (Military Intelligence) of the 10th Paratroop Division. Azzedine showed signs of willingness to cooperate with his captors, and agreed to write to his former chief, Si Mohamed, of Wilaya IV, calling upon him to surrender. Optimistically, Captain Marion sent Azzedine into the guerrilla-infested countryside south of Algiers to deliver the message, and he promptly disappeared.

Months later, Azzedine surfaced in Tunis, where, however, he was received not with enthusiasm but suspicion. The FLN took a long time to decide that he had not been turned around by the French during his imprison-

Within several weeks of his arrival, Si Azzedine was joined by another underground leader, Omar Oussedik, traveling under the *nom de guerre* of Captain Si Tayeb. Oussedik, former editor of *El Moudjahid*, the FLN's official newspaper, and an avowed Leftist, arrived as Azzedine's political adviser. However, from the start, Oussedik gave orders on his own without referring back to the major, and soon created an uproar in the reconstituted Zone through his extremist revolutionary position, the inflammatory slogans and inscriptions he ordered painted up, and the encouragement he gave to widespread premature requisitioning of *pied noir* apartments. The French thought of him as the driving force in the Zone, Azzedine as a mere figurehead. This was perhaps an extreme assessment, but there is no doubt the former deputy chief of Wilaya IV was considerably overshadowed by his stormy assistant.

In April, the Moslem leadership had promised European liberal friends and Frenchmen from France (whom they always considered as distinct from *pieds noirs*) that they would "clench their teeth and hold out." Independence was worth the high toll the OAS was taking in lives and property. But in the first days of May, the strain was obviously beginning to prove unendurable.

Discipline among Algiers' Moslem population of more than 200,-000, almost half of whom were concentrated in the Casbah, was being maintained in the teeth of extreme provocation.* Terrorism,

---

ment. Azzedine's position in the FLN remained precarious as late as 1962, and this need to redeem himself probably had something to do with his volunteering to reconstitute the Zone Autonome as OAS terrorism reached a climax.

The embarrassed French Army meanwhile claimed that Azzedine had been sincere in writing the surrender appeal and disappeared against his will, abducted by Wilaya IV guerrillas. Almost ten years later, Captain Marion, now retired from the Army, was unsure whether he had been made a fool of by Azzedine; but the evidence seems to indicate that he was.

* On May 3, 1962, a day after the dockside explosion, a stolen tank truck with 4,000 gallons of gas exploded on the heights above Algiers. OAS commandos had locked the steering wheel with a bicycle chain, then fled after they set the truck rolling downhill. They hoped that the explosion would send sheets of flame down upon the densely inhabited Casbah. Firemen's prompt work prevented this from happening, but the blast killed two, destroyed cars and telephone poles.

Several weeks earlier, on April 4, the OAS had already set some sort of record for provocation when a fifteen-man commando disguised as CRS troops drove up to Beau Fraisier clinic at dawn and began machine-gunning convalescents. Gunmen shot at random into beds. They killed ten patients and wounded twenty. Following the massacre, the commando left, in a ground-floor office, a thirty-pound plastique charge that demolished an entire wing of the building.

like many afflictions, tended to spawn among the weak and defenseless, in the slum quarters that were least capable of organizing effective resistance to it. It was a characteristic of this grisly period that, on both sides, the well-to-do were relatively exempt from attack. Instinctively, the Moslem bourgeoisie reacted to the breakdown of order like their European counterparts—sons of wealthy families were sent out of the country to pursue their studies; absolute commitments were avoided. But while wealthier Arabs could resort to the simple expedient of moving to the countryside to flee the terrorists, the poor had nowhere to go and no means of getting there; they remained jam-packed in low-income housing projects and the Casbah.

In a sense, the indiscriminate terrorism unleashed by Susini and Perez played into the FLN's hands, for instead of dispersing the Moslems and driving them into the streets, it concentrated them indoors in well-defined districts, where local political commissars and *responsables* found it easier to exercise discipline. One must not underrate the FLN's force of persuasion at this point; after seven years of war, it had grown from a minority group among the Moslems to a powerful political organization without serious rivals. The OAS murders and atrocities themselves, as has been suggested, strengthened the population's willingness to accept sacrifices. Nonetheless, it was remarkable that neighborhood chiefs managed to impose the iron discipline they did on their fearful and angry broods.

They brought out the Zone Autonome's small, precious hoard of arms left over from the Battle of Algiers, and formed shock groups in Belcourt, Climat de France and Mustapha to defend each area's perimeter. Moslem teen-agers, openly carrying pistols for the first time, patrolled all accesses to the Casbah and enforced strict orders to allow no Europeans to enter. (From this time onward, even journalists sympathetic to the FLN cause found the quarter closed to them.) Blood donors were recruited. Volunteers organized medical supplies and food relief for the virtually besieged population. To resolve a critical lack of fresh vegetables and fruits, the FLN—with cooperation from the *force locale*—dispatched an armed convoy on a shopping expedition to the municipal market; the trucks went and returned without OAS interference. Milk was obtained for children on the black market. Women whiled away the hours sewing FLN flags. Other volunteers, including several French doctors, improvised clinics for the wounded. It was a community effort—"the one time," André Pautard of *France-Soir* noted, "when the Algerian rebellion appeared to be a revolution."*

The older Moslem men submitted to the discipline this sort of life demanded without complaint. A problem undeniably existed, however, among the young, who listened with growing skepticism to the commissars' appeals to practice nonretaliation. One evening in early May, teen-age Arabs gathered with clubs and iron bars near the Place du Gouvernement, ready to invade the neighboring European waterfront district. Some tore down the barbed-wire rolls installed by the Army, and began stoning *pied noir* cars passing nearby. Hastily summoned French troops formed a human chain, hand-in-hand, until the partitions could be put back in place.

It was an eerie situation: while the Army acted as a buffer, and FLN leaders urged passive resistance, OAS commandos sought ever deadlier ways of goading the Moslems beyond reason into bloody reprisals.

It was past midnight when the Zone Autonome commissars arrived in secret at Vitalis Cros's villa in the European suburb of Hydra. He gave them *couscous* prepared by his wife, and listened with growing apprehension to what they said. Their plan was simple, and it confirmed the tip he had received that afternoon from Abderrahmane Farès, the president of the provisional executive. The *responsables* were planning a raid on Bab el Oued at daybreak, in which commandos would kill three times the total number of previous Moslem victims.

For the next hour, Cros tried to talk them out of it, but in vain.

Finally they offered to take him to the Casbah to meet their own leaders, but they insisted that he must come without escort or arms and trust them. Cros did not relish the idea, but nonetheless agreed.

A half hour later, after trudging through the silent Casbah, they entered a darkened, white house. In the patio the police prefect was given tea.

* A Franco-Algerian committee created in Paris launched an appeal for funds on May 25, to alleviate suffering in Moslem quarters of Algerian cities in the wake of terrorism, unemployment and shortage of medical supplies. The committee aptly noted: "Discipline cannot eternally replace lack of employment and insufficient sanitary means." Its members included Germaine Tillion, the ethnologist, former cabinet minister Maurice Schumann and Gaullist Jean-Claude Servan-Schreiber.

He stressed that the Moslems had won and needed only to keep their wits about them several more weeks until independence. But if they did not and carried out the massacre, he added, he would not be able to restrain the French Army from intervening on the *pieds noirs'* side.

Some of the men he was trying to convince were from the interior and spoke no French. They used roundabout and elaborate language, as simple men often will, and it took them two valuable hours—while time ran out—to explain their position, which was, essentially, that it was growing increasingly difficult to contain their own teen-agers. The raid represented a safety valve.

Finally—Cros claims—he bluffed and said, "Go ahead, kill five thousand or ten thousand if you want. But you will suffer the consequences."

They adjourned to another room, stayed there for a while, came back and said the raid was canceled; then some excused themselves and said they must hurry to issue orders; there were just three quarters of an hour remaining before the massacre was to start. It was dawn as Cros left the house. He returned to Hydra dazed.

But there is a limit to which a people's political sophistication can be tried.

The long-averted storm finally broke on May 14. It was, by coincidence, the holiday of Aid el Kedir, when Moslem families slaughter a sheep and portions of the roast are distributed to the needy. Beginning at five-thirty in the afternoon, in carefully synchronized attacks, cars with FLN commandos of three or four youths sped through the European quarters, machine-gunning bars, automobiles and passers-by.

The first attack occurred at El Biar, then more—twenty-eight, all told—from one end of the city to the other, in St.-Eugène, Bouzareah, La Redoute, Kouba.

One car screamed suicidally down the hillside, through an intersection, firing point-blank at the windshields of *pied noir* vehicles, before it crashed into a wall. From another car, Moslems dragged out four Europeans they had seized the day before, lined them up before a wall and shot them to death.

Panic broke out in downtown Algiers as word of the attacks spread. Quickly, the Army occupied Algiers' strategic heights and clamped a seven-o'clock curfew on the population. Within an hour and a half the hit-and-run raids ended. But twenty Europeans lay dead and eighty were wounded.

The riposte was far from being as spectacular as feared, and there was some doubt at first whether it was a self-contained action, or perhaps OAS provocation with the help of anti-FLN *harkis,* or the start of full-fledged civil war between the two communities. The next day, Si Azzedine assumed responsibility for the raids, which seemed to imply the last. In fact, he had not ordered or approved of them; local groups of youngsters had taken the initiative. From Tunis came quick support for their action; but Azzedine swiftly took measures to prevent any recurrence of the raids by tightening up discipline still further.

On the same day—May 15—there was jubilation within the OAS. Terrorism and provocation were beginning to pay off. The next step was to kill a still greater number of Moslems. There was to be no end to the deadly cycle of retaliation and counterretaliation until the reigning anarchy made a referendum altogether impossible.

That day, a homicidal attack occurred every ten minutes on the streets of Algiers.

23

The Judgment

THE ANCIENT and imposing hulk of the Palais de Justice, which stands on the Île de la Cité and is flanked by the Conciergerie and criminal police headquarters on the Quai des Orfèvres, generates an atmosphere of awesome retribution; justice here, in the shadow of rigid Roman law, is likely to be stern, and the dark massive structure is alive with the memory of politicians and power seekers who outreached themselves and came to grief at the hands of French society.

On May 16, Parisian onlookers watched and waited, contained behind iron palings, for justice, as each understood it, to take its course inside the Palais.

Parking in adjacent streets was prohibited. Police repeatedly checked the passes of those entering the somber corridor that leads to the Salle des Assises; they searched spectators and journalists —even judges and lawyers—for weapons. A magistrate in the full regalia of his office appeared to upbraid the police for jostling pe-destrians—and drew a reprimand upon himself from the Justice Ministry. The security measures were the strictest Paris had seen since the great collaboration trials of 1944–45.

When Salan rose in the dock to speak on the second day of his trial, an anticipatory hush stilled the courtroom. The nine judges in ermine capes and red robes—those who, with one exception, had sentenced Jouhaud to death—prosecution staff, witnesses, government observers, court reporters and caricaturists,* the young Army officers attending their first trial of a general—all leaned forward, straining to catch what they agreed must be the high point of the trial testimony.

Outside through the narrow ogival windows, one saw guards with Tommy guns patrolling nearby rooftops. The adjoining Gothic miniature of Sainte-Chapelle was closed to tourists. A dim, intense murmur rose from the cobblestoned yard, where police, CRS troops and black-jacketed *gardes mobiles* all waited.

"I am the chief of the OAS, hence my responsibility is complete," began Salan in his unmistakable high, harsh voice, reading from notes.

"I wanted to become a colonial officer," he declaimed in measured tones: "I became one. I fought to preserve for the *patrie* the empire of Gallieni, Lyautey and Father de Foucauld . . ."

For the next forty-five minutes, with several breaks, he read his prepared statement, the first draft of which he had certainly written, but whose final polished text seemed to owe a debt to the unhesitating hand of Maître Jean-Louis Tixier-Vignancour, his lawyer. It was a declaration intended to justify—in Salan's own mind and the audience's—everything he had done, whether criminal or not, successful or not, wise or not.

Reviewing his career and motivations, he centered his defense not on his revolt and subsequent depredations, but on the grand betrayal that, according to this version of the facts, had left him no alternative. He attacked the French government's policy of "genocide" toward the *pieds noirs,* its "cynical contempt for the most sacred commitments"—and "government," in Salan's mouth, meant, of course, de Gaulle. The man in the dock harked back again and again to May 13, 1958, to the integration policy endorsed by the *pieds noirs,* seemingly at the time by many Moslems, and indeed by de Gaulle himself, if his cry of *Vive l'Algérie française!* at Mostaganem meant anything—"It was the only possible policy . . . it was

* In France, as in the United States and many other countries, photographers are not allowed inside the courtroom; newspapers make do with caricaturists' pen-and-ink sketches to capture the trial atmosphere.

the only one that was legal." Salan here gave the words in his somewhat pebbly voice exceptional clarity, as if they could never be emphasized sufficiently, recalling the argument which everyone in the courtroom knew, but which by now seemed strangely so unavailing, that Article 72 of the French Constitution defined Algeria as being "made up of departments and communes . . . of the Republic." Thus, legally as well as morally and patriotically, his position until this moment was unassailable; he had done his duty as commander in chief, and he did not omit reminding the judges, a majority of whom were generals, that upon his recall to Paris in 1959 he had turned over a "more than favorable mitilary situation" into Challe's hands.

Why, then, had he stepped into a second career as outlaw? "Under no circumstances," he read aloud, "could I accept being considered as General de Gaulle's accomplice in the martyrdom of French Algeria and its delivery to the enemy. I became conscious of having been the dupe on May 13 of a frightful and sacrilegious farce." His fundamental error, he implied, consisted in "giving" de Gaulle power in 1958. For Salan believed this; like all half-truths, it possessed enormous attraction. "The government is responsible for the blood that is flowing," he said dully, "and above all he to whom I gave power."

He minimized his role in the April putsch: "I was not asked to take part in working out the plan . . . or its execution. . . . I want to point out that I initiated no action in the leadership or organization of the insurrection." On this score his resentment sounded loud and clear; he might be on trial for his life, but an old grudge against Challe still rankled and won some priority in his mind.

As for what had happened since the night of April 25, 1961, *and was still happening*—the cold-blooded fostering of civil war, the attempt to subvert the Army, the summary murders on a horrendous scale, the ruinous inflammation of racial antagonism—he owed an explanation, he said, "only to those suffering and dying for having believed in a broken promise and dishonored commitments."

With this he sat down and refused to answer further questions from the bench.

It was an unconventional performance, quite unlike anything one had expected of Le Chinois. Undoubtedly, Salan the general in the dock confronting his peers cut a more vigorous and plausible figure than "Soleil," the theatrically made-up furtive underground chief. "He seemed," noted one observer, not without malice, "better suited to posing for a bronze statue than playing at Robin Hood." Upper lip clean-shaven, ruddied by a year in the Algerian sun, spruce in a properly cut slate-gray suit, poker-faced, he stood stiff and impenitent in the dock, having resumed his true appearance as well as identity. Janet Flanner of *The New Yorker*, in a flash of intuition, compared him to an "elderly, pessimistic silver fox."

But those who had anticipated disclosures about the OAS's inner workings and strange, profitless campaign were left frustrated.

Salan stood indicted on four counts: attempt on the internal security of the state, incitement to rebellion and civil war, and constitution and command of armed bands (the last two of which were punishable by death). The government had flown thirty pounds of documents—dossiers, tracts, minutes—from Algiers to prosecute its case against him.

The opening day was taken up with defense delaying tactics over the court's competence;* but on the second day, the trial began to unfold in the grand manner. The government called four prosecution witnesses: General Charles Ailleret, Delegate General Jean Morin, former Algiers Police Prefect René Jannin (Vitalis Cros's predecessor), and *gendarmerie* general Bernard Cherasse—four officials who had suffered from the putsch and the OAS.

Of the four, Ailleret was the most brittle; he contemptuously referred to the man in the dock as "Salan," just the bleak name, as though he had never been, like Ailleret himself, commander in chief; and to the Organization as "bureaucratic terrorism . . . whose main concern was with the safety of the terrorists." Morin also delivered himself of the mortification the OAS had caused him ("it forgot the French of Algeria needed something other than murder, this was its worst crime"); and Jannin called it a "syndicate of crime devoted to hatred."

The official statistics Morin and Jannin cited could well justify their revulsion. The OAS had carried out more than 2,000 attacks,

---

* The defense sought to transfer the case from the jurisdiction of the Haut Tribunal Militaire on grounds that it was not empowered to judge acts committed after September 1961, the expiration date of de Gaulle's "special powers" under which the court was set up. The judges threw out this argument.

killed 1,400—of these, 85 percent were Moslems, which disposed of the romance that the Organization felt no animosity toward non-Europeans—and wounded more than four thousand. The Organization had set off 12,000 explosions, robbed banks of $8,000,000, and stolen at least 5,000 weapons of all sorts—machine guns, bazookas, Bren guns, automatics.* All this in one year's time! In a purely negative way, one could applaud the Organization's industriousness. And the general who claimed full responsibility for this havoc was no obscure figure from the bottom ranks of Algerian activism but a commended and respected officer known personally to judges and witnesses. No government could be expected to show much patience with him.

In the course of the trial one might have anticipated some stark explosion of pride or bitterness or grief as Salan sat quite alone in the dock with his unique view of all that had transpired since that moment when he had hurried across the Spanish frontier, unaware of all the consequences his single, impulsive step would entail. But nothing of the sort took place in the Palais; he remained enigmatic and aloof, at times as expressionless as though his face had been lifted. "Le Chinois" was a better description for him than ever was "Soleil."

And so, almost from the start, it became apparent that some indispensable element was lacking in the proceedings. This was, surely, the OAS's trial as much as Salan's. Removed from the seething political kettle of Algiers, it was now possible, in this courtroom, to take stock of what the OAS had attempted and actually done. Yet the indignant testimony and the dark statistics did not spring alive, the atmosphere remained muffled—perhaps, some suggested, because atrocities were commonplace since World War II. But the trial's abstract nature also stemmed from more specific reasons. As Jean-Marc Theolleyre, one of France's ablest court reporters, pointed out,† the prosecution was not interested in pinning down this or that particular OAS crime: no victim came forward with unendurable graphic details of terrorism; Algiers, sweltering

---

* The figures cited at the trial by Morin and Jannin varied. This was because Morin, for example, used statistics through March 24, 1962, the time of his departure, while Jannin cited statistics through April 1962, the date of Salan's capture. Moreover, some reports gave *plastiquage* figures for Algeria and the Paris region, while others included all of France. Unofficial estimates of deaths attributable to the OAS ran as high as 2,200.

† In his book, *Ces procès qui ébranlèrent la France.*

and murderous, was antiseptically remote. And, measured against a full year of military restiveness, open insurrection, street warfare and violence, a total of four witnesses seemed scarcely adequate in the balance. There was something altogether arbitrary about this number, and the choice of the four. Why had other high officials not been called? Disturbing allegations arose that the Army had ordered some officers not to appear in court. Prominent civil servants, like Jacques Foccart, Alexandre Sanguinetti and Michel Hacq, in a bland way typical of the Gaullist Establishment, overlooked summonses to testify.

The impression thus inevitably gained hold that the government wanted to scamp the hearings, that it was far from anxious to delve to the heart of the problem. There was to be no scraping for motives, no painting of a political climate. Salan was a common lawbreaker, who must, as de Gaulle had repeatedly warned, suffer punishment for his crimes. Manifestly, the government wanted no public review of the false starts and errors and turnabouts of its Algerian policy; what it wanted, in all simplicity, was a guilty verdict without ado—the presiding judge kept saying, "We'll never get through with this case"—of the sort meted out to Jouhaud. The government bore a real grudge against Salan, whom it viewed as a political general who had callously exploited the unsophisticated *pieds noirs'* hopes for an impossible result. The same could not be said, for instance, of Challe, a military general who had almost unwillingly kept his word to the colonels, lost his gamble and surrendered without bloodshed.

What ensued that week was a Parisian trial, *un procès parisien* in the same sense as *un gala parisien* or *une réception parisienne*. It was the talk of the town, that excited gossip; a spectacle for which women intrigued to get invitations; the Palais, a place to be seen —and it would be relegated from mind the week after. Instead of probing deep, the hearings produced a distinct air of evasiveness, which did not help the government's cause.

By the end of the first day, *Aurore*, catching the mood, observed: "A well-produced show, a well-filled theater and a very bad first act."

Salan realized what was happening, and appeared almost uninterested in the testimony. His depthless blue glance wandered around the courtroom without alighting on anybody or any one thing in particular. The outcome, after all, was easy to foretell.

The *pieds noirs* were preparing to leave. They spoke of nothing else—the men in cafés, where there was no lack of *pastis* or ice; the women in their kitchens and at market. Since the Rue d'Isly fusillade, their will was broken; and a new psychological jolt had just been furnished by the French cabinet's choice of July 1 as the referendum date. Some could not bring themselves to believe that independence, the referendum's foreseeable outcome, would take place in less than six weeks' time—the reality of disaster was, as usual, hard to swallow—but they were sick of terrorism, and afraid. The kidnaping of suspected activists was ominously up; an Army patrol had recently come upon the mutilated bodies of eight Europeans buried in mud and quicklime at a Moslem farm near Hussein Dey. The *pieds noirs* knew that international opinion condemned their participation in the OAS, and that henceforth they were utterly alone.

Five hundred miles of blue water—not an insurmountable distance—separated them from a France they had alternately fought for, looked up to, mistrusted and reviled, but never known at first hand; abruptly, now, it symbolized a badly needed minimum of security, a country with a future.

Susini, in the midst of all this, sought a way out. Gardy's idea of an Oran redoubt struck him as impractical—most Europeans would not be able to reach it through FLN-controlled areas, and work and housing would not be available for those who did. He realized that a slow but steady transformation was occurring among the *pied noir* professional cadres and *petits blancs,* who had been the mainstay of OAS action. They had backed the Organization to the hilt as long as it appeared to have a chance; but that chance was at an end. Belatedly, the more realistic members of the European community were beginning to think about ways of salvaging as much as possible from the general wreckage.

Susini's priority aim now was to discourage a mass exodus of *pieds noirs* that would mean delivering up the entire country to the Moslems; he wanted to gain time, to enable the OAS to escape with arms and funds intact; to exploit a possible split within the FLN, between Ben Khedda's moderate "pro-Western" faction and

Ben Bella's revolutionary-minded entourage; to have something to show his fellow *pieds noirs* to dissuade them from leaving; to carve out his own future in a new, independent Algeria.

To do these things, he would have to sue for at least temporary peace. He turned first to Abderrahmane Farès, the dapper round little Kabyle who presided over the provisional executive, as the logical channel to the FLN. Susini saw nothing contradictory about this step. He and the OAS had always claimed that they felt no hatred for the Moslems, and they cited the title of Jean Brune's book on Algeria, *Cette Haine qui ressemble à l'amour,* as the best summing-up of both sides' dual attitude (which did not, of course, prevent either from killing the other off). Long before the OAS, in the thick of war, the French Army had cultivated contacts, some secret, some not so secret, with the FLN, the aim always being a political deal to end the fighting. Susini regarded his current overtures as an extension of these earlier, military contacts.*

Farès, at any rate, promptly agreed to meet him. On May 18 Susini drove out to the quiet little village of L'Alma, twenty miles from Algiers, and a preliminary, unpublicized conversation be-

---

* Susini busied himself simultaneously with two other ambitious projects. The first was a scheme to set Degueldre free, and it can only be appreciated in light of Susini's steadfast admiration for the Delta chief; no similar escape plan was undertaken on Salan's behalf.

In early May, Susini earmarked $400,000 from OAS funds to finance the operation. Degueldre was to be poisoned (with his knowledge), then spirited away during the transfer from his cell to the prison infirmary, the one moment an action of this sort was possible in the case of a "maximum-security" prisoner. Several Paris gangsters were hired as intermediaries to offer guards at Santé Prison bribes of up to $80,000 apiece to relax their vigilance at the critical moment; they were also offered sets of false identity papers so that they could leave France immediately afterward. In mid-May, Nicole Gardy, Degueldre's mistress, arrived in Paris with a seventeen-man commando of Delta gunmen. For some reason, however, the funds were not transferred in time, and the guards were replaced by unbribable *gardes mobiles.* As a result, nothing came of the escape plan.

Susini gave the same commando a second assignment—an assassination attempt upon de Gaulle. The idea was to station a marksman using a rifle equipped with telescopic sights on a balcony of the Hotel Bristol, which stands only a few hundred yards up the Rue du Fabourg St.-Honoré from the Élysée Palace. The upper balconies enjoy an enfilade view of the street, and a marksman would have no difficulty picking off the occupant of an official open car. De Gaulle often used this route to return to the Élysée Palace.

An OAS militant betrayed this plan to the police, who collared the entire commando on May 22. The arrests frustrated what Susini described as the "best-organized assassination attempt against de Gaulle." It had been scheduled for the following day.

tween the two men occurred. This first contact was promising. Susini set forth the OAS's terms for a truce, Farès agreed to fly to Tunis to sound out the FLN. They initiated a draft protocol "subject to amendment," then clasped and embraced each other, Mediterranean-style. To prove his good faith—and indirectly show off the Organization's remaining strength—Susini tipped off Farès about an explosive charge imbedded in the walls of the Rocher Noir compound. Security patrols scurried to the spot, and indeed found plastique in the concrete; however, the threat was more spectacular than real, since Roger Caruana, a *pied noir* building contractor and one of Degueldre's aides, had omitted to add detonators to the charge.

Susini concurrently telephoned Jacques Chevallier, Algiers' former mayor, and appealed to him to exercise his good offices. In the mid-Fifties, Chevallier had carried out an energetic low-income housing program and sought to liberalize the city's municipal administration; unlike most *pieds noirs*, he retained considerable popularity in the Moslems' eyes as a sincere moderate pledged to peaceful coexistence between the two races. This could be invaluable when hard negotiations with the FLN began; Salan, months before, had tried to avail himself of the former mayor's political luster but had run into a polite refusal. This time—no doubt because he received unofficial encouragement from the Gaullist government—Chevallier, who was in Paris, agreed to serve as mediator. This brought a third man upon the scene: Jean-Marie Tiné, a *pied noir* industrialist and one of Chevallier's close friends, who likewise held liberal views uncharacteristic of the socially prominent milieu to which he belonged.*

Persuaded of the urgent need for a truce, Chevallier and Tiné flew into Algiers on May 26, saw Susini, then three days later lunched with Farès. They were taken aback by his eagerness to make a deal with the OAS, almost at any cost. Susini's demands at this stage were not modest: he wanted the referendum postponed and the creation of a seven-man National Directory, consisting of four FLN and three OAS members, to wield supreme authority over the provisional executive. The European community was to have a right of veto over all measures it considered harmful to its

---

* Tiné held the Coca-Cola concession for Algiers. In reprisal for his liberal stand, the *pieds noirs* undertook a boycott of Coca-Cola, just as they had previously boycotted Brigitte Bardot's films.

interests. A pact was to be concluded between Moslems and *pieds noirs*, represented respectively by the FLN and OAS—"between Algerians," as Susini liked to put it—which would bypass the Évian agreement and the French government. In return, Susini pledged OAS support for the new Algerian Republic.

An incurable wheeler and dealer, Farès urged his two visitors to trust his negotiating skill. He described the draft protocol he had initiated at L'Alma as being really a "basis for discussion." He had the backing of President Ben Khedda and several ministers in the Algerian Provisional Government, he claimed, and the *force locale*. Once negotiations with the OAS were successfully concluded—it would take a few days, at most—he would settle the Ben Bella problem.

Chevallier and Tiné thought Farès sincere, at least in his hope of playing a major role in reconciling the two enemy organizations; and his arguments were shrewder than they may have seemed at first glance. Susini by all accounts was ready to yield on a number of points in exchange for a face-saving agreement with the FLN. But on the other hand, Farès' apparent desire to use his position as a stepping-stone to the presidency of the new Algerian Republic left the two *pied noir* mediators with the uneasy feeling that considerable misunderstanding and mischief could arise out of the secret talks. Farès, moreover, seemed out of his league with OAS revolutionaries and gunmen.

As if aware of these misgivings, Farès that very day sent Susini a set of counterproposals "better suited to current circumstances," as he diplomatically phrased it. The notion of a Directory was discarded; so was the appointment of OAS members to the provisional executive; but Farès otherwise promised an enormous amount, notably an amnesty (in which all activists were vitally interested), a special status for the three cities of Algiers, Oran and Bône, where *pieds noirs* were predominant, and the incorporation of European units—a euphemism for the Deltas—into the *force locale* to maintain order.

Almost as soon as Farès had made this offer, Dr. Chawki Mostefai, a nationalist leader who spoke for the FLN with far more authority, issued a denial to newspapermen that secret talks were underway between the two organizations. Mostefai was in good faith; Farès had made commitments without informing him or obtaining Tunis's specific approval.

The denial created an uproar within the OAS. Had Farès tricked them to gain time? Without much conviction, Susini sought to placate the nervous Deltas. In truth, he had likewise overextended himself—by pinning too many hopes on Farès and by exaggerating his own backing within the Organization. Broizat and Gardes, to be sure, favored a negotiated truce; but Gardy disagreed violently, as did Argoud, who, from far-off West Germany, urged the OAS to attack Rocher Noir come what may! Godard forbore from expressing flat opposition, but showed no enthusiasm for the talks; French Algeria's fate as such interested him less than the defeat of the Gaullist government.

Aware of—or at any rate, suspecting—these divergencies within each camp, Chevallier and Tiné wondered with growing skepticism whether an agreement, though duly negotiated and signed, could be made to stick.

But if no truce were concluded, Algiers lay at the Deltas' mercy.

Colonel Henry Dufour arrived in Oran clandestinely. Dufour, former commander of the now-disbanded 1st Foreign Legion Paratroop Regiment, was serving—under a cloud of official distrust—with a French infantry brigade at Offenburg, West Germany. Here Military Security kept an eye on him—though, it developed, not a very close eye.

The Army's distrust dated back to Barricades Week in early 1960, when Dufour, whose activist ideas were notorious, had failed—deliberately, some charged—to bring his paratroopers to the support of the hard-pressed gendarmes under attack by European civilians; for this he had been bawled out by de Gaulle himself. Then, during the December 1960 *pied noir* demonstration, expecting a putsch to occur, he had made off with the regimental flag and stayed with local activists; when he returned crestfallen to his post several days later, he was placed under temporary arrest, before being transferred out of Algeria.

A willful but first-rate soldier, a jaunty officer respected and liked by his men, Dufour for more than a year now had hesitated about what course of action to follow; his sympathies went to the OAS, but he balked at open rebellion.

Then in April he received a letter from Salan, shortly before the latter's arrest, which painted a thoroughly gloomy picture of the situation in Algiers. This was followed by a second letter from Gardy, who hinted that three Foreign Legion regiments would be disposed to rise provided the colonel marched at their head. Dufour thereupon did what in others would have seemed utterly paradoxical. He chose this moment to desert. The desperate straits in which the Organization found itself at this late date did not deter him. On the contrary, they spurred him to kick over the traces. An impulsive, generous and straightforward man, he felt duty-bound to come to the aid of his beleaguered comrades in arms.

He obtained leave to visit his mother in Dijon, traveled instead to Paris, and through circuitous underground channels finally reached Oran. The OAS happily announced his entry into the movement's ranks.

His arrival alarmed Katz and gratified the *Oranais*, who expected the Foreign Legion to rise in Dufour's name. Dufour himself was convinced that, militarily, the notion of an Oran redoubt was feasible. The 1st Foreign Legion Infantry Regiment, a hotbed of activist feeling, was entrenched at Sidi bel Abbès. There was very little inclination here, among either Legionnaires or civilian inhabitants, to submit tamely to a Moslem takeover. But even the most bellicose officers set conditions for an eventual revolt: Oran must be defended tooth and nail, as though it were indeed a second Stalingrad; Europeans must be ready to fight to the last bullet; an independent Republic must be proclaimed.

With time running out and the *pieds noirs* showing signs of increasing lassitude, the chances of these conditions being filled were virtually nil. Dufour finally recognized this. As the second-ranking military man in the Oran Organization under Gardy, he drove to Algiers to seek support for the redoubt. Susini replied that he was agreeable to continuing the struggle, instead of negotiating with the FLN, if Dufour gave his word of honor as a soldier that the Foreign Legion would rise.

Dufour sprang to his feet, stood at attention and said, "The Legion? Here it is." And he made a disparaging sound.

"Then don't waste my time," answered Susini.

And so, although much was said and whispered about a redoubt, and many in France and even within the FLN thought it could succeed, first militarily, then politically, the idea died stillborn.

To this extent, Dufour's quixotic desertion had served no purpose. Among some disappointed *pieds noirs*, his stock fell in consequence. But he remained a key figure in the Oran OAS, a moderate element who counterbalanced Gardy's fanaticism.

By the sixth day of the trial, the press still unanimously believed that Salan would be found guilty, condemned to death and marched before a firing squad, although not all editorialists agreed that he should be. In spite of the government's best efforts to limit the trial's purview, charges and countercharges flew about Gaullist Algerian policy. At times, Salan and the OAS seemed to drown in the torrent of opinion about colonialization and integration. The Paris weekly *L'Express*, with its habit of seeking out a boldly fresh approach to the day's news, proclaimed: "De Gaulle is on trial . . . and History is the jury whose verdict is appealed to." This was pompous, but as events would demonstrate, close to the mark.

The gradual, subtle transformation of the trial from a criminal to a political one was the work of Salan's brilliant lawyer, Jean-Louis Tixier-Vignancour, inveterate defender of right-wing causes, a star performer at the bar, a hard-bitten and cagey veteran of courtroom skirmishes. He is a tight-knit, medium-sized man with an iron-gray crew cut and an intricate, mobile face as complicated as a road map, on which wrinkles and folds diverge and intersect unpredictably; but above all, he is a voice—a deep, vibrant, assertive, domineering voice, audible behind shut doors, that is squandered on anything less than a jury. It is a redoubtable voice, and to this superlative asset he adds, like bitters in a cocktail, a careful dash of hokum.

After citing one hundred thirty-two witnesses and being rebuffed by Chief Justice Charles Bornet, who said that he would decide whom to call "if their testimony appeared indispensable," Tixier-Vignancour summoned a total of sixty-three defense witnesses. Many were outstanding personalities in French life; there were generals and colonels galore, senators and deputies, and the widows of France's two illustrious World War II marshals, Leclerc and de Lattre de Tassigny. Practically none had been directly involved in the putsch, and all, of course, piously disclaimed a connection with the OAS, though they expressed sympathy for the way in which it was born and fought. Tens of thousands of words benumbed judges and spectators in the uncomfortable courtroom. One reporter wrote that it was "like wandering through a tunnel without end."

The witnesses expressed esteem for Salan, said agreeable things about his past record and noted understanding of his distress over the turn of events ever since Indochina. Salan, they said, had not betrayed the Army, he embodied its finest traditions. Not all on the witness stand were dull. A professor of political economy made the point that if this were solely a criminal trial, Salan should have been hauled up before the Court of Assizes in Algiers and judged by a jury of laymen. Dr. Georges Salan, the accused's brother, Gaullist and steadfast opponent of *Algérie française,* whose office in Nîmes OAS *plastiqueurs* had attacked as one of their first targets, made a considerable impression when he refused to denounce his older brother. "We are not that sort of family," he said simply. This did not get to the heart of the problem, but it undeniably created a ripple of feeling in the prisoner's favor. So did the testimony of Father Pascal, a Franciscan monk and former Army chaplain. Salan, under whom he had served in the 14th Infantry Division during World War II, had been chary, he said, of wasting his troops' lives and even the Germans'. And far from being a schemer, he had always been lucid and forthright in times of panic. "I understand him," the priest said briefly, "but cannot explain him to you."

Then General Maurice Valluy, one of the French Army's leading strategists, rose and said with genuine sorrow: "I wonder how we ever reached this point." Here, for once, a witness measured the scope of the tragedy, the *malaise* that had affected first the French Army in the field, then successively the *pieds noirs* and all France; this contribution was offset by the ludicrously one-sided testimony of others, like Father Louis Delarue, another Army chaplain, sixteen years with paratroop regiments in Indochina and Algeria, who had absorbed the paras' outlook more than the Church's. Brimming over with admiration for Salan, the priest insisted on a Christian's legitimate duty and right to fly to the aid of the oppressed. It turned out, however, that this concept was limited to Europeans who supported French Algeria; for when the public prosecutor questioned him about OAS attempts to finish off Yves Le Tac, a Gaullist, on a hospital sickbed, Delarue retorted: "Christian charity is all well and good, but justice first."

Throughout these six days of hearings, Tixier-Vignancour and the three other defense lawyers diligently mounted their attack, mostly by innuendo. Why, for instance, had *pieds noirs'* "love" for de Gaulle changed to "hatred"? How could the *barbouzes* operate in Algiers without government help?* Had not prosecution witnesses once proclaimed the "sacred right" to insurrection in defense of French Algeria? Former Justice Minister François Mitterand and former premier Michel Debré were called to the stand, in connection with the 1957 bazooka plot against Salan, in a transparent effort to pin the blame for this earlier violence on the Gaullists when they themselves were seeking power. Tixier-Vignancour growled and rasped, his robes flew about, he paced up and down, gave the prosecution lessons in grammar, mercilessly browbeat and heckled witnesses when he thought he could get away with it.

As defense testimony drew to an end, a general feeling existed that he had rendered one of his best courtroom performances on Salan's behalf, that in fact it had been a fair if unenlightening trial. If it had not been a great trial, it was due to Salan's silence and everybody's determination to beat about the bush, ignoring what was still happening in Algiers.

What happened now differed slightly from the schedule of events foreseen by the government. On Monday, May 21, through a source he declines to identify, Tixier-Vignancour learned of one judge's comment that the effect on the bench might have been more positive if the defense had stuck solely to the testimony of three witnesses— Salan's brother, General Valluy and Father Pascal.

On the basis of this unverifiable remark and slim hope, Tixier-Vignancour quickly requested and obtained the court's permission to put off his final plea by twenty-four hours. He spent the next day recasting his appeal, concentrating on an exegesis of what the three had said.

The public prosecutor, André Gavalda, was suffering from an attack of sciatica, and he delivered his summing-up seated, on the final day of the trial, May 23. In the earthy accent of southwestern France from which he springs, Gavalda spoke for two hours. It was a harsh, unremitting attack. He spoke of the OAS's "sly infil-

---

* The defense sought to stage a potentially embarrassing confrontation (for the government) between Ailleret, who said there were *barbouzes* in Algeria, and Morin, who said there was no such thing as "parallel police" in the territory. Under oath, Morin said carefully, "I'm not saying there were not men who fought directly against the OAS's killers; at all events, this did not come under the police." The bench turned down the request for a confrontation.

tration" of the schoolroom and the parish church, its attempt to "overthrow the government and put I don't know what in its place." He quoted Blaise Pascal, who wrote that "civil war is the worst of all evils."

After reviewing the OAS's obscure bloody history, Gavalda rose to his feet at the end, for the peroration, and then it was to accuse Salan of "wanting to be spared, but you spared nothing," and to make the damaging point that Salan had refused to call off further bloodshed. Gavalda waved aside all possible extenuating circumstances, yet oddly did not demand the death penalty in so many words. It fell short of this by a hair's breadth. "The only penalty I demand," he rumbled, "is an irrevocable (*irréversible*) penalty." Shriven of euphemism, the meaning was perfectly clear; yet the nuance appeared odd, in view of the prosecution's tone until now.

Then he wondered aloud whether Salan might not, through his obstinate silence, have forfeited God's mercy. The reaction in court was unfavorable. This was going too far, it was widely felt—Gavalda's preoccupation should properly be with human justice, not divine pardon. Salan, at any rate, shot back: "Dieu *vous* garde."

Then Tixier-Vignancour addressed the judges. His manner caused general surprise by its restraint; there was a striking absence of the oratorical fireworks with which he was associated; at times, indeed, he was subdued. Speaking in a soft voice and shying away from all frontal criticism of the government, he undertook a description of the Algerian political situation in which Salan, an honest soldier carrying out orders from above, had become entrapped. He implied that he was attempting to delineate not *the* truth but *a* truth. He appealed for mercy in the month of May, "*le printemps de Marie*." It was a happy inspiration, and he told this writer he had found it in a phrase of surrealist painter André Breton, who observed about Easter: "*Je hais cette grande croix noire jetée au travers du printemps* [I hate that huge black cross flung across the spring]." All told, Tixier-Vignancour spoke for three hours and ten minutes. It was a beautifully controlled plea.

Notwithstanding, no one expected it to make the slightest difference. The same judges, after all, had, for lesser offenses, condemned Jouhaud to death; they could not now very well step down from their earlier position.

The judges retired to deliberate.

At about 9 P.M. Salan dined with Tixier-Vignancour and his other lawyers in a basement cell of the Palais—the same cell where Pierre Laval had once been incarcerated. There was no doubt in Salan's mind that he was going to be sentenced to death. He reassured his defenders that he would face up to a firing squad without faltering.

Tixier-Vignancour continued to display confidence. "There was only one optimist at the trial—myself," he recalled later. Maître Bernard Le Coroller, a colleague, took him to task privately for cruelly bolstering Salan's morale when the cause was obviously lost. Tixier-Vignancour retorted there was a difference between the "professional optimism" any lawyer shows before his client, and the "reasonable optimism" he felt at dinner.

The judges remained closeted for two and a half hours. It was a half hour before midnight when they filed into the Salle des Assises and the presiding judge, Charles Bornet, began to read the verdict.

Bornet showed emotion, and as he tripped over the words, immediately the spectators knew something was up. To all six questions put to the court, one after another, which included a final, all-important one about extenuating circumstances that changed the import of the five preceding queries, he answered Yes.

It meant that Salan's life was saved.

Pandemonium of extraordinary dimensions broke out before Bornet could finish. Rightist spectators shouted encouragement and congratulations, they roared the "Marseillaise," they vaulted over benches and milled about the lawyers. They interpreted the verdict —accurately—as a vindication of the OAS and an unparalleled blow at de Gaulle. In their near-hysterical relief and joy, they overlooked the fact that Salan *was* found guilty on five counts and sentenced to life imprisonment; this seemed a trifle compared to what they had dreaded. The judges were so perturbed, so conscious of the judgment's spectacular nature—salutary or scandalous, according to one's views—that they neglected to confiscate Salan's property. Tixier-Vignancour swooned momentarily. In the tumult only one person retained complete, military control of himself—the defendant. At the end no more was known of his innermost feelings than at the start.

The judges' vote was and remains secret. At the outset, was it seven for the death penalty and two for outright acquittal, as Tixier-Vignancour believes? French law requires a simple majority among the judges to decide the vote. Those who argued in favor of extenuating circumstances became very persuasive. Did it then become five to four in favor of the sixth Yes? There was speculation that the shuffling of judges, the replacement of General Roger Gardet by General Max Gelée, who had refused to sit on the Jouhaud trial, transformed a progovernment majority into a minority. There was speculation, too, that the judges had condemned Jouhaud assuming that he would be reprieved, but that, since they could not make this assumption in Salan's case, they had moderated their judgment. However, this is slick reasoning and appears contrived. There were widespread rumors that Professor Louis Pasteur Vallery-Radot, eminent scientist and member of the Legion of Honor's governing board, threw his weight behind a crucial vote. It is impossible to say with absolute certainty. It *is* certain that several factors contributed to the bombshell verdict: for one, Salan's muteness in court spared him from identification with the horrors taking place in Algiers; for another, the obscurity that enveloped the bazooka plot, when Salan himself almost fell victim to the activists.

But above all, it was Tixier-Vignancour's handling of the defense, a triumph of shrewdness and courtroom intuition, that saved his client. That night, the lawyer exclaimed to a radio reporter, "This is the greatest trial of my life! I have become a Frenchman again!"

But at the Élysée Palace de Gaulle, who had just bid farewell to a state visitor, Mauritania's President Moktar Ould Daddah, blanched with awesome anger when an aide brought him the verdict. De Gaulle's wrath is often deliberate and artful, but this time the explosion was unpremeditated. Echoing Françoise Giroud's words in *L'Express*, he roared, "Those imbeciles didn't try Salan . . . they tried de Gaulle!"

24

The Flight

LONG BEFORE daybreak, they arrived at the pier with their baggage, and saw the ghostly white passenger ships moored to the quay, the *Kairouan, Cazalet, Ville de Tunis, El Djezair*. The fortunate few with tickets for the next sailing went aboard; the others remained disconsolate on the cement docks, awaiting their turn, which might come the next day or the day after.

The heat by midmorning became terrific. It was reflected from the basin in shimmering layers. Unshielded from the sun, men, women, children and pets prowled after water; but finding it was a problem: no facilities had been foreseen for so many. The noise and stench were overwhelming. The flight of the *pieds noirs* from Algeria had begun.*

At Maison Blanche airport, families camped overnight in fields adjacent to the runways or curled up on the tile floors of the waiting hall, to make sure their turn would not be lost the following day. Caravelles and DC-4s took off at intervals, but there never seemed to be space enough to take all aboard.

---

* After the Évian agreement, a newly created French government service, the Commission Générale aux Rapatriés, estimated that 150,000 *pieds noirs* would leave Algeria in orderly fashion during the next six months. Secretary of State for Repatriates Robert Boulin had reason to rue this figure later. By late May, Boulin said he expected 300,000 to leave. Even this figure fell far short of the mark; by June, 400,000 had departed.

In Oran, getting from the city to La Senia airport was risky. The road passed through Moslem neighborhoods, where signs declared, "FLN checkpoint." Here, Europeans suspected of participation in the OAS were sometimes forcibly removed from their cars, led off and never seen again.

By the end of May the *pieds noirs* were in full flight. Women, children, elderly people, followed by their menfolk, boarded ship and plane, first by the scores, then by hundreds, then thousands. There was no holding them back. Cattle boats, trawlers, motor barges and seagoing tugs crowded with refugees sailed as tides and winds dictated for the nearby Balearic Islands, the southern coast of Spain, the French Mediterranean cargo ports of Sète and Port Vendres, Marseilles. On some days there were eight thousand departures, but the figure rose as high as fifteen thousand. One of the biggest mass migrations in post-World War II history was now taking place out of the Algerian ports.*

Many of those massed at dock or airport had cleared out of isolated villages and plantations in the interior on a day's notice, at the Army's urgent behest, as the mood among the Moslems shifted and grew dangerous. Villagers and field workers whom the Europeans had known all their lives were powerless. Moslems no one knew—strangers, guerrilla fighters who turned up overnight from the *djebels*—gave orders to requisition and imprison. Appeals to the French Army to safeguard persons and property proved useless. Troops were under orders not to intervene; according to Évian, maintenance of order was entrusted exclusively to the Moslem *force locale*. So the Europeans began to evacuate the Hauts Plateaux, then the Mitidja plain and Oranie. Some drove off stiff and proud, heads held high, convinced of their innate superiority to the Arabs, as had been their ancestors upon arriving in the harsh, broiling Algerian hinterland; others left heartbroken, miserable and in a panic, their goods stored in their homes awaiting the inevitable looters. The old were the hardest-hit, uprooted, uncomprehending, experiencing an unsought transition from country to city, from Algeria to France. Many waited until the last moment to decide to leave—some had never set foot in France; others were returning for the first time since 1914.

---

* Of the total *pied noir* population of one million, 850,000 are estimated to have left. When India and Pakistan were formed in 1947, ten million persons were displaced.

The cities were bottlenecks through which the refugees flowed to the harbors. Along Rue Michelet in Algiers, shopwindow signs said "Annual Closing for Summer Vacation"; they misled no one. Schools were empty, public transportation was idle, long lines waited outside steamship company offices.* In European neighborhoods, young Moslems drew up lists of vacated apartments. Geneviève Borgen said the most characteristic sound in some streets was the noise of hammering, as families hastily nailed crates together.†

At the dockside, the departing *pied noirs* sheltered together, half expecting Moslem bands to burst through the gates and slaughter them or the OAS to bombard the port in a show of displeasure. Brand-new cars, refrigerators and washing machines gleamed in the sun, abandoned for lack of available hold space. Dogs and cats straying in search of food were everywhere; many, of every breed and size, were abandoned.

When the exodus showed no sign of abating, the French Red Cross and Catholic Welfare began to provide meals, tents, cots and medical treatment for the old and infirm and pregnant women.

While the *pieds noirs* waited, they talked. Most had backed the OAS through ignorance and for lack of other political outlets; now they suspected Susini and Perez of transferring funds abroad and leaving the entire European population in the lurch to face the Moslems' wrath. Myths had shattered one after another in quick succession during the spring: the Europeans' immunity from attack by the French Army; the OAS's invincibility; Salan's ability to perform miracles.

But another reason for flight went unuttered—the *pieds noirs'* own lack of total commitment to the defense of their homeland. The battle of the OAS was predicated on the European population's willingness to stand and fight and take its chances, but by 1962 the *pieds noirs* were skeptical and, above all, emotionally exhausted; they had lived through a succession of extraordinary experiences, from the exalting heights of May 1958 to the somber depression of the siege of Bab el Oued. Perhaps, from the start, they had been secretly convinced, in their innermost selves, that their cause was

---

* On May 23, recognizing the inevitable, the OAS for the first time had lifted its ban on departures. In Oran, a tract predicting a "violent, terrible and definitive battle" said women and children must be spared, but it strictly prohibited the departure of all men between the ages eighteen and sixty, and said those who violated the order would be considered deserters.

† In her book, *Journée calme . . . marquée par . . .*

doomed? This unavowed conviction is said to have motivated their panic-stricken cruelty and their strident pledges never to quit their native soil. Whether true or not at the beginning, this great, unspoken fear certainly became true as the spring drew to an end that year. And the alternatives no longer seemed altogether as black as before. The French government was offering them some financial assistance to help readjust. The prospect of unfriendly surroundings, grayer skies and material hardships was not enticing, but seemed decidedly preferable to the risks attached to sticking it out in independent Algeria. So the *pieds noirs* cracked and fled, in a fast-spreading stampede.

It need not have happened that way, cooperation and coexistence with the Moslem majority were possible at the outset, but required foresight, intelligence and cool heads. Instead, the *pieds noirs* had badly miscalculated de Gaulle's determination, the Moslems' strength and their own essential weakness. But as they massed on deck, hot, irritable and nervous, as the overcrowded ships cleared the breakwater and set course for Marseilles, they felt little regret or remorse for what could have been; their predominating emotion was resentment and apprehension, *"Algérie française"* lay bitter on their lips, a collapsed world, and they said to each other: "We are not repatriates but refugees, because we are not going to France but leaving it."

Susini reigned temporarily supreme. As the Terror in revolutionary Paris saw Robespierre and Saint-Just accumulate power by default through the elimination and disappearance of rivals, so a process of roughly the same sort occurred within Algiers' OAS. No one rose to challenge Jean-Jacques, the onetime student-association president, because his potential rivals, the colonels in particular, had never shouldered the burden of thinking out the situation; because he was glib, while they, politically, were almost inarticulate.

After munching sandwiches and catching a few hours' sleep at the Villa des Arcades, Susini passed all his waking hours, it seemed, racing from one urgent rendezvous to the next, accompanied by what remained of the OAS's general staff: Gardes, burned-out and aged, hair uncut, skinny "as a wolf," a study (to those who recalled the crisp colonel of Psychological Action days) in moral decay; Nocetti, unremarkable chief of the surviving Deltas; and Roger

Caruana, the *pied noir* building contractor, who all of a sudden had Susini's ear because he provided a direct channel to the Paris mediators, Chevallier and Tiné. It was a mediocre team compared to the constellation of bestarred generals and dedicated, ambitious civilians of a year before.

The fact that power had slipped into this new group's hands foretold the approaching end. Even Susini was beginning to have enough of Algiers' strong smell of defeat.

And indeed the white seaport at this moment incarnated nothing less than wholesale defeat. In the Jewish quarter around Rue de la Lyre, the still desolation was eloquent—a succession of looted, bombed-out stores whose proprietors had vanished. Elsewhere, a few merchants remained open, clearing out old stocks in an air of listlessness and indifference. Women wandered dazed through the scorched, acid-smelling streets, mindless of the sporadic dull boom of mortars and the tinkling of glass. Black OAS slogans splotched on bullet-marked stone walls no longer seemed relevant. Mounds of garbage grew higher; the Arab street cleaners had long since fled for their lives.

Hiding out somewhere in Algiers, Perez waited. It was May 31. There was still no break in the semisecret truce discussions, and time was growing short. Perez had set his own deadline at a meeting with Susini four days earlier: negotiations with the FLN must be concluded or broken off by June 1, to allow the Deltas a full thirty days before the referendum to destroy and withdraw in the event that no other solution was applicable. He had added a further condition: the provisional executive must recruit 12,000 Europeans under OAS command—more than half the *force locale's* total number—to help maintain order. The doctor did not really expect this exorbitant demand to be met. Placing little faith in Susini's contacts with Farès, his impulse was to get on with the business of total destruction.

Perez nurtured few illusions; ammunition was running low, the Organization was crumbling—in his own words, it was reduced to a "gigantic bluff." As far as he was concerned, the OAS had died as a military force on April 20, the date of Salan's arrest. But it still possessed a well-emplaced 60-mm. mortar in firing condition, and two hundred fifty shells that could wreak massive damage on Algiers' Moslem quarters—as well as a firm promise from European employees to blow up oil and gas installations in the Sahara at a given signal.

Perez's ideas reflected his earnest and violent simplicity. If serious guarantees could be obtained from Ben Khedda's Provisional Government, so much the better; but failing this, Algeria's economic infrastructure would be left in ashes. He planned, first, administrative sabotage—the destruction of government buildings and plants —then, as the last Europeans withdrew, generalized sabotage of personal property—"so that the Arabs would find nothing when they arrived in Algiers, not even faucets in the kitchen sinks."

To the victor would belong the ruins.

But on the afternoon of May 31, two pieces of bad news jarred him, almost simultaneously. Police had just arrested Nocetti during a raid; then he learned—and it struck him as unbelievable—that the Organization had ordered a unilateral truce effective that very evening, in Susini's and his own name, prior to a new meeting with Farès. There were no FLN guarantees in return, and he had not been informed beforehand of the decision.

In a confidential report an OAS colonel had once written: "Pride is the first thing that comes to mind in defining Jean-Claude Perez. His Spanish blood on both sides has marked and inhibited him." That evening, in an ominously restrained mood, Perez sought out Susini and asked him point-blank who had ordered the truce.

"Caruana," retorted Susini coldly.

Several hours later Perez put the same question to Caruana, who replied: "Susini."

The doctor was livid with anger. There was no way of getting a truthful answer, he concluded; and it was too late to recall the order.

In fact, it was Caruana who, at Chevallier's urging, had ordered all further attacks suspended as long as negotiations were underway.

The street scene that met Perez's eye illustrated what the truce's immediate consequences were likely to be. Reassured by the after-dark silence, in place of the dull boom of plastique, Algiers' remaining *pieds noirs* were assembled at café terraces; their will to fight appeared to be drowning in toast after toast to celebrate the end of the explosions. It seemed to Perez that the suspension of hostilities stripped the OAS of its last bargaining weapon.

Always overprompt to react, he might have been expected to take no notice of the truce order and implement his scorched-earth policy then and there. Significantly, he did nothing of the sort; his sole reaction was to summon six Delta chiefs the following morning to an apartment in La Redoute, where he told them that he would boycott further negotiations with Farès, and—unless the FLN provided a positive answer by June 4 to the OAS's proposals—withdraw his "revolutionary potential" from Algeria and pursue the underground war from a foreign base. In Perez's mouth this meant Spain, and "revolutionary potential" alluded to O.R.O.'s secret archives and Delta gunmen still personally loyal to him. It marked the first time an OAS leader had spoken so openly of retreat. The truth was that Perez's power within the Organization had virtually evaporated, and he had little choice. Moreover, a new danger threatened from another quarter: during the day, carrying out a concerted plan, gendarmes had raided one O.R.O. hideout after another in quick succession. Perez was certain that he had been betrayed.* From this point on, he moved nightly, on the run, expecting at any moment to fall victim either to the police or to Susini's long-standing antipathy; and the latter could be as deadly as the former.

On that same afternoon of June 1, police patrols carefully screened all motor traffic approaching El Bordj, Chevallier's family estate on the slopes of El Biar, the site chosen for the second meeting between Susini and Farès because of its relatively secluded character.

Shortly before 3 P.M., two cars drove up.

From the first stepped Farès, rotund and self-important, darting heavy-lidded, suspicious glances all about. Chevallier and Tiné, his hosts, thought of him more than ever as a Levantine merchant with a foot in both worlds—Arab and European.

From the second alighted Susini, pinched and cadaverously white, followed by Gardes and Caruana.

The negotiators trooped into Chevallier's sun-drenched study. Rival, machine-gun-toting OAS and FLN bodyguards spread out through the park; eventually, tiring of their work, they would set their weapons to rest against the estate's banana trees and chat peaceably together.

* Perez subsequently accused Nocetti, arrested that day, of giving his address to the police.

Inside, Susini spoke of the OAS's "good faith" in suspending terrorism and casually mentioned that it could resume on a moment's notice if no satisfactory agreement were worked out in the next few days. The Organization, he said, was still awaiting Tunis's reply.

Farès—in spite of Mostefai's public rebuff earlier in the week—exuded confidence. He would have a favorable answer within a week at most: as soon as the current plenary session of the National Council of the Algerian Revolution ended in Tripoli, a high-ranking FLN minister would fly to Rocher Noir and ratify the draft protocol with the OAS. Then Farès and Susini would make separate peace announcements. This would be followed by an appeal to hundreds of thousands of Moslems and *pieds noirs* to attend a reconciliation rally at the Forum, symbolically putting an end to seven years' hostility. The *pieds noirs* would even form a political party to defend their interests and cooperate with the new Algerian Republic.* In the midst of this verbal euphoria, Gardes briefly sounded a sour note: the *force locale* must henceforth, he demanded, sport red berets—the paratroopers' red berets associated with the torture-ridden Battle of Algiers—to win the population's respect. This incredible suggestion was turned down unanimously. Gardes by this time struck Tiné as being "no longer a soldier but a wreck from whom oozed moral and physical fatigue . . . the few times when he tried to speak, Susini unceremoniously cut him off"—an incarnation of the OAS's own tremendous weariness.

As it grew dark outside over Algiers' hills, the meeting broke up. Farès and Susini clapped each other on the back, promised to meet again on June 4, picked up their bodyguards and drove off in their respective directions down the steep roads. Chevallier and Tiné watched them go in silence. Nothing, really, had been settled.

The events of the next few days demonstrate the OAS's slipping hold on the situation. While Farès for the first time openly acknowledged that talks *were* taking place, and de Gaulle privately gave

---

* The name tentatively chosen for this party was RUAC (Rassemblement pour l'Unité de l'Algérie par la Coopération). Farès saw it as consisting of "respectable elements" of the *pied noir* community, and he urged Chevallier to head it. But Chevallier noted that the existence of an all-European party could be misconstrued as a new form of segregation. When the FLN ominously warned against the formation of a "racist party," the idea collapsed.

his assent to them,* Susini awaited Tunis's reply. He suspected that sharp differences of opinion within the Algerian Provisional Government about the advisability of dealing with the OAS must be delaying matters, and this surmise scarcely reassured him. He was playing an extremely tricky game that could backfire disastrously; he realized that if his gambit failed, Godard and Perez would end his temporary supremacy inside the Organization, liquidate him if necessary, and pour two hundred and fifty mortar shells on the Casbah.

As one day, then another, passed in silence, Susini's impatience became acute. His nervousness betrayed itself in a new pirate broadcast. In the absence of a positive reply from Tunis, the speaker warned, the OAS would "resume freedom of action as of zero hour, June 5."

June 5 came and went, and there was still no reply. A new meeting with Farès took place at Chevallier's house. This time there was no back-clapping or embracing—especially when Farès showed unmistakable signs of backing away from his earlier commitments.

White with fury, suspecting that he had been hoodwinked all along, Susini threatened, with as much violence as Perez, to blow up everything himself, on an Apocalyptic scale: to send rivers of ignited gasoline flowing down the Casbah's slopes; to use *pied noir* workers at the gas company to compress natural gas to the danger point, then set it on fire, annihilating Algiers; to dynamite hydroelectric dams and flood the Mitidja plain; to dispatch thirty teams of hand-picked saboteurs to wreck Algeria's harbors and airports; to blow up one hundred oil wells at Hassi Messaoud, in the desert— and to go down fighting amid the stark desolation.

All this proved too much for Farès: he stumbled out of the house aghast, without further comment. Sensing Susini's underlying desperation, Chevallier and Tiné did not take these threats lightly; they thought the OAS quite capable of carrying out part of its nihilistic program, but what could they do?

* The French cabinet was split in its attitude toward bilateral negotiations between the OAS and FLN. Algerian Affairs Minister Louis Joxe and High Commissioner Christian Fouchet reasoned that such negotiations—if they brought about a swift end to urban terrorism—were desirable, provided that basic provisions of the Évian agreement were not tampered with. Georges Pompidou, who had replaced Debré as premier, apparently took a hostile stand. De Gaulle agreed with Joxe and Fouchet.

Finally, at their repeated urging, Susini agreed to another twenty-four-hour reprieve, provided they undertook on their own responsibility—not Farès'—to get a binding reply from the FLN. Chevallier and Tiné breathed a bit easier. Undoubtedly this moment, when the threat of a holocaust loomed over Algiers, marked the apogee of the two men's mission as mediators.

There was another, unspoken reason for Susini's conciliatory attitude. He realized that systematic scorched-earth tactics, if implemented, would put an end forever to his hope of playing a role in emerging independent Algeria. His risky gambit consisted, therefore, of brandishing the threat without executing it—and preventing other, less political-minded OAS chiefs from doing so.

Consequently, during the day, he went to see Godard in his apartment on Avenue Pasteur. It was the first time the two men had seen each other in weeks.

Susini still had to take the colonel's reaction into account. He found him restive at the idea of new concessions and itching for an opportunity to fight to the very end. Susini retorted that the Deltas had few arms left and were threatened from one moment to the next with arrest by gendarmes or death by FLN bands; under the circumstances, further resistance appeared wasteful. Then, exasperated, he volunteered (if his version can be believed) to step down from command of the OAS.

"You don't know what the tricolor is," Godard snapped. "A flag is never lowered."

"I have run all kinds of risks—"

"That's open to question."

Susini observed coldly: "You're a brave man to say that now." And it was true that at this point Susini could have had almost any European in Algiers executed within hours on the strength of a brief oral order.

As they sized each other up, Gardes walked in, and it was on the hapless organizer of the Ouarsenis debacle that Godard's full wrath was vented. "How could you shake the hand of a dunghill like Tiné?" he exploded. According to Susini, although the two men were close friends they were at each other's throat before he could stop them. The incident pointed up the strain to which they were all subject now.

"Susini salaud! Susini salaud!" chanted the political inmates in Paris' Santé Prison upon learning of his negotiations with Farès.* The chant resounded along the filthy corridors.

But one prisoner whirled about in his cell and shouted to them to shut up. Susini had not betrayed a cause, he cried; there existed no other way out for the OAS. . . .

The prisoner was Degueldre.

Another person in Algiers expressed misgivings, less and less guardedly, about the negotiations underway with the FLN: Jean Sarradet, the *pied-noir student* leader whom the OAS had nearly ordered killed the winter before for insubordination.

For the preceding three months, Sarradet had, with the OAS's mixed blessings, run a hybrid political group of his own devising, the Union Générale des Travailleurs Français d'Algérie, into which Algeria's major trade-unions had theoretically fused to make common cause against a Moslem takeover. By April, Sarradet claimed the UGTA represented 450,000 *pied noir* workers in all branches of industry. He argued that the UGTA, as a legal movement uncompromised by assassination and terrorism, could usefully act as a front for the OAS in bargaining with the FLN, then become a focus for *pied noir* political activity in independent Algeria; but it could only perform this double role if it maintained a certain autonomy, to keep alive the fiction of its separate identity from the OAS. Godard and Perez grudgingly gave this line of reasoning their approval.

In fact, Sarradet promptly undertook a perilous game of the sort that had cost Leroy and Villar their lives in January. Accompanied by Anne Loesch and a band of eager *pied noir* students, he set about utilizing the UGTA not as an OAS front but as his own instrument of political power.

Informed of the Susini-Farès meetings, he pointed out to anyone who would listen that the OAS was dying and its guarantees worthless; the FLN might sign an agreement, but would be sure to repudiate it once its usefulness was over, on the grounds that the OAS did not represent the entire *pied noir* community. There was a

* "Susini the heel! Susini the heel!"

strong element of personal ambition in this; Sarradet was not above seeking to supplant Susini as the chief negotiator on the activist side. But the point he made contained a germ of truth.

Some time in mid-May, exhibiting an incredible mixture of recklessness and naïveté (and an overrated sense of his own importance), Sarradet secretly resumed contact—through a priest—with French officials at Rocher Noir. He asked for money to pay trade-union militants and his student followers, the disbanded Z Commandos; arms to defend themselves against the Deltas; and the promise of a post-independence amnesty. In return he proposed to set up the UGTA as a counterforce to the OAS. He also met secretly with two American officials: William Porter, the United States consul general in Algiers, and Bayard King, a political officer. Sarradet asked their help in obtaining an American guarantee of intervention in the event of Moslem reprisals against *pieds noirs*.

Days passed with no definite reply from Rocher Noir or the State Department. "If you want Susini and Godard killed, tell us where they are and we'll handle it for you," one of Fouchet's aides suggested. This in no way constituted the answer Sarradet wanted.

Finally he decided upon a spectacular, if essentially juvenile, gesture: he would call a press conference in Algiers, to publicize his demands and force the French authorities' hand.

On June 7, while armed students guarded the UGTA hall on Avenue Pasteur, Sarradet mounted a podium and addressed a roomful of French and foreign journalists. The taut, dark-haired student leader identified hmself as an OAS chieftain—which approximated the truth. "The OAS has lost," he declared, and appealed to all *pieds noirs* in a ringing summons to lay down their arms. *"Il est temps de déposer les armes au vestiaire,"** said Sarradet, self-consciously echoing old gangster films. The UGTA was ready to fly to Tunis to undertake direct negotiations with the FLN. He called on the French government to act as impartial mediator between the two racial communities, and idealistically proposed a new combat flag that would group the Moslem crescent, the Christian cross and the Jewish star on the same field! His plan, he added, represented the last chance of saving the *pied noir* population from catastrophe.

"Does Susini think that?" a journalist interrupted.

"I'm sure he does," replied Sarradet superbly. "He's an intelligent fellow."

---

* The best translation is: "Check your guns at the cloakroom."

Little further need be said about this press conference. Sarradet failed to understand that, less than a month before independence, the FLN had still less interest in negotiating with him than with the OAS.

Perhaps these high jinks might have made an impression on his audience, who were prepared to listen to the wildest proposals at this point, but as Sarradet spoke an enormous blast reverberated outside. Smoke began to seep into the hall. Down the street, the University of Algiers library, which housed 600,000 volumes, burned. So, in a matter of seconds, did two amphitheaters and a laboratory at the Faculty of Sciences. For the next half hour Sarradet stubbornly tried to make himself heard above the clang of firetrucks.

Within hours, an OAS pirate broadcast condemned him to death as a traitor.* But by this time Sarradet's ideas, and even his fate, counted for relatively little in the latest developments. Following the outbreak of arson on the university campus, the town hall and post office at El Biar caught fire. Two secondary schools blazed; a tax office and a wing of the Algiers Prefecture were in flames; mortar shells rained down on the Palais d'Été.

It was the OAS's answer to Tunis's silence. The scorched-earth policy had resumed in earnest. It would now take a providential man or event to save Algiers.

* Sarradet and Anne Loesch fled from Algiers after the press conference, taking a sack of arms with them, to a beach cottage owned by Sarradet's grandparents near Rocher Noir. Here, finally, the French authorities' reply to his scheme reached him: if he agreed to surrender and inform on other OAS leaders, he might benefit from extenuating circumstances before the law. Nothing came of this offer. Shortly afterward, Sarradet and Anne Loesch quietly shipped out of Algeria and settled down in France undisturbed by the police. Sarradet perished, asphyxiated by a gas leak, in December 1962.

25

The Forces of Destruction

THE PROVIDENTIAL man was Dr. Chawki Mostefai.

It was to Mostefai that Farès belatedly turned—prodded by Chevallier, Tiné and Fouchet—to extricate himself from his errors and break the deadlock. This was on June 6, hours before scorched-earth operations resumed, just as the OAS pirate broadcaster announced the collapse of bilateral truce negotiations and blamed it (unjustly) on the French government. "If we find ourselves in an impasse," the anonymous voice said, "it is because we cannot accept the Évian agreement as the sole guarantee of the European community's future. Consequently, as of tonight, the OAS resumes its freedom of action. Commandos should aim primarily at economic objectives. Further contact is forbidden at all levels with Rocher Noir officials." There was one loophole in this blood-and-thunder declaration: "A possibility still exists of negotiations between the two sides; but any future overtures, to be taken seriously, must come from official—we underline, official—representatives of the FLN."

This virtually excluded the discredited Farès, whose delaying tactics and personal ambition had exhausted everybody's patience; it was now Mostefai's turn to act, as the FLN's senior representative at Rocher Noir.

In 1954, when the Algerian rebellion began, he had been practicing medicine in Paris; he joined the nationalist movement, gave up his patients, settled in Tunis and subsequently headed the Algerian Provisional Government's permanent mission at Rabat, Morocco. Following the Évian agreement, he arrived in Algeria, assigned to the provisional executive as leader of the five-man FLN delegation. Tall, gaunt and reserved, the doctor impressed Frenchmen as one of the rare FLN leaders with a Western, practical cast of mind.

The very fact that Farès had made irresponsible commitments to the OAS came as an unwelcome revelation to Mostefai. He learned details of these commitments at the conclusion of a dinner given that night by Fouchet. For once, Mostefai's habitual self-control slipped; stiffly accusing Farès of "playing at soldier" and "treason," he declared in the presence of Fouchet, Chevallier and Tiné that he was not disposed to honor Farès' promises or bow to Susini's scorched-earth threats. The problem, unhappily, was not that simple, as the others hastened to point out: Algerian independence would inevitably be proclaimed after July 1—the referendum results left no doubt of that—but, should independence come about in the midst of total anarchy and violence, it might lead to a cancellation of short- and long-term French economic aid agreed upon at Évian. In Mostefai's view, this appeared to be the worst of all possible prospects for the new republic; if something useful could still be done to avert it, he was ready (with misgivings) to intervene—provided that, unlike Farès, he got a clear go-ahead from the FLN.

In short, the doctor agreed that evening to lend his weight to an ultimate attempt at reconciliation with the *pieds noirs*—a course of action not measurably different from Farès' efforts—but, being far more astute and experienced, Mostefai planned to attack the problem with greater circumspection and attention to form.

He lost no time. The next day, June 7, at noon, he left by plane for Tripoli, to seek an unambiguous answer from the FLN. Did it want to pursue negotiations with the OAS? Was it prepared to entrust him with a mission to that end? He flew off accompanied by a much-subdued Farès. Chevallier and Tiné did not join the party; the Europeans' presence, it was felt, would needlessly exacerbate matters.

In flight the two emissaries' Constellation developed engine trouble and made several forced landings. By the time they reached the Libyan capital, the congress of the National Council of the

Algerian Revolution, which had begun on May 27, was over and the delegations gone. The next morning the two men hastily flew back to Tunis. Here, while Farès remained penitently in the wings, Mostefai reviewed the case for a negotiated armistice with the OAS.

With independence less than three weeks off, he found the Algerian Provisional Government split in two over the problem, which accounted for its obstinate silence. Essentially, President Ben Khedda desired no contact—and certainly, no suspicion of a deal—with the crumbling Organization. The FLN bitterly blamed the French Army for allowing—through its tolerance toward the activists—the situation to degenerate to a point where such a deal was even remotely conceivable. Ben Bella's followers were still more hostile to a compromise with the OAS. Nonetheless, the problem existed: if, on dogmatic grounds, the nationalists refused all contact with Susini, they faced the prospect of a last, insane burst of sabotage, and perhaps—in Algiers' and Oran's streets—a pitched battle against suicidal Delta commandos.

Finally, after three days' cautious discussions, Mostefai won his case. Or so it seemed. The Algerian Provisional Government gave him full powers to negotiate, with the proviso (like the French government's) that there must be no tampering with the Évian agreement. Farès drew a sharp tongue-lashing and a warning to make no further unauthorized pledges. With this, the two men hastened back to Rocher Noir, where Mostefai asked for a written, up-dated résumé of the OAS's demands as the preliminary to a new meeting.

The list had no sooner been submitted than Ben Khedda, from Tunis, made a speech on June 13 that set things back where they had been at the outset. "We are witnessing a series of maneuvers aimed at sabotaging the Évian agreement by suggesting its revision to include extra guarantees for the Europeans. My government," Ben Khedda declared, "categorically excludes that possibility."

One reason for this sudden and potentially disastrous switch lay in the permanent Byzantine struggle for power within the Provisional Government; Ben Bella's influence was on the rise, Ben Khedda's was limited and he was forced to tack with prevailing winds. Accused by pro-Ben Bella forces of yielding to the "most gangrenous elements of colonialism," he had no choice but to denounce the OAS in public and repudiate any concessions beforehand. In addition, he was alarmed by Susini's latest list of demands, which included key posts for Europeans in Algeria's first independent government.*

When the text of Ben Khedda's speech began to move on the Rocher Noir teletype machine, Farès was in his office. His pudgy hands fell to his side, and he said, "This is the worst day of the negotiations." Mostefai blanched. For all his precautions, he—like Farès—had been disowned by his own side.

Within hours, the OAS voiced its disappointment. A pirate broadcaster commented with some candor: "Negotiations were underway between men of good will, in spite of de Gaulle . . . the negotiations' purpose was to fill in the blank spaces of the Évian agreement, which the *pied noir* community had no role in elaborating. . . . They were about to succeed when, to the FLN's own surprise, Ben Khedda made his declaration—there are thus two divergent forces within the Algerian Provisional Government, this may render even the Évian agreement null and void. In consequence, the high command of the secret army orders a speed-up and intensification of scorched-earth operations. . . ."

The next day, Perez's men ran amok in Algiers. They set fire to Social Security headquarters and the municipal waterworks office. Various stores burned. An explosion ripped apart the Prefecture. As walls caved in and flames shot up through the roof, jeering Europeans urged firemen to let the whole building go up in smoke.

Gloomily, Jacques Chevallier estimated there was now a five percent chance of a breakthrough before the "absolute deadline of June 15."

Once again, it was Mostefai who acted. He set out the same day to contact one nationalist leader who might still repair the damage—Belkacem Krim, the Provisional Government's vice-president, signer of the Évian agreement and one of the FLN's seven prestigious "historic chiefs" who had launched the 1954 revolt. Krim was politicking somewhere in the mountainous solitude of his native Kayblia, with the French government's tacit approval and in defiance of an OAS boast that he would never set foot alive on Algerian soil.

* Influenced by *pied noir* deputies Marc Lauriol and Robert Abdessalam, Susini asked for the Justice, Finance, Economic Affairs, Public Works and Saharan Affairs ministries; he also insisted that the prefects of Algiers and Oran must be Europeans.

Mostefai managed somehow—in one day's time!—to track down Krim in an isolated hamlet and obtain his backing for further negotiations with the OAS. Krim's position was simple: he thought the activists should be provided with a safety exit; it struck him as far preferable to further destruction. In advocating this policy, he also ran political risks, but then he had already displayed his courage by being the only FLN leader to put his signature on the Évian agreement.

Krim set one major condition on his approval: Mostefai must limit his contact with OAS members to the minimum.

Perez saw the situation now as a black-and-white choice between flight and a war of mutual extermination within the OAS leadership. The scorched-earth policy, to be sure, had resumed, but too late in the day. Susini's unilateral truce, as Perez saw it, was a tragic error that had wasted eight days of the thirty the Organization had left on June 1 to wrest concessions from the FLN. It struck the doctor that he could still attempt a last-minute purge; he reflected somberly on the feasibility of ordering the Deltas to assassinate Godard, Susini, Gardes and Caruana in one final swoop. He would have to strike fast; word reached him that his own life was in growing danger at Susini's hands.*

It boiled down to a stark choice—ordering more murder or beating a retreat. Probably because he was rattled, and by no means certain whose orders the Deltas would follow, Perez decided upon a hasty departure.

On June 14, accompanied by five followers, he went aboard a freighter in Algiers harbor with a counterfeit police card, ostensibly to inspect the cargo. With the crew's complicity the six men remained aboard when the ship sailed for Alicante. That day, Susini walked into a room where a number of Delta gunmen were assembled, and said curtly, "Jean-Claude has taken off. Good riddance."

In Alicante, Perez sat down and composed a letter in which he poured out his pent-up mortification and disillusions. He addressed it collectively to Susini and Godard—Godard, "who never commanded anything," and Susini "ready to betray one and all to become a minister in the Algerian Republic." The letter was rambling

---

* Perez's fears were not ill-founded. One of Susini's close friends has stated that he would have ordered Perez shot if the doctor had seriously hindered negotiations with the FLN.

and fiery. Perez accused both Jean-Jacques and the colonel of lack of courage, and justified his own flight from Algiers as the only rational step left, "to safeguard the lives of those we could no longer protect."

Then he added a sour comment on the ultimate battle to save French Algeria: "The stakes were high, and everything about the OAS was small." It was Perez's valedictory.

In Algiers, rumors immediately went round that the doctor had absconded with OAS funds totaling between $500,000 and $900,000.* He had, at any rate, not waited to see the outcome of negotiations with the FLN, and his flight left Susini more than ever in charge.

The next day, the OAS radio, which had been reporting on developments in both camps, with unusual accuracy, declared: "A ray of hope seems to exist. We are clinging to it."

The cause for this optimism was Mostefai's sudden decision to avail himself of Belkacem Krim's backing (in the event, this counted as much as Ben Khedda's support) and meet Susini without further delay. Susini agreed at once to come to a new rendezvous.

Chevallier's estate, besieged by journalists, was out of the question this time as a meeting place. The last-chance negotiations would take place in an apartment Tiné owned adjoining the semitropical gardens of the Hotel St.-Georges, an arrangement that afforded some privacy.

At four o'clock that afternoon, Mostefai arrived, with Farès in tow. Susini was waiting for him. Still conscientiously performing their role as mediators, Chevallier and Tiné sat down with the others at a long, rectangular table, and the meeting began. Once again, heavily armed bodyguards waited outside, bored and taciturn.

Susini spoke first. Seated inappropriately under a picture of the "Presentation of the Child Jesus," he held forth for two hours, explaining and justifying the OAS. He informed the imperturbable FLN doctor seated across the table that they were both revolution-

---

* Perez vigorously denied this in a letter addressed to *Paris-presse*, published on July 18, 1962: "If I'd had that sum at my disposal, I certainly would not have kept it in Algiers and I would have taken it with me for the revolutionary war we are carrying on."

aries, hence could understand one another. He made few specific demands. With his usual bland cocksureness, he went so far as to reject grandly the suggestion of double nationality for those *pieds noirs* who remained in Algeria; in fact, it would be undesirable, he added; those who stayed on, like himself, planned to become true Algerians and burn their bridges with France. The others in the room registered some incredulity at this, since the prospect of retaining French nationality in an emerging, poverty-ridden underdeveloped country was not one to be lightly sacrificed. Did Susini claim to speak for all *pieds noirs?* But at this point, launched upon wave after wave of rhetoric, he could not be stopped.

An armistice must be proclaimed, he declared; but ways and means of enforcing it could be worked out later. Ignoring the inherent contradiction with what the OAS had always preached, he concluded by calling for a "democratic, popular and secular Republic." He gave some of those present the impression that he was making a dead-earnest bid to obtain a cabinet post in independent Algeria's first government.

"He could have said it all in ten minutes," snapped Tiné. But it was Susini's great moment, the apotheosis of his clandestine career, when, seated face-to-face with an FLN negotiator, he outdid the other in his profession of fraternal, Yugoslav-style socialism. Susini's problem all along had been to fight on the wrong side of the lines, a would-be revolutionary devoting his entire force to a counterrevolutionary goal. It was one of many bizarre contradictions that bedeviled the OAS to the end.

Mostefai took just ten minutes to reply. He stressed that the new country should be "born in peace," but, in spite of Susini's prodding, he declined to sign anything. It was out of the question, furthermore, for Belkacem Krim to put his initials to a document, since this might constitute FLN recognition of the OAS. Each negotiator would merely broadcast an armistice appeal to his own community, the texts to be drafted jointly. This was as far as Mostefai would go.

The meeting thus broke up inconclusively, with Susini promising a yes-or-no answer within twenty-four hours. He had accepted Mostefai's bleak judgment on the OAS's nonexistence without demur.

The question arose whether Godard would respect a cease-fire. Turning to Caruana, who had waited in the apartment without participating in the talks, Susini implied that in the event of refusal, Godard would be liquidated.

When the meeting ended, Farès embraced Susini. There is no record of Mostefai having done so.

During the night the precarious "basis for an agreement between Algerians," as Susini called it, nearly broke down. At eight o'clock an unusually heavy charge of dynamite devastated Algiers' new Town Hall, a solid, white, three-story structure on the waterfront between the Prefecture and the Hotel Aletti. The explosion literally ripped the building apart from top to bottom. The ceiling caved in, beams buckled, trapping young soldiers of the 9th Zouaves on guard duty inside; their cries could be heard under the rubble. At least one soldier was dead and forty-three wounded. It was the biggest explosion Algiers had known.

Not far away, another series of blasts destroyed three operating rooms and X-ray installations at Mustapha Hospital. Diehard OAS commandos were pursuing the scorched-earth policy up to the last moment, and there was no certitude that Susini could still restrain them.

He was aware that he had very little to show for a full month's bargaining. That night, at the Villa des Arcades, he drew up two columns on a sheet of paper, one listing the advantages and disadvantages of a cease-fire, the other, of continued scorced-earth operations. As Susini saw it, the decision was not an easy one.

Early the next morning, in a more relaxed mood, he informed Chevallier, who came to see him, that he had decided in favor of a cease-fire. But there was still one final hitch. When Susini cast an eye on the armistice appeal Mostefai planned to read over the government radio, he balked; it referred to FLN contacts in the preceding weeks with "representatives of European opinion," but it omitted all reference to the OAS as such. In the course of a month's strenuous negotiations Susini had retreated from virtually all his major demands; he was not prepared to yield on this minor point.

When Tiné heard of this unforeseen development, he thought incredulously that the hard-won armistice "hung by a thread—or rather, by a comma." It appeared likely that Susini was bluffing by now; he disposed of very few forces and little remaining time to wreck the Casbah and the Sahara pipelines; some Delta commandos had fled, others were disbanded. Still, the risks involved in calling his bluff seemed terrible.

Throughout the following, fateful night of June 16 Chevallier—encouraged by Tiné—stayed up, drafting one clause after another that could satisfy Susini's vanity without nettling Mostefai. At daybreak, after further last-minute coming and going within Algiers, a compromise formula was adopted: "The FLN has consulted with European trade-union leaders, members of the liberal professions, *and in particular with chiefs of the OAS*," the statement would say. It was a minuscule concession to Susini's sense of the fitness of things and his sense of history.

At 1 P.M on June 17, Mostefai delivered his appeal on the state-run radio. The brunt of his message was: "The past is the past; let peace and security return." He called upon Europeans to join Moslems in the constructive task of building a common future. But the speech contained no reference to an "agreement between Algerians," and significantly he made no promises about the *pieds noirs'* future, except to grant them the "right" of joining the *force locale*. This must have been cold comfort for those who believed until the last moment in Susini's ability to work miracles.*

Susini followed Mostefai at eight o'clock over the pirate transmitter. His message was terse. He endorsed the doctor's declaration and said that Algeria could become a great nation if the *pieds noirs* joined without mental reservations in the task of national renewal. He gave orders effective at midnight for the OAS to cease fighting and stop further destruction, but he called on the population to remain vigilant.

After several gongs, an unidentified voice read out the sort of cryptic operational message the activists had always delighted in but which meant so much less than met the eye—"*Pour le renard des sables: les briquets ne doivent pas être allumés ce soir* [For the desert fox: the lighters must not be lit tonight]." This did not refer to cancellation of sabotage of the Sahara oil wells, as one might have assumed, but to a pirate broadcast.

Neither cease-fire appeal caused much surprise in Paris. The French government knew beforehand what Mostefai planned to say over the air; officials at Rocher Noir had counseled him and "inspired" certain passages.

As for Susini, what else could he say?

* In fact, no Europeans volunteered for the *force locale*.

France's widely read yearbook, *L'Année politique*, described the tenuous agreement thus obtained with the FLN as "a quasi-political victory for the OAS." It is hard to accept this judgment.

Susini's partisans have since claimed that it would have been criminal not to exploit the slightest possibility of bringing into being a Franco-Moslem republic, even though the chances of success were admittedly minimal. The armistice itself, they argue, allowed the atmosphere in inflamed, neurotic Algiers to cool off during the short interval before independence, and thus warded off a head-on racial collision, a new Saint Bartholomew's Day Massacre. Finally, by negotiating, Susini bought time and enabled the commandos to make their getaway.

There is some truth in these arguments. But it must also be noted that Susini settled for next to nothing of what he wanted at his final, decisive meeting with Mostefai. He failed to obtain recognition of the OAS as a political entity; postponement of the independence referendum; or a veto over future Algerian legislation that affected *pied noir* interests. All he obtained, indeed, were soothing words and a bare, face-saving reference to the Organization in Mostefai's speech. Moreover, it is not at all sure that the cease-fire prevented an ultimate racial clash; that none took place was due, it seems, primarily to the Moslems' preoccupation with other problems and to the *pieds noirs'* rapid departure.

Susini's strategy of promoting a "pro-Western" faction within the FLN also came to nothing. He proved direly misinformed about the staying power of Ben Khedda's Provisional Government, as became apparent shortly, when Ben Bella, who had refused point-blank to negotiate with the OAS,* swept his rivals from the field and Ben Khedda's government into oblivion. Within a month of independence, Susini bitterly confessed that he had overestimated Ben Khedda's influence; that his hopes of helping forge a Western-oriented Algeria had "dissolved like soap bubbles."

Frenchmen hostile to the OAS wrote off the Susini-Mostefai ne-

---

* On June 17, Ben Bella issued a communiqué claiming that the "Algerian Provisional Government had decided . . . before the Tripoli meeting . . . to reject any idea of talks with the OAS." As far as can be ascertained, Ben Bella planned to wait until Independence Day, then smash the OAS by force.

gotiations as much ado about nothing, another bit of psychological warfare in which the dupes were, once more, the *pieds noirs*.

The harshest criticism came from the Canary Islands, where café-keeper Joseph Ortiz accused Susini of "criminal folly." Ortiz took violent exception to the June 17 armistice because it destroyed once and for all the Organization's assiduously cultivated image of uncompromising resistance to the FLN. He wrote, "The OAS died of this crime more than of its defeat."

Slowly, the roadblocks came down. The curfew was lifted. Army troops with buckets of whitewash smudged out the year-old OAS slogans in black—*"Vive Salan, OAS vaincra!"* Near the Forum, where just a week before it would have been unthinkable to encounter a Moslem who valued his life, Arab boys traced green-painted appeals to vote Yes in the forthcoming referendum, and other slogans—*Vive la Liberté* and *OAS vaincue!*

Some *pieds noirs* began timidly to converse with Moslems on the sun-beaten streets. For the first time in months European journalists ventured into the Casbah and found posters affixed to blue-daubed doors for a rugby match the following weekend between local youths and *djounouds* ("guerrillas") from the hinterland. Tiné thought: Politics in this country are like the climate: one moment stormy, then, without transition, blue skies.

Jacques Chevallier, his fellow mediator, addressed an appeal in turn to the *pieds noirs*, and pleaded with them to stay in their native land—or return to it, in the case of those who had left—now that the terrible times of hatred and revolt were past. He employed lyric language that they as Mediterraneans presumably understood; he spoke of the turquoise sea, the orange trees and olive groves of the Sahel, sunrise . . . Many lauded the speech, but, like Susini's efforts, it came too late; few changed their plans because of it.

At Bab el Oued a group of *petits blancs*—all from the neighborhood—soaked the posts and crossbeams of the wooden market hall with gasoline. As flames soared about the structure where they had until recently purchased poultry and fish and vegetables, the departing inhabitants in a frenzy began to throw books, photographs, chairs, keepsakes and mementoes into the blazing heap. Then they stepped back and watched the flames, transfixed. . . .

The pestilence in Algiers was, to all intents and purposes, over.

The sign on the road leading into Oran had once read: *"Hertz—Location de Voitures."* Now the letters were blacked out, except for the *o* and *a* in "location" and the *s* in "voitures." As one drove into the city, huge posters proclaimed:

Ordre
Avenir
Sécurité.

Order, the Future, Security. . . . At a barbed-wire entanglement, a Foreign Legion colonel was funneling pedestrians from a Moslem into a European neighborhood when a *pied noir* youngster approached and, at point-blank range, shot him dead.

Two days later, June 15, General Philippe Genestet, the newly arrived, fifty-six-year-old Army Corps commander, went to Baudens Military Hospital to pay final respects to the dead officer. He was greeted at the main gate by the senior Medical Corps representative, Colonel Mabille. As they crossed the courtyard, a door in one pavilion flew open and a Legionnaire deserter stepped out and opened fire, then fled before hospital guards could be alerted. The general and colonel crumbled to the ground, the latter fatally wounded several hundred feet from the spot where he had scoffed the winter before at Police Prefect Pierre Le Thiais's prediction that this was the place where one of them would be assassinated.*

It had taken the Oran OAS only a day to decide that it would not observe Susini's cease-fire. On June 18, a pirate broadcast an-

---

* Genestet lingered several days after the attack, then also succumbed. His assassination was apparently an error: the intended victim was the much-hated General Katz. Katz subsequently described the double attack at Oran's military hospital as "a murder plot worthy of Hitchcock." According to this version, the OAS shot the Foreign Legion officer, Lieutenant Colonel André Mariot, solely to lure Katz to the funeral chapel. He indeed made plans to go to the hospital, then suddenly canceled his visit when he learned that his regular four-man armed escort had been borrowed by a civilian official. Genestet went and was killed.

When Katz finally went to the hospital, it was to pay respects not to one dead officer but to two, with a third on the critical list. At a subsequent funeral Mass at Oran Cathedral, officers felt relatively safe indoors, but were worried when they came outdoors and passed a cloister behind which OAS gunmen could easily have ambushed them. As it was, no further attacks occurred. OAS sources have confirmed that the ambush that took Genestet's life was intended for Katz.

nounced that the "June 17 agreement applied only to the Algiers area," that in Oranie, "where the situation was different," the battle continued. And two days later, Oran's powerful coordinating committee of trade-unions rejected the "vague and imprecise promises" contained in the Algiers truce "signed by certain OAS leaders concerned more with defending their own interests than protecting those of the French in Algeria, France and the West." The only valid guarantee for the *pieds noirs,* the trade-union communiqué predicted, would be a federal Algeria made up of autonomous states, with the European minority recognized as a special ethnic group.

To those who recalled the FLN's steadfast refusal during the drawn-out Lugrin and Évian negotiations to grant the *pieds noirs* a privileged status—and who noted that Algeria's vast Moslem majority was under no compulsion to bargain a week before independence—this last-minute attempt to revive Salan's old notion of a federated Algeria appeared insane. But life in Oran now verged on the lunatic. The forces of destruction here were proving far more powerful than in Algiers.

The new Oran Prefecture, the city's pride, rose in splendid uselessness. Several times Prefect René Thomas and his aides had come under OAS machine-gun fire from a building directly across the way as they went to lunch down the fifteenth-floor corridor past a huge plate-glass window. Now they stayed away from the top-story restaurant, and took meals in the basement with CRS troops assigned to the protection of the building. A few civil servants, men alone without their families, slept in the Prefecture, changed rooms every night and washed down with *eau de Vittel;* the OAS had long since cut the water supply.

Father de la Parre, the priest who kept a diary of Oran life during these closing days, made an entry of unconsciously grim humor: "I have just passed a burned-out apartment house and watched a shoe store being looted; at a distance I saw several murders. People seem nervous."

The Oran OAS was pursuing twin goals—organizing its retreat, while dreaming of leaving behind a wide swath of sabotage. Charles Micheletti, Gardy's civilian deputy, was adamant on this score. A retreating army, he repeated, blows up its stores to prevent them from falling into the hands of the enemy . . . and to the end this hard-pressed businessman persisted in the dangerous illusion that the ragtag band of the terrorists under his orders constituted an army. As for the Moslems, he was temperamentally incapable of regarding them otherwise than as foes.

By late June Micheletti still commanded several small but fanatical sabotage teams composed of Legionnaire deserters and *Oranais* of Spanish blood. Confident that the *clan espagnol*, as it was called, could inflict heavy casualties on the FLN before going down, he made careful plans to fight it out to the end, and ordered explosive charges placed in Oran's main power plant, its hospitals and clinics, and above all the Shell gas tanks located directly behind Moslem-inhabited Ville Nouvelle. On Independence Day the FLN would inherit a city reduced to desolation.

Micheletti himself prepared for the end in a feverish, unhealthy state. A friend found him unrecognizable—pallid, wild-eyed and fat ("he had put on forty pounds from compulsive overeating"). He was dangerously close to nervous collapse.

The end was approaching. In another week Oran—and all Algeria —would cease being French. The streets leading to the port were full of motorized Legionnaires, honking *"Algérie française"* on their way to embark for France. Refugees from the interior crowded downtown restaurants. Long lines of Europeans formed to withdraw their savings from the main Caisse d'Épargne. The FLN administered Ville Nouvelle as a sort of autonomous Arab enclave; Moslem employees on the city payroll continued to draw their pay, provided they worked where they were and did not venture downtown. The city was swept by rumors: that banknotes of the Banque d'Algérie were no longer being accepted in France; that the FLN was about to forbid further departures; that the United States Sixth Fleet was under steam to come to the *pieds noirs'* rescue; that Bidault and Soustelle had formed a new Government of French Algeria in Lisbon.

Evenings, some hostesses organized farewell parties for the officers of departing regiments—as though the far-flung empire of jungle and desert still thrived and the officers were bound for a new tour of duty in another territory. Nicole Monier, the girl who had acted as Jouhaud's liaison agent, went to one such party where champagne and whisky flowed. She thought: *La perte de l'Algérie est pire que la perte d'un parent.**

Ex-colonel Henry Dufour's feelings were less simple than Micheletti's. He had set June 24 as a deadline for a series of last-minute demands—notably, his own appointment as commander of Oran's *force locale,* as a guarantee that Europeans' legal rights would be respected after the referendum. Dufour thought of this idea as eminently realistic, and was amazed when no one else appeared to. Oran would never lay down arms, he vowed, unless this condition were met.

Nonetheless, the colonel had increasing doubts about continuing a doomed struggle. Destruction for destruction's sake struck him as pointless. In this he was influenced by an open letter Salan had just dispatched from his solitary cell at Santé Prison, urging all *pieds noirs* to "have the courage" to adapt to a new situation, cease further hostilities and remain peaceably in a "fraternal Algeria."† There was to be no territorial redoubt; Salan's letter explicitly advised against it.

Dufour waited tensely for a reply from Rocher Noir to his proposition. He realized that he was involved in a dramatic race against time—not so much because of the FLN's imminent arrival in the city as because of Micheletti's destructive urge. But no reply was forthcoming from the provisional executive. Although Dufour did not fully realize it, the time was past for further bargaining. Neither the FLN nor the French government wanted to undertake a whole new round of negotiations with the shrunken kernel of resistance the Oran OAS represented. It had been one thing to deal—reluctantly—with Susini, who claimed to speak for the remains of a once-formidable national organization; it was quite another, to make an effort to appease a small band of terrorists on their last legs. From Algiers, Mostefai coldly announced that he would make no trip to Oran to try to duplicate the June 17 truce. As far as the FLN was concerned, his agreement with Susini applied to all Algeria; if Gardy and Micheletti refused to honor it, this constituted an internal problem for the OAS.

* "Losing Algeria is worse than losing a relative."
† Salan's appeal was published by Agence France-Presse on June 22.

French officials at Rocher Noir thought the real task now consisted of calming Oran's population and isolating the handful of discredited OAS leaders.

On June 25, at five o'clock in the afternoon, following three plastique explosions, fire broke out in the oil-storage tanks of British Petroleum at the port. A three-hundred-foot-high tower of smoke rose steadily into the sky. Two and a half million gallons of fuel oil were aflame, and fire threatened adjacent depots. Passenger and freight ships in the harbor, including those used to evacuate *pieds noirs*, hurriedly lifted anchor and gained the roadstead. Fortunately the wind was blowing seaward, which prevented the fire from spreading to the city.

Pieds noirs crowded the waterfront to watch the gigantic blaze. They shouted with joy, and jeered at soldiers trying to redirect traffic away from the port. In the intense heat and odor of diesel-oil fumes, hundreds of sightseers moved about antlike, fascinated by the pagan spectacle.

The flames cauterized the *pieds noirs'* wounds.

Next day, the main post office containing the telephone exchange was blown up. Oran was isolated, except for Army field lines, from the rest of the world.

At one clinic a solitary nurse remained on duty, caring for the wounded and rolling up the dead in bedsheets; all the European doctors were gone. Rats scuttered through the unclean streets in broad daylight.

With the blowing up of the telephone exchange, the fire alarm no longer sounded at station houses. Two of Oran's biggest bakeries were on fire, and for the first time the threat loomed of a shortage of bread.

At the port, the British Petroleum fire roared unchecked. Oil particles filtered through window chinks into apartments. The blaze was visible ten miles away. A sooty pall obscured the horizon, the sun could be seen only as a dim disc, and people commented on the rarity of this in summer.

It was Operation Apocalypse, the operation Micheletti (and Degueldre and Perez) had dreamed of—a twilight of colonial gods.

In the blackened city Dufour abruptly gave up the struggle.

That afternoon he went round to Gardy's secret command post. The door was locked, and no one replied—an air of desolation already hung over the apartment. The last of the OAS generals had slipped away, out of the city and Algeria, for good, with several commandos.

If Dufour's mind still needed making up, this development did it. He agreed to meet with Pierre Laffont, former deputy and liberal editor of *L'Écho d'Oran,* who had suddenly emerged as the leading figure among a group of Oran liberals seeking to spare their city further wreckage, in much the same way as Jacques Chevallier had mediated in Algiers.

Laffont, a reflective and intelligent man, told the colonel that as a senior French Army officer he could not allow the European population trapped in Oran by lack of ships and planes to confront the very real possibility of famine and epidemics. Dufour listened closely. He promised nothing, but said to Laffont before leaving, "I hope to see you again under different circumstances."

Then he returned to his apartment and recorded a terse, sober appeal to the "special sections of the secret army" to suspend further destruction that "could add to our compatriots' calvary." The wording was subtle. It meant that official buildings could still be blown up at will, since these were now useless to the European population, but not gas tanks, power plants and water-pumping stations, which Micheletti had listed as legitimate targets. Dufour reasoned that these installations could be of use until the last *pied noir* left Oran.

However, to get his appeal broadcast, he needed Micheletti's approval. Micheletti controlled the pirate transmitter, and asked to see the text.

"I don't have to submit it to your censorship," Dufour said.

"Then it doesn't get on the air," Micheletti replied.

The colonel stalked out. He could think of only one solution. During the evening he saw Laffont again. Laffont went immediately to Katz's headquarters at the Prefecture and arranged to have the order transmitted on Army facilities. It was broadcast at 10:30 P.M.

As soon as it was aired, *Oranais* heard Micheletti's voice on the pirate channel denouncing "certain officers' treason" and calling for a fight to the very end.

Explosions resounded that night in Oran. All street lights were extinguished. Young *pi₂d noir* hoodlums prowled through the abandoned European working-class suburbs of Gambetta, St.-Eugène, Lamur and Lyautey, looting stores, firing into apartments. As bystanders watched powerlessly, they invaded one of the city's fire-gutted bakeries, split open flour sacks and strewed the contents on the ground.

Dufour's appeal had had little effect, and the outcome was still in doubt.

The end—the real end—came all of a sudden and surprised all those unaware of the secret, urgent mediation taking place in the city.

On June 27, Laffont held another meeting—this time with Micheletti himself. There are no written documents to prove exactly what transpired between the two men, or to what extent the liberal newspaper publisher spoke for the French government. Laffont says he merely urged Micheletti to leave and avoid Moslem reprisals while it was still possible. Micheletti claims that he agreed to retreat with his remaining commandos provided that Katz authorized several boats to sail without papers. If not, there would be a final burst of fireworks. But for all his white-hot ranting, Micheletti recognized that further action would be suicidal; Salan had spoken out against continued hostilities, Gardy was gone, and Dufour could no longer be counted on.

Some time that day, Micheletti quietly ordered ten volunteers to remain behind in Oran to blow up the War Monument after independence, but canceled instructions for widespread sabotage. Presumably he had received the assurances he wanted about his own safety. That evening, at eight o'clock, he too went on the air.

It was the last pirate broadcast the *pieds noirs* would hear, and it was widely listened to. The long battle was over, Micheletti conceded: the Army and the Foreign Legion had failed to throw in their lot with the defenders of the "last bastion of the West." There was no recourse but to withdraw—"Our fight is hopeless and unresolvable. *Tout est fini. Adieu, Algérie!* May God's will be done." At the end his voice broke; this overwrought, stout businessman with limited military capability who had read too much about guerrilla warfare was sobbing as the OAS went off the airwaves in Oran forever.

The broadcast was the signal for the mass flight of the remaining commandos. Urban desperadoes, they sprang from the local population, and now merged effortlessly among the fleeing *pieds noirs*.

At dawn next morning, dozens of young terrorists piled into fishing smacks, pleasure boats, any available craft leaving for Spain, often without water, food or change of clothes, but with their most precious belongings, a crudely counterfeited passport and a gun. Some actually turned over Bren guns and stores of plastique to gendarmes they felt they could trust, to maintain order against the encroaching Moslems.

Many shipped out from the sheltered little harbor of Arzew, east of Oran beyond Pointe Canastel, tucked in an indentation of the coast, and similar coves and inlets—ideal localities for inconspicuous departures. Ships from Oran waited for dusk, then slipped back into shore and took them aboard. The commandos fled—though they did not always realize it—with Katz's full knowledge and approval of what they were up to. He was glad to be rid of them—it seemed more important than laying his hands on a few—and when an aide arrived at the Prefecture with news of Micheletti's departure on a trawler bound for Alicante, Katz's ugly features cracked into a jagged smile.

"Goodbye to the Pied Piper," he growled.

Before he left his apartment, Godard read through the newspaper a last time. It carried the final appeal Susini had addressed to the *pieds noirs* on the Algerian Television sound channel thirty-six hours before the referendum. As he read the text, Godard thought that he could almost hear the well-modulated, smoothly flowing voice. Susini was still in Algiers, as busy as ever on the eve of independence, politicking on behalf of the "agreement between Algerians." Godard did not know exactly where he was, and no longer cared.

"Algerian men and women!" the speech began. "With how much faith and stubborn determination you fought and suffered so that this country, which is ours, could remain our motherland! Fighting has ceased because we have obtained from those who were our enemies recognition of our honorable struggle and a guarantee of our rights. On June 17 the OAS–FLN agreement, authenticated in the eyes of the entire world, laid the basis for a new . . . Algeria in which the place of each is assured . . ."

Godard smiled. He thought of the rising number of kidnapings and car thefts and expropriations attributed to the FLN. His packed bag stood near the door.

". . . the new Algeria must be built with all those who extend their hand to us. Nothing can be founded on negation, abstention or pusillanimity. In two days' time I ask all to say Yes to the Algeria of June 17, the Algeria of courage, progress and fraternity!" Godard crumpled the newspaper and flung it to the floor.

Outdoors, Algiers sweltered in the Mediterranean summer heat. As the colonel came outside, he saw up the street the burned-out shell of the Algiers University library. At one of the few café terraces still open, the only patrons were a few young soldiers from France and some foreign journalists looking for someone to interview. But it was almost as difficult now in Algiers to find a member of the OAS as it had been to find a Nazi in Germany at war's end. Military vehicles rumbled down the street. Godard passed the singed complex of municipal and government buildings along the waterfront. Inside there was dead silence, the offices were vacant, a solitary pair of woman's heels clicked down empty, echoing corridors. One hundred and thirty-two years' French presence was drawing to an end in utter silence and resignation. Downtown Algiers was a dead city.

An hour later, he strode through the port. A heavy-set, sick-looking man in his early fifties hurried to keep up with him; it was the former Colonel Roland Vaudrey, Godard's deputy four years before at the Algiers Sûreté, the man who had called upon the *pieds noirs* to demonstrate at Rue d'Isly.

Soon they reached the basin where freighters bound for foreign ports were tied up, and found the ship they were looking for. French police and customs officials had vanished. Only a few incurious idlers hung about. No one questioned the lithe military-looking man or his sick companion. Together they clambered up the gangplank and went on deck.

That night, June 29, the freighter lifted anchor and sailed for Greece.

That same night, a nine-meter sailing boat also cleared the port. It was bound for Palma de Majorca, one hundred eighty-five miles away. The *pied noir* owner motioned to his sole passenger and close friend, ex-Colonel Jean Gardes. They looked back several times at the white city rising tier upon tier from the dark water.

At Oran's Prefecture a meeting was being held of town leaders, shipowners, industrialists, trade-federation members—pillars of "respectable" *pied noir* society, who had financed and abetted the OAS without becoming openly compromised in its killings. They waited with some nervousness for their unaccustomed guests. Finally, after a forty-five–minute delay, the eight FLN delegates shambled in— dirty, ill-clad uncomfortable-looking guerrillas, whose chief, Si Othomane, the administrator of Ville Nouvelle, brusquely saluted the assembled Europeans. Visibly he was as ill at ease as his hosts.

It was an inauspicious beginning for the newly created Franco-Moslem Reconciliation Committee. To cross the European quarter and reach the Prefecture unharmed, the FLN group had come escorted by three French officers, a humiliation they were unlikely to forget.

But soon, as both sides plunged into a discussion of plans for future cooperation, the tension subsided. *Pieds noirs* and Moslems exchanged cigarettes. At the end of the two-hour meeting, Si Othomane said, in a voice trembling with emotion: "You are all Algerians. We are ready to greet you in our neighborhood. Let us wipe out the past!"

Katz, who was there, thought with amazement, *It's as if nothing had ever happened.*

The next morning, June 30, Monseigneur Bernard Lacaste, Archbishop of Oran and onetime champion of *Algérie française,* mounted a podium at the Place des Armes, where corpses of murdered European liberals had been publicly displayed not so long before, and addressed the assembled *pieds noirs* on the virtues of charity and forbearance. It was the last day of French Algeria.

At six-thirty the same morning, Dufour gathered with a small group of followers on the deserted quay. He had waited till the last day to make sure that Micheletti did not change his mind and launch a wave of terror attacks to disrupt the referendum.

No one at the pier said much, no one had much to say; everyone instinctively whispered, persuaded there were Moslem snipers in the area. An eerie tomblike silence lay across the docks and vast, emptied warehouses. Not a single car moved in the port. The fire at the British Petroleum dump had consumed itself, but the early-morning breeze still stank of oil fumes.

They walked down the docks in search of the boat that would carry them to safety in Spain. Finally they found it—an old, rusting tub used for hauling sand and gravel up the coast, that looked full of leaks and woes. Once aboard, they met the skipper, a *pied noir* none of them knew, who had volunteered for the task: a ragged and impressive figure in a rumpled sports jacket, a pair of opera glasses strung from his neck in place of binoculars. He announced briefly that he would set course due north for Cartagena, less than one hundred twenty miles away, hoping to do ten knots an hour and make landfall at eight in the evening—*inch' Allah!* They derived some comfort from the thought that by sticking more or less to their course they must arrive somewhere in view of the Spanish coast.

The boat sailed. As they cleared the breakwater they saw a French soldier placidly fishing from the rocks, and Dufour's men shook their fists at him. He looked at them without interest and made no gesture in reply.

They began to crowd aft round the taffrail for a last look at the row of glistening white skyscrapers along the Front de Mer and the Virgin of Santa Cruz, the statue raised by the people of Oran on the tawny hilltop of Murdjadjo that dominates the entire serene gulf. Soon Dufour ordered them below decks until they were past the territorial limit, although inwardly he thought the danger would not end then; the French Navy would hardly be deterred by their being on the high seas if it decided to hail and intercept them. He remained alone topsides.

The *pied noir* skipper suddenly pointed out the silhouette of two warships on the horizon. Dufour felt a moment of panic. "They're Spanish," the skipper said. And soon it became evident that this, indeed, was what they were, two Navy vessels escorting the Alicante-Ceuta ferryboat detoured from its normal run to evacuate Spanish nationals from fire-scorched Oran. There was nothing to fear from Franco's warships.

The cloud cover broke, the sun suddenly sparkled on the water, the breeze smelled warm. The neutral sea bore the ship northward on an even keel.

After a while Dufour's men came back on deck. They were leaving Africa's troubles astern in the green fleeting wash. Did the thought occur to them that the OAS's battle had been limited to murder and destruction? Apparently not. Dufour thought of Algeria's jumbled white cities with their flawed sense of tolerance and their stubborn, generous friendships, their admirable striving after sunlight and life and their political imbecility. He shook his head. A year's struggle for nothing.

They enjoyed a following sea, calm and regular. Once, French Navy planes flew over the ship but did not return.

That evening, on schedule, lights came into view—tiny, scattered and remote in the faint bluish land mist, then more and more at the foot of mountains and in capacious bays—and from nautical charts they recognized the outline of the coast of Spain.

The boat lay to in the roadstead. Next morning they sailed into the busy harbor of Cartagena and obtained authorization from the *capitanería* to disembark.

The fountains on the palm-bordered Esplanada played freshly in the early summer morning. They were escorted to an improvised reception center in a hangar, where Navy officers, customs officials and Cruz Roja ambulances and nurses awaited the crews of the little desperate boats arriving from Algeria. Parched and frozen, they were given hot soup and were told that they enjoyed the status of political refugees and could remain without cost for the next two or three days in Cartagena. Then they would have to fend for themselves.

The authorities showed a notable lack of interest in their forged papers, but one port official processing the fugitives asked Dufour with some humor why he had left Algeria and what he had come to do in Spain. The colonel's jauntiness had temporarily deserted him; he was incredibly weary. He looked at the man and replied, "Do you ever read a newspaper?"

Then he picked up his bag and started off down the unfamiliar street.

EPILOGUE

On July 1, 1962, of six and a half million eligible Algerians—Moslems and *pieds noirs*—5,975,581 voted for independence. All seven legally registered parties taking part in the referendum campaign had advocated casting a white "Yes" ballot in reply to the question, "Do you want Algeria to become an independent state cooperating with France under terms defined by the Évian agreement of March 19?"*

The Moslem population chose independence by an overwhelming proportion that amounted to 99.8 percent of the ballots cast and 79 percent of the registered voters. The number of orange "No" ballots was negligible—16,534—but in numerous European quarters of Algeria's main cities residents stuffed blank slips into the ballot box to show disapproval of the proceedings. Nevertheless, more Europeans than had been expected voted "Yes"—in some cases expressly, they claimed, to avoid future reprisals at the hands of the FLN.

* The absence of any choice other than independence, such as limited home rule or federal ties with France, drew outraged protests from the Right, which accused de Gaulle of blandly scrapping his own triptych of solutions to the Algerian question propounded in 1959—integration, association, independence.

The Right observed that the referendum, in practice, denied any voice to the Sahara population, which had no close ties with Arabs and Kabyles on the coast and perhaps did not want complete severance of ties with France: this minority's wishes were buried in the mass of Moslem votes. (FLN control over the Sahara was spotty, and in some areas its campaign on behalf of independence began only twenty-four hours before the self-determination vote.)

That evening the Casbah staged open-air entertainments to which foreign correspondents were admitted. The neighborhood's maze of steep alleyways was ablaze with lights in coffeehouses and pastry shops; balconies were festooned with green, white and red decorations; once-outlawed FLN flags hung from every rooftop. At the access to the European quarter, Arab youths and girls clambered atop cars and wildly Twisted the night away. *Pied noir* spectators turned away in anger.

During the next forty-eight hours the celebrating continued uninterrupted. Triumphant truck-borne Moslem crowds from the squalid, disinherited shantytowns of Belcourt and Clos Salembier invaded downtown Algiers and reached the waterfront, ululating, clapping and screaming *"El Djez-a-ir. Ya ya!"* In Oran, Arab women belly-danced inexhaustibly in the Place des Victoires. French flags lay discarded in dustbins, torn and dirty. Algerian banners snapped and strained from the War Monument, which, contrary to Micheletti's instruction, stood intact.

In spite of the remaining European's vivid fears, no major outbreak of racial violence took place. *Pieds noirs* wandered, for the most part dazed and ignored, through the milling Moslem street crowd. But everybody was aware that the carefree joyful atmosphere lay at the mercy of the first gunshot.*

---

* Violence broke out on July 5 in Oran. An independence parade was coming to an end before the Hôtel de Ville, when bursts of gunfire occurred shortly after noon. The Arab crowd concluded that OAS diehards were firing on them from rooftops, and reacted menacingly. Europeans fled for cover, but confused shooting lasted until three in the afternoon, and it was not until four o'clock that police intervened. By this time, ninety-five persons lay dead, including at least twenty *pieds noirs*, and many more Europeans were missing.

Following French officials' immediate representations to Ben Bella, some *pieds noirs* were released from Ville Nouvelle, where they had been taken, held in cellars and unmercifully beaten. The fate of others has never been resolved.

As in the case of Rue d'Isly, the immediate cause for the massacre was hard to ascertain. It is possible that *pied noir* bystanders were caught in cross fire when violence flared up between Ben Bella and Ben Khedda factions. It is certain that a handful of OAS volunteers remained in Oran, bent on making trouble, and young Arab hoodlums were also on the rampage. Eyewitnesses noted that the Moslem crowd was at an extreme pitch of excitement: five days' unaccustomed idleness and celebrating were bound to lead to an incident.

The impression made on the *pieds noirs* after a brief renewal of confidence was disastrous. *Algérie française* had died emotionally on the pavements of Rue d'Isly; the prospect of Franco-Moslem coexistence in independent Algeria crumbled in the streets of Oran on July 5.

In Paris, independence was a perfunctory formality. On July 3 the cabinet met and went over the referendum results. A light rain fell in the courtyard of the Élysée Palace, where journalists waited: at length a spokesman emerged and read a solemn proclamation. It ran to a mere fourteen lines and said in essence that France recognized the independence of Algeria's fifteen departments. It was 10:40 A.M.

Inside, deliberately playing down the moment's historic significance, de Gaulle met with his old friend and guest, Chancellor Konrad Adenauer, and retraced the Grand Design of Gaullist foreign policy which the Algerian War could no longer disrupt.

Workmen were raising a white-and-blue dais for the official dinner that night.

Susini lingered in Algiers, a haunted, inquisitive figure, alternately attracted and repelled by what he saw. Boyhood, young manhood, the first eighteen years of his life were inseparably associated with the *pied-noir* seaport; now he witnessed its swift metamorphosis into an Arab city. Moslems occupied Bab el Oued. The Otomatic and the Cafeteria, former hangouts of youthful OAS killers, became, respectively, Cercle Taleb Abderrahmane and Cercle Tahar Chefai, in honor of martyred nationalist students. Rue d'Isly itself, where *pieds noirs* had fallen disbelievingly under the fire of French Army patrols, underwent a change of name and habitués, and became Rue Abane Ramdane, a shopping favorite of Arab women.

The last leader of the OAS was not molested. He remained in contact with Farès and Mostefai. Tiné saw him one day driving through downtown traffic—a balding youngish man who had come illusorily close to fulfilling his vision of counterrevolutionary decision in the streets and who still dreamed of playing a role in independent Algeria.

But a day came, not long afterward—in July—when he was turned away from the executive offices at Rocher Noir. It was painfully obvious that his presence was an embarrassment to all. Then one afternoon he passed several Arab girls in European clothes chattering excitedly as they stood on a street corner. And suddenly it was like being a stranger in his own home, and he had no desire to remain.

He sailed for Italy, accompanied by Broizat, with only one regret: that during his entire youth in Algeria he had never once set foot inside the Casbah, never made a trip into the Sahara; all he knew, in fact, of the immense land were the coastal cities and the adjacent strip of valley cultivated and irrigated by *pieds noirs*.

Like a particularly wrathful tornado, the Organization had come spontaneously into being, marched destructively up and down Algeria, flattening whatever lay in its path, then receded and vanished over the horizon, leaving an uncertain calm in its wake.

The OAS dispersed. Gardes reached Madrid, where he joined Perez and that ghost of pre-May 1958 activism, Dr. Bernard Lefèvre. From somewhere in Spain, Gardy announced his entry into Bidault's new National Council of Resistance. Micheletti lay low in Almería.

The rank-and-file scattered for safety to different parts of Europe. Deltas from Algiers landed at Marseilles, then moved on to pre-arranged hideouts and rendezvous points in the southeast, the southwest and Paris. Those from Oran sailed into Spanish ports; some stayed in Alicante, one commando regrouped at San Sebastián, then attempted to slip into France, but several hours after illegally crossing the frontier all were under arrest.

The Deltas at large were in a state of hypertension, bewildered by their utter defeat, quarrelsome, and soon hard pressed for means to survive. Some had received three months' pay, and instructions not to show themselves but to await orders. Almost all congregated where there was hope of collecting money from former chiefs. Very rapidly a majority lost interest in politics and turned to an ingrained Delta habit: in Marseilles, six bank holdups in six hours' time were laid to the newcomers from Algeria.* But once removed from native surroundings, they showed no aptitude for crime or concealment; their *pied noir* accent gave them away, and they could not resist brawling with any North African Arab they came across; in Spain a language problem occasionally cropped up.

---

* " . . . It is estimated that 85 percent of the persons arrested in France during July and August 1962 for theft of arms or money were members or former members of the OAS." (Marie-Thérèse Lancelot, *Organisation Armée Secrète*)

Police estimated that returning Deltas, who merged with the fleeing *pied noir* population as a whole, smuggled 20,000 weapons into mainland France, concealed in baggage, furniture crates and ship holds.

The Spanish police regularly tossed a few into prison for cooling-off periods. In France, they fell afoul of the law through barroom gossip and bragging, and their ranks were soon depleted.

For all without exception it was a brutal awakening; torn from the bravado of urban guerrilla raids, they were thrust back into the daily competitiveness of industrialized societies. But in time they settled down.

Franco's government released the Madrid activists—Lagaillarde, Ortiz, Lacheroy—from their nine-month exile in the Canaries on the day Algerian independence was proclaimed.

Degueldre did not survive the fall of French Algeria by long. His trial took place on June 27 and 28 in barracks at the Fort de Vincennes, in eastern Paris. After the surprise verdict in Salan's trial, de Gaulle had ordered the High Military Tribunal, his own creation, abolished, and replaced by a new five-man Military Court of Justice. It was before this special jurisdiction that Degueldre appeared in summer khakis of the Foreign Legion: a grim-jawed figure whose bloody reputation created a chill even in these austere surroundings. He was defended by the ubiquitous Tixier-Vignancour and Denise Macaigne, a woman lawyer.

Edgard de Larminat, a five-star general appointed to preside over the new court, had been hospitalized the evening before, his nerves affected by the defense's violent pretrial attack on his impartiality.* Thus, that morning, a new judge, General Roger Charles Gardet, sat on the bench. This still did not appease the defense, which charged that grounds for "legitimate suspicion" of Gardet's impartiality also existed (since he had sentenced Jouhaud to death):

* It was de Larminat who, the year before, had said publicly that he knew no honorable way out but suicide for the unsuccessful fomentors of the April putsch. A stanch Gaullist, he had headed Free French forces who surrounded and took a German pocket of resistance at Royan, in western France, in 1944. With extreme reluctance, but under considerable pressure from de Gaulle, he had agreed to head up the Military Court of Justice. The defense made use of a contemporary World War II report, from General Georges Catroux to de Gaulle, which declared that de Larminat was suffering from mental weakness that could have catastrophic consequences on military operations. Use of this report apparently put an unbearable strain on de Larminat, who four days later, on June 30, 1962, committed suicide in his apartment after sending de Gaulle a terse three-sentence letter saying that he could not measure up to the duty imposed on him.

the two lawyers moved for the appointment of still a third judge. When this tactic failed, they did an unusual thing: they appeared before the court not in barristers' robes but in mufti, "not as lawyers but as human beings," and cited a precedent during the Paris Commune and "antique custom." In effect, this meant that Degueldre would go undefended.

And undefended he went, refusing to answer Gardet's questions and making no serious effort to save himself. One must conclude from what ensued that the French Army's network of friendships did not apply to a junior officer who had risen from the ranks in a Legion regiment and whose very nationality was obscure. No generals, no illustrious widows, no fellow lieutenants came forward to testify on his behalf. The defense, challenging the court's competence, declined to plead substantive questions. The government called only four prosecution witnesses; they were sworn in and heard within the day. The public prosecutor, in summing up, described the defendant as a "hired killer." It was justice at its speediest. The next day, the court found the prisoner guilty of participation in ten murders and sentenced him to death.

Upon hearing the verdict, Degueldre smiled.

Following his trial he was held in solitary confinement, the only inmate of the death block at Fresnes Prison. He was as fatalistic and individualistic as ever. When he learned of fellow prisoners' plans to launch a hunger strike in protest at the sentence, he observed: "There'll be no strike for me." On some days he would dance a little jig and talk of his coming execution, convincing the guards that he was mad. Two days before his death he wrote an exceedingly curious letter, which seems to betray signs of acute schizophrenia. It refers to Roger, who is "detached from all that is occurring about him." Susini has said that his friend was sweating with horror when he wrote it.

Some thought Degueldre would be reprieved, since the Organization he incarnated no longer existed and the cause he killed for lay in ruins; but, although French judges had found extenuating circumstances for Salan, and Jouhaud was saved from a firing squad *in extremis* through Vatican pressure,* there would be no reprieve for Delta, the loneliest of terrorists.

---

* In the immediate wake of the Salan trial, de Gaulle's irritation was such that persistent rumors circulated at the Palais de Justice that Jouhaud was to

At dawn on July 6 Degueldre was marched before a firing squad at Fort d'Ivry in the woods of Marly le Roi, west of Paris, where Jouhaud was to have been executed. The tall ex-lieutenant sang the "Marseillaise," and said he was proud to die having kept the oath not to deliver Algeria to the FLN. Gardet, the presiding judge, contrary to custom, did not attend the execution. A salvo rang out and Degueldre crumpled to the ground. The officer in charge came up and delivered the traditional *coup de grâce*. Tixier-Vignancour, who remained on the spot, charged that the shot struck not the head but the shoulder of his client, that he was still breathing and in pain for several minutes before he expired.

The extreme-Right press subsequently made a halfhearted attempt to build up Degueldre as a bigger-than-lifesize legend, "the first martyr of the European cause." But while Rightist admirers kept alive his memory, Joseph Ortiz caustically noted from Spain that Madrid's OAS leaders, with the exception of Lacheroy, danced and enjoyed themselves as usual on the night of Degueldre's death . . . creating a deplorable impression among their Spanish acquaintances.

As with everything else about this cryptic and ferocious figure, his death resolved no questions. He is buried in the cemetery of Thiais, outside Paris, in the *Carré des Suppliciés*, the plot reserved for executed men.

---

be shot on Saturday, May 26, although several hundred letters had reached the Élysée Palace urging clemency. More than half the cabinet, including Premier Pompidou, intervened on Jouhaud's behalf, arguing that the nation's and the Army's unity must be preserved; that a time for reconciliation was at hand as the war drew to a close. Justice Minister Jean Foyer sought to resign rather than see the sentence carried out. To all this, de Gaulle turned a deaf ear and insisted that the case must be judged on the basis of the state's higher interests.

On May 25 a number of measures were taken to prepare the execution. A coffin of Jouhaud's size was readied; the chaplain at Fresnes Prison was alerted to be available some time past midnight.

According to Maître Bernard Le Coroller and other sources, the Vatican intervened in diplomatic but no uncertain terms. Pompidou reintervened, as did other high French officials, who emphatically urged de Gaulle to reconsider, pointing out that the execution would be a serious political mistake. The general summoned to designate the firing squad refused to do so.

Some time during the evening of May 25, the preparations were canceled. Jouhaud himself was fully aware of how close he came to being shot. At the end of that harrowing evening, he observed, "I've just come back from a long trip."

"French Algeria died badly," wrote John Cairns.* "The whole episode constituted perhaps the most sordid and pathetic event in the long twilight of colonialism." The experience was traumatic, leaving psychological scars that have not healed.

De Gaulle's preponderant role in this major historical transformation can be summed up briefly: except for a few notable instances of floundering, he operated deftly, with the objective precision of a surgeon removing a tumor. From his point of view, Algeria had to be got rid of, to save the French from prolonged bloodletting and self-division. So he acted, not always charitably, very often brutally; yet he undoubtedly carried out a policy that at the end corresponded to a deep popular longing. Former Premier Edgar Faure concluded: "A considerable portion of the French approved of de Gaulle for having delivered the country *at whatever price* from a malady that was consuming it."

The question one can legitimately raise is whether this twin deliverance—of the Algerians from French rule, of the French from the hornet's nest of Algeria—could have been accomplished with less blood and bitterness. The answer appears to be that all parties involved committed tragic miscalculations, underestimating their adversaries' emotional involvement and stubbornness, while overestimating their own ability to force the issue at little cost. This judgment applies to de Gaulle, his government, the OAS, the *pieds noirs* and the FLN. At the risk of stating the obvious, one must say that every one had dirty hands in the affair; during that final year Algeria was a vast *foire d'empoigne*, a free-for-all, where each tried to cheat the other, a cursed land.

In addition, one must note that no wholly satisfactory explanation —except obstinacy—has been offered of de Gaulle's refusal to make peace with the *wilayas* (through Si Salah and Si Mohamed) in 1960, a course that would have spared Algeria more than a year of war and the rise of the OAS. Or of his stalling, when the OAS was growing in numbers and fanaticism, on FLN claims to the Sahara, although he was already prepared to cede the area and knew that doing so could curtail the war.

This much said, it is evident that decolonialization is not, and cannot ever be, a honey-smooth process.

* In "Algeria: The Last Ordeal," *International Journal* (Toronto), Spring 1962.

"To the extent that the OAS was an attempt to maintain French sovereignty in Algeria," wrote Roland Gaucher, "the consequences of its defeat are irreversible."* The tricolor is not likely ever to fly again over Algiers. In 1968 it was estimated that the former European population of a million had dropped to 80,000, of whom most were too old or too sick to be transplanted; the vital elements among the *pieds noirs* are gone forever.

They arrived in France tagged as fascists, losers and murderous-minded, backward-looking accomplices of the OAS. Their assumption that they deserved special treatment due to hardships endured caused exasperation among Frenchmen, although some thought that their migration was preferable in the long run. For had they remained in newly independent Algeria, they would have created a thorny problem as a large restless minority. Moreover, as sworn enemies of the Gaullist regime, they would undoubtedly have wielded their influence to aggravate relations with France.

Many settled in Marseilles, Fréjus, Nice and Toulouse; some struck out northward without joy, away from the sun. Local communities gave them considerable assistance, in the form of transportation allowances, housing and insurance loans, subsidies for skilled workers to adapt to new trades; but red tape and the unexpected number of refugees jammed improvised machinery, and payments were slow. And aid was not always altruistic; many a mayor and municipal councilor had an eye cocked on the potential votes this influx represented.†

The attitude of the *pieds noirs* themselves was one of distrust and resentment, lassitude and inability at first to cope with new circumstances. There was undying rancor against de Gaulle, who had betrayed them, and disillusionment with the OAS, which had let them down—far more, in fact, than anger with the Moslems. The *pieds noirs* felt keenly unwanted. But as time passed, their native tenacity

---

* Roland Gaucher, *Les Terroristes*.
† The French government, on April 2, 1962, extended to French nationals of Algeria and the Sahara provisions of a 1961 decree for the welcome and reinstallation of French returning from overseas territories such as Morocco.
Many *pieds noirs* from Oran settled in Spain, where their arrival coincided with that country's tourist boom. Others moved to Argentina and Canada. A minority returned to Algeria after independence. This attempt to find a new *modus vivendi* in their old homeland almost invariably failed. They found the country radically changed.

and industriousness came to the fore; they invested shrewdly and worked hard, and many have prospered. Their children, raised in France, now ask: "Well, what were we doing there in the first place? It belonged to *them*, after all."

After deluding themselves that a cease-fire would never be signed with the FLN, the *pieds noirs* awoke to a sense of mortal danger very late in the day. And when they did, their sense of urgency was fragmented, bred by local conditions, instead of reflecting awareness of an over-all problem. Oran, for example, was confident that with Mers el Kebir near by it would never be abandoned, and its interest in Algiers' plight was limited.

There was also considerable truth in Perez's charge that the *pieds noirs* showed little taste for dying. In this respect, the myth of a New Israel—of an entire people under arms protecting its frontiers —never sprang to life. Bab el Oued was the only pitched battle, and even here a stout fight to the finish was not put up, resistance melted as soon as the Army used force. There was a subsequent outcry about persecution, but it was oppression of a short-lived and relatively benevolent nature. If the *pieds noirs* had really been persecuted the world would have sympathized; committees would have been formed, appeals launched, letters of protest published— the extensive mid-twentieth-century machinery for special causes would have begun operating. The *pieds noirs* saw themselves as underdogs but never managed to persuade the world of this; in fact, a contrary impression arose—with much basis in truth—of selfish grasping of outdated privileges.

In retrospect, it would seem that the *pieds noirs'* biggest error was, paradoxically, to think too much along French lines. The average settler relied on the French Army to protect him, come hell or high water—in brief, on an outside force he could not control. When it came time to choose, the Army—by this time a very different creature from what it had been in the days of May 1958 under the spur of the politically indoctrinated colonels—prudently chose to obey the traditional source of authority, the home government. It was not till desperately late in the day that the concept of an independent *pied noir* republic was seriously advocated.

In moments of candor *pieds noirs* admit today that the slogan *Algérie française* was inaccurate. What they really wanted was some sort of guarantee that they could remain on viable terms in their birthplace; whether it endured under French sovereignty was secondary. The strongest ties were to a specific piece of real estate, not to the tricolor. Here many were at cross purposes with the OAS colonels' nationalistic creed.

The OAS represented the rear-guard action of a battle fought to preserve the last major territory that belonged to the once far-flung French colonial empire, a battle waged militarily and politically for seven years in the mountains and eroded gullies of Kabylia and the Constantinois; the Casbah, and diplomatic hotel suites in Paris, Tunis and Switzerland, then at the end on the pavements of Algiers and Oran. But this ultimate phase came too late, and—with the exception of Salan, Susini and Godard—it was entrusted to mediocrities. For some fourteen months the OAS waged an improvised, uncoordinated, apolitical struggle to defend "men, principle and a flag"; but from the outset the Organization represented a vastly outnumbered minority, and in the end it went down to defeat unable to overcome its initial strategic disadvantage.

It has been argued that time worked against the OAS,* but in the final analysis it is unlikely that more time would have changed the outcome. One hundred percent *pied noir* enrollment in OAS cells, instead of sixty percent, for instance, could not alter the basic strategic situation. Barring a stroke of fortune, the OAS was foredoomed.

As a movement, it degenerated inexorably from a high-minded attempt to conserve France's last strategic bastion in Africa to corner-boy sadism. Increasingly it was boxed up, reduced, left in irresponsible hands; former Rightist supporters turned away nauseated by its excesses. Only a handful of quarreling subalterns stuck it out to the bitter, ruinous end.

Still, as Gaucher noted, just as lessons learned from the nineteenth-century Commune de Paris were not lost a half century later on the Russian Bolsheviks, so the tactical lessons drawn from the OAS's struggle as an urban guerrilla force will be studied and presumably applied elsewhere in the world. The Organization introduced no new concepts of house-to-house fighting or intelligence-

---

* Susini stresses, in his *Histoire de l'OAS*, that the "secret army" had only one year in which to organize.

gathering, but some of its psychological-warfare innovations were ingenious.

For all its skillfulness, however, the OAS was opposed by a determined government, with greater freedom of action, broader resources and more political astuteness. The underground war ultimately proved that, while one thousand men may perpetrate extensive material damage and commit a lot of murders, there is a limit to their destructiveness if resolutely opposed. The Moslems' instinctive and formidable discipline contributed equally to checkmating the OAS.

In rebuttal to Perez, it can be said that the Organization failed to give the *pieds noirs* purposeful leadership and an example of combativity. It shied away from combat against regular *wilaya* units. As one hostile critic noted, if Delta commandos wanted to resist to the death, they needed only to stay in Oran after July 1; but by that date nearly all had fled. Not a single OAS chief fell fighting in the streets; not one, for that matter, went bankrupt.

There was another reason for the OAS's defeat: its lack of discipline and its uninterrupted internal bickering. To which the OAS's defenders retort that it was vanquished less by its own weaknesses than by the Army's betrayal. But to have placed faith in the officer corps *after the putsch of April 1961* was, to say the least, naïve.

In a broader perspective, the French Right misrepresented the OAS's character. Depicting it as a gallant rear-guard action was, perhaps, understandable; but it was specious thinking when writers hailed the Organization as marking "the first time, in France, that revolutionary methods were grafted onto a nationalist movement."[*] No matter to what degree it borrowed from Viet Minh and FLN tactics, the OAS's basic aims remained counterrevolutionary, and the methods were always bent to this end. The movement became tagged as fascist in the public's eyes for sound reasons: the pernicious support of extreme-Right groups; OAS leaders' admiration for the Spanish Falange; the Madrid faction's ultrareactionary political philosophy.

The consequences of decolonialization did not altogether bear out the Right's dire predictions. Algeria, to be sure, foundered almost immediately in poverty, administrative chaos and political instabil-

---

[*] Fabrice Laroche and François d'Orcival, *Le Courage est leur patrie.*

ity. Throughout the summer and fall of 1962, Ben Bella consolidated power, crushed democratic liberties, drove many of the original FLN chiefs into exile, imprisonment or disgrace, instituted a far-from-viable "Arab Socialism" and aligned the country with other ill-governed lands of the underdeveloped world. The dismal result, in terms of squandered funds and unfulfilled prospects, justified Belkacem Krim's ironic contention, "Seven years of independence have been far harder to bear than seven years to attain it." But the much-feared Communist takeover of North Africa has not ensued; France, rather than the Communist world, continues to donate a lion's share of economic aid to the Algerian Republic, and French cultural and educational influence remain predominant.

Long after independence, the death throes of the OAS continued. The remnants of the Algerian Organization merged with Bidault's National Council of Resistance; the ex-premier was flanked by Argoud and Sergent, both still at large. But after July 1, activism had lost its original purpose and no voices were raised for a military reconquest of the lost province. From somewhere in Europe, the CNR's clandestine "central information agency" outlined the new goals as being the overthrow of the Gaullist regime and the restoration of "legality" through an Army-backed Government of Public Safety.

If the activists had failed beforehand, there was scant hope of their succeeding now. Yet they persisted with sabotage and terrorism. There were at least three further attempts on de Gaulle's life. The attack that came closest to putting an end to the Fifth Republic occurred on August 22, 1962, when fifteen men ambushed the presidential motorcade as it sped through the southern Parisian suburb of Petit Clamart en route to Villacoublay airport. This was a far more practiced and coordinated attempt than the Pont-sur-Seine affair. The ringleader, Lieutenant Colonel Jean-Marie Bastien-Thiéry, a military engineer assigned to the Air Ministry, had laid his plans with care and posted men and vehicles in a semicircle around a strategic intersection from which it was virtually impossible for the intended victims to escape alive. But one accomplice's hesitation in opening fire provided a few seconds' delay during which the convoy roared past the trap to safety. Nonetheless, twelve machine-gun slugs pierced the body of the presidential car, one within an inch of de Gaulle's head. The *attentat* touched off a priority manhunt, and the extent of police penetration of extremist networks in France was revealed when all the would-be assassins were identified within a month.

Then, in February 1963, police uncovered and smashed in time a second plot to kill the General by long-range rifle fire while he attended ceremonies at the École Militaire, in Paris. A year later, de Gaulle visited the Mont Faron war memorial near Toulon, and detectives found a bomb planted in a flower vase that was to be exploded by a short-wave radio signal. More arrests followed. All three abortive attempts were laid to the National Council of Resistance or one of its offshoots.

Meanwhile, OAS survivors maintained nuisance activity: weapons were stolen from Army bases, cars were set afire in Paris and windshields were stoned, apparently as vengeance on Metropolitan Frenchmen who had watched the loss of Algeria passively.

In Spain, Perez railed vigorously against those who thought of giving up the struggle. The flight from Algeria was, he announced in his usual bombastic style, a mere matter of "retiring to other theaters of operations." In Alicante he set up reserve commandos drawn from a hard core of O.R.O. members, and organized a "general staff" to analyze what had misfired in Algeria and dabble in revolutionary theory. But a day dawned—to be precise, January 17, 1965—when, after much soul-searching, a brief expulsion to South America and a tussle with Swiss police in the railway station at Geneva, Perez announced that he was no longer an activist. "A chief must be in a position to reward and punish," he said; visibly, no OAS leader still wielded such power.

He settled down in a seaside villa near Tarragona, and consulted Spanish ecclesiastical authorities about the spiritual justification for his terrorist actions in Algiers. He was asked whether no other way of tackling the problem existed. In reply, he claimed no other way was practicable.

The doctor's case is singular. In the summer of 1967 he told this writer: "I derived no gratification whatever from clandestine life. . . . A man very quickly becomes an animal leading this sort of life." But he still speaks with a certain icy hostility about victims of Delta operations who were, or were alleged to have been, "reds"; in such unguarded moments, passions of the Spanish Civil War rise unambiguously to the surface.

He has since resumed medical practice.

In West Germany, Argoud—"the most ambitious of the OAS colonels"—was also for continuing the struggle in July 1962, although his followers melted away in the months following independence, not solely because French Algeria was dead, but because they lacked a secure foreign base, were numerically weak and spent most of their time dodging host countries' police. In February 1963, in a seriocomic episode, plainclothes agents of French Military Security kidnaped the ex-colonel during the pre-Lenten Fasching winter carnival in Munich, spirited him across the Rhine in the dead of night, and delivered him trussed and helpless next door to Paris police headquarters.

After Argoud's abduction, Jean-Marie Curutchet, Sergent's deputy in charge of Metropolitan terrorism, panicked and fled to Italy, where he naïvely struck a deal with the French Embassy to go into exile in South America in return for his passage and a small monthly subsidy. On November 29, 1963, he boarded an Alitalia plane bound for Uruguay. At a stopover in Dakar, local gendarmes came aboard, seized him and, by prearrangement, turned him over to the French.

Both Argoud and Curutchet were sentenced to life imprisonment.

Other prominent OAS leaders remained safely out of the law's reach—Dufour, Broizat, Achard, de La Bigne in Spain; Godard in Belgium; Sergent in Belgium and Holland; both Gardes and Gardy in Argentina. Jacques Soustelle, who had never belonged to the OAS, continued to rail at de Gaulle's government from Switzerland. But Argoud's capture split the National Council of Resistance wide open. Not a single leader felt safe any more; Bidault himself skipped off to Brazil, and it marked the end of significant organized clandestine action mounted from abroad. Politicians and businessmen who covertly or overtly had backed the Organization gradually withdrew their support, and the vast majority of Frenchmen, with the complex and costly Algerian problem solved, saw no need for a Government of Public Safety. The sound of plastique was heard with decreasing frequency in France. There came a day, July 11, 1963, more than a year after independence, after which the Paris Prefecture reported no more right-wing *plastiquages.**

---

* Prefecture officials consider the last OAS plastique attack occurred on this date against local Gaullist (UNR) headquarters in Levallois-Perret, a Paris suburb.

Throughout the same period French police, with no further in-hibitions about *Algérie française*, continued to break up activist networks, while French courts tackled the proliferating backlog of OAS cases.

Only a few judgments need be cited here. Philippe Castille, for his role as technical adviser during Paris' "Blue Night," received a twenty-year term, and Jean-Marie Vincent, head of the *plastiqueurs* who had blinded Delphine Renard in one eye, life imprisonment. André Canal was sentenced to death, but then was reprieved by de Gaulle. Bastien-Thiéry was executed on March 11, 1963; this brought to four the number of OAS men legally put to death. The Right charged the Gaullist government with executing solely scape-goats devoid of influence or backing—a lieutenant whose career was passed entirely in the Foreign Legion (Degueldre); a lieutenant colonel of engineers who was a technician more than a career officer (Bastien-Thiéry); a Legionnaire noncom and foreigner to boot (Dovecar) and an obscure *pied noir* insurance agent (Piegts), both condemned for their role in Gavoury's murder. Still, by the yard-stick of OAS terrorism, this figure seemed restrained and showed no particular official bloodthirstiness.

As time passed, de Gaulle pardoned the putschist generals—first Zeller, then Challe and Jouhaud. Salan alone remained locked up in Tulle Prison, in central France, engaged in drafting his memoirs, visited regularly by his wife and daughter but seemingly without prospect of parole.

Then in the late spring of 1968, following a new challenge to his authority from combined students and workers on the Left, de Gaulle hastily and cynically pardoned Salan, Argoud, Curutchet and nine other OAS members still in prison. Bidault was allowed to return from exile. Controlled by an overwhelming Gaullist majority, the National Assembly, on July 13, the eve of the national holiday, extended the provisions of two existing amnesty laws to all activists, which meant, in effect, restoration of their civic rights and exemp-tion from further prosecution for all criminal acts committed "in connection with events in Algeria."* The slate was wiped clean.

---

* According to official statistics, 3,471 persons benefited from this general amnesty. Four persons were excepted from it, including Pierre Lagaillarde, who had fled to Spain during the Barricades Trial.

Shortly afterward, almost all OAS members who had been tried *in absentia* and were living abroad returned to France.

There was such a strong flavor of political opportunism in these measures that they produced considerable discomfort—though no downright disloyalty—among Gaullists who had fought the secret army.

After his departure from Algeria, Susini settled in a suburb of Rome, and proceeded, at the rate of three pages a day, to write the first volume of his highly subjective and opinionated history of the OAS. In it he ridiculed Perez's role and disparaged Godard's.*

Meanwhile he dodged with alacrity gangs of resentful OAS militants who traveled to Rome (*"et ce n'était pas pour lui dire bonjour"*), attracted by tales of two and a half million dollars he had allegedly spirited out of Algeria.

In 1968 he returned to France. He says that he would like to reenter politics.

Salan lives in retirement in Paris. He has regained the sprightly vigor of his Indochinese days, his silver mane is still profuse. On a visitor he makes an impression of being energetic and decisive, untouched by the prison years, except perhaps for an accentuated reluctance to reveal his true thoughts.

He sits in his Right Bank apartment amid heavy bourgeois furniture, miniature Buddhas, muted sounds made by a servant somewhere, stiffly leans forward, clasps his hands together and explains earnestly the unfolding of that unaccountable final year.

He is not a man who says *"mea culpa."* Even in connection with tactics, he does not acknowledge many errors; he explains what happened in terms of shortages, and his view is essentially military. The reason for the OAS's defeat lay above all "in France's desire to give up Algeria," and within this context it was a foredoomed battle waged to show the *pieds noirs* they were not abandoned. More than just a *baroud d'honneur,* a "final skirmish," it was *une bataille pour l'honneur,* a "battle for honor's sake"; he stresses this distinction. The one aspect he is loath to discuss is blind terrorism; this, in its worst phase, he points out, occurred after his arrest.

* The French government seized the book as soon as it appeared for sale in November 1963, and ordered cuts. The second volume has not been published.

For the rest, his position has not changed significantly. What he did was necessary, he believes, and not so badly executed in terms of the monumental difficulties involved—"There were problems, as in any resistance movement. If they were brought under control, it was because I was there. I was the only one with enough authority to do so. I *was* the OAS. The proof? When I was arrested it collapsed."

He looks with disfavor upon those who have prattled about the Organization and its secrets. Susini's name irritates him; but for Godard—as a proficient military man—he has distinct praise.

That the end of French Algeria—the manner as much as the fact of its collapse—left its mark on France's body politic, the Army, the youth of the country seems undeniable. For one thing, both pro- and anti-government forces acquired a perhaps ineradicable habit of fighting in the dark, abetted by underworld confederates; traces of this deformation cropped up in the murky and still unresolved 1965 Ben Barka case.*

The impact of Algeria's loss was so great at the time that immediately afterward there was a conscious national effort by the French to erase this painful chapter from the mass memory and turn to other projects. "It will take perhaps a generation to forget this drama of decolonialization. . . . It is indispensable for the French to set their ideas in order and face reality." These were sentiments expressed in June 1962 by editorialist J. R. Tournoux; but he did not reckon with the fact that things go fast these days. Passions have cooled—no one now could arouse the French to the same pitch of emotion, on either side, about Djibouti or Réunion or even Martinique—but a residue of unmistakable regret and distaste lingers.

Like the Hotel Princesa in Madrid, where it all began, the OAS no longer exists. But "study groups" of former members remain in

* Medhi Ben Barka, an exiled Moroccan liberal leader, was kidnaped in broad daylight off the streets of Paris on October 29, 1965, and never seen again. A subsequent widespread investigation indicated collusion between SDECE (French counterespionage), some of its part-time agents drawn from the Parisian underworld, and police tipsters recruited in the same milieu. Moroccan Interior Ministry officials—and Frenchmen connected with the anti-OAS *barbouzes*—were also reported implicated in Ben Barka's disappearance and presumed murder.

close touch, and talk intermittently of new political action—purely aboveboard, they claim—to steer the country in a Rightward direction.

Lost causes are always unpopular, and the OAS passed out of the picture in 1962–63 with decisive finality.

The only monument to it are the black capital letters O A S, which, only partially washed away by winter rains, still deface some walls of the Sixteenth Arrondissement in Paris.

But even now, on wet evenings, over a glass of Ricard, around the hushed plazas of Alicante, nostalgia for the white coastal cities, the immense bluish mountain ranges, the spectacular dawns, the freedom of Africa suddenly pierces one of the *pieds noirs* who fought with the OAS. He is young and dirt-poor, wears a torn shirt and filthy pants, and has fashioned a new life for himself where he disembarked in confusion and bitterness in 1962. Yet something of the rough past lingers, his views have not changed all that much. Clapping his hand to his heart with no trace of self-consciousness, before returning to his game of cards with his Spanish partners, he proclaims: *"La France est ma terre."*

BIBLIOGRAPHY

Azeau, Henri, *Révolte militaire: Alger, 22 Avril 1961.* Paris: Plon, 1961.
Behr, Edward, *The Algerian Problem.* London: Hodder and Stoughton, 1961.
Bidault, Georges, *D'Une Résistance à l'autre.* Paris: Les Presses du Siècle, 1965.
Borgen, Geneviève, *Journée calme . . . marquée par . . .* Paris: Collection Alternances, 1964.
Bromberger, Merry and Serge, *Barricades et colonels.* Paris: Fayard, 1960.
Brune, Jean, *Interdit aux chiens et aux français.* Paris: La Table Ronde, 1967.
———— *Cette Haine qui ressemble à l'amour.* Paris: La Table Ronde, 1961.
Buchard, Robert, *Organisation Armée Secrète.* Paris: Albin-Michel, 1963.
Buron, Robert, *Carnets politiques de la guerre d'Algérie.* Paris: Plon, 1965.
Chaffard, Georges, *Les Carnets secrets de la décolonisation.* Paris: Calmann-Lévy, 1967.
Dauer, Jacques, and Rodet, Michel, *Les Orphelins du Gaullisme.* Paris: Julliard, 1962.
Duchemin, Jacques, *Histoire du F.L.N.* Paris: La Table Ronde, 1962.
Dupuy, Marie-Thérèse, *Fors l'Honneur.* Paris, 1963.
Fauvet, Jacques, and Planchais, Jean, *La Fronde des généraux.* Paris: Arthaud, 1961.
Favrod, Charles-Henri, *Le F.L.N. et l'Algérie.* Paris: Plon, 1962.
Ferrandi, Jean, *Les Officiers français face au Viet Minh.* Paris: Fayard, 1966.

Figuéras, André, *Salan, Raoul, ex-général* . . . Paris: La Table Ronde, 1965.

Furniss, Edgar, *De Gaulle and the French Army.* New York: Twentieth Century Fund, 1964.

Gallagher, Charles, *The United States and North Africa.* Cambridge: Harvard University Press, 1963.

Gaucher, Roland, *Les Terroristes.* Paris: Albin-Michel, 1965.

Gauvin, Jean, *Le Procès Vanuxem.* Paris: Éditions Saint-Just, 1963.

Girardet, Raoul, *La Crise militaire française.* Paris: Armand Colin, 1964.

Jacob, Alain, *D'Une Algérie à l'autre.* Paris: Grasset, 1963.

Jaffre, Yves-Frédéric, *Les Tribunanux d'exception.* Paris: Nouvelle Éditions Latines, 1962.

Kayonakis, Nicolas, *Derniers Châteaux en Espagne.* Paris: La Table Ronde, 1967.

Kraft, Joseph, *The Struggle for Algeria.* New York: Doubleday, 1961.

Kelly, George, *Lost Soldiers.* Cambridge: M.I.T. Press, 1965.

la Gorce, Paul-Marie de, *De Gaulle entre deux mondes.* Paris: Fayard, 1964.

Lancelot, Marie-Thérèse, *Organisation Armée Secrète,* 2 vols. Paris: Fondation Nationale des Sciences Politiques, 1963.

Laparre, Fernand de, R.P., *Journal d'un prêtre en Algérie: Oran 1961–62.* Paris: Éditions du Fuseau, 1964.

Laroche, Fabrice, *Salan devant l'opinion.* Paris: Éditions Saint-Just, 1963.

———— and Orcival, François d', *Le Courage est leur patrie.* Paris, 1965.

Lentin, Albert-Paul, *L'Algérie entre deux mondes,* Vol. 1, *Le Dernier Quart d'heure.* Paris: Julliard, 1963.

Loesch, Anne, *La Valise et le cercueil.* Paris: Plon, 1963.

Monteil, Vincent, *Soldat de fortune.* Paris: Grasset, 1966.

Morland, Barangé, and Martinez (pen names of three officials of the French Ministry of the Interior), *Histoire de l'Organisation de l'Armée Secrète.* Paris: Julliard, 1964.

Naegelen, Marcel-Edmond, *Une Route plus large que longue.* Paris: Laffont, 1965.

Nicol, Axel, *La Bataille de l'OAS.* Paris: Les Sept Couleurs, 1962.

OAS parle. Paris: Julliard, 1964.

Ortiz, Joseph, *Les Combats.* Paris: Éditions de la Pensée Moderne, 1964.

Paillat, Claude, *Dossiers secrets de l'Algérie,* Vols. 1 and 2. Paris: Les Presses de la Cité, 1962.

Reimbold, Jean, *Pour Avoir dit non.* Paris: La Table Ronde, 1966.

Roy, Jules, *War in Algeria.* Gloucester, Mass.: Peter Smith, 1965.

Sergent, Pierre, *Ma Peau au bout de mes idées.* Paris: La Table Ronde, 1967.

———— *La Bataille.* Paris: La Table Ronde, 1968.

Servan-Schreiber, Jean-Jacques, *Lieutenant in Algeria.* New York: Knopf, 1957.

Soustelle, Jacques, *L'Espérance trahie.* Paris: Éditions de l'Alma, 1962.

———— *Sur une Route nouvelle.* Paris: Éditions du Fuseau, 1964.

Sulzberger, Cyrus L., *The Test: De Gaulle and Algeria.* New York: Harcourt, 1962.

Susini, Jean-Jacques, *Histoire de l'OAS*. Paris: La Table Ronde, 1963. Though it is highly opinionated and often errs by omission, this book is fascinating reading for those interested in an insider's view of the OAS. But Volume 1 carries the story only through September 1961; Volume 2 has never been published.

Terrenoire, Louis, *De Gaulle et l'Algérie*. Paris: Fayard, 1964.

Theolleyre, Jean-Marc, *Ces Procès qui ébranlèrent la France*. Paris: Grasset, 1966.

Tislenkoff, Alexandre, *J'Accuse Lemarchand*. Paris: Éditions Saint-Just, 1966. This was seized by French authorities after a court judgment. It can be consulted in some libraries.

Tournoux, J. R., *L'Histoire secrète*. Paris: Plon, 1962.

———— *La Tragédie du général*. Paris: Plon, 1967.

Press

Throughout 1961–63 leading French newspapers and periodicals carried numerous articles on the OAS and Algeria. The following are of special interest:

Bardèche, Maurice, "Une Fille pour du Vent," *Défense de l'Occident*, March–April 1962.

Bitterlin, Lucien, "Journal d'un barbouze," *Esprit*, November 1966.

Cairns, John, "Algeria: The Last Ordeal," *International Journal* (Toronto), Spring 1962.

Fauvet, Jacques, "D'Un Putsch à l'autre," *Le Monde*, October 20, 1961.

Gabilly, Marcel, "L'Équipée d'Alger," *La Revue de Paris*, June 1961.

Girardet, Raoul, "Sur une Cérémonie militaire," *Combat*, November 24, December 11–12, 1961.

Mermoz, Gilles, "Connaissances de l'OAS," *Écrits de Paris*, October and November, 1962.

———— "Erreurs de l'OAS," *Écrits de Paris*, March 1963.

Montfort, Colonel, "La Situation militaire en Algérie," *Revue Militaire Suisse*, February 1962.

Nef, La (Paris), special issues—*L'Armée française* (July–September 1961)

———— *Histoire de la guerre d'Algérie suivie d'une histoire de l'OAS* (October 1962–January 1963)

———— *La Police en France* (June–September 1963)

Tribune Socialiste, special issue—*Où en est l'OAS?* (November 1962)

Miscellaneous

Gaulle, Charles de, *Major Addresses, Statements and Press Conferences, May 1958–January 1964*. Service de Presse et d'Information, French Embassy, New York.

Stenographic transcripts of the court trials of Generals Challe, Zeller, Jouhaud, Salan, and subordinate French officers. Paris: Nouvelles Éditions Latines, 1961–65.

LIST OF MAJOR DATES

May 13, 1958—Outbreak of European settlers' insurrection in Algiers leads to the collapse of the French Fourth Republic and de Gaulle's return to power.

September 16, 1959—De Gaulle's self-determination speech, offering three solutions to the Algerian problem: integration, association, independence.

January 24–29, 1960—Barricades Week. European settlers, with the passive complicity of French Army units, raise barricades in Algiers and defy the government for one week.

November 4, 1960—Barricades Trial. Nineteen activists are indicted for an attempt on the security of the state during Barricades Week; sixteen go on trial before a military court in Paris, three are at large.

December 9–11, 1960—European street demonstrations and Moslem counterdemonstrations in Algiers. FLN flags appear openly in Moslem neighborhoods.

1961

January 8—French voters approve de Gaulle's Algerian policy in referendum.

Early February—Formation of the OAS in Madrid.

March 2—Barricades Trial ends. Lagaillarde, Susini and three other defendants have already fled to Spain.

April 11—De Gaulle, during press conference, forecasts a "sovereign" Algerian state.

April 22–25—Generals' putsch in Algeria.

May 5—First of several secret meetings in Algiers at which activist officers and civilians re-form OAS and vow to fight on.

May 20—French and FLN delegates meet to negotiate cease-fire at Évian. French government orders unilateral truce in the field.

May 29–31—Challe and Zeller, tried before a military court, receive prison terms.

June 13—Breakoff of cease-fire negotiations at Évian.

July 10—Salan, Jouhaud and colonels who took part in the putsch are sentenced to death *in absentia*. Salan is rumored to be in hiding somewhere on the Mitidja plain, south of Algiers.

July 19—Cease-fire negotiations resume at Lugrin, near Évian.

July 28—Lugrin talks are suspended.

August 5—First OAS pirate broadcast in Algiers. Throughout the month, the OAS steps up fund raising, distribution of tracts, and plastique explosions.

August 26—Ben Khedda replaces Ferhat Abbas as president of the Algerian Provisional Government, with mission to conclude peace negotiations with French within six months.

Early September—Salan returns to Algiers.

September 5—De Gaulle, during press conference, indicates willingness to make concessions on the future status of the Sahara.

September 8—Unsuccessful attempt on de Gaulle's life at Pont-sur-Seine.

September 20—General Ailleret issues Order of the Day to French Army to cooperate with police in stamping out the OAS.

October 4—Spanish government arrests leaders of the "Madrid OAS."

November 8–9—Right-wing deputies defend the OAS cause during a National Assembly debate. The so-called "Salan amendment," providing for mobilization of several classes of European reservists in Algeria, gets 80 votes but is defeated.

Mid-November—Arrival of *barbouzes* in Algiers, to combat the OAS.

November 19—"Delta" gunmen assassinate William Levy, secretary general of the Socialist party of Algiers. Levy is the most prominent victim during a week marked by OAS assassinations of Europeans and Moslems.

November 22—De Gaulle summons 2,000 French Army officers to Strasbourg, stresses their duty is to obey and employs celebrated phrase about "lost soldiers."

December 19—French trade-unions call protest strike against OAS.

1962

January 4—Salan orders "general mobilization" of all Europeans in Algeria.

Mid-January—Rumors in Algiers of a "second putsch."

January 25—A bomb devastates a villa occupied by *barbouzes* in El Biar, killing fourteen.

February 8—In Paris, anti-OAS demonstrators clash with police at Charonne Métro station; eight are killed.

February 13—An estimated 500,000 attend funeral procession for the eight victims of Charonne street fighting, in the biggest turnout Paris has seen since the Liberation.

February 11–19—French and FLN negotiators meet secretly at Les Rousses, near the Swiss frontier, to prepare new cease-fire negotiations.

March 7—Cease-fire negotiations begin at Évian.

March 19—Cease-fire becomes effective at noon, ending Algerian War. Salan orders start of "harassing operations" to block the cease-fire.

March 22—Bab-el-Oued uprising, followed by week-long siege of the neighborhood.

March 25—Jouhaud arrested in Oran.

March 26—French Army troops fire on European civilians in Rue d'Isly, Algiers.

April 7—Provisional executive is installed at Rocher Noir and prepares for independence referendum. Degueldre is arrested in Algiers.

April 8—French voters in referendum approve Évian agreement.

April 20—Salan arrested in Algiers on Good Friday.

May 15—The bloodiest day in French Algeria's final year: OAS and FLN commandos attack victims every fifteen minutes in the streets of Algiers.

Late May—Mass exodus of Europeans from Algeria's hinterland and coastal cities to France.

May 23—Military court, in surprise decision, finds extenuating circumstances for Salan and sentences him to life imprisonment instead of death.

May 18–June 17—Series of secret meetings between Susini, Farès, Chevallier, Tiné, in attempt to end terrorism.

June 17—Susini and Mostefai, in separate radio statements, announce OAS–FLN truce.

June 18—Oran OAS says it does not recognize truce.

June 25—OAS blows up oil dumps in Oran harbor.

June 26—Dufour orders cessation of OAS sabotage.

June 27—Military court sentences Degueldre to death.

July 1—Ninety-one percent of registered voters in Algeria vote for independence.

July 3—Algeria's independence proclaimed.

INDEX

[*Page numbers in italics denote photographs.*]

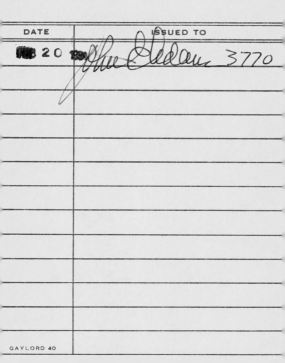

DATE	ISSUED TO
FEB 20 199	_(signature)_ 3770

DATE	ISSUED TO

PRINTED
IN
U.S.A.

Henissart

Wolves in the city